FOR KATIE

2018

Athelstan's World

First in the
Celtic King Saga

M. F. Harding

Athelstan's World

First published by
Triskelion Press Publications Co.
Campbell River BC V9W 1C6
2018

ISBN: 978-09959344-1-2 (sc)
ISBN: 978-09959344-0-5 (e)

First Published and Printed in
Canada and the United States of America

First Edition August 2018

Dedication

This is dedicated to the loving memory of Sally Woodfield.
This book would not have been possible without you.

Acknowledgements

I would like to thank my wife Barbara who patiently guided me through every word of this book as it now appears. You were wise with your criticism, unyielding with your corrections, and kind with your praise.

Thanks to my publisher, Triskelion Publications for seeing the value in my work.

I would like to thank Kailee Noel Smith, John Lennon and Coby Treadway. The generous donation of both your time and your unique creativity helped determine the direction of this story early on. Stalwart friends such as you are a rare gift for anyone and I am grateful to have had you with me.

I want to also thank the photographer for the image used for the cover.

I give my unswerving gratitude to my proof–readers. Barbara Wyatt and Helen Dolhanyk. You turned this work from gibberish into English – no small feat if I do say so myself.

My thanks also to The Druidry Handbook, by John Michael Greer for rituals, poetry and prayers; The Druids, by Peter Berresford Ellis for content; The Celtic Druid's Year, by John King for timelines; Bracken Books, Celtic Myths and Legends for just that and; The Druids, TD Kendrick for historical accuracy. My undying thanks to Philip Carr-Gomm for a lifetime of inspiration and wisdom. You are indeed a blessing.

Prologue

Wild is my name.

I am a child of the wind in the trees, of the sunshine and of the pouring rain.

Myth sired me and the earth bore me.

This spirit beats with the heart of the wolf and with the wings of the raven.

The moon, the stars, and the seasons propel me.

The storms of winter rage within me, yet my aspect is of a tranquil pond.

Colour me with the greens of spring grasses and the blues of the deepest seas.

Listen for me in the nightingale's song and in the random flutter of a butterfly.

Feel me in the hoar frost of winter and in the burning sun of summer.

See me in the eyes of the newborn fawn and in the gaze of the owl.

I am but a single leaf in an endless forest of trees.

Should I fall, others will stand.

I shall never perish.

Nothing can kill the spirit of life that rages me.

I rejoice in life.

I am its guardian and its defender.

I am of the elder race of Celts.

I am eternal.

Chapter One

The General growled with impotent rage as he watched another of his clansman die on the spike of a Roman lance. A west wind blew warm and humid through the Celt's long, hair. It smelled of thyme, cold iron, and old leather. A soft tinkling sound could also be heard. It was a curiously gentle sound, in stark contrast to the clash of swords on shields and the screams of dying men and horses. Enameled amulets and talismans decorated with colourful, intricate patterns clanged together like soft wind chimes. These disks were braided into the thick blonde hair of a Celtic General. Each fluttered with the summer breeze. Black raven feathers were also woven into his hair, moustache and beard. It gave the barbarian General a fearsome look; a look accentuated by the ill-concealed fury in his eyes.

Above their heads, the ravens and storm crows that attended every battle circled and screeched their impatience over their impending carrion meal below.

"I have seen enough!" Athelstan growled over the din of battle. "Commander Cedric, sound the retreat. Get my men out of there." Another grim-faced man stood beside his leader, defiant in the face of Rome's might, looking southward from atop the rough-hewn marble walls of the sprawling hill fort of Milan. Cedric raised a hand and heralds blew long blasts from their war–horns. The noise voiced the screeching discordance of defeat.

Battle had raged amid the leafy stands of maple ash and aromatic cedars that dotted the golden and ruddy–coloured grasses of the surrounding valley. At their backs, towering, white-capped mountains glowered down on the carnage like disapproving sentinels. Their snowy heads and shoulders stood naked. Scented pine forests draped their knees and toes. All the land to the south of them fell away in low hills and undulating ridges. The Alps shed melt water in countless streams towards the lazy twists and turns of the Po River.

South of the hill fort, near the Po, the ground became boggy. It descended into the bug–infested swamps. Alders and birches formed thick groves in these lush lowlands. Clear creeks and swampy tributaries obscured by perpetual mists wandered downward only to lose themselves on their way to the great flow.

General Athelstan of the clan Epona, stood six feet, one inch tall and had the lean musculature of a veteran soldier. He was used to the hardships of battle, pain, and death. Blue tattoos in dots, slashes, and whorls of power decorated the exposed parts of his shoulders. He also bore silver rings and armbands of his station as Clan chieftain. His chest and back were armoured in square enamelled copper plates wired onto laminated linen laid over a jerkin of layered felt. A simple blue and green–checkered cloak was laced at his neck. Coating all, from helm to boots, was the blood – Roman blood. The cost of the Roman victory had been high on both sides.

It was the afternoon of Midsummer Solstice day, fourteen years after the death of Alexander the Great. Battle with two Roman legions had been joined at dawn. He had watched as wave after wave of fearless Celtic fighters crashed and broke against the solid shield walls of Roman phalanxes. Cavalry charges would open great rents in the Roman lines but these invaders were well trained. These openings closed on all sides, creating death traps for any horse, or soldier locked within.

The massed Celtic charges, meant to overwhelm and scatter enemies, fared little better. The enemies shield walls bristling with twelve–foot spears proved all but impossible to penetrate. Romans also interlocked their wide shields overhead turning aside the clouds of arrows fired from the city walls. Catapults were the Celt's only effective weapon but the city's defenders had too few of them to stem the tide of the determined Legions and their Commander. The architect of all this death and horror was none other than Papirius Aurelius Cursor. He was Proconsul of Rome. His leering hawk–nosed visage was one Athelstan would never forget. He was an effeminate looking man, much used to ease and privilege. He directed the assault from a decorative pavilion situated well to the rear of the fighting.

A heavy scowl furrowed Athelstan's brow. Pale blue eyes squinted to slits against the wind as he surveyed the ruination of his troops. Smoke from the many trench fires lit by retreating troops coiled over the landscape before him, leaving a black, oily stain on the ground. The air was filled with choking smoke. Athelstan descended the walls and mounted a massive white warhorse named Maehadren. Covered in dry sweat and congealed human blood, he rode towards the Royal compound in the city centre. He galloped through a burning maze of half-collapsed buildings. His blood was up.

At his back, a fierce, proud, and noble people – the Senone Celts, were retreating before an inferior foe. In front of him was the cause of this madness and slaughter, his half-brother Trahearn Livy, the Senone King. He stood huddled with his new advisors. They were all laughing.

The original plan had worked well enough and much-needed information about Roman tactics had been learned, but Athelstan seethed at how many of his men had fallen to obtain it. It was clear after three hours, that they had nothing more to gain by fighting. Their fight today was not about keeping their homeland. To let this slaughter continue unabated was inexcusable. Eight thousand good men – entire families, had died without purpose in this meaningless delaying action. Delaying what? Agreement to leave this land and fight Rome the following spring had been made months ago. The evacuation had begun at once and now, save for the army, Milan was all but deserted. Nothing could be gained by continuing to fight a battle they had intended to lose from the outset. Athelstan knew it and so should have Trahearn.

This year was a Golden Year for the Senone Celts and, it was a very special time of pilgrimages and religious festivals. It occurred every nineteen years and major Druidic holidays were celebrated during these years. For a fortnight convoys of wagons, entire clans had left Milan. The Senone nation was on the move either by horse or by foot. The population journeyed to the sea and boarded ships for western Macedonia and one of the most sacred of all Senone places, Gwennderion Glade.

The Romans needed to believe they won through superior force of arms and the Celts knew they had to leave them with that impression. This lie was essential.

Athelstan reined Maehadren to a halt before the Royal Standard of King Trahearn. Vaulting from the saddle before the King, he grabbed his half-brother and bellowed into his face.

"What have you done to my men?" He shook with fury and pointed towards the fires and his beaten army. "Thousands have died because of you!" Spittle spattered the Kings face as he bellowed at him.

Trahearn, in turn, grabbed Athelstan and roared back at him. "Your men? Who are you? I am King! I command here and these are my men. I rule, not you! You would do well to remember that!" Trahearn snarled back into Athelstan's face. Trahearn read the defiance in his General. He leaned even closer and sneered, "Do you dare to challenge…"

Athelstan had just watched many fine men die. He had killed a dozen Romans himself and his bloodlust was up. Madness claimed him. He slammed a mighty fist into Trahearn's jaw sending him sprawling to the ground. With a feral roar, Athelstan charged.

He did not get far. He was intercepted by Trahearn's guards and was borne to the ground thrashing but not before three of them fell to broken bones and smashed teeth. Trahearn, dazed, rose to his feet, rubbing at a purple spot on his jaw and stood over the apoplectic Celt.

"You dare question ME?" The King thundered. "You dare assault ME? Have you lost your mind? You have your orders. Get on your horse and be gone. Maybe those Spartans will teach you some discipline." He kicked Athelstan in the ribs – hard. There was a crunching sound and the wind rushed from the Generals lungs. The King turned and with casual indifference, strode away. His guards formed a rear guard against further attack.

Athelstan lay there wheezing and coughing up bright red bubbles of blood. It was Athelstan's own cousin, Commander Cedric Epona, who helped Athelstan stand. The grizzled old warrior steadied him as he struggled to re-mount Maehadren.

"Watch for me at Samhain old friend and wish me luck," he gasped at Cedric.

"General… Cousin, he broke your ribs and you are bleeding inside. You have to get help from the witches or…"Athelstan knew what the bloody bubbles meant as well as the next man. He was going to die a slow and painful death coughing his life away in a dwindling effort to breathe. He would drown in his own blood. With sadness, he shook his head. His King had been noticeably changing of late. He was far less patient, harder to deal with, prone to violent explosions without cause and he was losing his ability to reason. The multitude of dead littering the battlefield was proof of that. A year ago, Trahearn would never have allowed such a slaughter.

"I have my orders Cedric and you have yours. My path takes me to Sparta and I will go as commanded. I am a soldier first Cedric, just like you. If that means my life, then so be it. I am but a single leaf in a forest of trees. If I fall, another will complete what I have begun." Another painful paroxysm of coughing erupted from the Senone General. Flecks of blood spotted Maehadren's white neck and mane.

Looking across the emptying battlefield, he could see that the evacuation of Milan was all but complete. The last of the refugees trundled away with wagons, carts and on foot toward the mountains north of the city. The screams of the wounded men and beasts left on the field grew less and less - as they were dispatched one by one. Rome had won the day. It galled the General. With a single word from Trahearn, he could have swept this Roman rabble away like so much smoke on the wind.

"Rome has won a small skirmish here, but this war is only just begun. This is our land and it will be ours again I swear it!" he muttered savagely and spat more bloody red foam from his mouth. The Celtic exodus northward out of the Po River valley was heartbreaking to watch. Turning his back finally on the smoke and the ruins of his home, he began his solitary journey due east along the line of the Alps Italia towards the seaside port of Ravenna.

Chapter Two

The sun was low in the sky and Athelstan heaved another rattling gasp. He slumped over Maehadren's neck and coughed up more pink froth. The endless journey of nights and days had redefined the word agony in his mind. He coughed up thick bloody foam. The spreading purple bruise on his side burned like fire. Every breath he took had become a gargantuan struggle. How he came to be travelling this rough dense forest mountain trail he could not say. Reality waned days ago and he travelled in the land of dream. Every bump and jolt brought low exhausted groans from his lips. His lung was punctured and he knew it. He was dying and he knew that too.

The pale lights he could see in the spaces between the trees, he believed, must be the campfires of his long departed ancestors. In his tortured mind, he welcomed falling into their warm embrace. Soon he would fly to them on the wings of the raven. The sacred bird would carry him into the next world and a new life. He did not fear his death, quite the opposite. It was his firm belief that he was immortal as were all his people. Life for him was a never-ending journey, not a destination; so, he bore a calm smile as this mortal life neared its end. All that remained was for him to wait for the last of his strength to fail. When it finally did, he slipped from Maehadren onto the ground with a jarring crash and gentle blackness engulfed him.

It was a shapeless, lightless void where he floated. There was no sound, no sight, and no sensation of any kind. How long he floated, he could not say but the peace and contentment of this place were soothing.

Was there music in the void? There was music. Music? He could hear voices in the music. It sounded like voices. Was it just one voice, or was it music? Was there more than one voice? Were the voices singing? It did not seem so. These voices were demanding an answer. Musical voices demanding that he answer a question. Was there a question? Was there an answer? Every question had an answer. Answers were questions – infinite in number and evenly paired. An answer to what question he could not say. He did not want to listen. He did not need to listen, but even so, he began to listen. He began to focus. He began to live.

"Can you see it? Celtic man, can you see it?" What an odd question to ask in the blind and shapeless void.

"What? Can I see what? I see nothing." Athelstan's mind answered the question with other questions. What kind of questions were these? He would ignore these questions. Were these question he could ignore? He was blind and mute and he experienced only the void. He liked the void. He did not like -

questions.

"Celtic man, can you see the green meadow in your mind?" asked these odd musical voices again. One voice would start the question and another, almost identical voice, would take over the asking of the question. Finally, the first voice would finish the question. What sort of question needed two voices?

A dream awakened in his mind. His dream eyes opened and indeed, he gazed upon a sloping green meadow covered in spring blooms through which a gentle stream danced. A rich forest smelling of humus and green leaves surrounded him and the air was filled with the most fantastically coloured birds. A magical snowfall of pollen and lighter than air seedpods on tiny white wings swirled all around him. The sun, borne upon a warm gentle breeze, caressed his face.

"Can you see the green meadow Celtic Man?"

"Yes. I see the meadow," he answered the voices out loud this time. His voice sounded like a harsh growl when compared to the clear, song-like quality of the others.

"Good… good. What else do you see Celtic man? Look around at your surroundings. Do you see any animals near you?" It actually sounded like two people were speaking but were sharing the task equally. The two voices seemed the same yet each had an indefinable difference he could not entirely grasp. His Gods, he concluded, were guiding him now. He followed their lead and looked around.

"Animals? Yes, there are animals."

"Which animals do you see? Describe the ones nearest to you."

"I see hart and badger," his voice a rough whisper. His throat burned as he spoke. "Hare and the raven walk together. A bear travels through the glade but does not tarry and wolf reclines contented in the sunshine. swifts and martins sing to us all while newt looks under the leaves for something he has lost long ago and cannot find."

Those soothing voices continued, "These are your animal spirits and they are your guides, Celtic Man. Which one of them is the closest to you now?"

He cast about. His eyes settled on the wolf with its pale-grey fur and grey-blue eyes. wolf stood and stretched in a deep respectful bow before padding over to Athelstan and sitting down beside him. Intelligent eyes looked at him.

"Wolf is beside me," he breathed.

"Very good Celtic man, he is a powerful spirit guide and healer. You are in need of both. It is the Wolf–God Phaelan that will help you now. He is your heart; his spirit possesses your soul. He will never lead you astray. Listen to him always Celtic Man. Do you understand?"

Athelstan nodded weakly, "I understand."

His hands were buried deep into the neck fur of wolf and he scratched the beast behind the ears like a beloved dog. Wolf allowed the attention for a while, then stood and sprang away.

"Where are you going?" croaked Athelstan with undisguised alarm.

"You and he are the wolf. Wolves run. Run with him, Celtic man. Run! Can you feel the wind? What do you see?" The voices faded to silence.

"I, I see…" he began. It was never clear to him later if he spoke further or simply allowed the dream vision to unfold in silence.

Transformed, he leapt after wolf, chasing him across the meadow and into the trees at a phenomenal speed. Over roots, under branches, they raced and howled their feral delight as the ancient boles flashed past. The forest suddenly ended, opening again onto a long flat grassy plain that stretched for leagues. They ran faster now with the unfettered abandon given every wild creature. Man in his quest for dominance had forsaken that freedom. To have it returned to him now, like this, was a gift beyond measure. A gift he felt he would hold onto for the rest of his days.

They ran until the grasses finally ended in sky. The ground dropped away suddenly. Transformed again into a raven, he soared over the countryside on the black wings. The pair shot out over a vast ocean of blue-green water and it sparkled in the bright sunlight. Floating above the world, he soared and swooped, performing an aerial dance reserved only for winged creatures. Exaltation was his and it carried him away.

"Can you see it, Celtic man?" prompted the soothing voices again.

"What? See what?" he asked.

"The island beneath you, do you see it?"

From high above, he saw an island – a vivid green slash against that impossibly vibrant blue sea. He spiralled down towards it, letting the wind caress his blue-black wings.

"Yes, I see it."

"Your destiny awaits you there, Celtic man. Follow your heart wherever it leads you: it will show you your future. Listen always to your inner voice. It is the one voice in this life that will never lie to you. Behold…"

The island grew larger as he swooped down towards it. Mountains and river valleys crisscrossed its vast surface and he found he was skimming the treetops weaving a gentle path along one such river. As the ground rose, the water became wilder and the surrounding forest grew darker and more foreboding.

Far in the distance, the hearth fires of his long-departed family members blazed brightly. The glow of those fires passed beneath him, he could see the ancestors were arrayed for war. Then his people were suddenly all behind him and he could see their foe. This enemy was not Roman but some much darker threat. A sinister black-clad army marched towards his family. As it advanced, the lush forest vanished, swallowed up by the relentless advance of a desert of shifting lifeless sand.

Cold anger filled him at the sight and he flew lower still to see the faces of this dark foe. However, they had no faces, only blank empty hoods.

One powerful leader seated upon a black steed directed this sprawling hoard. Athelstan swooped towards this cloaked and hooded commander. The dark hood turned towards him as he approached and a near-skeletal hand pointed, beckoning him to come. A cold hollow laughter rose to greet him. This faceless enemy reached for his cowl, threw it off, revealing there was nothing at all inside. The cloak collapsed in a shapeless empty heap onto the ground. Only the laughter remained.

The dream ended abruptly and there was a physical jolt as his spirit slammed back into his mortal body. The odd voices returned.

"He's waking up. That is a good sign. Celtic Man, can you hear us? Wake up," commanded that song–like voice. The Gods had sent him back to the world. It would seem he was destined to live after all.

A low groan was all the answer he could muster, his side ached and his tongue was thick and pasty. A warm salty broth trickled past his lips. It tasted like rabbit, wild onion and oregano. It was beyond delicious. He realised at once that he was starving. A second warm drizzle followed the first and Athelstan opened his eyes a crack.

What he saw caused him to blink twice in an effort to focus. He believed he was seeing double. A slender white-haired woman with a pinched face and long slender nose leaned over him with a wooden bowl and beside her sat a mirror image of the first, save for the bowl. Each woman had one brown and one blue eye, one having a brown left eye and the other a brown right eye. He screwed his eyes shut hoping to clear this disturbing double vision, but the pair was still there when he re–opened them.

With a slight frown, he croaked weakly, "Two? There are two of you… right?"

"Two!" They answered together nodding. Kind smiles lit their faces. "You did not hurt your head, after all, just your ribs. We are sisters if you must know. Twins," they said simultaneously. Both ladies giggled at this.

"Where am I?" He tried to sit up, but an overwhelming wave of dizziness swept over him and he collapsed back onto the crude cot – head aching unmercifully.

"Learn from that, Celtic Man. It will take a day, or two for the Poppy Sap to leave you completely." The pair spoke in a back and forth chorus. He looked from one woman to the other as they seamlessly helped each other speak. One would start a phrase and the other would pick it up after only a few words and they would alternate back and forth until the thought was completed. Each seemed to know what the other would say and when. It was a bit disturbing, to say the least. "To answer your question you are in the mountains well north of Milan. Rhaetia to be precise."

"Rhaetia? I am named Athelstan," The two white-haired women nodded but remained silent.

More clear broth was raised to his mouth and for a time he ate in silence. He reached for his left side with a groan and found it was heavily bandaged and wrapped in white linen. He frowned as he remembered what had happened.

Pausing in his meal, he blinked several times only now comprehending what they were saying and asked, "Poppy Sap?"

"Yes, we had to keep you asleep until you were well enough to wake up. You had a torn lung and two broken ribs. We cut you open to set the bones and stop the bleeding inside. You very nearly died." Nodding weakly, he reached for the bowl, raised it to his lips and began taking slow sips. He found it disturbing trying to watch these two sisters speak. His eyes were forced to dart back and forth. It was beginning to make him feel dizzy and nauseated. Their explanation made absolutely no sense to him.

"Finish the bowl if you can and then try to get some sleep. You will feel better in the morning. I think it's time to go and sing to Pinky again." The twins left him alone with his rabbit soup and a head full of questions. He was weak and tired and tomorrow did seem like a better time to find the answers to those questions. The warmth from the soup soon lulled him. After a few minutes, clear alto voices singing long forgotten lullabies filled the evening air and he fell back to sleep listening to the strangely haunting harmony in the distance.

It was a rapid crunching and chewing sound that roused him from his slumber. Even through closed eyes, he could tell it was a bright summer morning. His eyes opened and focused on an astonishing sight. A small red squirrel sat nestled into his long reddish–blonde beard. It was chewing and filling its cheek pouches with apple seeds. The squirrel turned suddenly, sat up and looked Athelstan squarely in the eye. He devoured another apple seed at high speed. Then with a sharp squeak, he scampered out through an open window in a frantic rush, apple seeds, bushy tail and all.

Sitting up slowly this time, he stretched his back and shoulders. It was as though he had not used them for weeks and each joint creaked and popped in protest. His ribs still ached but even if he had been asleep for a few days, his side should have hurt far worse than this. He was also alone. The two odd women from his dream were gone. With a sigh, he realised he had another mystery, or two to solve. His brain felt as fuzzy as his tongue.

He discovered he was naked beneath the heavy white furs save for the thick padding wrapped securely around his ribs. He stood and hammered the top of his head on one of the low rafters. The explosion of stars made him sit back down heavily letting the accompanying wave of dizziness pass. This long low house was not built for someone his size. He had always towered over most men of his day by a full half foot. For the first time, he let his eyes wander over the interior of this strange little house. His long low cot was tucked into one of the back corners where the sharply sloping roof came close to touching the ground. This steep angle would help shed snow and deflect winds common in an alpine, or northern setting. It was similar to the house he was born into. What was he doing in the mountains? He should be near the sea. Questions were beginning to pile up like firewood.

The walls, rafters and ridgepole were festooned with every sort of herb, root, mushroom and moss. Swallows and purple martins nested in the higher rafters and three tiny bats found suitable refuge behind a crude, crooked cupboard near one of the doors. The level surfaces were no different and contained clutter beyond anything Athelstan had ever seen. Barrels and clay amphorae were jammed into every available nook and cranny, while other spots on the floor were piled high with sacks, baskets and boxes containing all manner of mysteriously aromatic substances.

While the back wall had no windows, the same could not be said about the others. He counted ten windows of all different sizes and shapes as well as two doors; one at either end of the building. It was almost as though each window was designed with a different function in mind. Looking up he tried to stand again, this time with far better results. He carefully untied the bandages covering his ribs. He peeled away an oily poultice to reveal a large yellowish mark and several well-healed scars. He probed his wound with some confusion. Something was not right here.

Still in a half–crouch, he wrapped the huge white bed fur around his shoulders and stepped outside. He was looking south down into a long valley surrounded by towering snow-capped mountain peaks. Icy streams from the high melting snows fed a wide river that meandered through the fertile grasslands far below. The cabin sat on a flat bench of land overlooking the valley floor and someone had transformed this wild land into a spectacular garden.

Aside from the riotous blaze of flower and herbal beds, clumps of vegetables filled every available space between the fruit and nut trees. These plantings were purposely random and the whole seemed to blend in seamlessly with their wild surroundings. It was a pleasant change from the endless rows of crops common to farms in the Po Valley. It was the most idyllic place he had ever seen. However, where was this place?

He walked around back and found more terraced gardens in the sloping hills above as well as several long barns of similar construction to the odd house. The twins who fed him soup were nowhere to be seen and he was beginning to suspect they really were a dream. If so, who had bandaged his ribs?

Finally, near the edge of the tree line, he spotted one of the ladies on all fours using a digging stick in one of the gardens. A movement behind her stopped his heart. Three bears, a large one and two smaller, emerged from the cover of trees and slowly approached her. He cast about for a weapon, he could wield against a bear – but found none. He started to hurry towards her and opened his mouth to warn her when she looked around and saw them as well. Her reaction brought him to a complete halt.

It was clear she was motioning the three beasts to hurry up and then bade them stop and sit, which all three did. For the next ten minutes, he watched her, hand feed potatoes and carrots to these three beasts. Then with the same absolute authority, she shooed them back into the trees and in a twinkling were gone. That was when he closed his mouth.

"Never seen that before, eh, Boy?" He must have jumped a foot at the sudden voice behind him. The other aged sister had somehow appeared like magic and her left arm was casually draped over the neck of a black-tailed deer. It ate walnuts and green grapes she produced from her apron pocket.

"Or this either for that matter," he stated with growing astonishment. "What is this place and who are you two?" He glanced back up the hill and saw the sister coming back down the hill.

"I am called Ratia and that is my sister Ludmilla. My, my – you are a big one!" She was appraising him like some prize steer and he could not help but smile at her. Her tone was gentle and kind.

"I am somehow heartened to find that you each can talk independently of the other. I had begun to wonder." Ratia took his hand and started towards one of the barns.

"Ludmilla is still mouthing my words even from up there. We have always talked like that and its part of the reason you find us living here. It disturbs other people as well."

Ludmilla caught up finally and repeated. "My, my but you are a big one." Athelstan had to smile at the pair. They were so connected, so alike.

"I am called Athelstan." The corner of his mouth twitched into a half grin. "I am a General in the Senone Army." The sisters looked at each other and nodded.

"Yes, we remember. We are old – not deaf. Greynoc was right; he said you are a Senone from the Po Valley – beaten by Rome and set adrift upon the world. We are very glad Pinky brought you here for you would have died had he not." This had already become a very confusing conversation. Athelstan had already decided he was still alive and he must have dreamed the black army of hooded soldiers. He had also decided these two ladies were very real.

"He? Was he right? Who said I was a Senone? What is a Greynoc and who is Pinky? I do not see anyone here but you two and you of course," he referred to the young deer that seemed quite content to have its neck and ears stroked as they walked towards a long low barn-like structure. It sat some distance up the hill from the house. A flood of questions had begun to pour out of him.

"The Hidden Ones told us who you were, but we did not believe them. Then we learned of Rome's attack on the Po Valley and we knew then you were fleeing the destruction of your city." The two women nodded simultaneously. Athelstan blinked at the two and started to laugh.

"The Hidden Ones? That is very good. You mean the Invisible Ones as we reckon them. Of course, everyone knows they belong to the land of Sidhe – they are the fairy–folk. I did not just sprout out of a cabbage patch. You must know they are not real." He was still chuckling when they approached the large entrance to the barn. The twins spoke.

"Do not be so certain about that. We found you lying in a cabbage patch. Did you hear that Greynoc? You are not real, what do you make of that I wonder?" She addressed a low bush growing to one side of the open doorway.

A snort of pure derision was heard. "Well, that is disturbing but I hardly care what this witless oaf thinks is real, or not. I am reasonably certain that I am real. I am not too certain about him yet."

Athelstan jumped at the gruff male voice and watched in astonishment as a bush stood up and transformed into a most curious looking little man. He was about five feet tall and covered with leaves, twigs, mosses, and feathers. His face, hands, and arms were covered in black and green tree moulds, carefully applied in a mottled pattern and even his eyebrows were festooned with fern fronds and grasses. He looked like a part of the living forest. He was also glaring at Athelstan.

"You… you people are real!" the Senone blurted out.

"So I have been told," an annoyed Greynoc retorted.

"You are one of the Invisible People… Then you are this Pinky, the one who brought me here, the one they sing to?" he blurted out perplexed.

"Hardly. I would kill any man who would dare call me 'Pinky'," he glared at the twins. "It is a terrible name for an animal." He turned on his heel and ducked into the barn followed by Ratia. "See Gentle Mother, I told you these Senones were not very smart. It is why they live on flat ground. At least this one was smart enough to flee from the Romans. They are still beating the bushes for stragglers from the war. It is a wise man who knows when he is beaten. It is not unmanly to yield to fear after all." At this point, Ludmilla caught up with them and winked silently at Athelstan as she too plunged into the darkness of the barn.

Athelstan was left standing outside with the Black-Tailed deer nudging him for more grapes. He gathered the white fur around his nakedness and followed them into the barn.

"I am a Warrior. I do not FLEE from Romans... I do not run from any fight – ever! I FEAR NOTHING!" Even though he was flabbergasted and a bit incensed, he found suddenly that he was speaking to no one. Greynoc's voice carried out from inside the barn.

"Then you are also a fool," he said flatly.

Chapter Three

"I am NOT a fool! Will someone tell me who in all Tartarus is this Pinky you keep talking about?" The deer followed him into the barn and disappeared into the gloom at the back. Athelstan was getting annoyed and his voice showed it. He came to a stop with his feet planted in the fresh rushes covering the floor and let his eyes adjust to the sudden darkness inside. The two women exchanged amused glances. Greynoc had a half smile, half-scowl on his twig and moss covered face and the witch twins were beaming. They all looked at him expectantly.

"What?" he barked and then his eyes refocused on the rear of the long narrow barn. His mouth fell open in astonishment. A thunderous whinny shook the rafters as the great warhorse pranced forward out of the deep gloom, hooves pounded on the wooden floor. The beast was full of excitement.

"Maehadren?" Athelstan exclaimed with a mixture of surprise and delight. He had been certain that he had seen the last of his old friend along with his armour and weapons, clothing and silver; thieves were everywhere. It was a poignant reunion between horse and master. The great warhorse bowed to Athelstan before nuzzling him backwards several steps with his soft nose. He puffed huge gusts of air from his flaring nostrils and tossed his head with one deafening whinny after another.

"Peace old friend, I did not abandon you by choice," he was being sniffed and drooled on as his long–time friend made certain Athelstan was still well.

"Oh, he knows that. He has been looking in on you through a window every day since you arrived. He watched over you while you recovered," the twins explained.

"Never seen the like myself," snorted Greynoc. Athelstan was scratching Maehadren's forehead. "That is one very loyal creature, Senone. He must have been delivered to you by the very hand of the Goddess Epona." Greynoc had a genuine smile on his face or was it a grimace. It was difficult to tell behind all the camouflage.

"I would not doubt it. Yet, I am curious how you were able to approach him. He is shy of people and so far I have been the only one who has ever touched him and gotten away with it." He was stroking Maehadren's long neck when the great head swung around and trapped Athelstan between his head and shoulder. He was getting a horse–hug and the force of it drove the wind from his lungs. His ribs ached and he had to elbow the huge beast before it let him loose.

"Easy you, great slack lout, you. I'm glad to see you too," he gave a sidelong to Ratia and Ludmilla. "How were you able to get near him? He is a singular demon when the mood is upon him."

He noticed the trio exchanging glances. "We sing to him of course," they chorused. Their eyes danced and twinkled with childlike mischief.

"You sing to this – to this giant Buggerlugs? This is Pinky? This is the Pinky you have been singing too?" They all laughed and nodded with some vigor. Athelstan blinked before joining in.

"But his name is Maehadren, why do you call him Pinky?" Athelstan was confused.

"Ahhh, but we did not know that, did we? He could not tell us his name, could he? Neither could you. When he found us, he was rider–less and reddish–pink from all the blood you spit up over his head and neck. He led us back to you lying in our cabbages and Greynoc's people helped us get you back here. Maehadren here was a bit shy of us at first but once he saw us with Stander, the Black–tail, he calmed right down. After that it took but a few songs and a pocketful of sugar–plums and dried apples; he was as gentle as a fuzzy bunny." The twins were giggling like little girls and Athelstan could hardly resist laughing with them. He fixed a withering gaze on Maehadren. The horse turned his head and lowered it as if abashed.

"You shameless…!" Athelstan scolded. "Sugar plums and apples? Singing?" The great head lowered even more. "You would desert me for sweet plums, apples, and gentle song after only a few days… I declare!" Maehadren knew his master's tone and shoved him with his snout. The horse trumpeted and shook his mighty head. Greynoc put up a hand.

"Athelstan, my large warrior-cousin, you have been here for a bit longer than just a few days," Greynoc said seriously. "It was two days before the full moon of your month of Tinne when you arrived on our Gentle Sister's doorstep. That moon has now waned to new and has again waxed to full twice since. This night is the full moon of Coll. You have been kept asleep and hand fed liquids for sixty–two days General," the Chieftain commented gravely. "Nothing could have been done differently. You live and everything beyond that is a trivial matter; would you not agree?"

Athelstan was stunned and tried to get his mind around this revelation. Sixty–two days? This is the month of Coll? He shook his head. He had wasted a month in his quest, lying sound asleep being tended to like an infant by two witches and this mythical fairy chieftain. Who would believe such a tale? Certainly not his insane king.

With lips pressed into a thin hard line, he placed a hand on Greynoc's shoulder and nodded. "I agree, Lord Greynoc. Life is always best, but what of my clothes and gear? Were they lost? I would hate to travel to Sparta dressed only in this white fur." He looked down. It trailed along the ground behind him and offered only the barest coverage in front. He held it closed with both hands.

"I'm not certain if their elderly King Leonidas ll of Sparta would survive such a sight as this." Laughter erupted again. Any sense of actual modesty was alien to them all.

"Your possessions are in Pinky's... ah rather, in Maehadren's stall. Maehadren!" Greynoc nodded solemnly. "Tis a fitting name for this magnificent animal." The chieftain looked at the majestic creature with an expression of awe. "Yes... he is a most remarkable horse... too bad he will be leaving soon." He let his hand gently slide from shoulder to flank and the horse shivered in delight. The three watched Athelstan locate his clothing; they continued talking as he dressed.

"Athelstan, you do realise that we had no choice but to keep you here like this? If there had been any other way we would have chosen it gladly." Ratia and her sister seemed quite concerned he understood their motives.

He smiled at them over the walls of the stall while pulling a long–sleeved white shirt over his head. He fluffed out his beard and moustache over the white material.

"Peace Gentle Mothers, My Lord Greynoc! I am more grateful to you than you will ever know. My mission may have been delayed by two moons but that is a small matter and easily remedied," he shook his head again in disbelief. "I have no doubt, had it not been for your kindness towards someone you did not know, that my mission would already be at an end. You have given my people a chance. Whether I succeed or die is again up to me and I shall always be grateful to you for that chance."

He pulled up long woolen blue and green check pants and laced leather boots in place. Out of habit, he slipped two long, delicately etched skinning knives into each boot and stepped back out to meet them. He left his armour and weapons where they leaned against the back wall of the stall. He would have no need of them in this friendly, cosy glade.

"Why is it too bad Maehadren is leaving? He is deadly at both ends and bloody uncomfortable in the middle. I cannot imagine how he has wormed his way into your hearts so quickly," he chuckled.

"He shits!" they said gravely serious. Athelstan's face fell into a mask of confusion. He considered himself rather clever but this was like getting a 'yes' to the question 'why is the sky blue?'

"He shits... yes... he does quite a lot of that. It is why I do not let him stand near my board while I eat" he opened his hands and shrugged his shoulders in confusion and the action caused his three new friends to laugh.

"We gather it up and spread it on our gardens. It makes everything grow bigger and faster. Here taste this." Ludmilla reached into her deep basket and took out a length of vine bearing fat globes of red fruit. His eyes narrowed as he spied one of the leaves.

"Thank you – no. That is the fruit of a Nightshade plant. They are poisonous."

"No! It is, but this plant is not poisonous This fruit is sweet." Ratia took a big bite from the ruby globe and juice dribbled down her chin as she chewed and swallowed. With an intense look, she dipped a finger into the red flesh and held it out for him to taste.

"Do you not trust us?" they asked.

Dubiously, Athelstan sniffed it. He tasted it with his tongue and braced for the bitter, drying feeling associated with nightshade poisons, paused a moment smacking his lips, then devoured the sweet and succulent morsel. "That is really very good," he chewed and mopped juice from his wild beard. "What do you call it?"

"Tow May Tow!" the three said in unison. Athelstan mouthed the odd word several times and licked his fingers clean.

"So the Horse Goddess Epona has turned the poison of this fruit sweet through Maehadren's shit?" They nodded. He also nodded his understanding. "I am never surprised but always amazed at Her power and Her love for us. We are the most blessed of all people are we not?"

"It has always been so, my giant friend," admitted Greynoc. He placed his hand on Athelstan's forearm.

The twins were already walking away with Stander in hot pursuit of more treats leaving the two very different men alone to talk. He took a closer look at this odd Rhaetian chieftain and noticed he was a much older man than he had first appeared.

At twenty-seven, Athelstan was in his absolute prime and by age forty he would be considered old. It was difficult to tell through his camouflage, but Greynoc was venerable. He had more that fifty winters of experience behind those wise eyes; he was ancient for these times. Yet, his twinkling brown eyes still held the light of wonderment so often reserved for the very young. He was a living enigma to the mountain-bred Senone and Athelstan would take great pleasure should he ever get the chance to unravel the mysteries of this man's life story.

"You have not asked about Milan yet, First General of the Senones, Half brother to the King. Does the Senone nation now forsake that land? Will you just leave the Romans there unchallenged? We are many here in Rhaetia but even so, we will not be able to contain the Romans forever." Greynoc was blunt and now the young Senone felt like a mouse caught in the gaze of a cat.

"You are well informed," said Athelstan. Greynoc simply stared at him.

"That land is our home. We shall reclaim it!" Athelstan stated. "No, we will not leave them unchallenged for long. The timing of their raid was very well considered. It is a Golden year and our people travel far to the east for our Samhain festival… as we have done since time began. They knew that and arrived as we were leaving. Cowards… I stayed with a token force to cover the people as they left Milan," he issued a dangerous growl of frustration that caused Greynoc's eyes to rise slightly. "We have emptied all of our cities. Ravenna chief among them."

"I have heard."

"The Senones will be back, but not until spring, or early summer now. We are forced to winter at Gwennderion Glade during such migrations. It is the only place where our nation can comfortably spend a winter. However, you may be certain of this, Rome shall pay for this treachery. Greynoc, I know these Romans. I have had many dealings with them over the years and this I do know about them. They are greedy like little children, but in all things, they use great caution. Romans are not stupid people; they will hold on to what they have won and strangle the life out of it before they turn their eyes further northward. Rome will not assault a mountain kingdom like Rhaetia in winter. They are not crazy. We have an old saying 'Hard times do not last, determined people do.' Rome will be taught once again what determined people are capable of – when pushed." Athelstan scowled back at the Chieftain.

"I know of Gwennderion Glade in Alexander's Macedonia," he said casually. "But something else troubles you; something beyond the raid, something far more personal." Greynoc was blunt and intuitive... a side effect of his great age. "Your face shows it. Tell me what it is. Perhaps I can help in some small way." Greynoc spoke with soft authority and great confidence.

Athelstan had felt comfortable with this fairy–chieftain immediately and after a moment, he nodded almost imperceptibly. "Our wise Druids tell many a fanciful tale of the magical Hidden Ones and there is one thing that is present in all the stories, 'Trying to deceive the Hidden Ones is like trying to hold back a river with a broom.'"

A low chuckle rumbled behind Greynoc's beard.

Athelstan let out a long sigh and turned his attention to Maehadren. "Trahearn Livy is my king... my half–brother – my friend. We grew up together, played and laughed, drank and tasted women together. He once broke my nose while I was brawling with him. Being nobles we were schooled in Latin, Greek, the numbers and we were trained in the ways of war; as it has always been for boys such as us – noble caste."

He paused and a fond memory tugged at his lips. "We even stole strawberries together. Can you understand what it is to be inseparable from someone? Well, that was the two of us. Where there was one, the other was not far. His enemies were my enemies and together we were invincible."

Greynoc sat down in the rushes on the floor watching as Athelstan began to examine Maehadren in minute detail. It was a meticulous process. He began with the eyes, ears, nose, mouth and teeth. He moved down the neck and felt each leg and hoof. His hand brushed over the ribs and under the belly before moving to the rump and hind legs. He spent the rest of his time searching for knots and burrs in Maehadren's white mane and tail. He found none. The twins had taken good care of him.

All the while Athelstan talked and throughout Greynoc listened in silence.

"Four years ago his father King Brennus died and Trahearn Livy became our king. He has always been quick–witted, clever and fair. His hand is made of stone when needed, but he loves his family and his people and would die to protect them – I know that. He ruled with kindness and wisdom and all Senone loved and trusted him. He may very well be the greatest man I have ever known."

Athelstan and Greynoc traced the same design in the air; a Celtic air sigil to the honoured dead; in tribute to the King Brennus.

Finished with Maehadren he turned back to face Greynoc. "He is going mad from a sickness and I do not know what to do about it." There was a long pause as the old man frowned down at the straw and sweet rushes he sat on. Then he looked up at the young General leveling a shrewd gaze upon him.

"Oh yes you do!" he said accusingly. "You know what you must do about it – what you want is someone to give you permission to do it."

Athelstan stood dumbfounded. It was not the response he was expecting.

"Come now my boy, I might be an old man, but I can still read a man's true colours. I can tell you are neither a dullard nor an idiot. For you to speak of this to me now means you have thought long and hard on the matter already. This madness you speak of did not come upon him swiftly but in spare inches at a time. His mind has been fading for months now has it not?"

Athelstan nodded sadly.

"You know what is at stake and what will come from your inaction. Aside from some sage advice, I cannot help you decide what you need to do. Only you can give yourself the permission to do what must be done. So what is your decision?" Greynoc's eyes bored into those of the younger Senone and Athelstan nodded silently.

"He must be removed from the throne for all our sakes."

"Then do it!" There was a tinge of sadness in the chieftain's voice. "Will you sit and sing a lament for the dead with me? Your King and brother deserve no less." The large Celt sat and began a long slow dirge with Greynoc. Tears flowed from eyes both old and young but their voices did not falter. When the song had ended, Greynoc nodded at Athelstan.

"There is a saying among us Rhaetians. 'A man must become what he dreams and that dream will be reflected in his actions.' You dream wisely, Athelstan of Senone." A statement offered no room for contradiction.

"Rhaetians?" Athelstan asked.

Greynoc stood "You might know us better as Swiss." Athelstan nodded his understanding.

"This is Rhaetia? I thought the twins were mistaken. I have travelled far from my intended course." Greynoc nodded and stood.

"You can thank Maehadren for that. He was drawn to the twin's magic. Come along. Let us see what is for breakfast." The two strolled out of the barn into the bright sunshine and Athelstan moaned and stretched his aching side. He leaned over to one side then the other and caught a flash of red through the hazel trees off to the west of the orchards. He straightened and saw it again. "I wonder what... that... red... thing?"

He froze in horror as he realised what was coming up the forest track. He grabbed Greynoc's leafy collar and propelled him back into the barn. Greynoc protested but he was weightless in the grip of the huge Senone.

"Romans!" He spat before dashing towards Maehadren's stall for his weapons. Armour took time to put on so he grabbed his sword and shield and turned towards the door.

"Wait, Athelstan, what are you going to do?"

He stopped and blinked at Greynoc.

"What in all Tartarus you think I am going to do? I know what these monsters will do to the twins – old or not, they are women and they will all take their turn. I will die before they lay a hand on either of them. Now get out of my way."

Greynoc grabbed Athelstan's wrist in a vice–like grip and growled softly. "If you die they will have their way with them regardless. Dying to protect friends is hardly a way to win a war. Make the Romans die protecting their families seems a far better choice to me. Think for a minute, Athelstan! You forget where you are – boy. The twins will be fine, just relax. Things will work out for the best... they always do."

The confidence in Greynoc's voice was unmistakable. Athelstan for his own part did not relish a pitched battled with nine hardened Roman soldiers on an empty stomach. That Tow May Tow seemed very far away now. They watched from the shadows as a mounted commander in his red cloak and gold armour, along with eight armed and armoured foot soldiers, closed on the twins cabin. The leader dismounted and strode up to the door with a superior swagger. He pounded on the doorframe and bellowed. "Sicco! Mondo!" (Out! Now!)

Athelstan grimaced and held his breath as the Roman waited. Then the door slowly opened and Ludmilla and Ratia were roughly hauled out of their house and pushed to their knees in front of the commander with swords at their throats.

"Haaaa antiquis dominas. Quatinus e' Senone Athelstan?" He was asking the 'old women' where Athelstan was in Latin. One of the sisters cowered and pointed at the barn. Athelstan's shoulders dropped. A fight was inevitable now. Yet, he would not fault the old witch. She had her sister to consider and she did what she must. The alternative would have been immediate death for them both had she not spoken. Now, she could look forward to a long slow one, nailed to a cross instead.

The Romans spread out as they approached the barn, commander in the rear. There was no doubt that their quarry knew they were here so stealth was replaced by sensible tactics.

"Athelstan of Senone, come out! You are under arrest for crimes against Rome!" he called out in flawless Latin. He used that haughty tone, one that always grated on Athelstan's ears.

"They're all yours my boy," whispered Greynoc with a wide smile.

"Oh… you are too kind. Perhaps you might join me out there. Nine against one is somewhat unfair after all." His tone dripped with sarcasm.

Greynoc shook his head with a bright grin. "Unfair yes, but I grieve that they will not have time to go for more men." Athelstan frowned at that for a moment, then swung his blade up onto his shoulder and casually took a step, or two outside. He made certain that the bulk of the building was behind him so he could not be surrounded. However, after so long laying asleep and still weakened from his ordeal, his sword felt clumsy and heavy in his hands.

"I am Athelstan!" He said in equally flawless Latin. "What do the dogs of Rome want with me?" His sword felt awkward and ill-balanced. He swung it like a farmer would wield a hoe.

The commander was sickened to hear his glorious Latin language being uttered by an animal and his face showed it.

"The Proconsul Papirius Aurelius Cursor has issued an order for your arrest for making war upon the northern Legions of Roma. You will be brought before him to answer for your crimes before you are executed. Now lay that sword down and come along. My orders say alive, or dead and I care not which."

There was pure loathing in the Commander's voice plus the unmistakable glint of the predator in his eyes as he sensed the Celt's weakened condition. Confidence at a quick kill oozed from his every pore. Athelstan also took measure of this man quickly. He was of noble birth and came to his present rank by appointment rather than by merit, or skill. He would not dirty his hands in this fight. His left cuff concealed a perfumed and powdered handkerchief used to block out unpleasant odours. He was an ineffectual, effeminate, fop in armour bought with family wealth. He was accustomed to having his orders obeyed without question and controlled his men using fear rather than respect. He was not a danger. His Contubernium of eight men was another matter entirely. These were well–trained and merciless killers.

Bushy blonde eyebrows lifted in mock surprise. "Oh the Proconsul wants to take council with me, does he? Well, I have never heard the like." Sarcasm dripped from every word. "You may tell him that we will indeed have a nice long talk, but at the moment I have pressing business elsewhere. I shall make it a point to ask for him the moment I arrive in Rome and we can have our little chat. Afterwards, his and your world will be burned to as he's around his ears. It saddens me to think you will not be alive to witness that blessed event." Athelstan had taken this time to assess the nine men facing him. He was in a very bad spot and he knew it. Whatever might be said about Romans, they were perhaps the best–trained soldiers on earth. He would need more than luck in order to eat that promised breakfast.

"Advance!" The mounted commander ordered. "Give him no quarter!"

Athelstan raised his sword in shaking hands while taking a defensive stance and waited for a hated enemy to come close enough to engage. He might visit paradise this morning but so would some of these Romans. He smiled grimly at the idea. Death could not frighten Athelstan. He was a Celt and so, in his mind, immortal. Only one thing frightened him – failure. The troop moved as one and closed on the Senone. The Celt held his long sword one–handed in the high guard position and raised his shield.

When the soldiers had closed to within ten feet of Athelstan, he heard the clear, sharp bugle of some unknown bird directly behind him. It was clear, crisp and perfect. He jumped in surprise. What had just made that sound? Before the echo died, a sudden flurry of tiny white–feathered arrows filled the air. Eight Roman soldiers collapsed to the ground as one. Since he was still mounted, the commander had further to fall but he hit the ground just the same and he was just as dead as his soldiers. Each had been slain by dozens of the short slender shafts. Athelstan glanced around at the nine corpses. He reversed his weapon point down, leaned on the pommel of his sword and cleared his throat.

Greynoc casually joined him outside. He looked around Athelstan's left side with raised fern–frond eyebrows. He then looked up at a thoroughly astonished Athelstan. The Celt looked around and began to notice there were actually hundreds of Greynoc's people in and around the buildings, gardens and surrounding forest. Hedgerows and leafy shrubs disentangled to reveal hundreds of men armed with short bows. Some of them were hidden in the trees and bushes. Others were decorated with trees and bushes. A few of the trees and bushes did not move. They were actually real trees and bushes.

It was quite impossible to tell shrubbery from man unless they decided to move. The significance of this ability was not lost on Athelstan.

"See, you forget where you are my giant friend. I command here, not them" he turned a squint eye up at the Senone. "Not you either. You will do well to remember that my boy."

"Hrumph!" Athelstan grunted.

"Is there anything else I can do for you, you know, while I still have my sword out?" Athelstan asked, still looking about in with growing realisation.

The Romans had died all in a single heartbeat and now Hidden Ones began the job of removing weapons, armour, and valuables.

"Nothing that I can think of my boy," the Chieftain said casually. "Besides, I am starved what about you?" Athelstan watched as Greynoc stepped over a dead soldier and headed back towards the witches cabin.

"I could - eat…" he said absently as he watched Greynoc's men clear the courtyard of corpses. There was nothing left to do but to follow the chieftain downhill.

Chapter Four

It had been more than an ample breakfast. He eyed the bowl containing the warm roasted Tow May Tows but simply could not manage another bite. Eggs, wild boar meat, boiled roots and hot flatbreads rounded out the substantial breakfast he shared with his hosts.

He turned to Greynoc. "What was that strange whistle I heard you use?"

"A Swans Song. Black Swans sing that very song just before they die." He nodded sagely.

Athelstan thought about that for a moment with a frown. "No, they don't. Swans hiss, they don't sing."

"Oh, then perhaps the next time your life is in danger, I will be sure to hiss instead." Greynoc hissed and it was almost inaudible.

"I see your point. Use the Swan's song to your heart's content. Who am I to argue? Still, I would have liked to have a quiet chat with our dearly departed legionnaires out there. We might have learned a great deal."

"So, you would rather I had let them kill you?" Greynoc queried past another mouthful of the boar. A wry grin crossed the Athelstan's face and he grunted at the humour. Ludmilla, Ratia, and Greynoc looked at him gravely.

"No, no, you did what you felt you had to in order to protect Ratia, Ludmilla, and your people. I shall not fault you for doing your job as the leader, Greynoc. I am a Clan Chieftain too." Athelstan returned their serious looks each in their turn. Greynoc had no idea what he had just done – but Athelstan did.

"Rome, despite its many faults is renowned for its organisation and discipline. It is the very backbone of their society – especially their military. It is my belief that they all defecate in perfectly straight rows and only when they are commanded to do so." This got a quiet laugh from his audience.

"Greynoc, let me ask you something. What do you know for certain about the Roman military?" he asked casually.

The Rhaetian Chieftain frowned and the fern fronds that were his eyebrows knitted together. "They are organised into vast Legions numbering between four to five thousand men. A Legate commands each Legion. Each Legate answers to and is directed by the Emperor and the Roman Senate." Greynoc stated with conviction.

Athelstan looked at the ageing Rhaetian and nodded ever so slowly. "That is right, sometimes," he responded kindly. "They may appear to operate like that, but more often they do not. At the Legion level, they act more like separate countries with the Legate being a kind of dictator. Some Legates listen to the Senate while others do not. Political intrigue is a way of life with no one being safe from the assassin's blade. Yet, each citizen holds a fierce loyalty to Rome and its high ideals of Empire and Republic. Atop that, they are convinced that theirs is the superior way of life. It makes them a very dangerous foe."

Stunned silence greeted this. Athelstan continued. "Despite what they might think of themselves they are still quite unique in many ways. The Roman Army, as it actually exists, is constructed entirely of Contuberniums, eight men led by a Decanus - a Commander like this group today."

He pointed towards the door. "That! That is the Roman Army, eight men, and a leader. Every other subgroup, regardless of its size, or skill level, is based on this simple design of eight men and one leader. Bloody ingenious when you think about it." The three leaned forward as Athelstan spoke. He was speaking very softly, a skill he had developed to focus his listener's attention more fully.

"Additional Contuberia, along with non–combatant personnel totalling one hundred souls forms a Centuria, two Centuria forms a Cohort. The list goes on and on I am afraid. These tiny compact units can group together and act as one single entity, your legion," He gestured towards Greynoc. "Or they can separate and fan out to search huge areas very effectively. In doing so the army takes on all the characteristics of a cat with its many whiskers searching for mice."

Ratia was frowning now, she was either lost, or she was beginning to see where this was headed.

"Each unit is like a single whisker. If a cat loses a piece of a whisker, its loss goes completely unnoticed. So too with Rome, the loss of several men is meaningless. On the other hand, if a mouse were to pluck that same whisker out, or if we were to kill an entire Contubernium, the cat would instantly know where to look for that mouse, would it not?"

Athelstan stopped and let the room go silent.

The twins each raised a hand to their mouths in shock. Greynoc frowned and nodded slowly.

"Then if what you say is true, Rome is the cat, we plucked a whisker and you are the mouse," Greynoc stated slowly as realisation dawned on him.

A light moan of despair escaped Ratia and both old women looked at Athelstan.

He nodded.

"So you are saying Romans will come here looking for those men? Greynoc asked.

"The Romans will mount a search when those nine men out there do not report back, yes. They are very good about such things," he admitted flatly.

The twins began to cry quietly. "Sister, we will have to leave our home. Where will we go? They will come looking for Athelstan and these men and when they do not find them…" They left off speaking and began to scurry around as if trying to pack and flee in an instant.

"What will they do to us? We cannot leave our home." They wailed in unison; eyes wide in panic.

Greynoc gathered them both up in his arms stroking their hair. They clung to him for comfort but both women were now badly frightened. The very idea of a Legion of five thousand hideous murdering animals invading their tranquil valley was beyond unthinkable.

Athelstan suddenly felt terrible for being the cause of all this; especially after their overwhelming kindness to him. "Ludmilla, Ratia, please calm down. While it is true Rome will find me eventually, it will be at a time and a place of MY choosing. They certainly will not find me here. Listen to me!" It was a command and they calmed down a bit.

"All is hardly doom and gloom, ladies. Tell me, have either of you ever misplaced an object and spent the time to look for it?" The twins still clung to Greynoc for comfort and nodded.

"Have you noticed that you always find it in the last place you look?" They nodded again a confused frown on their faces. His steady gaze and soft voice and confident tone were having a soothing effect – it always did.

"Do you know why that is?" They shook their heads again.

"That is so, because once you find what it is you are looking for – you stop looking. Don't you? So it shall be with the Romans."

They blinked and nodded but they were clearly confused.

"Their scouts will find these men long before they come anywhere near this valley. You will be perfectly safe right here. Do you understand?" They shook their heads unsure.

A serene calm descended upon Athelstan as it often did during stressful times. It helped him think more clearly and although the Poppy Sap still affected him, his mind was already beginning to clear. He looked at these gentle Rhaetians and an old story suddenly occurred to him.

"Ummm. In the stories of my people where they regard the Invisible People, it is often said that they can still manipulate the old powers of… magic. Is that just another myth, or is your magic real?" he asked simply.

"Magic? Real?" Ludmilla was outraged, daubing at her teary eyes with a ragged cuff. "What do you think has kept you alive this last two months, bloody fruit flies and mud? Of course, the old magic is real! However, you just answer me this, young man, how do you expect magic to keep all of Rome from finding our valley? How does magic stop them from looking for you?" There was outrage mixed with their anxiety.

A cunning smile slowly covered Athelstan's face as he was being rebuked and it did not waver in the slightest after they had stopped. "Oh it will not stop them from looking for me, but it can stop them from searching these mountains."

It was now their turn to frown. "WHAT?" they demanded in unison.

"Have I mentioned yet…" he paused for effect. "How superstitious our Roman brethren are?" They shook their heads confused and it was clear by their expressions they believed he was crazy.

However, he was far from crazy. Athelstan had not become the First

General of a vast Celtic army by accident. In fact, he possessed an agile and cunning mind. Atop that, he recognised a deadly weapon when one was presented to him.

"I would ask you to think about this for a moment. Romans are cripplingly superstitious people. They have deities, daemons and night terrors, both real and imagined, beyond count. They fear them all," he looked at the witches.

"Ladies, you know how the ancient magic functions. We can force their minds to believe anything we want if we present them with the proper set of circumstances. That is the key." Greynoc was frowning.

"Combine the elements of magic, Greynoc's camouflage, with Roman superstition and we have created a devastating weapon that a few men can use against many. We will take these dead Romans deeper into the mountains to the west and bury them in a rockslide. Wound and release the horse where it can be easily found. Once the beast is located, they will begin a systematic search and the dead will be quickly found. It will be reported back, as a simple accident. They will have found the missing men they are looking for and they will have a very plausible explanation for their deaths. Like you, once they find what they are looking for, they will stop looking. Rome will have no reason to look here at all. While they are in the hills, if we can make them believe that evil spirits inhabit these mountains, they will not willingly return. Moan, laugh, sing, wail and send a few well-timed rockslides down upon them and that should be more than enough to convince them the mountains are haunted. You must remain absolutely hidden for any of this to work." Greynoc slowly began to smile at the simplicity of the plan. It was a wicked grin and it was infectious.

"I know the perfect place. We shall see to it, Athelstan. You only just awoke. You still need time to regain your strength," Greynoc admonished and the still teary–eyed the sisters nodded their agreement.

He looked at each one of them and sighed. He knew they were right. "That is probably wise, but there must be something I can do around here to thank you."

The twins exchanged glances and a small nod.

"Yes? What would you like done?" Athelstan prompted. Greynoc rolled his eyes. The twins looked at each other again with sly smiles. He frowned slightly. "Do not worry, despite my ribs, I am pretty tough. What do you need me to do for you?"

Ludmilla stepped forward and whispered into Athelstan's ear. His eyes widened in absolute astonishment. He looked at Ratia who nodded.

"Are you serious?" he asked knowing they were. They both nodded.

Greynoc made for the door. "I should go now," he said.

"NO! Wait!" Athelstan exclaimed.

"Sorry General, I have business to attend to... ahhh... dead Roman business – that sort of thing. I am far too old for..." he waggled his finger at the two women. "You are on your own my boy," he blurted out as he made good his escape. The cabin door swung wide open.

"But..." He looked back at the two witches who were gazing at him expectantly. He sighed. Sex was a common form of payment in the Celtic world.

He could pay them now, or he could wait and pay them in the next life.

"I was thinking more along the lines of chopping some wood, or something…" he tried, but they were already reaching for his hands. The door slammed shut.

Chapter Five

Evening fell. Athelstan found himself chuckling as his axe met log with a loud crack. His ribs ached and his back muscles burned from two months of disuse. Sweat streamed off his bare torso like rainwater but still, he was smiling. It felt good to work out the stiff joints and tendons. Greynoc and his men had left with the dead by midday and he assured Athelstan it would be several days before they returned.

He scooped up another armload of split wood and stacked it neatly on the growing pile before hoisting another log onto the block. He split it asunder with a mighty stroke of the axe. Wiping a tangle of hair from his brow he peered at the sinking sun. Every muscle glistened in the rosy alpine glow.

"I think that will be enough, for now, Athelstan. You should come in and eat," the elderly twins chorused sweetly.

Dinner was the usual abundant affair. With the help of Greynoc's Invisible People, the twins never wanted for wild game and their benefactors never wanted for spiritual guidance. Once the table was cleared of wooden platters and thanks for the abundance was given to Mother Earth. Ratia and Ludmilla sat facing him. He watched as the women sat quietly for a short time. They calmed their breathing and relaxed.

"What are you doing?" he asked softly.

Ratia spoke. "Ever since we were little girls we have been considered – strange. Our appearance and the way we speak was what set us apart from our family and the Rhaetian people. We are not sure how you will react to what we are about to tell you, but we feel we must."

"Athelstan, we are able to see things and know things that others do not. It has frightened many powerful people in the past and that is why we live here alone." They spoke in low tones as if embarrassed somehow.

"I had wondered why you would be so far from any village or town, but you two do not seem terribly frightening to me. You can tell me anything you like. You cannot frighten someone like me."

They looked at each other and silently agreed. Ludmilla spoke first. "You must know that everything in this world has a spirit that emanates a light; rocks, trees and animals... people too."

Athelstan nodded. This was common knowledge in his belief system.

"We can see this light and the light of your spirit is particularly bright – blinding in fact. There is a great deal of inner strength and fire in you." Ratia looked up. "Yes, yes... I will in a minute, now shush!" He frowned and looked behind him. They were alone in the room.

"Who are you talking to?" he asked softly. The twins glanced at each other.

"We also see those who have departed from this world. Those who stand with their ancestors."

"Athelstan, your father, and grandfather stand behind you right now. We can see them and they can speak with us. But...." They exchanged a strange look. His eyes widened. It was exceptionally rare that Druids could see the next world as well as this one. The unknown had always fascinated him and he would hardly pass up this chance to learn more.

"But...?" he prompted.

"This is very strange. They bring with them a strong and mighty warrior. He stands with them, shoulder to shoulder in fact. It is your family members who have brought him here. This is very odd, but he is a very powerful departed spirit. We do not know if this is a good or bad sign. He seems very insistent to communicate something to you directly." They abruptly started to speak with a single voice. Gone was the back and forth of their normal speech. Both women spoke simultaneously.

"Can you see him now?" he asked intrigued.

"Yes. He stands by your right shoulder." Athelstan looked around and saw nothing.

"Can you describe him for me?"

"He is a Great Spirit. He is tall and very handsome, like you, but with a prominent nose. He has dark hair, thick – wild looking and he has a trimmed beard. He does not appear to be Celt. He could be a Guardian Spirit. Do you know who this might be?" they asked together.

He shook his head slowly as he searched his memory. "No, I do not," he would have remembered someone who looked like that. The twins froze and a faraway look came over the pair.

"Wolf! Phae-lan. He is saying something but... we do not understand. We do not understand you, say it again." They addressed the spirit directly; another frozen moment followed.

"He wishes to speak to you. Will you hear his words?" the twins asked.

Thinking for a moment, Athelstan nodded, "I... Yes, of course, I will hear him." The pair then stopped all movement for a few seconds. He saw

Goosebumps rise on their arms and sweat glistened on their lips and brows. They let out a long-held breath.

"He is saying something like... Canete Cara Calla Homo. Dee Leap Hairy Chan–dan. The twins shook their heads in unison, paused a moment and repeated it.

"Hmmm we do not understand that language and he is not translating it either. Both women looked abashed. He is showing us a man with no face, or perhaps a man who is hidden. That is very disturbing. Do you know who this could be?"

Athelstan was startled. "No. The first part sounds like Latin. Do you speak Latin?"

They shook their heads.

"It translates to something like 'Beware, a man with a hood', the last part means nothing in Latin. Could it be a name?"

"Usually we receive messages from ordinary folk, tinkers, cooks, farmers and such but we have never seen such a collection of powerful souls before. It is like being in the presence of Kings; or Gods."

Once again, they looked past him and shivered. "Yes, we will tell him." The twins still spoke in unison. Two voices one message.

"The Wolf Spirit is showing us a thrice–saved life that will alter your path forever. He is showing us the numbers three, four and seven relate to this thrice–saved life,"

"Do you know who he is referring to?" Athelstan shook his head perplexed. "We see that he is handing you two items very, delicate items of great value." They shook their heads in confusion. "We do not understand what he is showing us. It is not money. He clutches one to his chest and the other he crumbles to dust. One is a treasure, one is a curse." They went still again as they listened to the voices.

"Your grandfather shows us a hidden enemy reaching out for you. He is saying, beware the unseen enemy, for he hunts this treasure as well. He is cunning and ruthless. Only countering his cunning with greater cunning, his ruthlessness with mercilessness, will you gain the treasure for your own. You must not fail in this, or the treasure will tarnish, fade and be of no value. Seek the aid of the Guardian."

The twins stopped again.

"What does this mean? What kind of treasure? What kind of curse? Who is this Guardian?" Athelstan was understandably puzzled. These women spoke using metaphors when delivering their messages from beyond since it was often how they received them. They shook their heads.

"That is all they say, a great treasure, an equally great curse, and the guardian. They repeat it over and over." Ratia suddenly looked down almost under the table with her far away eyes. Her sister's eyes followed.

"Yes my dears, would you like to say something too?" Ratia asked. There was another pause before Ratia and Ludmilla both looked up and laughed.

"We have two very pretty girls here who say you are going to be their Father. They say not yet, but they can wait. They say they are going to be daddy's little Princesses." Ratia looked back down at the invisible children. "I am sure you will, little darlings. He will be very fortunate indeed to have such sweet souls as daughters." They paused again as they listened to the messages.

"Oh my! Athelstan, your father is showing me more girls, a great many young girls. Are you married, do you already have children?"

He shook his head. He liked children well enough and they seemed comfortable around him but he never gave children of his own much consideration.

"They are telling us that they will all come into your possession. Treat them with care and kindness."

"All of them? I do not collect girls and my father knows full well I will not own slaves, so I have no idea what that means," he said.

Their eyes suddenly cleared. "Well, it would seem that is all they have to say; they are gone now. Did any of that make sense to you?" Their normal mode of back and forth speech returned.

"Not much, save the unseen enemy. I can only think it must be Rome that they were referring too. Cunning and ruthless, that is Rome alright."

Ratia and Ludmilla just nodded.

"But it is this treasure and this Guardian that has me the most puzzled. What could they possibly have meant? More to the point, who could this 'Man with the Hood' be? You do not speak Latin?"

"Not a word. Athelstan, sometimes it is difficult to say what they are showing us, but rest assured everything will become plain in time. This reading dealt with things that are yet to occur, so they are far less clear."

"It seems am going to have daughters – two at least, but maybe dozens. How? I am not married," he stated.

"Yet!" They smirked. "You are not married yet."

Almost a week had passed since Greynoc and his people left with the dead Romans. During these lazy days, he worked tirelessly preparing the cabin for winter. He split and stacked wood to his own height along the length of the cabin. He helped till the fields for late season plantings, harvested herbs, and mushrooms for drying. They sat through the evenings telling stories of myth and legend. He played on a simple wooden flute and sang the old songs taught by the bards. It was a very restful time for him. Day by day he grew stronger.

He learned many mysteries of the centuries-old healing arts and studied as the twins taught him the workings of Celtic magic. Magic, he found, was surprisingly simple once its secrets were revealed. Everything had a trick that either fooled the eye, fooled the mind or both.

He was an attentive student and learned quickly. He learned the first rule of magic. Focus the people's attention on one hand while doing the trick secretly with the other. Soon he was making small objects appear and disappear. He learned to read the bones and tea dregs. They taught him in depth the secrets usually known only to the Gods, and the power of the elements. In time, he understood enough to make fire from earth and make water from the air. To his Celtic mind, the connections between the Gods, the elements, and the living world were obvious and tangible.

The morning of his sixth day in the company of the twins dawned bright and clear. It would undoubtedly be another hot one. Greynoc and his people had returned that morning. He and his men had given the Roman army a very simple puzzle to solve. The twin's hidden valley was safe – for now.

He stood beside a fully laden Maehadren and embraced his new friends one final time.

"I cannot stay any longer, Gentle Mothers," he explained. Maehadren danced from foot to foot anxious to leave. "Every minute I remain here puts you all in more danger. I will not do that to you. I must get as far from here as I can, as quickly as I can. My enemies will be led on quite a chase I can tell you that. Besides my journey has been delayed far too long as it is," he kissed Ludmilla and Ratia and what words could not say, their tears spoke in their place. He clasped arms with Greynoc.

"Farewell my boy and keep your backside out of trouble!" he elder Rhaetian Chieftain said gravely.

"My backside will have to fend for itself Hidden One. Just you keep these two ladies safe Greynoc, for they are a treasure beyond measure," Athelstan said solemnly.

"I shall my Senone friend. Remember the lessons they have taught you. One day their magic will save your life – they have foreseen it."

Ludmilla sniffed and wiped her nose with her dirty sleeve. "We have packed food and spring water for ten days if you are frugal," they stated as he mounted Maehadren. Two pairs of eyes widened and they said suddenly, "Oh we almost forgot."

Ratia turned and ducked inside. In a moment, she returned with the white bearskin from his bed. It had been trimmed and sewn to form a massive cloak. With it, they had a glittering, silver torque. It bore two horse heads. It was beautifully carved. Athelstan's eyes widened with astonishment.

"So you stay warm in faraway Hellas," they explained. He examined the generous gift and marvelled that such a treasure rested in such a plain cottage.

"Where did...?" he began. The twins exchanged what could only be called knowing grins.

"It belonged to King Brennus. It was in recognition of our rather special talents. He was quite taken by us once." They were smiling now as the memory returned. Brennus was his King's own Grandfather. He was the man who sacked Rome and demanded tribute in gold seventy years earlier. It was a princely gift.

"I cannot take this treasure away from you. He gave it to you," he stated.

"And now we are giving it to you. What use is it to us now? Besides who better than you should have it?"

He had no answer and accepted the gift graciously.

"I cannot thank you properly for such a treasure or for my life. Thank you. Farewell, for now, Gentle Mothers. Look for me in the spring."

"Look for us in winter," they stated in unison. He looked at them both for one last moment.

All the words had finally been spoken. The big horse turned a walnut sized eye upon Greynoc and the twins and then did a most remarkable thing. He bowed to them and his nose almost touched the ground between his front hooves. Ludmilla reached into her pocket and fed him a dried apple patting him kindly. Athelstan nodded to his new friends, wheeled Maehadren around and left the twins' valley far behind.

✝

Night blooming jasmine's sweet scent clung to the thick night fog with a cloying sweetness. The odour vied for dominance with the smells of wood smoke, roasting meats, horse dung and the warm summer rains. Every branch and leaf pearled with moisture. Spider webs glittered in the dim light with a diamond's sparkle. It was a perfectly magical evening for an outdoor festival.

The hilltop on which it was being held sat three leagues north of Rome and thrust its proud head high over the spot where the salt road, Via Salaria crossed the Tiber River. This place was where the Senone armies of Brennus defeated the legions of Rome eighty–five years earlier as a prelude to the sack of the great city. Now, on this night, Romans feasted and sacrificed bulls to Fortuna, their fickle Goddess of Fate. As it was here, so it was also in the Celtic world; Aerten always favoured the bold. Who Fate would favour this night was a question soon to be answered.

The sounds of music and joyous laughter grew ever louder as the band of Goths closed like a fell omen upon the unsuspecting Romans utterly immersed in their festival of Lucaria. The Goths feet and weapons were wrapped in dark cloth to muffle sound and eliminate reflections; their faces smeared with black soot to the same end. They looked like demons, risen from Hades and were advancing with a single-minded murderous intent.

These horse lords whispered a prayer to Epona, the horse Goddess and then slipped slowly and quietly through the picketed mounts. They crept soundlessly towards the tired and distracted Roman guards. Long rune– covered knives slipped from soft leather sheaths and were swiftly wielded with deadly efficacy. The first to die did so easily. Their throats slit with neither hew nor cry issued. They crumpled inert upon the ground, resting motionless there like individual islands of flesh in slowly expanding lakes of blood.

Bonfires blazed in the distance and dancers in flowing gowns twirled and flowed as if spawned by the very fog itself. The Goths paused a moment to watch the lights as blood drooled from their knives like some macabre syrup. Then they turned their attention to the many pavilions nearby. Their prizes were asleep within guarded by mothers, nannies, and drunken old men. Speed was their ally and the dark tide separated each towards a separate tented sanctuary.

Constantina gasped as an unimagined horror bore down on her. A nightingales' warble masked the sound and lent its voice to the gaiety outdoors. Such a sweet innocent sound. Such a terrible result. As one, the Goths struck and in doing so, they took their prizes and insured that nothing would ever be the same in Rome again.

In a far distant corner of the world, sat a land of sun-baked red sand and grey rock. It was so hot it could kill a man in a few short hours. Men and women alike were swaddled in thick white robes from head to toe. Scarves pulled over their noses and mouths helped keep the omnipresent sand at bay. Nestled in the towering highlands of Jeru–Salam, a green oasis named Axum basked in the shadow of the cliffs. Here, a toehold of life eked out an existence.

It was a walled city tucked in a valley between rocky desolate hills and at the nexus of trade routes. One from the Red Sea to the east, another from the subcontinent of Africa to the south, a third running north to the Nile River and Egypt and a final route travelling northeast to the Egypt capital of Meroe. The shale and mortar walls enclosed a few dozen buildings with a grand palace at its centre serving as both a mercantile headquarters and a royal residence.

Seated in near darkness was the enigmatic ruler of Axum. A self-proclaimed king, unseen but only a select few, presided over all facets of life here. A candle sconce guttered and smoked on either side of his ornately carved throne. They cast a weak wavering light, a non–light. Here he awaited news.

Unannounced, a small door opened at the far end of the room and a dark figure was briefly silhouetted before the door closed again. Unseen sandals scraped the flagstones as the figure approached. When the ghost-like being finally entered the dim candlelight, he knelt and touched his head to the floor in abeyance. "I bring profoundly humble greetings most Exalted One," declared the man in a muffled voice.

"Speak," hissed the swaddled King. The prostrate form rose but did not stand. To do so would mean instant death.

"Your operation against Hellas is going well, Exalted One. As you predicted, the Roman expansion north is also proceeding as planned."

"Vut of 'The One'? Is she encountering any difficulties?" "None as of her last message Exalted One." "And The Other, has she been found yet? Vhy is she not in chains
before me? I have plans for her," his odd accent dripped with menace. The kneeling man drew a shaky breath. "There is a report that she was taken, but not by us. Word has arrived that she, with a number of other
prisoners, have been sighted somewhere near Sparta." He trembled visibly. A long silence followed this.

"This is distressing news. Who gives you these reports?"

"Two naval captains, Exalted One. They hang on the flaying racks even as I humbly speak. We shall know the truth soon."

"Send vord to our friend, Cassander of Macedon, that I am coming. Suggest to him that Athens is now ripe for the picking. Tell him nothing more. Prepare for Our journey to Hellas."

"What of the two captains, Exalted One?"

"Let them speak all before you let them die. Promote their seconds, but impress upon them that failure is dealt with most harshly. Tell Acaph I have a task for him. Now be gone. Your presence soils my mood," he commanded.

The prostrate man backed out of the light still on his knees, head close to the floor. Only when he was in total darkness did he rise to leave the throne room. When he was gone, the hooded man raised a pale skeletal thin finger.

"Orders, Exalted One?" came a soft response from one side of the room.

"Vait until he has carried out my orders – then kill him. Allow Acaph to approach unhindered. He vill find her for us."

Chapter Six

Inhaling deeply the crisp tang of salty sea air, Athelstan rode down towards a bustling seaside city. Avoiding the many Roman patrols was not easy. He was nearly caught several times.

He had left the twins and Greynoc behind many days ago. Now he picked his way carefully down the rugged east coast of Italia. He quietly moved through the quiet nameless fishing villages until he came to the city of Ravenna. Farms, peasant huts, and fishmongers comprised the bulk of the inhabitants and businesses. Most were on stilts amid a warren of winding streets and waterways. Since trade with Macedonian Hellas had been established, a large thriving port was established itself. Ravenna was two thousand years old before Athelstan first drew breath in this world. Fortresses of stone and houses built on stilts dotted the marshy landscape. It possessed a deep–water harbour. It was the oldest inhabited city-state in all Italia. This was 'Senone' territory. Its harbour and its busy dock were his ultimate destination.

Romans would be watching all the ports for any sign of fleeing Celtic soldiers. If he were spotted, his death would inevitably result. He crept along the storage buildings, keeping hidden behind the towering heaps of trade goods waiting stacked on the dock. He led Maehadren, avoiding all contact with people. The pair stopped in one of the narrow alleyways formed by sacks of grain ready for export and the rough-hewn walls of one of the long low storage sheds. Now they would wait for dark.

Carefully Athelstan peeked out from his hiding place. Nine ships lay alongside one of the docks, Each ship was a microcosm of activity. Three ships were Greek and two were Roman. The remainder came from Carthage, Egypt, Galilee, and Crete. It was a well-organized operation. The outer harbour was dotted with many other ships at anchor, waiting for a space to open up. All goods loaded for export were neatly organised by type and separated by narrow east-west corridors. Raw materials like logs, grains, unbleached wool, and metal ores were all neatly arranged at the north end wharf. Finished products and trade goods like textiles, smelted iron, tin, wine, beer, and salted meats were at the south end. Off-loaded products were piled in the middle section and the majority of the activity occurred here. Gangs of slaves loaded wagons to haul the goods to the central market.

Romans directed the hundreds of slaves toiling to load and unload the ships. Some stood sentry while others patrolled the wharf from end to end. Getting aboard a ship here would not be easy. In sharp contrast to the brutal conditions endured by slaves, was the sound of running, laughing children. He returned to the security of the grain sacks to wait. With an almost casual slash of his knife, Athelstan cut open one of the sacks. As the wheat poured out, Maehadren lowered his head to enjoy his treat.

"Marbog, quick, hide here!" Came a shrill cry. It was immediately punctuated by the slap of running feet. More surprising was that it was spoken in Gaelic. Pressed back against the wall of wheat sacks, Athelstan awaited the inevitable. Two small sandy-haired boys backed into the same hiding spot occupied by the Senone General. Both continued looking back in the direction they had just come from when strong hands closed on their shoulders.

Squeals of surprise erupted from both of them as Athelstan turned them around to have a look. They were dressed like Roman children with togas cinched at the waist and lace-up sandals but that was where all resemblance ended. These shaggy-haired freckle-faced boys looked up at him with their bright blue eyes in silent shock. They were obviously brothers.

"Samhaich! (Quiet!)" he hissed. The boys nodded and were instantly silent.

He addressed them in Gaelic with a sharp whisper. "What are you doing here?"

"Playing!" There was an uncomfortable silence as Athelstan scowled at the two. "We're playing hide and find… with our friends. Honestly!" one boy whispered back.

"No, no no. In Ravenna, what are you doing here?"

"We live here."

"What are your names?"

"I am called Derfel of the Mallo clan and this is my brother Marbog. Our father was Clan Chief Bransar Mallo." He glanced over his shoulder quickly at his brother. "Oi, I know you! They are looking for you everywhere, General - Sir."

"How do you know me?" Athelstan's frown grew deeper.

"Everyone knows you. You are General Athelstan. My father served in your army with Captain Cedric's infantry unit during the battle of Milan. He pointed you out to us once and said. 'That is General Athelstan' he says to me. 'He is a great leader and a good man.'"

The boy was clearly proud of his father, as it should be.

"It is not my army Derfel. It is our army – yours and mine."

He released the pair.

"Where is your father now? Why are not you travelling with him? You should be half way to the Glade by now," he dreaded the answer. Too many good men had been lost at Milan.

Marbog spoke up. "He is in the next world with grandfather and my two uncles. Mother was told that he fought with great bravery and died with honour. We wanted to join the army and fight too, but Father said we're too young."

It warmed the General's heart to hear such talk. It was touching, that even after such a dreadful loss, the boy could speak of his father with such pride and reverence. He knelt in front of Derfel and Marbog.

"You are good boys – worthy of the name Mallo. I knew your father well and what they said about him is true. He was kind, honest and fair. His blood and his spirit burn brightly in you boys. His passing has cost us a great man, but it has provided us with two new ones. Your father would be proud of you, as proud of you, as I am. The name Bransar Mallo shall be spoken in the rolls of the honoured dead," Athelstan said solemnly.

"Tell me, where is your mother, Lytheria?" Athelstan tried not to show any eagerness. He knew Lytheria years ago before she had met and married Bransar Mallo.

"She works as a nanny for the new Prefect here," Derfel piped up quickly. His voice was loud and shrill.

"Shhhh!"

He began again in a whisper, "She works as a…" Athelstan nodded and waved him silent.

"Who in the new Prefect? What is his name?"

"Artivus Scævola."

"Who else were you playing with just now? Are there any Roman children with you?"

Both boys spat their disgust.

"I see! I need your help boys. I have to find a ship bound for Hellas and get aboard without attracting too much attention. Do you know if there is one leaving today?"

"Yes, the one with the blue and white sails." Young Marbog offered the information with a hopeful expression but received a punch on the shoulder from Derfel.

"All Greek ships have blue and white sails, Marbog. Think!" He let his little brother do just that while he rubbed his sore shoulder.

Marbog grinned suddenly. "Oh yeah, that is right they do. It is the third one along from this end. That one," he pointed.

Marbog was pointing at a huge Greek Bireme. It indeed had blue and white striped sails neatly furled along a cross-spar. Its bow and stern were gracefully curved upward high over the roof of the upper deck of oar-holes. The stern beam had a curious rectangular hole cut through it just above deck level. It was roughly two hands wide and the length of a man's arm high. Athelstan presumed it was to see through. This opening was not mirrored at the prow.

Marbog was still explaining, "A fat loud–mouthed captain named Piros owns it. You know he only has three fingers on his left hand. He smells of fish and some kind of awful cheese."

"Greeks all smell of fish," Derfel made a face.

"Anyway," Marbog continued, "the ship is one of those long narrow ones with two sets of oars. It's not like those other Greek cargo ships at all. So far, it has been loaded with twenty barrels of salted pork, thirty-two bundles of finished linen and fifty bales of raw wool. Sixty–eight amphorae of lamp oil, four hundredweight bags of salt, ninety barrels of red wine and beer, dried apples, walnuts, one hundred twenty-five sheaves of hay and one hundred fifty iron bars; the long ones." He counted the items on his fingers and nodded with satisfaction once he was done. "It is still practically empty. Captain Piros says he is leaving as soon as can find eighteen replacement slaves for the oars."

Athelstan was astonished. "Marbog, how do you know all that so exactly?" he asked.

"He told me."

"Why would the Captain tell you this?"

"I asked him."

"You asked him, I see."

"It wouldn't matter either way General, he remembers everything he sees and hears. He can be a real anchor sometimes," his older brother commented.

"An anchor? That may be, but not today he isn't." Athelstan countered with a smile. He looked the two boys over with a critical eye.

"Why are you wearing togas?" he queried.

"If we wear our Clan colours we cannot do anything. The Romans bully and kick us. They will not let us play anywhere. If we wear these togas, then we are invisible to them and we can play anywhere we want."

"Invisible? How would you boys like to pay those mean Romans back for all their bullying?"

"How?" asked Marbog.

"Yes!" Derfel said with more certainty. The excitement in their eyes was obvious.

"First, I need a good place to hide Maehadren until we are ready." The huge horse gulped down mouthfuls of the grain from the torn sack.

"Second, you need to gather up your friends. We will need all of them."

"You can hide Maehadren inside here," Derfel indicated the wooden storage shed behind him. "Follow me," he stepped out from behind the sacks of wheat glanced up the narrow row separating the wheat from the oat sacks and froze. Heavy footsteps could be heard approaching.

"You! What are you doing back there?" The perfect Latin was spoken by a rough voice with an imperious tone. Athelstan lifted his right foot and drew his long skinning knife from its sheath. With a finger, he motioned Marbog to silence and pulled him back against the sacks of grain.

"Nothing sir," was Derfel's reply. He took another two steps and disappeared from the guard's view. He turned quickly and waited. A second later an armed Roman sentry, replete with bronze armour and brightly plumed helm, hurried around the corner and grabbed Derfel by the shoulder. He shook the boy and cuffed him hard sending him sprawling. Derfel bounced back to his feet.

Athelstan followed the Roman into the narrow space between grain sacks and the wooden shed.

"I asked you what you are doing back here, now answer me, boy!" His hand rose to strike the boy again. Derfel's face was now a mask of defiance. The blow never fell.

A powerful hand closed on the Romans' wrist and twisted it backwards. He yanked the surprised guard around. The Roman stared with astonishment at an enraged Celt.

"He – is - with – me!" Athelstan growled into the guard's surprised face. The surprise was quickly replaced by sudden shock and agony. With savage brutality, Athelstan drove a slender blade upward through the soft flesh under the guard's jaw before the guard could react. It crunched through the upper palate and into his brain behind his eyes.

There was a pause as the man's eyes rolled inward toward his nose. He gaped and moved his jaw as if trying to speak or yell for help. Athelstan twisted the blade roughly and the Guard collapsed, gushing blood from his mouth and nose, coating the Celt's hand and arm. More blood spattered across Athelstan's chest. Derfel turned white at the sight of a man being killed in such a way. Marbog joined his brother staring down at the dead man. The General cleaned his knife on the dead Roman's cloak and re-sheathed it.

Without warning, Marbog kicked the Roman in the chest and spat on him. Derfel seized Marbog and pulled him back roughly.

"Do not do that!" he admonished.

"I did not mean anything!" Marbog began in protest.

"Your brother is right Marbog," Athelstan said softly. "Nothing can be gained by punishing the dead. They are beyond learning the lessons you seek to teach them. Besides, there is no honour in it and we are a people who hold honour above all things. A man only dies once and it is important that he does it well."

Athelstan hoisted the dead guard onto Maehadren's rump and emptied the remainder of the ripped wheat sack onto the pool of blood. He tucked the empty sack into his tunic. The boys led the General past some loose piles of wood near the shed's north doors. A moment later, they stood in a dark windowless storage building. It took several seconds for their eyes to adjust.

"Go find your friends. Bring them here, but do it quietly. Do not tell them why, just bring them."

The boys slipped back out. Athelstan dragged the man off his horse, trussed him up in the empty sack, and deposited him under a tangled heap of dry rope. He made a quick inventory of the shed contents. It was a catchall of garbage and broken bits of ship's detritus. Items too spoiled for export found their way into the shed. His nose wrinkled at the stench of rotting food. He noted several items that held promise - mouldy rope and six amphorae of rendered fat. The oil was now rancid; it was useless for cooking. Nevertheless, it would still burn.

A slow trickle of boys began to arrive and they gathered in a group around Athelstan. Stern eyes beneath a heavy brow swept the tiny congregation. Eleven grubby–faced boys ranging in age from about seven to nine stood in a semi-circle around the Senone General.

"I am Athelstan and I am looking for an army of brave men to help me strike a blow against this Roman occupation. Do you know where I might find such a group?"

Derfel looked left and then right before stepping forward.

"What are your orders, General? You waste time by asking. What you require already stands before you," Derfel stood, his feet wide apart and hands on his hips. He bore a serious expression. Athelstan smiled in spite of himself.

"I see. You boys were told you are too little to become warriors, is that true?" Heads nodded reluctantly and some chins dropped. Derfel remained stoic and did not react. Athelstan continued.

"In the next few minutes, we will prove that assessment to be wrong. You men are already warriors and have been so from the moment you drew your first breath. You will remain so until you draw your last. You are Senone. That is our way." Derfel and one of the older boys rapidly quelled brief cheering.

"It is my intention to board one of those ships bound for Hellas. At first, a distraction was what I had in mind. I meant to trick the Roman guards and board a ship secretly. Now I'm not so sure that would work, so..." He looked into each face.

"Instead I mean to kill them. I mean to kill as many of them as I can. Would you like to help?" Their agreement was unanimous. Their fearlessness caused him some concern. What he had planned would be dangerous for these children, so he took great care in describing the plan. Once he was certain they understood it completely, he set them to work.

They soaked lengths of dry, rotten rope with the rancid oil and laid them carefully on the walls behind the mountains of debris. A second rope was stretched between two full amphorae of oil. It was set as a trip wire at the midpoint of the shed where the path between the piles of debris was narrowest. The oil containers were set in such a way that they would smash open when they fell. Strips of oil-soaked sailcloth ran from the rear door to the perimeter ropes. He inspected the work carefully, encouraging the boys in their smelly task. When everything was to his liking, he created a torch with a broken lashing pin and a length of oiled cloth.

"We are ready. You have done well. Now all that is left is for you to tell the Romans I am in here. Tell them you have seen me bring my horse inside here and then I want you to run home and stay there." A raised finger silenced a chorus of protest.

"It is important you do this. You have done all you can for now. I do not want any of you near here once this begins. That is an order, men!"

They all reluctantly nodded. Athelstan clasped forearms with each boy thanking them for their help. Derfel and Marbog were last among them.

"Derfel, you are a leader if I have ever seen one. Lead these boys and do whatever you can to vex the Romans. Do not target their food, all that will happen is they will steal yours. Use Marbog as your advisor and listen to him. He is very clever, as clever as anyone I have ever met. I wish there was more time to instruct you lads properly. Just choose your targets with great care. Make your father and the clan Mallo proud. Now go with Epona."

They bowed and left.

Once gone, he took 'iron to flint' and set a sparked to the torch. Maehadren was packed and ready to leave. All that remained was to wait. He did not have to wait long. The doors at the far end of the cluttered shed flew open and a dozen or more soldiers rushed in.

"You there! Hold! You are under arrest for crimes against the Empire." The Centurion commanded imperiously. They rushed forward eager to capture the Senone General. No one noticed the trip rope. "Drop that torch!"

"As you wish Commander," Athelstan said in a calm baritone. He let the burning brand fall from his hand onto the oil–soaked cloth. The fire took hold of the cloth immediately and spread outward quickly along the oiled ropes. The ropes along the exterior caught fire easily and the flames swept rapidly along the walls setting the various piles of clutter ablaze. The running soldiers reached the midway point of the shed and tripped over the rope. Two amphorae flew off their perches crashing and spewing oil all over them and onto the floor. Several soldiers skidded on the slippery surface and fell to the ground.

The fire grew to a roaring blaze between Athelstan and the Romans. Only now, did the soldiers realise their peril? Two of them were already beating the flames licking at their cloaks. Fire exploded up the walls and had passed the troop of soldiers on either side. The shed was filling with thick choking smoke as orders to retreat were coughed out. Athelstan saw the far doors being wedged closed by the boys. No exit remained as flames sprang up around the doomed Romans.

"I would love to stay and chat with you Centurion, but you do not have that kind of time. Perhaps we shall talk in the next life."

He and Maehadren left the burning shed by the rear doors and braced them closed with some of the loose boards. Screams of terror and agony rose in a ghastly chorus before the noise abruptly ended. A cry of 'Fire' was taken up and all eyes were focused on the burning shed.

Athelstan calmly turned Maehadren toward the large Greek bireme selected by Marbog and simply led him aboard. Crew and dockworkers alike scattered and skittered out of the way, as the warhorse charged up the gangplank. One poor soul caught between a crush of people and this massive white horse, dove into the harbour to avoid being trampled. Chaos had erupted on the dock behind him as Athelstan tied Maehadren off to the simple main mast between the two decks of rowers, where he stood and awaited the Captains pleasure.

Chapter Seven

The Captain was a rather excitable man – to say the least! The instant the Celt charged aboard, a squat round-bellied man launched a furious tirade at horse and rider in a very colourful mix of Greek and Phoenician. All work aboard had initially stopped to watch the fire, but now not a single man dared move as their captain closed on the Celt. He rounded Maehadren's rump and skidded to a stop. Aside from his physical appearance, Athelstan emitted an aura of absolute authority. The 'barbarian' leaned forward and spoke to the captain briefly. The words were so soft that none but the captain heard what was said.

"Captain Piros, it might be a good idea for you to cast off immediately. Once our Roman brethren discover what has happened here, they will be quite harsh with anyone helping me. I'm sure you do not want to look at this fine ship from atop a cross."

"You are responsible for the fire?" Piros asked.

"Yes, I am. It might interest you to know, I trapped a dozen or more of those Romans inside… we are at war after all."

"AT WAR? Here on MY ship?"

"That's is how it works Captain. They kill my people, I kill their people. The last one to fall, loses." Piros looked at the flames as they engulfed the shed and began to spread across the wharf.

"A dozen, or more you say?"

"It was the best I could do given the shortness of time."

A slow smile spread across the captains disfigured face.

"I can pay for safe passage to Sparta," Athelstan stated.

Piros accepted a small token from the Celt. His eyes widened briefly when he glanced at the pale green gemstone. Large faceted Moldavite spheres were rare in the extreme. This one stone alone could buy a fleet of ships like this one. The captain nodded his head slowly and scanned the dock. A full cohort of Roman soldiers arrived at a run from the town proper once they spotted the thick smoke. They began to mobilise firefighting activity by emptying all the ships of slaves and workers to form bucket lines. Piros took a long hard look at Athelstan as if trying to gauge something intangible in him.

"Who are you?" Piros asked finally.

"Wild is what I am! Who I am is my own business for the moment."

"Wild? What kind of name is that? Where did you come from? What in bloody Tartarus is going on here?"

"Calm yourself… Captain. I wish we had the time to explore these important questions in more detail, but sadly, at the moment, we do not. I might suggest that whatever it is you plan to do – now - would be a good time to do it."

"Is it possible?" he muttered, looking Athelstan over with narrowed eyes. Then his voice boomed out.

"Get your horse aft and keep it out of the way, or I will toss you both into the sea." Turning away from Athelstan, Piros began shouting orders at his crew, breaking the spell. "Raise the gangplank! Cast off the lines. Make ready to raise the sail. Oarsmen, put your backs into it, I want to be clear of the Ravenna lagoon within the hour!"

A frenzy of activity ensued as fifty men pushed off from the dock using long oars. The heavy ship slowly inched away. Athelstan led Maehadren to the stern of the ship and tied him off to the rail. One of the sailors tapped Athelstan on the leg and handed him a short bow with two arrows. The Celt took the gift with a quick wink.

"Wait! Greek vessel Aphrodite… Stop!" Some local Roman official issued these imperious commandments from the shore. "Your ship has not been cleared to leave. We need your crew to help fight the fire. Unshackle your slaves and have them come ashore immediately. You must wait for inspection regardless." His shrill voice was grating.

Other ships' crews were being forced by soldiers to help fight the fire, but Piros was having none of it. "Not on your wine-soaked life! I will not risk my ship, or any of my crew fighting a fire that, clearly, is not my problem. I wish you luck putting that out, but we are leaving," Piros shouted back in terrible Latin. The excited official had caught sight of Athelstan and Maehadren.

"Bring your ship back alongside and release that prisoner to me, or you will be boarded and imprisoned."

"Prisoner? What prisoner? What are you babbling about you witless drone? I have no prisoners aboard my ship. Only free men serve aboard Aphrodite. Busy yourself elsewhere." Piros said.

"Him!" The Roman pointed at Athelstan. "He is an enemy of the State and he is under arrest." The Celt listened to the exchange but remained silent. He was calmly stringing the bow and nocked an arrow.

"He might be an enemy of your state, but he's not an enemy of mine. Since I have no way of determining the truth of your claim, I have no choice but to declare that so long as he is aboard this vessel he is under the protection of the Queen of Corinth. If that is not to your liking, you and your government may take it up with her and mine."

"Now just a moment. I am in charge of this dock and it is I who says when a ship may leave. I command you to…" An arrow suddenly materialised in the middle of the Dock Masters forehead. He stopped speaking and fell stiff-legged backwards onto the dock.

44

With a casual wave of his two-fingered hand, he dismissed the dead official. In Captain Piro's opinion, their conversation had ended some time ago.

Without so much as a glance at Athelstan, Piros turned his attention to the crew. "Pull to Starboard! Push to Port!" He commanded and the one hundred oars on the right side and one hundred oars on the left dipped into the water as one; the bow of the ship pivoted smartly away from the dock. Once clear, both sides pulled and with every pull, the two decks of oarsmen propelled the bireme forward. The wharf dwindled in the distance as the stiff breeze took hold of the blue and white striped sail.

It snapped sharply like a huge whip, driving the groaning ship relentlessly onward. Horns of alarm sounded from the shore and other horns repeated the alert up and down the coast. The sound echoed across the water alerting the Roman warships anchored at sea to stop any vessel trying to leave. It would be quite a gauntlet for this tiny ship to run. Piros glared at Athelstan and the Celt shrugged spreading his hands before patting his sword. Piro's glare became a reluctant grin; then it was gone.

At first glance, Captain Piro's bireme was much the same as any other Greek ship. There were the usual two decks of rowers on each side with fifty-two benches per deck. Two slaves manned each oar, totalling four hundred and sixteen rowers in all. Four officers, a drummer, a tillerman, a wood wright, a blacksmith, and twenty sailors to operate the fixed square sail rounded out the crew.

Athelstan noticed, upon closer examination, that there was something very odd about this ship, its captain, and its crew. These galley slaves lacked the beaten and dejected expressions usual for slaves. There was fire in their eyes. Missing too, were the brutal overseers wielding whips or flails on the slaves' bloody, tattered backs. None of the slaves was chained to their benches either. He looked closer and discovered that each man had armour and weapons carefully hidden beneath each bench. These men were not slaves; they were Greek marines. The Aphrodite was a Corinthian Warship.

A drum kept a rhythmic cadence for the rowers and the ship fairly flew across the choppy water. Athelstan's long hair lifted into a wild halo around his head in the freshening wind. The Aphrodite swept southwest along a long stone breakwater before turning east heading for a gap between it and another similar wall. Two large naval vessels sat at anchor blocking the opening. With a simple hand signal from Piros, the rowers began to don their armour, helmets, and weapons. Athelstan came to stand beside the pock-faced Captain at the bow. There was no free oar-bench for him to use.

"It would be best if you make certain your horse is well secured. I intend to ram one of those ships and sink it. They will board us in numbers, of course, so you might want to get ready for a fight."

"Ram it? Ram it with what?" Athelstan swallowed nervously. He was beginning to have a bad feeling. Piros leaned over the prow of the ship and pointed down. The curved prow cut through the water like a knife sending plumes of white to either side. Athelstan looked deeper into the water. He saw a heavy bronze battering ram attached to the keel timbers jutting ten feet beyond the bow of the ship.

"You cannot be serious?" He turned to find he addressed thin air. Piros already stood amidships atop the roof protecting the port side rowers. He was seeing to preparations for battle. Everything not part of the ship was being lashed down. Flying debris would be deadly.

Athelstan prepared for a fight. He drew his long sword giving it a few test swings. One of the marines near him was chuckling.

"You cannot be swinging a great cleaver around here my giant friend! You'll chop down the bloody mast with that. Never fought aboard a ship before have you?" The Celt shook his head with a scowl.

Like all the marines, he was buckling on a sturdy vest of overlapping leather scales. It fell to just above his loins and left both arms and legs bare. Even if Athelstan did not look into the marine's eyes, the scars on his shoulders marked him as a seasoned veteran.

"That sword will be too long and cumbersome for the kind of close fighting that happens at sea. Short weapons are the best," he gestured with his Xiphos. It was short, less than half the length of the Celt's long heavy blade. It was narrow at the hilt and widened slightly as it approached the tip. A groove was ground along its length on either side to let blood gush out and make it easier to remove from a body. With a few stabs, slashes and feints he demonstrated some of the basic ideas behind fighting on a pitching deck.

"Hold your shield arm up for balance like this and keep up on the balls of your feet. Stay back and wait for your opening. Oh, and whatever you do, do not miss because you can be certain, your opponent will not. These are Romans." He handed Athelstan his own Xiphos. The Celt was about to protest when the marine bent down and produced another from under one of the benches.

He patted the weapon. "I never leave home without it. The Gods protect you Celt!" he said unsheathing the spare weapon with a flourish.

"Yes," he answered honestly, "they always do."

The Greek marine graced the Celt with an odd look before swaggering toward the bow. Athelstan followed him somewhat unsteadily. The sailors were quickly lowering and lashing down the sail. They could not risk it being damaged in the collision. The rowers redoubled their efforts and the Aphrodite charged towards the huge Roman ship.

The smaller Greek ship aimed directly towards the Roman trireme's vulnerable side. Like a cavalry charge, the last few seconds before impact were painfully slow. Then they experienced a shuddering, crunching, grinding crash. Even braced for the collision Athelstan was thrown off his feet. Many of the oars on the Roman ship snapped like twigs, littering Aphrodite's deck with deadly spinning splinters of wood. A shower of spears thrown from the enemy vessel preceded uncounted coils of ropes with three-pronged hooks and grappling poles that rained down from above. The iron hooks bit deep into the wooden decks of the Greek vessel locking the two ships together.

A swarm of Greek marines rushed forward to engage the Romans who swung across to capture Piro's ship. The confident attackers were shocked to find a highly trained fighting force awaiting them instead of a merchant crew and slaves. It was fierce and bloody work. Teams of knife-wielding men cut the grappling lines as quickly as they could. A skeleton crew of rowers from the lower deck began to pull the Greek ship away from the now holed Roman trireme. It was already listing badly with tonnes of water rushing in through the gaping hole below the water line. Piros needed to get the Aphrodite clear of the dying ship in case it rolled over onto the smaller Greek vessel. The irreparable hole in the side of the larger vessel spelled doom for the Trireme. It took on water at a frightening rate.

One sailor engaged Athelstan almost immediately. The skilled sailor forced the larger Celt backwards as he pressed home his ferocious attack. Athelstan knew there was nothing more dangerous than a man with nothing to lose.

The Roman was slender without being slight. All of his movements were efficiently designed for combat on a pitching rolling deck. He launched a withering assault. A savage thrust from the Roman gladius was barely turned aside by the chain mail vest the Celt wore. It was very difficult to find an opening past the square Roman shield.

By now the Roman knew his own ship was sinking. It must have been obvious to him that he could not return there, so he fought with relentless desperation. In truth, it was all the Celt could do to ward off the endless rain of blows with his small leather shield. He could find no opening whatsoever past the Romans' defences.

Screams filled the air in counterpoint to the ringing of weapons on shields. Some were screams of rage; others were screams of agony. A few were screams giving orders and fewer still were screams of victory. In any close–quarter fight, timing was everything. After an interminable time, the Roman began to tire; Athelstan finally saw his opening. He ducked inside an overhand blow and drove his Xiphos into the Romans' upper thigh. Wounded, he lurched backwards but the damage was done. Athelstan dispatched his foe with a quick slash to the throat.

Heaving for breath, Athelstan looked up in time to see the Roman Trireme turn turtle, pitching a thousand men into the merciless sea to drown. The fight aboard the Greek ship was nearing an end as those men who stoically remained at the oars, turned their vessel towards open water and freedom. A second Roman trireme struggled to turn its wide body and give chase. All things being equal this would be a short race. No quarter was given to those surviving Romans sailors. They were simply hacked to death and tossed over the side. The extra weight was a hindrance.

The square sail was raised and unfurled again allowing the long, slender Greek ship to surge forward. Half the crew still manned the oars; the others tended to the dead and wounded Greeks. Athelstan helped clear Aphrodite's decks of shattered wood as well as dead and dying Romans.

The wind filled the three sails of the second Roman warship with explosive bangs that echoed across the sea. Its three decks of oars dipped and rose rhythmically in and out of the water making the behemoth look as if it walked across the sea like some evil spider. Slowly, inexorably it closed the distance between them.

A frantic scurry of activity was taking place on the raised rear deck. Pre-shaped timbers were brought aft and men were hammering thick wooden arms into pre-drilled holes in sides of the upswept stern. They locked them in place with wooden pins. A triangular stand with a longboard was set in place directly in line with the rectangular opening. The two legs of the stand were fitted neatly into square holes in the deck. Cross braces anchored the sides together. Ropes, wheels and a long pole with a metal ring on one end were assembled on this odd framework forming a squat but powerful looking bow. The horizontal rope that stretched from the ends of the squat arms was pulled back with a winch and fitted into a notch in the longboard. The tension on the rope must have been tremendous.

Coal fires guttered in two iron braziers on either side of the tiller. Men mouths of amphorae filled with oil and delivered them up to the bow's crew. Athelstan watched as the oiled wool was wrapped around one end of long javelins lit from one of the braziers and was fitted onto the rope-triggers' metal ring. It was a perfect fit.

The trireme loomed larger and larger but captain Piros waited until it closed to less than three hundred feet from the stern of his own ship.

"Fire!" He thundered suddenly. A heavy thud shook the entire ship as the catapult launched its burning projectile high into the air. It left a delicate trail of smoke as it sped through the air. A second blazing javelin was released and then a third but only at Piro's deafening command. He waited patiently judging the pitch and roll of his ship. He only issued his command when he knew the aft deck was in its correct position.

Each of the deadly missiles found a target on the Roman ship. One glanced off the starboard rail and skewered an oarsman. A second landed in the space between the rowers just short of the mast. It took several seconds for the smoke to rise above the main deck but when it did, it was oily and black. The third missed the upper mast by inches and exploded on the upper deck aft. The flames spread quickly.

The ship slowed and turned to port, then, all at once, flames overtook the vessel entirely. Spinning towers of fire twisted and danced a hundred feet in the air above the tall masts. Thick black smoke rolled and coiled many hundreds of feet above that. Romans dove into the rough sea to escape the flames, the slaves manning the oars were left chained to their benches; their death was assured. Those in the water would drown; those who stayed aboard would burn. Piros left the doomed ship in his wake. Open sea was before him, and he set a course south-east.

Chapter Eight

Great reverence was given the Greeks who died during the battle. Prayers were recited to the Gods and their brows were anointed with oils. Then, one by one their bodies were commended into the sea they loved. Athelstan stood in silent tribute to the fallen simply bowing his head to each spirit lost. As it happened, the warship Aphrodite was the flagship of the Corinthian navy and 'Captain' Piros was the Admiral who commanded that fleet. When Athelstan received his invitation to dine with Aphrodite's officers that evening; he knew it was not a request.

After all the officers were seated, Piros rose to his feet.

Admiral Piros looked at the Celt over a goblet of wine. "Perhaps you might be kind enough to tell me why I have just given nineteen of my best men to Poseidon and risked five hundred others not to mention my ship, to help you flee the Empire of Rome. I can assure you Keltoi, we do have the time to discuss these matters in great detail now." Piros was not amused and his four officers seemed equally annoyed.

"Captain Piros, I am always grieved when good men fall. Today is no exception." Athelstan reached into his tunic and withdrew a scroll, which he slid across the pitching and rolling table. "This might help explain that your actions today were the correct ones," he offered.

"What is this?" Raw annoyance tainted Piro's voice. Athelstan simply gestured for him to read. The Celt waited as he read the document. Raised eyebrows replaced the scowl. Piros looked up slowly and let the document slip through his fingers.

"Where did you get this? Who are you? Be warned I will not tolerate any more riddles from you."

"I received that document from the hand of Trahearn Livy the Senone King. My instructions are to present it to King Leonidas ll of Sparta. I am General Athelstan. I command the Senone multitude."

"Admiral, that is the same name…" began one of the younger officers.

Piros silenced the officer with only a glance. The officer reddened. Piros

49

sat and stared at the scroll in front of him for a very long time.

He looked up at Athelstan and fixed him with a dark intelligent gaze.

"No! You are not. You cannot possibly be Athelstan. The Senone General is dead. He perished in the wilderness after the battle of Milan. So I ask you again, who are you and where did you get this?" The captain studied the Celt's reaction closely.

"It is true I was wounded during the battle. It is true that I very nearly walked the paths through paradise. I am back to health and now I have resumed my journey." To emphasize the point he stood and reached for the tails of his shirt. The four officers quickly stood and drew their Xiphos ready to defend their Captain. A slow frown crossed Athelstan's face. He opened his arms.

"When a man comes to the table of friends he brings neither weapons nor an impure heart. To do otherwise would be… uncivilised, would it not?" It was a rhetorical question.

With a gesture from Piros, the four men sat but did not relax. A smile and a nod greeted the gesture of trust. Athelstan raised his shirt and showed his ribs on the left side. A long scar with evenly spaced holes to either side where quills and twine had held the wound closed, was offered for close inspection by the seamen.

"I have never seen… Who did this to you?" Piros leaned forward. He still sounded gruff but there was a distinct hint of fascination in the question.

"The witches of Rhaetia," he responded as though that answered the question. Piros glanced at his men before settling back into his chair letting an amused grin spread across his face.

"Witches? You expect me to believe that witches sewed you up like sail cloth? I suppose they used magic." The men chortled.

"Yes, with magic. How else? I was dying after all."

"I am not the bumpkin I must seem to be. Witches are a myth. Everyone knows there is no such thing as witches or magic. Our physicians are, as yet, incapable of this and we have the most advanced medical system in the known world." Piros countered.

"Oh? I would not tell the Witches that." Athelstan warned with a quiet chuckle. "They might turn you into something… unnatural."

Piros slammed a fist down on the table and everything jumped. "Enough!" he roared. "I will not be mocked aboard my own ship SIR! It is well within my rights to have you thrown over the side for risking this vessel and crew. This meeting is a courtesy, nothing more. Now answer the question!"

It was a low growl that rumbled in the Celt's chest. "You would not have this ship but for me and the men, I command. You are not a stupid man so I will not treat you as one. You have watched the Greek city-states of Italia fall to Rome's legions one by one. Where were you, Admiral Piros of Corinth, when Taras fell this spring?" Piros sprang to his feet.

"How dare you? I will not…" He roared.

"SIT – down Admiral! It is I who speaks now." They glared at each other with murder in their eyes. His officers stood weapons drawn. He ignored them.

"I said sit down and sit your men down before I send them all to Tartarus with surprised expressions on their faces." Piros sank back into his chair slowly motioning his men to do the same.

"Let me tell you where I was – thank you for asking. I was there. I watched eight hundred and seventy-two of my men, good men, family men all, fight and die to hold back three entire Roman legions, so the Greek citizens of Taras could be safely evacuated by sea. King Molossus personally thanked my King for his help. I was there when he did so. Who do you suppose has kept those Romans bottled up in Italia all these years? Fairies spreading their magic dust? Hardly. It has been men – brave men like the nineteen who fell today and the five hundred gathered here that did not," he gestured to include the entire ship's complement then leaned forward and placed both hands flat on the table and stood.

"You mourn less than a score of men, Admiral. I mourn thousands! So pardon me for not apologising because I fight wars that I must win for your sake as well as mine own. I am Athelstan, First General of the Senone Army and I will defend that truth against anyone who claims that I am not." There was a growing menace in his voice as he glared at Piros. Athelstan's patience was at an end.

Piros also glared at Athelstan and slowly stood. There was a long moment of hushed indecision. Then Piros smiled and sat.

"Pray, sit down General," Piros said softly. "Have some wine." It was an easy gesture of his hand that finally diffused the tension. Athelstan sat and raised the goblet to his lips. An officer stood and opened the door. Food was brought in and laid on the table – roast goat, black bread and roasted carrots.

"I was at Taras, General like you were. Who do you suppose commanded the evacuation? Welcome aboard the Aphrodite, General Athelstan. Of course, I knew who you were the moment you boarded, I have been ordered to watch for you and render any aid I could." Piros said with some hauteur. "However my instructions are to bring you directly to Corinth."

"So all this was what, a test?" Athelstan asked. Piros nodded slightly. "You play a perilous game Admiral."

"So do you General. I think now we understand each other quite well, do we not?" A wry smile tugged at the Celt's moustache and for a time he turned his attention to the roasted goat and cabbage.

With a tiny sip of wine, Athelstan pushed his board away and began to speak softly.

"I thank you for your hospitality. I hope I might return the favour one day soon." Piros inclined his head. The Celt continued.

"You must realise by now, I seek military help for an overland assault on the fortified city of Milan; my home. Corinth is not noted for its armies. I believe I must go directly to Sparta and speak with the Spartan King instead – I do not say this to offend."

"And no offence is taken. It is no secret that our navy is our strength, it is true, but Queen Kratesipolis wishes to take council with a Barbarian Gaul."

"We refer to ourselves as Senone Celts, Admiral. Gauls and Goths may look similar but we are actually quite different."

"My apologies General, I meant no offence; with a Senone Celt rather. I would hate to advise her that you refused to see her."

"No offence is taken sir and I shall not prove you false in the face of your Queen's commands. I would be honoured to meet with her. You may tell your Queen I will attend her at her convenience as soon as my business with Sparta is concluded. However, I must first complete what I have been directed to do by my own King. "

That was acceptable to Piros and the conversation turned to the battle of Milan. The men were interested in every detail; Athelstan did not disappoint them. He sent for his boot knife and let them examine the intricate designs running the length of the blade.

When the dinner concluded, Athelstan was assigned a small room below decks in which to sleep and stow his gear. Throughout the ten-day journey across the Adriatic, he fed Maehadren dried apples and fresh hay. One handful of oats a day kept his coat a shimmering white. Dung was flung overboard and he toiled to keep the deck boards spotless. It was not by accident that the Celt loved this magnificent steed. His people worshipped Epona, the White Horse Goddess. It was a thriving and widespread religion among the Senone people. Maehadren was as much a God in Athelstan's eyes as he was a horse and the Celt treated the beast accordingly.

Many of the Greek sailors doted on Maehadren as well by slipping sweet treats to the spoiled horse when they thought Athelstan was not looking. Often horses did not do well on sea voyages and to have a warhorse of Maehadren's calibre aboard a warship, was a rare occurrence, to say the least.

The days were clear and sunny. Athelstan could usually be found standing like a statue in the prow, once he had overcome the disturbing motion of the ship and the vomiting had ended.

Athelstan thoroughly enjoyed the trip. He relished the crisp tang in the air and the salty sea spray. He could watch for hours in rapt fascination as dolphins rode and played in Aphrodite's bow wake. They called to him with their shrill laughing voices and waved up at him with their fins. A human voice startled him.

"Have you given them names yet? I could not help notice you have been watching these dolphins for days." Piros stood grinning at the Celt. Athelstan laughed.

"Why would I do that? They have names of their own already."

The Admiral found that funny. "They are just stupid fish, they do not have names. Only people have names."

"I have been rejoicing in them and I can tell you they are far from stupid fish. In fact, they are not fish at all. They breathe air. Fish breathe water. I have been watching them very carefully. It's quite possible these animals are smarter than we are."

"Ha! That is where you are wrong Celt. Look at them. They do not even have the good sense to stay out of the way of a moving ship."

"Have you ever hit one?" He gave Piros a sidelong glance.

"Hit one?" He frowned at the odd question looking down into the water. "Well no…"

Athelstan looked back into the water. "You never shall either. Listen to them Admiral; they are laughing and playing like children do. What you hear is the voice of Nehalennia, Goddess of seafarers. So long as she leads you, all your journeys will be safe ones."

"I am convinced Nehalennia Goddess of the sea abides within these magnificent creatures. They probably think the Aphrodite is some slow moving, wooden cousin of theirs." Athelstan had a serene face. "Admiral Piros, only intelligent creatures have the need for play; wolves, otters, foxes, even people; we all need to play. Fish, bugs, trees; none of them play. They have no need. Dolphins, on the other hand, seem to play most of the time so, by my reckoning, they must be very intelligent indeed."

"I was warned you were an odd man with strange ways, General. I am relieved I was not lied to." Piros looked into the water at the dolphins for a time before shaking his head. He mouthed a silent prayer before heading aft.

Under full sail, they made good time. After ten long nights and days of sailing over the blue-green Ægean Sea, they rounded the south cape of Akra Tainaron. This was his first glimpse of Lacedaemon. Here is where the mighty city-state of Sparta lay.

Three hours later, the coastal breakwater of Yithion could finally be seen. They slipped into the calm waters of the harbour. It was a confusing tangle of masts and sails. Pennants were strung across ropes on ships from many strange lands. The sights and smells of this Greek port were exotic to Athelstan's nose. The warship moored at the southern end of the harbour and the cacophony of Sparta's bustling seaport assailed his senses.

Athelstan bade farewell to Piros and the crew of the Aphrodite, took Maehadren's reins, and disembarked the ship to begin his land journey from Yithion north to Sparta. He wound his way along the docks through the stacks of crates, bales, wagons and sledges; all seeming randomly scattered. Hundreds of people scurried here and there, loading and unloading ships from a dozen nations. Many gaped at him with wide-eyed surprise as he led the great white horse among them. Few, if any, had ever seen someone who looked even remotely like him. Athelstan avoided eye contact but a ghastly shrieking caught his attention. His mood darkened by what he saw.

He came to a stop and watched for a moment while a heavy-set man, whipped a grubby slave girl unmercifully. She howled and pleaded for mercy as she scrambled to avoid the stinging lash. The wielder of the whip was skilled, powerful and merciless.

Athelstan dismounted and shouldered his way through the crush of cheering bloodthirsty spectators. The bull of a man with the whip had his back to Athelstan and as the long lash was brought back for yet another crippling blow on the prostrate girl, the Celt simply stepped forward and grabbed the blood-soaked end. He easily yanked it out of the man's hand. The overseer suddenly tipped off balance, fell on his ample rump with a thud. Athelstan tossed the whip aside with a grimace of disgust. The girl lay motionless.

"That will do," he growled in his heavily accented Greek. A gasp rippled through the crowd and he felt them stiffen in fear. As the man scrambled to his feet Athelstan bent over the prone girl but he saw she was already dead. Her eyes had that dull vacant look to them. He gently laid her head back down and wiped some of the dirt from her cheek and nose. She now stood with her departed family members. This life of pain and degradation was finally over.

With a sudden howl of rage, the overseer leapt up to face the bearded Celt, balled up his fists and charged. Both the man's fists slammed into Athelstan jaw with two mighty blows. Athelstan's head snapped from one side to the other, only to rotate back towards the bewildered dock master. The Celt towered several inches above this man. A dark, almost feral look lit the Celt's face. The Greek swung again and the Celt blocked the punch and lashed out with his ham-like fist. The overseer dropped wobbly-kneed with a heavy thump. He rubbed his jaw and shook the stars from his head.

The Greek stood and grabbed a baling–hook, then charged the Celt again, this time with murderous intent. Athelstan had been in fights like this since he was little. Single combat was an integral part of his culture. He never backed down. As the man rushed in Athelstan moved forward like a cat. He stepped inside the weapons deadly arc. A howl of pure hatred tore out of the Celt. He could not abide cruelty towards the weak and he absolutely detested bullies.

Now inside the overseer's attack, Athelstan's left hand grabbed a greasy knot of hair then pulled it backwards and down. The brute's chin rose skyward. He struggled to recover and be free of the Celt's iron grip. At the same instant, with his other fist, Athelstan delivered a devastating overhand blow to the man's centre of his upturned forehead – like a blacksmith would hammer glowing iron. A loud, sickening crunch could be heard and the overseer's body went suddenly limp. His life of cruelty was also at an end.

Still holding the knot of hair, Athelstan drew the long rune–covered knife from his boot and calmly decapitated him to gasps of shock and horror from the growing crowd. The headless body dropped away and then he looked at the disembodied head for a moment before tossing it casually into the sea. A weak cheer rose from the workers nearby. Clearly, this man had not been well liked.

"Small wonder," he muttered into his beard. The gathered crowd made a wide path so he could mount Maehadren. They turned as one towards the city proper and left the docks behind.

The city of Yithion was small and compact. The dockyards opened onto a fresh–air market teeming with people. Exotic food, drink and products from all over the known world were for sale here and the merchants did a thriving business. The incident at the docks had not faded from Athelstan's mind when he heard something else that caused him to turn in his saddle.

Chapter Nine

"Stop! Thief! He stole my figs!" someone bellowed. Athelstan caught sight of a brief struggle between a fat man and a young boy.

Athelstan's eyes scanned the crowd briefly and he watched as the grubby youth in a torn toga came dashing towards him. The man had melted away quickly into the crowd. The young boy was running hard, with an expression of terror on his face. Curly, blonde hair was tucked tightly under a wide-brimmed hat. He dodged and darted past surprised onlookers in the crowded market, bearing an armload of fruit – presumably stolen. A corpulent, balding merchant, dressed in a dozen yards of blue and white material, was chasing him as best he could. However, with the boy's long stride and the merchant's advanced weight, it was no contest. The merchant was losing ground with every waddling, jiggling step he took. In a few moments, the boy would be swallowed up in the crowd and out of sight of his pursuer entirely, when suddenly someone tripped him and he fell in a sprawling pile on the flagstones. The armload of fruit scattered in all directions. Rough hands grasped him as he tried to bolt again. They held him firm until the furious merchant came to a puffing wheezing halt. The fig merchant cuffed the boy hard and his hat flew to the ground. Long, fine curls cascaded down the thief's back

"This is a girl!" someone exclaimed. "What are you trying to do dressed like that?"

She was yanked around to face the Merchant and her face bore an expression of abject terror. A crowd was quickly gathering.

"A girl? Thieving bitch!" he spat and cuffed her again across the cheek. "I will have your hand for this! I will see you skinned alive!"

The girl struggled to free herself and bit down hard on one of her captor's hands. She received another painful smack for her troubles.

"Fetch the guards," someone demanded, but there was no need, as a pair of armed men in Spartan uniforms arrived on the scene.

"What is going on here?" one of the soldiers demanded in a loud voice.

"She is a thief," the merchant accused pointing a finger in the girl's face. She nearly bit that off too.

"I am a thiefless – not. Man gave," she snarled in dreadful Greek.

"Silence! Who is your master slave?"

"No slave! I free–girl, myself stolen past weeks. They stolen my person. Seven of ourselves stolen weeks ago, brought here badly. To home we must travel quickly," she said nodding.

The merchant was not even listening. "Look at all this fruit she stole. It is ruined. I want her hand for this."

"No!" she screamed shaking her blonde locks vigorously.

Accusations and denials filled the air from a dozen or more voices in an ear-numbing cacophony. Greeks were the undisputed masters at the art of arguing. Athelstan sat quietly aboard Maehadren watching this scene unfold. The girl's Greek was oddly accented and she was not entirely fluent. Her explanation was also far from clear but he did hear phrases like 'the poor little ones' and 'stolen my person'. None of it seemed to make much sense but it was clearly entertaining the crowd as much as it was enraging the guards. They began to push the crowd and demanding they make room. She started to sob.

"You have to let me go," she pleaded.

Athelstan sat back in his saddle with a visible start. She spoke perfect Latin. This girl was Roman. He glanced around again. If there were Romans here, he could be in grave danger. This was their style, create a diversion first and strike second.

"What is language?" demanded the Greek guard.

"Justice! Justice," the merchant screeched. "I want her flayed! I want her hand! I want her crucified!" The Merchant's bellowed.

"No. My fault it is not. Run from bad men. The poor little ones need eating soon," the girl pleaded again in her broken Greek.

"So you are a runaway slave. Who is your master?" howled the merchant.

"Shut up, both of you! I have heard enough," the exasperated guard growled. "You are coming with us." He had her arms pinned behind her back and yanked her around to drag her off. "And you," he aimed a stubby finger at the Merchant, "need to file a formal complaint…"

"I do not have time to file a complaint. I want justice done here and now." The crowd seemed to agree and began to grow angry.

"No complaint? Then she goes free – here and now. So choose. Come to the garrison. We will hold her there. Then you can have your justice done. Clear? The rest of you get back to work, ya hear?" The conversation was clearly over. The guard fell into step with his partner hustling the girl along with them. The merchant departed, grumbling. The crowd slowly dispersed into groups but continued to argue the matter, at some length.

Athelstan was suddenly torn between his duty to his King and his duty to his Druidic faith. Choosing one threatened the other. On one hand, if he just went to Sparta and attended to his mission, then this girl would most certainly die. If on the other hand, he intervened on the girl's behalf, he would almost certainly become a criminal under Spartan law, which would threaten both of their lives.

How could he even contemplate the later? She was Roman after all. This fact could prove serious indeed. Defend and protect the weak was the mantra hammered into his brain by the Druids since he was a child. It would seem he had little choice. A growl of frustration escaped him. Those close enough to hear him took several steps back. It would seem Greeks did not growl.

A Celt's curiosity is a powerful force and he found himself following the trio at a discreet distance as they bundled their prisoner along. He was torn between his duty to his King and their mission, his need to question this girl, and the Druidic faith that required him to help this girl. Choosing one, threatened the other and for a moment, he was gripped with indecision.

A moment came when the prisoner felt the time was ripe to make a final bid for escape. She twisted violently, broke their grip. She took to her heels back in the direction she came. The guards were caught off balance for the briefest of moments, before taking up the chase. As fate would have it, she collided with Maehadren slowing her sufficiently for the guards to catch up. She looked up at Athelstan as they grabbed her.

"Succurro." It was a plea for help.

With a slight nod, he answered. "Patentia," he replied in Latin. His choice had been made. Her shocked expression was fleeting and she sagged in defeat as they roughly wheeled her around and dragged her into the Spartan guardhouse. The looks on the guard's faces spoke volumes as to the fate that awaited her. He was a soldier and had seen that look countless times; that look of lust and domination so common to victors in the field. He knew her chances were not good. If he intervened directly now, he would certainly be branded a criminal under Spartan law and his mission would be over. He was forced to wait, however not for very long.

A few minutes passed and three guards reappeared. They dragged her by the hair and she struggled helplessly. Her arms were cruelly tied behind her back. She was unceremoniously thrown into the back of a hay wagon. One guard jumped into the back beside her while two other guards sat in front. One took up the reigns and their cart was on its way.

"Fiat mihi exponere…" She tried again to explain in flawless Latin. Hers was not the accent of the streets either. She had obviously been schooled.

"Silence!" The guard cuffed her backhanded across the face. Athelstan flinched at the power of the blow and his grip on the knife tightened involuntarily.

Athelstan followed as discreetly as possible riding Maehadren north out of Yithion. He stayed well back amid the throngs of wagons and other foot traffic bound to and from Sparta. They said they were going to take her to their jail, but looking at the men holding her; that seemed unlikely. One guard kept looking into the back of the wagon while the other one trussed her up more securely. Athelstan had seen that look in men before. He knew their minds. To them, she was merely a street urchin, a runaway slave. She had no value to them, beyond the carnal. They would each take their turns raping her, then murder her when they were done. He tried to keep within earshot.

It hardly mattered if he heard them, or not. Athelstan knew what he must do. His personal sense of honour deeply rooted in Druidic faith demanded he take this girl from these men before any more harm was done to her. Abuse of the helpless was a dishonourable act, so by that measure, he was free to act on the girl's behalf and rid Gaia of these evil and wicked men. No other action was now possible, or acceptable for him. In matters of Druidic Law, there was only good or bad – right or wrong – white or black. There was no grey at all. That he was in Hellas with different laws and customs, mattered not.

For a second time, she tried to reason with the guard. "Truth I tell," she spoke some Greek words well enough, but could not converse very clearly.

"I do service to you. You listen at me."

"Oh, you'll do more than one 'service' to us alright." Guffaws of laughter filled the wagon.

She looked around quickly and spied Athelstan following. He raised a finger to his lips urging her to be silent.

The girl turned back to her captors. "Non-furtum facies pro me…" she began again but was cuffed into silence.

The Celt was fairly seething at this unnecessarily brutal treatment. She had just said that she 'did not steal for herself', then for whom? "Little ones? Little what? At this point, it was difficult to know.

Dizzy, she struggled to her knees. She raised her head just in time to see the man's fist slam into her right eye. She toppled back out of the wagon into the dirt on the side of the road. The guard jumped off and tossed the unconscious girl back into the wagon like so much rubbish. Athelstan very nearly intervened right there.

"You are a runaway slave and that's how we're going to tell it," he said with a snarl.

"Before we get paid and you lose that hand, you are going to give us a prize of another sort."

'Stay out of business that does not concern you.' Athelstan heard the words of Caileigh, the Epona clan's Arch–Druidess, echoing in his mind. She was the power in the Celtic world. Kings may rule but this Druidess's word was absolute law. When she realised that Athelstan would be travelling to Sparta in search of help against Rome, she sat him down and had a long talk with him about how he should act in foreign lands. This 'girl' was clearly 'business' that did not concern him, but still, he watched this sickening scene unfold.

A full hay wagon pulled onto the road blocking his view of the guards and their captive. He followed at a steady pace but once around the bend, the soldiers were nowhere to be seen. He doubled back quickly. He searched both sides of the road until he found a set of tracks leading away from the road north into a dense orchard of figs. It was a narrow track that disappeared quickly into the gloom.

His mind returned to Caileigh's warning. 'Stay out of business that does not concern you.' It rang in his head giving him another moment of pause. Surely, the Arch–Druidess had not imagined this. However, she had wagged her bony finger under his nose when she said it. She meant every word literally. She was like that - abrupt and literal. He heaved a sigh. It was quite likely that once she discovered he had disobeyed her she would use her magic to turn him into something slimy and unnatural. It would seem in this case, the Druidic law was somewhat unclear.

He continued fifty yards past the wagon track before he wheeled Maehadren to the right plunging into the rows of fig trees. He moved through the tangle of wide leaves and around the low branches as quickly as he could, hoping the line of trees followed a straight line. He suspected it would. Greeks seemed so linear that way.

A sound filtered through the trees – guttural laughter muffled by the dense foliage and Athelstan smiled, or more accurately, grimaced wickedly. They were close. Slowly he angled Maehadren back towards the narrow track. When he found it, the wagon was still some distance away. He backed away from the road and waited for it to arrive.

The men were drinking now. His nostrils flared. Even from this distance, he could smell them. Soon her torment would begin. The girl's death would follow soon after that. He could hear the wagon trundle closer and closer and when the noses of the horses finally came into view past the screen of leaves, he urged Maehadren up onto the road and came to a complete stop, barring the way. The wagon team shied away from the sudden appearance of the huge white warhorse. The wagon lurched to a stop.

The surprised drivers had not expected any company and did not mind showing it. They sputtered with drunken outrage.

"Tartarus!" the driver shouted. "What have we here? What do you think you are doing? Get out of the way Keltoi, if you know what is good for you. We got official state business to take care of. Move that ugly nag off the road!"

Silence was all they got from the Celt. He did not even look at them; rather he sat staring into the trees on the far side of the orchard track. The silence grew increasingly awkward. The Greeks looked at each other then back at the Senone in astonishment. Even the draft horses were getting nervous.

"You there! Get out of the way, I say!" Still, Athelstan offered no reaction whatsoever. It was as though, to him, they were simply not there. The guard in the back had his prize half stripped and was tugging at his own loincloth when the wagon had suddenly stopped.

The guard stood. "I'm talking to you. Are you deaf? Move aside!"

As slowly as the sun rises in the morning, Athelstan's head turned to face the wagon driver. He bore the intense expression of a hungry owl staring at a mouse. The guard sank back in his seat.

"Let – her – go!" the Celt said slowly in his heavily accented Greek. There was a moment of utter silence before the driver recovered his wits. He shook his head as if to dispel some perceived wizardry.

"What? Let her go? Who do you think you are? Give me your name!" The driver stood to get a better look at this strange man. Athelstan continued to stare at the driver but remained silent.

"Name! What is your name?"

"WILD!" Athelstan thundered. He issued a positively feral snarl. His ice-blue eyes glittered.

The easily startled draft horses reared and danced back a pace or two in fright. Even the guards jumped at the explosive outburst. Maehadren remained as still as if he had been carved from the very bones of the earth.

"Malaka!" the trio exclaimed in unison.

"Let – her – go." His quiet voice had returned but now he was certain he had focused their attention.

"Ohhh, this is going to be a real pleasure. I have not hacked a foreign asshole to bits in days," spat the driver as he descended from the wagon in a mighty leap. The Greek soldier drew his Xiphos and closed on Athelstan. He was a thick-armed, stocky man with a shock of straight black hair, greying slightly at the temples.

"Sabaid Maehadren!" Athelstan whispered in Gaelic for Maehadren to defend himself. The horse spun on his rear hooves and lashed out with his front hooves at the approaching man. There was a pair of horrible crunching sounds in rapid succession as each front hoof connected with the man's head. The impact lifted the man from his feet. He skidded to a stop in a fetid, muck-filled ditch at the side of the track. A warhorse's front hooves are their primary weapons and Maehadren had been very well trained.

The remaining pair of Spartans looked at each other and then at their dead comrade in shock.

Athelstan now glared at the two remaining men. They looked away from their dead friend and back at the Celt with pure hatred.

"I said, let – her – go. Do it now. I'll not tell you again." His voice had returned to a bare whisper, but in the still orchard, it suddenly sounded very loud indeed.

Chapter Ten

The remaining two guards' duty was clear and they tried avenging the sudden death of their comrade, but they had no chance against such an efficient, killing machine. It was a ferocious two on one fight. These were skilled warriors – but in the end, the Greek's short Xiphos were simply no match for the five–foot long, rune-covered blade favoured by the Senone General. Athelstan hoisted headless Greek bodies back into the wagon and gently lifted an unconscious girl out of it. He did not steal the horses. Instead, he unhitched them, swatted their rumps. They disappeared down the track at a trot. He did not loot the corpses either. It lacked honour.

She was small in stature and light as a feather. He doubted she stood five feet tall. After cutting her bonds, he sat this strange looking thief on the ground letting her rest against one of the heavy wagon wheels.

He tugged her floppy trousers back into place, re-tied the cord, and stuffed her blonde curls back into her hat. Despite the bruises, her features were delicate, with broad cheekbones, narrow upturned nose, full lips, and a narrow chin. Her blue eyes were large and set wide apart. They were framed with impossibly long, dark lashes.

A leather pouch was tied around her waist under her clothing. Inside there were nine Roman coins. They were newly minted and made of fine silver.

"If you have silver coins, why were you stealing figs in the marketplace? Or were you stealing coins and figs?"

He replaced the coins into her pouch and straightened the rest of her clothing. She was dressed like a Helot – a Greek peasant boy, for some reason. Were these the only clothes she could steal? Was this a disguise meant to fool someone?

There was something very odd here. Everything about her appearance screamed beggar or runaway slave. Everything about her manner and accent screamed privilege, so which was the truth? If she was indeed a slave, these coins could hardly be hers. If she was nobility from Rome, then how did she come to be dressed like this Greek beggar boy? He was not certain how much she might remember about recent events. He decided to let her maintain her beggar boy disguise.

Still, he needed to unravel this puzzle quickly. Hellas was not a safe place to be alone, pretty and on the run. Someone had already discovered her secret once. He figured it out the moment he saw her. It was only a matter of time before someone else did. There was a strange tale woven into this girl and her few precious possessions. She had said some very odd things earlier, which might simply be poor phrasing of a language she was not familiar with. Or, perhaps it was something else. Athelstan could not resist a good mystery. He concluded that whoever she was, someone of high rank, a Senator, or merchant perhaps, was probably looking for her. It would seem he was now firmly mired in, 'business that did not concern him'.

The other issue was what he would do if she were part of some vanguard of Roman soldiers hunting him. Even now, they might be closing the net.

Occasionally her dazed and glassy eyes would open but they refused to focus. They were a rich blue with darker specks in. They had a translucent – almost bottomless quality. He had never seen such a colour – not even in all the blues of the sky. What worried him was that her pupils were not even. He had seen men die with no other injury save this.

He turned her lolling head this way and that. He examined her closely. He felt around for other injuries like broken ribs but found none. By the size of her breasts and narrow hips, she looked like a girl of about between thirteen and fifteen years. The left side of her jaw was bruised, swollen and her lip still bled a bit. There was a little knot under her left eye and a large one above her right. He wiped away the blood with the cuff of his white linen shirt and waited for her to regain her senses. Her eyes fluttered open and shut several times as she fought to wake up.

When she did finally focus on him, her eyes widened in surprise. A small squeak of shock escaped her before she passed out once again. His brow furrowed.

After a moment, or two, she lifted her head again and now her expression cleared a bit.

He took her face in his hands and lightly tapped her cheeks. When her eyes open, her expression cleared a bit. Her glassy eyes changed to show determination. He smiled. Yes, a warrior's spirit was exactly what she had.

"Geia sas. Hello. Welcome back. Do not be afraid. You are safe now. Do you understand me?" He spoke in his heavily accented Greek. He chose not to use Latin for the moment since it would be a clear giveaway that he was from the north of Italy and an enemy of Rome. She blinked at him. Her brain might take a while to get working properly. Her hand went to the side of her face and she winced.

"Moraine na piantan?" He tried Gaelic asking if she was in much pain but she still responded with a blank stare. "Vides," he repeated again in Latin; still nothing.

"Elliniká? Greek? Do – you – speak – Greek?" He spoke louder and slower in spite of himself, but when she cringed away from the sound, he shook his head. He was talking to her like an idiot.

She looked sick and dizzy and her eyes were still not focusing well. He had seen this many times in soldiers with head wounds. It was rarely a good sign and

Athelstan was worried. He failed to save one poor spirit today and he was not prepared to lose a second. He shook his head. He was panicking; that was not like him. He was just going to have to let her recover in her own time, which meant they would have to stay put for the time being.

So far, it looked as though she could still barely see, let alone think. It was all she could do to remain conscious. He looked up and down the orchard trail. Nothing moved in either direction. This was good. This was the hottest time of day in southern Hellas. He knew that Spartans usually take shelter from the brutal sun during midday. Under this cool canopy of fig trees, they were safe for the moment.

It just was then that he realised what this poor battered, girl might think, seeing a wild-haired, fur–covered Celt hovering over her. If other people's reactions were any measure, she might very well die of fright. He decided to play a rather simple character for her. It would give her less reason to fear him and since he had no intention of harming her; trust might come quicker.

Those eyes were finally focusing and she did shrink back from him. Athelstan asked again. "Greek? Milás Elliniká? he asked again. "Do – you – speak – Greek?"

"Nai, Yes, a little bit," she said weakly, her voice slurring the word. When she tried to speak, only a hiss and rough gurgle came out. She tried again. A sound left her mouth this time. Not quite her real voice perhaps, but it did what it was meant to do.

"Yes, some Greek," she said with a strange inflexion in her pronunciation. Who was he to criticise? His accent was little better.

'Good.' Athelstan thought. He nodded and beamed what he hoped was a friendly smile at her. At least they had a language in common.

He issued a soft whistle and Maehadren walked forward. The sound caused her to squeeze her eyes shut and hold her head with a low moan. "Sios," he said in Gaelic and the great beast knelt. Her gaze shifted from Athelstan to his horse and back again.

"Your head, hurt bad?" He made a punching motion towards his own chin. She nodded weakly before clapping her hands over her aching eyes in an effort to stop the dizziness that motion caused.

"Dizzy, not good. Rest now."

He looked at her partially with concern and partially in amazement. Despite the pain, he could tell she was curious. She was still fighting to try to sit forward and get up.

He retrieved a skin of water from Maehadren's shoulder pack. Holding the tip to her lips he said. "Drink."

She eyed him cautiously before tipping her head back allowing the cool liquid to dribble past her lips and relieve her parched dry throat. He pulled the water skin back several times letting the liquid settle in her stomach before giving her more.

"Athelstan – me," he stated, pointing at his chest. "To ónomá sas? Your name boy," he asked pointing at her. He did not want her to worry about her disguise. He feared she might try to bolt if she did.

She simply blinked at him and studied his face with naked astonishment. Shaky fingers rose of their own volition and touched his beard, moustache, and several of the amulets woven into his hair. With effort, she pulled her hand away.

"Thank you," she said to him.

"Welcome – you," he nodded seriously. It was easy for Athelstan to replace Greek words for Gaelic. With his own thick accent, it made him sound simple and slow.

He offered her a few more sips of the water. Soon her eyes were finally able to stay open long enough to meet his steadily. He noticed clarity returning as well. She was clearly scared of him. He was going to have to do something about that.

Until he learned more about this girl he would keep this up.

She was staring at him now, presumably trying to determine if he was one of the brutes that attacked her, or perhaps even if he was a slaver. His head involuntarily shook in negation to her unasked question and his lips bore a kind smile.

Clearly, Athelstan was something entirely new to her; and in truth, she was as much a mystery to him. He had to suppress a smile as he watched her struggle inwardly.

"Who are you?" she asked still not giving her name. "Why did you do this?"

He mouthed her words and puzzled them out for a moment.

"This I not do. This I stop. Athelstan – me," he tapped his chest with a finger and nodded. By her reaction, it was not the response she was hoping for.

"I thank you, Athelstan. You did not need to…" She faltered and licked her split, swollen lip. While her Greek was heavily inflected, she had a soft voice with a musical accent as she spoke. When she said 'I' it sounded more like 'ahh' and when she said 'not' it was a long and drawn out 'naught'. He let her drink from the skin.

"You did not need…" She began again but stopped when he put his finger to her lips.

"Yes, I did," he whispered with a serious look. His simpleton ruse was gone for a moment.

Confusion and some trepidation crawled across her features as she scanned his face closely before she slowly nodded her thanks.

He nodded back. Athelstan stood, picked a handful of ripe figs and smiled. "Tá tú tuillte acu tar éis an tsaoil," he said in his native tongue. "You have earned them, after all."

Gaelic was so much easier to speak; he had slipped into it without thinking. It must have sounded like pure gibberish to his still stunned companion.

"Eat," he said again in his battered Greek. His smile widened as she smiled back. With some hesitation, she reached for the figs. She ate and winced each time she bit down, but her hunger clearly eclipsed her sore jaw. He gave her more water until she waved him off. "Enough."

"You stand?" He asked glancing quickly about. "Because we have absolutely got to get away from here and right now," he completed his phrase in Gaelic and did not care if she understood.

The 'boy' did smile, then nodded with a big sigh. He helped her stand on wobbly legs.

"Steady now!" he cautioned and stood looking once more into the wagon and its cargo of butchered guards.

She went to rummage in the wagon as well but turned away unsteadily once she saw its grisly contents. She was obviously not good with blood and death. Her face turned ashen and she vomited.

"You look upon the face of a righteous killing. The innocent should never be abused. This was necessary. Do you understand." he said accidentally letting his ruse drop again by speaking in flawless Greek. He lifted her chin so she could look into his eyes. "Do you understand?"

"Yes. I understand." The events of the morning seemed to return and her smile was sudden, wide and happy. Obviously forgetting her disguise, she hugged him tight and kissed his bearded cheek

"Hrumph" Athelstan was surprised at the kiss. He turned his still nameless charge away from the death wagon and motioned that she was to ride Maehadren.

The horse cast a dubious eye at the girl. Athelstan could not help but stare. Even dressed as a guttersnipe, she was lovely.

"No biting!" he admonished Maehadren in Gaelic since it was the only language the horse understood.

"You ride," he finally managed.

She shook her head in negation and wobbled slightly when she did. A strong hand tightened on Athelstan's arm as she fought to remain standing on unsteady legs. He, in turn, wrapped an arm around her waist and walked with her slowly as she struggled to remain upright.

Swaying like a drunk, she used Maehadren's rump for balance. He was smiling at her in spite of himself.

"I not ride. Walk better."

"No walk, you ride. Seating, the world will spin not." Once again, he cast about for witnesses. There were none, but he knew that would not last. Someone had built this road, perhaps even one of the dead guard's families. It was best that they not remain to find out.

He saw her contemplating his words, but yet she still shook her head no. "Must leave now. Big importance. My thanking you now." Athelstan was not really listening to her. Grabbing the disguised girl by the waist, he hoisted her up and onto Maehadren's broad shoulders, then vaulted up behind her.

"Grab here and here and hold on. You will not fall off," he forced her to grab handfuls of Maehadren's golden mane and circled her waist with a strong arm. Even without him holding her, she was in no danger of falling off. Maehadren would make it his job to see she remained aboard. He suddenly realised he had spoken in perfect Greek again. He was going to have to watch his speech more closely.

"No. Must not. No ride with you." When her head dipped forward, he knew she had not noticed the verbal slips either time he had done it. He knew his charge just needed to find a quiet place to sit and rest her eyes. He saw her rub her aching eyes and tenderly probe her jaw.

"Ionnsaigh Air!" Responding to Athelstan's commanding tone, Maehadren wheeled and headed off the road back into the trees.

Since he hardly needed handholds to stay aboard, he used both hands to wrap his passenger in the white bearskin cloak given him by the twins. The air was dry and oppressively hot even under the trees but he could feel her shivering. Whether it was from being aboard Maehadren, or from the shock of her attack, he could not tell. He held her as still as possible and kept her warm.

Who was this strange girl and why did she need a disguise so desperately that even a bad one sufficed? Where was it she needed to go so urgently?

Athelstan knew that getting away from here was more important than this fugitive's headache. Murdering Spartan citizens was definitely frowned upon. Heliots were state-owned serfs and never possessed weapons, or had access to horses. Only citizens like Spartiates or Mothakes, non–Spartan free men, raised as Spartans, had that kind of wealth. It was also widely understood that Celtic warriors behead the wicked and the unjust. Athelstan quickly reasoned that anyone seeing a large, heavily armed Celt riding a white horse away from a town containing four headless citizens, would almost certainly remember it. He had picked on the wrong people and needed to avoid all contact with the local population until he could bring his case for help to the Spartan King personally. Even then, his fate would be far from certain.

As they rode, his thoughts returned to the things she said when he first met her. 'I am free–girl myself stolen weeks ago. They stolen my person. Seven of ourselves stolen weeks ago, brought here badly.' 'Run from bad men. The poor little ones need eating soon.' None of this made any sense. It would help if they could speak more freely in a language they both understood well. However, getting away from here was more important than anything else now.

In the west, a formidable line of snow-capped mountains ran roughly northeast. While it would be effortless for Athelstan to evade pursuit in their forested slopes, he doubted if his young companion could survive such a journey. To the east, the coastline curved gently away past a line of low rocky hills. He had seen as much from the ship. He took a moment to consider the options before heading northeast away from Sparta.

He stayed in the trees, avoiding easier routes in favour of concealment. Orchards were perched on terraced hills, interspersed with small stands of trees. Maehadren easily manoeuvred the rocky terrain as they charted a circuitous route past the many farmhouses. Soon Yithion, the wagon, and its ghastly cargo were left far behind.

He brought Maehadren to a stop near a small stream. He needed to let the great beast rest. Dismounting, he lifted the girl from the simple saddle. Maehadren immediately went to graze and drink. His guest curled up against a shady tree and closed her eyes. A stray lock of hair slipped from her hat to cover one closed eye. He could not help but smile at just how angelic she looked. She looked like the children from his people. Pushing the hair back behind her ear,

Athelstan left her to sleep against the tree. She had earned this rest. As soon as his hands left her, her eyes fluttered open. She was just about to speak when he placed a finger to her lips silencing her.

He needed to look around and indicated his intention silently with his fingers. She nodded weakly. She seemed grateful to finally be motionless.

The air held the tang of fish and salt so he knew the coastline was very close now. They had travelled far enough that it was worth the risk of coming into the open for a look at the land. He climbed a sharp rocky hill spotted with dry scrub brush and scanned the surroundings.

He immediately sank into a crouch like an animal. Before him, the blue-green waters of the bay of Lakonikos stretched to the horizon in the south-east. The rugged hills fell away to a sandy shoreline that curved gently away to the northeast. Sea grasses and stunted trees leaned away from the water under the constant force of the wind. In the far mists to the east lay another range of mountains. Two mountain chains formed two of the four fingers of land that thrust their way southward into the Mediterranean Sea. Where these two ranges met sat Sparta and the last hope for his nation.

"Kir Ree! Kir Ree!" Seagulls hovered motionless in the stiff breeze and called their greetings down to Athelstan. Mouthing a silent Celtic prayer for abundance, he then returned his attention to the immediate landscape around him.

Before beginning his journey to Hellas, he and his commanders poured over the crude maps of Peloponnesia and he committed them to memory. A river lay in front of them to the east; he believed it was named Eurotas. It emptied into Lakonikos Bay. It was the source of fresh water for Sparta. He also knew that around the far side of the huge bay sat another port town of Asopos. If he could get across that river, it might be argued that they had come north from Asopos.

He slipped back down the hill and kept low, using what little cover he could find. The girl was sleeping soundly when he returned; Maehadren kept a close watch while grazing nearby. Lifting her into the saddle caused her to moan and awaken, but once on the move again she quickly fell back to sleep.

It was well past midday when they struck out again. Two choices presented themselves; head due east over rough terrain, or head south directly for the coast. The first would take time but would guarantee they would remain unseen the other offered speed. Given the way the bruise on her right eye was swelling plus the fact she was having difficulty keeping her eyes open, he decided that their need for speed far outweighed their need for stealth. She required a place to lie down and recover. He turned towards the south and the Laconian Gulf.

Gleaming white sandy beaches disappeared in the distance as they rode east through the gentle surf. Even under the merciless afternoon sun, the moist sea air was refreshing after the dry dusty air under the trees. The girl shifted position with a contented sigh and let the cool wind and sea spray hit her face. Always alert, Athelstan's keen eyes scanned the shoreline for any sign of people who might mark their passage. He saw none but knew that meant nothing.

The setting sun at their backs cast an almost magical light on the landscape. Orange sand and yellow flowers glowed with a divine brilliance. The shore grasses, the gnarled twisted branches of the stunted trees caught that bright evening fire and seemed to beam their light back at the Gods.

Hellas was truly a blessed land in so many ways. Its sights, smells and sounds all seemed crisper andcleaner here. Athelstan was inwardly glad he had come. He would learn as much as he could here. Despite the rugged beauty, the inhabitants of Sparta were survivors. Their history was filled with victories against superior forces and overwhelming odds.

Rome was just such a threat to Senone and he needed any advantage he could find if he was going to remove them from his homeland.

A low rumble – almost a growl rose in his throat as he contemplated Rome. His companion moaned in response. He shushed her back to sleep and she contentedly nestled back into the crook of his arm. A bright orange ball of fire was starting to set in the western sky when they came to the mouth of the river Eurotas. While it was not the mighty Po River roaring down out of the mountains of his homeland, it was still too deep to cross without a bridge. Orchards covered the western riverbank. After a few minutes, they shuffled to a stop up a long row of orange trees. Maehadren was quickly unpacked and turned loose to graze.

He retrieved a long package wrapped in an oiled skin from one of the packs and came to squat in front of his companion. Sleepy, bleary eyes still fought to focus on him as he tilted her head and gently probed her jaw and cheek with his meaty finger.

"Hurt bad your jaw?" he asked. He hoped just these few words would maintain his ruse of not speaking Latin well. The instant he touched her jaw she slapped him hard. He sat with a thud.

"Stop" she demanded. She tried to stand up. The movement caused her head to spin once again. She sank down, her head again resting against the tree.

He would have chuckled, but all he could muster was a smirk. Her slap had connected well.

Her eyes fluttered open. "Me excusatum," she whispered. "Yes, hurt bad." She probed the aching jaw herself and felt inside her mouth for any loose teeth.

He started to chuckle and she graced him with another staggeringly beautiful smile and joined him with a delightful laugh of her own. Her eyes were piercing and he was surprised at how difficult it was for him not to stare at her.

"Name. I no call you 'Boy'." She drew back and a frown creased her brow. Self-consciously she reached up and touched her hat.

"Con...stan," she began cryptically. He arched an eyebrow and cocked his head to one side like a curious dog. "...tine," she concluded halfheartedly. "Con – stantine. Yes, I am Constantine." she said with only slightly more conviction. A sigh of exhaustion wracked her and she settled herself more comfortably against the tree.

Athelstan said nothing. He simply looked at her with a steady, unflinching, unblinking stare. She glanced this way and that briefly, before returning his relentless stare. She licked dry lips but still, he sat motionless in front of her... staring.

"Constantine," she whispered more to herself than out loud and it dripped with bitterness. "Friends call me Connie." The Celt remained unmoving for several seconds. He held her gaze unflinchingly.

"I friend of Constantine?" Athelstan asked.

She shrugged and looked at him directly. "Are you?" There was a long silence as the two measured each other for the first time.

A brief nod from her answered the question and broke the spell. "Connie," the deep baritone rumbled in his chest. "Connie I call you."

He had to let her maintain the illusion of being a boy, if only for her benefit. She was a curiosity to be sure, even to him. Here was a boy who was really a girl; smelling not of sweat and piss, but of exotic scents. She had money but tried to run with stolen figs. If she was from a political, or merchant family, were they looking for her? Where were her guards, protectors, fancy clothes, and slaves? He could scarcely afford for her Roman friends to find him all alone in the wild. He could not let her go any more than he could let her stay. Killing her and burying her here was not an option either. No mistake, there was both a mystery and a conundrum here. He liked mysteries but not conundrums. Both were dangerous, but for very different reasons.

So here they sat, a fine pair indeed. One was a strange thief, the other a murdering barbarian, hiding in an orange grove, each wondering whom the other one really was. If it were not so deadly serious, it might have actually been funny.

He finally opened the package and there were dozens of wrapped items inside – gifts of healing from Ratia and Ludmilla. He selected two tightly wrapped leaf packets and opened the first. In it was a sticky ointment that smelled of balsam, mint oil, and cloves. He took a daub and held it up to her nose for her to smell. The sharp fumes would clear the fogginess in her head quickly as she inhaled. He touched a tiny amount to her upper lip and rewrapped the salve in its leaf. The strong smell of the ointment in her nose caused her eyes to water. She tried to move back in an attempt to get away from it. The tree she was propped against prevented it.

He opened the second and in it were dozens of tiny leaf packets, each tied delicately with a slender blade of grass. Once again, he selected one and rewrapped the others. This he handed to her. He made a chewing motion and pointed to the leaf pack. "Stop pain. Chew," he pointed at her cheek and nodded.

Connie wiped her face. It was clear she was studying him. She took the leaf from him, sniffed it and then began to chew. She winced as the pain in her jaw erupted again.

"Ouch! Thank you." Slender fingers cupped her cheek and she began to probe her jaw again.

He wrapped the heavy white bearskin over her shoulders, then made her lean forward as he tucked it around her.

"Suck good, yes," her eyes widened and he watched her stiffen. It took him a second to realise what had just flashed through her mind.

"No, no!" He exclaimed waving a hand back and forth. "Leaves! If chew hurt, then suck," he chuckled again.

He repacked the oiled skin and unpacked a larger bundle. He returned with it and a skin of mead. The girl watched him closely, clearly ready to strike out at any moment.

Without flourish, he unrolled it on the ground. Contained within were spiced goat, dried boar meat, flatbread, cheese, olives, and figs. There was also a healthy supply of those sweet red Tow May Tows. "Eat. Drink. We stay night here," he said simply.

She nodded then tore into the deliciously spiced food. She acted like she had not eaten in days.

Several blonde curls had slipped free of her hat again. She abruptly stopped chewing and stared at him with a puzzled look.

"You rescue I. I am thief – why?" she asked him in broken Greek.

"Not thief." He settled more comfortably on the ground. Why indeed? That was the real question. He had been specifically warned not to do what he had just done and now even the one he saved was demanding an explanation. In truth, now that he pondered it, he could not come up with a good answer. The treaties he bore from the time of Alexander proved that officers of the Celtic armies were capable of dispensing justice in times of war. However, it was not entirely specific. It presumed that they could dispense justice among their own people. He rather doubted it extended to Greek dockworkers or to Spartan guards in times of peace.

He shook his head and chose not to answer. "Eat. Sleep. Safe now. We try talk tomorrow."

"You should not have. You do not know what you have done."

"I know," he grunted. Had she an expression of concern? For him or for herself?

Connie bent to her meal. He watched her eat with a ravenous abandon and noticed her eyes rarely strayed from him. He studied the girl as she ate and poured some water on a clean rough rag. Her face was smudged and covered in dirt. He gently rubbed a smudge from her nose.

She swatted at his hand.

He handed Connie the cloth and when it looked as if she would do nothing, he waggled his finger at her forehead indicating it could use some work as well. With a sigh, she began to wipe away the smudges on her face and he was nearly struck dumb with just how beautiful she was. Blinking to shake off the effect, he handed her a skin of honey wine and settled down against an adjacent tree. A look of gratitude flashed his way as she washed her face, arms, and hands.

Ever since childhood, he had been in the habit of rescuing things that needed help. It began with a hedgehog. What followed was an endless stream of creatures. Many bit him for his trouble. Now, it would seem, he was beginning to collect people. He hoped this girl didn't bite.

He was tired! He tugged off his white bloodstained shirt. It felt good to stretch his shoulders and back. His physique was hardly lost on the teenager. Beneath the shirt was a leather vest covered in heavy overlapping chainmail rings. Intricate blue tattoos in swirls and knots, so complex that they vexed the eye, covered much of his upper arms and shoulders. Connie tried not to let on she was watching, but she was.

He pretended not to notice, but he did. Once settled back against his own tree, he heaved a deep sigh. He could see she was tense and he knew she needed sleep. Was she tense due to her injuries? She seemed to be doing much better. He realised she was probably frightened of this wild-haired tattooed Celt – rightly so, too. She had probably never seen a Celt before. He had to get her to relax enough to really sleep.

In a flash of inspiration, Athelstan unstrapped a long boot knife from his left leg. She sat up and clutched the fur more tightly around her. All he did was simply toss the long sheathed blade onto the ground beside her. "Yours now. Use wisely."

The girl picked up the weapon and drew the blade. Even in the waning light, she could see it was covered in designs, cunningly engraved onto its surface. She pulled it under the fur then settled back again. Athelstan nodded at her and did the same.

In a deep resonant baritone, he began to sing softly. The words were Gaelic and the tune had a soothing lilt to it. As he sang, he watched her in fascination. Dressed as a guttersnipe, her every move and gesture screamed wealth and privilege. So, what had brought her here pretending to be a thief and a beggar? Could she actually be a lady of privilege, or was she some elaborate spy in the employ of Rome? Both scenarios seemed equally likely.

He had to get her talking. 'Perhaps tomorrow,' he thought to himself.

He nodded as he continued to sing the sweet Celtic lullaby. The song was actually about a group of new army recruits, at a whorehouse where they could get serviced. Since it was obvious she did not understand the words of the song what harm would it do? It had a nice simple melody. Her drooping eyes showed it was having the desired effect. It was helping her relax enough to sleep.

'...Athasp, athasp mo lom beig masans...' he sang the chorus. '...Next, next, my bare little bottoms...' it went and he smiled as he realised she was beginning to hum along before she closed her eyes and drifted into a peaceful and hopefully, recuperative sleep

Chapter Eleven

She awoke with a start before dawn. Peeking out of her white fur cocoon, her eyes fixed on Athelstan sitting up asleep against his tree. She looked around quickly and clasped her hand to the back of her stiff neck.

The long knife he had given her, lent her some sense of comfort. She got up holding the sharp blade in front of her and listened to his breathing. She debated whether to simply stab him and be done with it. Even in the early morning light, she could make out his features. His bushy eyebrows, moustache, and beard gave him an animal-like appearance.

It was said that the sleeping face, whether it be good, or evil, was a person's true face. It was a measure of his soul. She stepped a bit closer. Her hand tightened on the handle of the knife. She would kill him should it become necessary.

A careful examination of the savage's sleeping face began. There were soft laugh lines around the Celt's eyes and a few frown lines upon his brow. The corners of his mouth turned up slightly and an aura of quiet confidence seemed to cloak him, even as he slept. She finally came to some decision and let out a nervous breath, then backed away from him slowly and headed towards the river.

He slowly came out of his long sleep just as the first rays of light began to break over the horizon and stretched his aching neck and shoulders. It took him a moment to realise that the girl was gone. He looked around quickly. The fur cloak was at the base of the tree in a pile and Maehadren was some distance away quietly cropping the verge at the base of the orange trees. A soft growl escaped the Celt as the events of the previous day came back to him. Maehadren stamped a foot in warning; its alert ears pointed to the south. Someone was approaching from the south. Athelstan relaxed believing that Connie was returning from her morning ablutions.

It was his first mistake.

He took a moment to gather up the dew–covered cloak and shake it out. He fastened it back over his shoulders with the torc given to him by the twins. Then he saw a movement through the trees. It was not the girl. It was three men and they crept between the boles carefully avoiding making any noise. The Celt went into a crouch. He had been found.

"Droga!" he cursed in frustration.

"Amddiffyn y ferch!" he whispered in Gaelic at Maehadren and the horse bowed his head, turned, and headed for the river to find his young companion. The soldiers were clearly trained and were trying to flank him. Athelstan, in turn, backed away from the trio who were still some fifty yards away and moved to the northeast, away from the river. He did not want to be surrounded.

That was his second mistake.

The three Spartans began to press their advantage and broke into a run. They closed the distance quickly while still keeping tree trunks between them and their prey. Athelstan knew that circling would do no good. They could shift position as easily as he could and he would still need to deal with these three soldiers who clearly knew their business.

Then there was a change in their tactics. He continued to back up. His foe stopped following. He wondered why when he saw one of the men look up into the canopy of leaves over his head. He also stopped and risked a quick glance over his shoulder.

That was his final mistake.

A weighted net was tossed down at him from above with marvellous accuracy. He had only enough time to drop to one knee before the tangle of knots engulfed him. He had been herded to this spot with practised skill so others, hidden overhead could capture him.

Now he was angry. He drew his remaining boot knife and slashed upwards with the sharp blade. The knots of the crude net parted easily. He simply stepped through the rent and stood. A blow from a wooden cudgel glanced off the back of his head. Other soldiers had dropped from the branches of the tree behind him. He spun quickly.

He hammered a fourth 'net-wielding' man solidly in the side of the head with the butt of his knife. He tumbled to the ground stunned. A fifth man was still too far out of reach. Momentum turned him towards the original three spearmen. Their spears were levelled and they were approaching at a full charge. When the first one arrived, Athelstan grabbed the spear shaft with his left hand. The sharp spear point ground hard against his mail–covered ribs. With his right hand, he shattered the shaft two feet from the end. An elbow blow directed at the jaw of this warrior missed. Athelstan continued to turn.

The Celt was planning to stab the fifth man from the tree with either his knife or the spear point. Something that sounded like a bee buzzed past his ear followed by a hollow thud. That second man from the trees fell backwards and his club fell beside him. Athelstan had just enough time to face the second spearman and watch him throw his spear directly at the Celt's face. Athelstan moved his head violently to the right and the spear grazed his ear. A moment later, that charging spearman hit him low and bore him to the ground.

The last spearman, only a step behind his comrade, raised his weapon to deliver the killing blow when Athelstan heard a second hollow thud. The warrior paused and his arms dropped to his side. The spear fell from numb fingers, his chin dropped to his chest, and he fell like a post unconscious atop his friend and Athelstan.

The Celt twisted violently and shook free of the two warriors. He clamped two meaty paws onto their throats. For the first time, he got a better look at his opponents and was truly startled to discover they were little more than boys. He stood and hoisted the pair off their feet.

"Are you insane?" he bellowed at them. "I might have killed you all."

"We are Spartan," croaked one angry boy through clenched teeth. They gripped Athelstan's wrists with both hands and struggled in vain to free himself. The other hunter lay crumpled on the ground where he fell.

"Same bloody thing!" Athelstan grumbled.

The first tree–boy, who clubbed him, staggered to his feet somewhat unsteadily and raised a spear. He looked past Athelstan and slowly set the spear back down on the ground. A large lump was rising just above his left ear.

Athelstan risked a quick glance over his shoulder and to his astonishment saw Constantina standing twenty paces away. She was wagging a finger back and forth in negation and swinging a loaded sling over her head.

"YOU?" he blurted out in Latin.

"Well it certainly wasn't your horse, now was it." She retorted with no small amount of venom.

He turned back to the boys and roared in Greek, "SIT!" He flung the two he was holding onto the ground. Both landed in a sprawl and sat up quickly. The one standing sat. They all glared at the Celt with hatred. Two others lay motionless, face down in the dirt.

Connie joined him. "You speak very good Latin for – a Barbarian," she sneered in her native tongue.

He nodded without looking at her. "Greek, the Celtic tongue, and several other languages too as it turns out."

"When were you going to tell me you spoke Latin like a citizen. How long were you going to make me struggle in Greek?

"About as long as it took for you to tell me the truth – boy. Now shush!"

"SHUSH?" she exclaimed.

"Yes, shush." He turned a frightful gaze upon her with his ice–blue eyes. "It means stop talking."

Connie's mouth opened but no sound came out for a moment. "I see. Well, you're very welcome."

He smiled. "So I have been told."

He turned his attention back to the children. "Who are you?"

"We are Spartan," was the retort.

"Yes, you said that already."

"Why do you not kill us?"

"I do not kill children. Which makes me curious, why are children running around hunting people?"

"They are not children; they are Spartan Soldiers," came a deeper voice from behind several trees. Connie and Athelstan turned to face the newcomer. Athelstan took a step back. Connie began to twirl the sling again.

"Yes," he repeated, "they are learning how to become Spartan Soldiers and failing miserably it would seem."

"We are not finished yet Lord Mikonos."

"Yes, you are. Take the wounded back to camp." He looked at Athelstan. "Unless you actually do want to kill this bunch, in which case, go ahead. He will wait."

"Who will wait?" asked Athelstan.

"He." The stranger pointed to himself.

Athelstan frowned in confusion.

"No?" asked Lord Mikonos, "very well then, GO! He will deal with you later."

The boys did as they were commanded. They grabbed the two who were hurt and began to drag them to the east away from the river. None seemed too happy about any of this. 'Constantine' and Athelstan glared at this odd man. He was resplendent in shiny armour chased with gold and decorated with blue and red. Beneath, he wore finery that one might see in a royal court, rather than in an orange grove in the countryside. The man paid the pair no mind at all. He calmly watched the boys limp towards wherever home was.

When they were totally out of sight, he turned with a stylish sweep of his arm and struck an idiotic pose. He looked Athelstan and Connie up and down and seemed quite unfazed by the daunting Celt. He sniffed, with an air of superiority.

"Dip–me!" he exclaimed, waving a bejewelled hand at the pair, then placed his index finger on his temple as if thinking. Athelstan and Connie exchanged confused glances. There was an awkward pause.

"In what?" the Celt asked.

"In what?" the man queried.

"Yes, in what? You just asked me to dip you in something. What?"

A forced and insincere giggle escaped the Greek. "Oh, that must be what passes for humour in your... your pack... your herd... wherever it is you - squat. Yes. Very clever indeed. He must remember that. No, He is some confused. Five of His young charges bested by a Barbarian and this stripling. How is that possible He wonders."

Athelstan chuckled wryly. "Oh. He wonders that does He. You sent them to waylay and murder us. The mystery is solved save for the question of why. So, Why?"

"Murder you? Oh my dear Barbarian," his nose rose in haughty disquiet. "Perish the thought. Dip–me! He only sends them forth to generate income and wreak havoc. It was they who failed. No Matter. No harm was done."

"No matter? No Harm?" Athelstan blinked.

Connie was hopping with agitation and fury. "Oh, just let me bounce a rock off his head. He sounds crazy to me." Connie offered.

"In a minute perhaps," he told Connie.

"We are simple travellers. People who try to murder me and," he jerked his head at Connie, "'the stripling' here, do so at their own bloody peril. Now I demand an explanation. What is going on here?"

"You? Demand? Have a care! He will explain nothing to one such as you. You presume upon familiarity with This Person and that will not stand. That will not stand at all. It is a Spartan Prince you address. Know your place, base creature!"

"Still," he paused in reflection, "He can see how you might believe you have been wronged." The Prince stepped forward.

"You now have been granted the singular honour and privilege of making the acquaintance of His august self Mikonos Arios, Commander, and Prince of Sparta. You may now kiss His ring." He held out his hand and averted his gaze. "Oh, do try not to soil it will you." He said with an expression of disgust.

"I will try my best." Athelstan glanced at Connie and rolled his eyes. Connie was trying not to smirk. She just knew what was coming. The angry Celt lashed out and grabbed the Spartans extended hand from wrist to fingertips in a crushing grip. The smug expression vanished from Mikonos's face and it was instantly replaced by one of pain.

"Release His hand immediately! You know not whom you handle!" he shrieked.

"'HE' is whom I handle." The Celt thought about what he had just said. "Who I handle? Whom I handle?" He looked at Connie, "Who, or whom?"

Connie shouted, "Whom cares! I don't care."

"Quite right." he turned back to Mikonos, "Whom indeed." Athelstan was switching from Latin to Greek and back again smoothly.

"I handle 'HE', Mikonos Ari... whatever it was, Commander and Prince of Sparta. I know who HE is. I also know HE is going to answer my questions, now isn't HE?" Mikonos hopped about helplessly trying in vain to pull his hand out of the massive paw.

"Come with me!" Athelstan said. He jerked Mikonos towards one of the trees and slammed him hard against it. Undoubtedly some of his pristine armour got dented. He tore the helmet off his head and flung it. It glanced off another tree and bounced away. Connie bent and collected the broken spear tip and a fair sized rock.

"What are you going to do with that?" Athelstan asked in Latin.

She tapped the spear tip against Mikonos' privates and said, "I haven't decided yet. I have some questions of my own, thank you very much. That is a you should learn." Athelstan translated. Mikonos looked bewildered.

Athelstan nodded absently, then glanced back at Connie who was wearing a coy yet somewhat wicked smile.

"Let HIM GO, this instant!" Mikonos wailed. "To harm someone of the Royal House is punishable by death, or worse! You are breaking HIS hand!"

he squealed. His eyes darted from one to the other.

"Would you rather I grabbed you by the face?"

"Yes," Connie piped up in Latin. "Grab him by the face." Her smile got wider. Athelstan looked down at her with exasperation.

She shook her head and shrugged, "Just trying to be supportive is all," then scuffed the ground with her foot. "Ask him what they do with the girls they capture," Connie asked.

"I don't need to ask him that, now do I? If there were young ladies present, they would not have to fear louts like these, would they Connie?" He looked at her sidelong and watched her blush bright red. "Something you would like to add? It is not like you would be telling me anything I do not already know."

"What do you know?" she was incensed.

"Plenty," Athelstan countered.

"Let it go," Mikonos wailed.

"Shush!" Athelstan admonished still looking at Connie. She really was very beautiful.

"I am going to ask," his gaze once again fell on Mikonos, "Three questions and you are going answer truthfully. Do you understand?"

"YOU CAN NOT SPEAK to this Royal Person like…" Athelstan slammed the hand against the tree again and tightened his grip. Mikonos howled in pain.

"Do – You – Understand?"

"Yes."

"Good. I would just hate to strip you naked, skin you alive and give your clothes to the whores of Sparta… just hate it. In fact," he looked away absently, "I don't believe I have ever skinned a Greek." He turned to Connie with an inquiring expression. "Have you ever skinned a Greek?" he asked in Latin.

"Not since I was a child, no." She began to examine the captive top to bottom, front to back. "I forget where to start. Sorry." Mikonos shook uncontrollably and a puddle of urine formed at his feet.

"Oh, that IS too bad. Still, if we started in the crotch and worked our way outward from there… Yes, I think that might work."

"It might indeed," she agreed.

"No! I will tell you anything." Mikonos mewed.

"Hmmm? Oh yes. Where was I? Who is your father?"

"Atiphates, younger brother to the King Cleomenes II."

"So, you are a Prince in name only. Who sent you to find me?"

"No one. Those boys found you by chance." Athelstan said nothing but leaned in until their noses nearly touched.

"Seriously, no one was sent to find you. In truth, we came here for the oranges."

"Last question. Why should I let you live? You seem to be quite an ugly bag of mostly blood."

"He is… He is Royal. You must not kill Him. If they find His body, the whole army will hunt you down and kill you.

"Like you just tried to do to us? I think not. Besides, the pile of meat I would leave here could hardly be identified as a person let alone a Prince."

"He can pay in gold!" Mikonos said hopefully.

"No, HE can pay in blood," Connie stepped forward and jammed the tip of the spear past his teeth. Mikonos turned his head away as she brought the rock up and hammered the broken wooden end hard. The iron tip went through his cheek and bit deeply into the tree. He let out a deafening scream. For good measure, she pounded the rock against the shaft twice more. Athelstan released the hand and took a step back.

"There," she exclaimed. "Let's get away from here. IT," she waggled a finger at Mikonos, "sickens me!"

"Absolutely," Athelstan agreed quietly.

"Here." She held up his knife, "Take it. I have nowhere to carry this." He slipped it back into his boot with a nod. He was fighting not to smile. She had fire this one did. What she had done to Mikonos had surprised him and he was not easily surprised. They collected Maehadren and rode north. Mikonos's screaming faded and soon the river was all that could be heard.

After an hour of riding, they had left the cultivated lands of farms and groves behind entering a wild and rocky valley. He kept the river that ran south towards the sea on his right shoulder and followed it upstream. Wild groves of oak and elm crowded the riverbank in places. It was down into one of these that Athelstan urged Maehadren.

The sun was getting lower in the sky when the river turned a sharp corner and widened. He made a decision to cross here and make camp for the night. He angled Maehadren into the water.

"What are you doing?" she asked into his ear.

We will cross here and make camp for the night. We both smell wrong and now is a good time to bathe and correct that. That hunting party may have found us by smell."

"Bathe? NO!"

"Bathe – YES." He neared the far shore and pushed her off the horse and into the water. She landed with a terrific splash and disappeared from sight. He followed her into the water and waited for her to come up sputtering and cursing with fury. Her hat was floating away and her long blonde hair hung to her waist.

"So, tell me little girl, why so desperate to look like a boy? Who hunts you?" His look was intense and unlike most people, she did not flinch away from it. Athelstan was immediately intrigued.

Her almond eyes narrowed dangerously. Her eyes flashed and she said, "Why did you do that, you… you Mongrel! Who and what I am is none of your business. I will tell you nothing."

"Mongrel am I?" he replied and released her shoulders. "Very well then, but before we travel one more foot, you are absolutely going to bathe. If you are so determined to play the part, it's time you started to walk, talk, act and smell like a boy," he rummaged in a pack and produced a greenish ball. It was waxy and smelled of lavender and thyme.

"It is called soap."

"I know what it is called!"

"Then make use of it. All over, especially… down there." Still standing waist deep, he pointed below the water line and waggled his finger. "Everywhere. I will wait."

She hurled the soap back at him with all her might and it struck him in the chest like a rock. She turned towards shore. He caught her arm again spun her around and with his free hand dunked her completely underwater. When he hauled her back up, he applied soap to her hair and began to scrub. This was maddening. Athelstan enjoyed both fear and respect from some of the most dangerous warriors on earth and it would be a fine day indeed when some slip of a girl could defy the one who commanded 'The Multitude'.

"How dare you! How dare you touch me? I swear if I had that dagger I would carve out a suitable spot in your chest where you could put that soap!" She was outraged.

"Sadly you do not have a dagger at the moment, but after you wash I will happily let you try." he dunked her again.

The girl backed away, fists raised, ready to defend herself.

Athelstan was further intrigued. Whoever this girl was, judging from her stance, someone had taught how to fight. He shook the water from his eyes.

"Listen, I do not care if you want to kill me when all this is over, but make no mistake, one of two things is about to happen here. You are either going to wash that foreign stink off yourself so we can have some hope of not being tracked, or I leave you here to whatever fate might claim you. Choose now." He reached out for her arm. She pulled away.

An exclamation of outrage escaped her. "Foreign stink?" she howled. "I am not the one who stinks of wet bear and old horse!" she shrieked.

"You're right," he asked simply. He began to wash as well.

"I am not trying to be cruel. I am trying to avoid being found just like you are. That is why I saved you from those men yesterday. I was not going to allow them to harm you further. It is my way. It is our way."

Her clear blue eyes blinked up at him.

"I do not know who is hunting you. In truth, I do not care. They will not find either of us if I can help it. If you believe nothing else I say, believe that."

Wrapping her arms protectively across her chest, she took an involuntary step forward and Athelstan drew her close and let her sob. He gently stroked her hair. This moment did not last long. She pushed away from him suddenly and before he could stop her, she dunked herself underwater. He saw the surface ripple. Athelstan reached beneath the water, grabbed her by the wrist and pulled her back out. He held her against him by her shoulders. He opened his mouth to speak, but before he could speak, she said.

"You have already robbed me of my security, do you plan to take my dignity as well?"

"I will never do that. I would rather die first. You are alive now because I chose to preserve your dignity."

"I will bathe myself, please leave me alone."

He handed her the soap.

"Please, would you tell me one thing? What is your real name?" He exuded a quiet strength.

Her whole body shook softly.

"My name is Constantina."

He inclined his head in respect. "Be assured Constantina of Rome, I am only interested in your honesty. I thank you for that," he turned his back to her. "You cannot know this yet, but I rank personal honour above all other things. I am duty-bound to protect you and I will see you safely to your destination… wherever that may be provided you will allow it." He turned and led Maehadren across the river to the eastern bank.

She nodded, stood straight, tall and proud. Stripping off the ragged clothing she had been wearing, she began to scrub.

Athelstan replayed her words. Not much to go on yet, but every little bit of the puzzle helped to fill in the whole. Her name was Constantina. It was a Roman name. What was she doing here alone in Greece? He left her to bathe alone and he went in search of firewood.

There was plenty and he had picked this spot on the river for that very reason. That hunting party had taught him a thing, or two. Spartan boys were formed into gangs at a very young age and survived on their own wits in the wild for ten years, or more. They lived and became soldiers, or they died. Where these child strongholds existed, no firewood would litter the riverbank. It would have been used up long ago. Here they were safe from prying eyes – at least for now.

He set about making a small hot blaze that gave off little smoke. With his knife, he cut up some cured meat and placed it in a simple iron pot of water. He added some rosemary, along with a small sack of fresh greens, pigweed, and lemongrass he had collected while gathering wood. He set it on the fire to boil. Throughout the preparations, he had his back to the river and he ignored the girl bathing behind him.

He rummaged and pulled out a set of brown trousers and a heavy linen shirt. He laid them out on the warm rocks and waited for her to finish.

When she was done, Connie gathered up her clothing and made her way to the shore. Her long damp hair flowed over her shoulders; the pile of clothing covering her body

"Feeling a bit better?" he asked. "I have left you some dry clothes if you like. We can cut sleeves and cuffs to fit. I'm afraid we will need to burn yours, they will be recognized." After she slipped on the voluminous shirt, he laid her old wet clothing close to the coals allowing them to sizzle and burn.

He filled a cup with the steaming soup before handing it to her wrapped in a clean rough cloth. "I think you have more than earned a hot meal. Here, careful not to burn your mouth," he had a kind look.

When he offered her food, she shook her head.

"No thank you."

It was not lost on Athelstan the fact that she had not answered his question about feeling better. He poured a cup of soup for himself.

"We still have a long ride ahead and you really should eat. I suspect you have not had a good meal in a while. Please try to eat something. You know, sometimes I command rather than ask, it is often the way of a... of a soldier. I do not mean to be abrupt, but we need to face a rather stark reality here, one you may not be completely aware of."

He began to stroke his moustache. It was an unconscious act he often performed while organizing his thoughts.

"You know that the three men who captured you in Yithion are dead?" he asked quietly.

"I do."

"And you know that I had to kill them in order to rescue you? I need an answer, Connie. You were more than just a bit addled yesterday." His face was calm and again he gestured for her to try the soup. "Do you remember?"

Connie sat down with her knees to her chest and her arms wrapped around her legs. She looked almost shy, timid. Her hair was beginning to dry in the gentle wind and her eyes were still somewhat red. Had she been crying?

"I do," was all she said gingerly sipping the hot soup.

"Good. I had to know you did not think that was a dream. What you do not know, is they were not the first men I killed in Yithion yesterday. An overseer on the docks took offence to something I did." His eyes never left hers, he watched as she listened to his story.

"They were evil and wicked men Connie and by my code, their actions warranted death. I dispensed justice – nothing more," he showed no remorse for these killings – in his mind, they were justified. "Another thing you should know is that I am a Celt and we behead wicked men – all of them, every time. My religion demands this so the wicked cannot find their ancestors and cannot return to wreak more evil and havoc upon the innocents of this world. I believed from the moment I saw you that you are just such an innocent. That is something we are known for and only an idiot would fail to connect the two incidents yesterday. Do you understand so far?" She nodded but still did not look at him. He was glad to see her finally begin to eat. He would wait until she was full before he had a bite.

"I understand. I will leave. I do not want you captured because of me. I can take care of myself," her voice was soft but it was far from defeated.

"I have no doubt you can; you will remain with me regardless. You are neither a burden nor will you slow me down. I cannot abandon you until I am satisfied you are safe. It is our way – the way of honour. Besides, I am beginning to like your company."

"I thank you for your help thus far, unfortunately, I cannot pay you with anything other than my body and that will not happen." She looked at him closely. "I warn you now, if you attempt to take that from me I will kill you in your sleep."

A soft low chuckle escaped the Celt and he shook his head. "I require no payment from you or anyone. Just the doing of a thing is reward enough. I have known you were a girl from the moment I laid eyes on you at the market. I am hardly the hayseed you take me for," he cocked his head at this strange girl with her odd ideas. "You will find your body and your virtue are quite safe from me. I do not lie and I have told you, I do not lust after children."

With a sigh, he realised what she must think of him some brutal savage creature who kills indiscriminately and captures lost girls.

"Children?" she repeated with some confusion.

"Are you afraid of me?" he asked suddenly. She looked at him and her pretty brow furrowed in thought for a moment.

"No. I am not afraid of you. I suppose I should be, but no," she answered in her sweetly accented Greek.

"I am glad of that. So I think you should know one last thing. I have told you I am Celt. You are a Roman."

"Yes, so?"

"I am a soldier."

"… and?"

"You do not know, do you?"

"Know what?"

"Since the spring, our two governments are at war."

"Pah!" she snorted with derision. "Men and your precious wars. You go play at war somewhere else and leave me out of it. War, what a useless pastime." There was honest indifference in her tone. He read her expression. It was perhaps the first purely truthful, unguarded thing she had said to him. He simply had to laugh.

"You are absolutely right, child. It is a useless pastime and I am the first to admit it."

Her eyes suddenly met his and she cocked her head as if confused. "You keep talking like I am a little girl. How old do you think I am?" she demanded suddenly. Her round eyes studied his bearded face.

"By your height and shape, I would give you fifteen winters, no more," he answered. Connie's eyebrows rose in surprise and a smirk graced her delicate features. She said nothing.

"What?" he queried. She just shook her head and casually waved a hand in a dismissive manner.

"I am glad you are not afraid of me. I am hardly a monster, but I simply will not tolerate abuse of the helpless. You asked me earlier why I did this. Why did I kill those three men? I will not allow someone to be raped and murdered when I can prevent it. So I prevented it." Athelstan was serious now and offered Connie another steaming cup of the soup.

"It is not necessary to explain," she said taking the food. She ate it with obvious hunger but still retained an air of elegance, even as the broth ran down her chin. He trimmed the legs of the trousers and shirt as she ate.

"Yes, Connie, I think it is. I think you deserve to know who and what I am and what you might expect of me and now you do. So do we still ride together?" he asked.

"Yes, if you promise not to dunk me in the river again," her mouth turned up a bit at the corner and her face transformed into a thing of astonishing beauty.

"Alright, I promise," he laughed. "I only hope that one day you will forgive me for that."

"But my disguise remains. If that is a problem then I will travel alone," she said.

"The disguise remains," he agreed. "Who are you hiding from?"

"That is none of your concern." Connie looked at him with a smile. "Have I ever skinned a Greek! REALLY?" she snorted with bell-like laughter. He simply shrugged his shoulders.

She grabbed the trousers and stood. The shirt he gave her dropped to mid-thigh.

His eyes watched her walk away. Honorable, or not, he was far from immune to those slender muscular legs and soft sway of her hips. He shook his head in an effort to banish those kinds of thoughts. Her curly blonde ringlets were bouncing with every step. Connie headed upstream along the riverbank.

She glanced back over her shoulder at him. It was the most sensual gaze he had ever seen. Athelstan let her alone with her thoughts and brought the pot with the soup to his lips absently. He yelped as the hot metal burned him. The pot dropped and the soup went everywhere. "DROGA!" She simply smiled and kept walking

He remembered Caileigh's words go through his head again. 'Keep clear of business that does not concern you.' Well so much for that. With a sigh, he drew a boot knife and carefully began to cut off his full beard. With fresh pine sap, he glued the blonde curls into the cap and trimmed it in the style of Greek boys – straight in front and longer in the back.

When she returned from her walk, it took over an hour to perfect her 'boy' look. He had braided her hair and tucked it down the back of the shirt.

"Do you think this is going to work?" she asked.

"It will suffice unless someone looks closely," he answered then went to work with white ash and black charcoal from the fire.

Greynoc's brief tutelage was more than helpful. He darkened her eyes and lightened her cheekbones. The swollen eye was very tender. He accentuated her jawline with the coal and blended it in. A few random smudges later and people would be hard-pressed to tell she was anything but a grubby, pale peasant lad of fourteen, or fifteen years.

Once he was satisfied her disguise was as good as he could make it, Connie took up his knife and sat in front of Athelstan. She reached over to lift his chin.

"Is it your intention to cut my throat and leave my entrails to bake on a hot rock in the sun?" he asked. A surprised giggle escaped her. It sounded like music to his spirit.

"It is not!" she stated flatly before catching the joke. She swatted him on the arm and her eyes narrowed. "Unless you would like me to."

He shook his head. "No, I like my entrails right where they are thank you."

"See was that so hard?"

"What?"

"You said 'Thank You'," his smile was victorious. "I mean to fix that scruffy beard of yours. It is… well, it is uneven, now hold still." His eyes narrowed and he pulled back.

"You ask me to trust my life to you, did you not? Now it is time for you to trust me, Athelstan."

His mouth opened and shut again. It was the first time she had used his name. He did not think she knew it. In response, he lifted his head exposing his neck.

Cool steady fingers pressed his sharp knife against the skin of his throat. A frown creased her brow and she reached for the ball of soap. With some softening in river water, she managed to cover his face with lather. In very short order with deliberate strokes, she removed the remaining beard. She trimmed the ends of the moustaches so they hung just to the point of his chin and leaned back to appraise her work.

"There, that is much better. You do not look half so scary now… Hmmm, you might actually lean a little towards handsome if you were not such a…."

"Mongrel?" he helped, flashing a sly grin.

She met his eyes and blushed at her bold statement. "I am sorry I called you that. What possessed me to blurt that out I will never know."

"I am not sorry. It is fitting somehow," he was smiling widely.

She swatted his shoulder playfully. Connie made a close examination of his face.

"What do you see?"

The question seemed to catch her by surprise her by surprise.

"You are not at all what I expected. We should go!" She stood.

He called after her, "I think we have gone far enough for one day. We will rest here and let you get your strength back. We can continue our journey in the morning."

"Are we really at war?" she asked with a frown.

All he could do was nod.

"It doesn't feel like it to me." She stared at him for a very long time.

Chapter Twelve

The following day the change in terrain was startling. The once gentle river now raged through a deeply cut canyon. The sandy beaches were now replaced by water-polished rocks. Connie rode as Athelstan led his horse, picking his way carefully around some of the larger obstructions. His attention kept shifting from Connie to the riverbed, to the high canyon walls on the western shore of the river.

It did not take a genius to see the Celt was tense. He felt confined and for the last few hours, he knew in his bones they were being followed. Even Maehadren tossed his head and issued blasts of air from his nostrils. A soft hand on the horse's muzzle helped to quiet the uncomfortable animal.

"Not my imagination then? How many?" he asked in Gaelic. The horse shook its head repeatedly and snorted again. Athelstan got his answer. He decided to call a halt. He had hoped this was not a mistake. Romans could be fiercely determined when the mood was on them and the Gods alone knew he had given them cause for just such a determination.

Both horse and young rider needed to cool down.

"What is wrong?" She had to speak loudly to be heard over the roar of the river.

"Not your concern. Here is a good place for a rest." He had picked a one hundred foot long swirling backwater to stop. There was a sandy beach and a good cover of trees to shield them from prying eyes.

He looked up at the canyon walls above as he helped Connie dismount. He unstrapped the heavy bags from the horse's rump letting the Maehadren drink.

"I thought you might be hungry. Either way, you have earned a rest." Clouds had slowly thickened all day. Sniffing the air, he knew there would be a storm.

"Will we have to ride through the rain?" she asked looking up. He nodded absently. She did not take her eyes off him.

"When are you going to tell me what is wrong?"

He looked at her with some surprise. "We are being followed. I am afraid I may have underestimated a very persistent and dangerous foe. I did not think they could pick up my trail so quickly," he placed a hand on her shoulder. "I am sorry I have wrapped you up in all this."

Connie shrugged. "It is me they are after. Besides what is done is done. How many are there?" she asked. He silently held four fingers to his chest.

He had her look at the canyon rim about a league distant. Small shapes could be seen creeping through the trees high above. He bent over and spoke quietly into her ear.

"They are no danger to us at the moment. It is impossible for them to cross the river here. They will need to cross over to our side at some point, or we over to theirs. I would like to know where they are when that happens. Now, stretch your legs and have something to eat. Once we can get free of this canyon we can have these Romans chasing their own tails in short order," he gave her a warm smile. "After all, they're hunting a wild beast."

"So first I am a little girl and now I am a wild beast?"

"What makes you so certain they hunt you?" he asked and then saw her smile.

"If they do catch us it will be comforting to know that I will have company hanging there on the cross," Connie said, her smile gone.

She nodded then bent to take a sip of river water. He could tell she was worried and a rest would not help. "Shall I catch us some fish?"

She was an amazing girl. Even with unknown, presumably dangerous men within hailing distance, she had found something that would take both their minds off the situation for a few minutes. "Yes, I think that would be fine. Perhaps you might show me how you plan to do that."

Connie stripped off her hat and sandals then waded into an eddy of the swiftly moving river slowly taking a crouching position scanning for fish.

Following her example, he took up a position several feet in front of her then put his hands in the water like he was being shown. In an undignified crouch, he watched Connie and waited. He looked up at her and noticed the shirt did little to cover her chest. He felt a tug in his loins and decided to return his eyes back to the water.

She glanced at him and smiled. She waited until a school of fish to begin to swim between their legs and called. "Now!" and reached forward to grab a fish.

He saw the fish and at her command grabbed the nearest one. A cascade of water erupted from his hands that washed over Connie in a huge wave. No fish appeared at all. The motion pitched the Celt off balance and after a vain struggle to remain standing, disappeared in a massive splash under the water.

Connie, also off balance, tumbled forward and landed atop him. He surfaced sputtering and laughing all at the same time.

"Takes some practice I presume," he laughed.

"Apparently so," she giggled.

He sat laughing with water streaming from his moustache and hair. With a playful motion, he splashed her again. "Shall we try again?" he asked offering her his hand.

She splashed him back. "Think you can handle it old man?"

He grinned showing a full set of brilliantly white teeth. "Old man? Oh, you insolent young whelp. Here, just help this old Mongrel to his feet; I will show you what an old man can do."

Connie laughed, splashed him again and dove under the water.

He stood, stumbled and dove in after her. She was a powerful swimmer. Only with a herculean, effort was he able to close the distance between them. He seized a foot yanking her back dunking her under. After a brief struggle, he found her pressed against his chest blinking; her long lashes drooling water. She just kissed him.

It was the last thing Athelstan expected. Yet, when she did, his mind shut down and his body reacted.

Connie's arms came up to encircle his neck; her breasts pressing hard against him. Before he realised it, she had wrapped both her legs around his waist. It was a profoundly passionate embrace.

When the kiss broke he stared at her in stunned silence. He brushed a dripping tangle of hair from her face. She felt so good against him and his heart hammered in his chest. He was quite powerless in her embrace. It was as if his will power had utterly vanished and the world narrowed to such an extent that only her eyes remained. His grip on her waist tightened and he fought the urge to kiss her again. It was a fight he lost. Their lips met again but now there was a savage hunger in the touch. It was like falling from a very great height - a very great height indeed.

Connie could only stare at him. His lips found hers again and her fingers slipped deep into the strands of his hair. Her grip was strong and hard; her legs tightened around him; her body ground against him. He responded to her touch, her taste and her fingers in his hair. She felt like pure clean water in a pool of clinging muck. His tongue sought out hers and his eyes closed. He drifted on a cloud buoyed up by his rising passion. His breath came faster and faster and his hands began to slide down her back. He cupped her buttocks and pulled her closer. He could scarcely think about what he was doing, he just let the animal within him run free.

Connie looked into his eyes and shook her head. "Stop!"

He blinked twice and reality crashed back into his brain. He let her sink back into the water. "I do not know… I mean it was not my intention to… I mean," he stammered.

She pushed away from him and began to back away. "Do not do that ever again. Never again!" Connie swam away disappearing up stream.

He was embarrassed at the rebuke and was instantly furious with himself. He had broken his word to her already. First telling her, he had no interest in children and now, to do this was beyond dishonourable. She was quite right of course. Yet, where she had touched him still felt like he had been burned. Somewhere deep inside he knew he would never forget that burning touch or those soft lips.

It seemed to take all his efforts to wade ashore. Should he say something to her? He felt that nothing would help repair her trust in him.

Athelstan sat on a large flat rock and buried his face in his hands. He felt miserable. He had wanted her so intensely that all other thoughts fled. No other woman had ever done that to him and she was just a girl. He had no right to do what he had done and she was right to push him away. For all his life, he was convinced he was in total control of his actions but this girl had proved this belief wrong in only a few seconds. Did he actually kiss her? Did she kiss him? He could not remember.

His morose reverie ended sharply as he remembered the men following them. He had to find Connie and quickly. He found her a few hundred yards down stream. She was crying and it drove home the fullness of his deceit.

He walked up to her and said. "Connie, I am sorry. That was not my intent. I cannot explain my actions except to say they will not be repeated. We have to go now." He scanned the cliffs across the river but could see no sign of their pursuers.

Connie did not look at him. She could not look at him. "But it was – alright," she said softly.

"I just need you to know this. I will be here for you when you need an ear or a kind word. You understand? No matter what."

She never looked at him but allowed him to lead her back to Maehadren. This quiet acceptance only added to his guilt.

They continued their journey in silence; each wrapped in their own thoughts. A spattering of rain began to fall and Athelstan finally climbed aboard Maehadren behind Connie. He wrapped her in the white fur and they picked their way out of the canyon. The river valley swung away to the southwest but he continued the journey north crossing a wide grassy plain. The land descended and as expected a rough narrow bridge spanned the river two miles further upstream. The wide curve on the western side of the river added over ten miles to their enemy's route.

The sound of rain and the roar of the rushing water deadened the hollow sound of Maehadren's hooves on the boards and the pair rode towards the town. She had not said a word since leaving the river and he feared she might never speak to him again.

Night had fallen an hour ago and only now did he begin to see the outlying homes and farms of a small village. The sky had finally opened and a heavy cold rain fell. They had been in the saddle for a long time taking only one other short rest around mid–afternoon. They traveled north and concealed their tracks in the river where they could. They followed the main road when there was no other choice. Now they were traveling directly towards Sparta and hopefully the salvation of his people.

Connie, now cocooned in the white bear skin, had rested her head against his shoulder not long after dark and was dozing now. Lights of a small farming village began to twinkle in the distance and a few minutes later Athelstan turned Maehadren out of the rain and into a warm, dry, common stable.

Two stable boys, brothers by the look of them, craned their necks looking down from the upper hayloft to see who had arrived. When it was not someone from the area, they scrambled down a sturdy wall ladder and ran to grab Maehadren's reins.

"STOP!" Athelstan boomed and the pair skidded to a halt, still several feet from the reach of Maehadren's deadly hooves. "He's a bit touchy lads, I will see to him if you do not mind."

He climbed wearily from the saddle and pulled Connie off as well. "Sit here," he indicated a low mound of hay and she did.

"Say that is a real shiner you have there!" offered the younger brother looking at Connie's swollen cheek and eye. It had turned an ugly shade of purple. "How–ja get that?" The pair cast a dubious eye at Athelstan. Brutality was all too common here. Yet in spite of that, the pair seemed eager to talk – any stranger was a welcome distraction from the plodding monotony of life in rural Hellas.

"I'm Mitzu and this is my brother Athios. What is your name? You guys are from a different country are you not? Hey, look at how pale his hands are. You should get out in the sun more."

Connie looked up at the two boys and smiled softly.

"Mitzu and Athios right?" Athelstan inquired.

The boys looked back up at the giant Celt in wonder and nodded. "My friend Connie here has been through a lot today and he really needs some sleep. I have an idea, now stay right there. My horse IS dangerous. I mean it," he glared at the boys and received grave nods in response.

He opened a saddlebag and rummaged about. He removed two copper disks the size of their palms. One side was covered with brightly coloured enamel and the other side had a Celtic Ogham letter engraved onto it. He handed one to each boy and watched their glittering eyes as they examined the shiny prizes. The copper alone would seem like a fortune to them.

"You boys can keep these for awhile. Look at them closely, see how they were made; dream about them, make up stories about them if you must. If you can tell ME what I am and where I am from by the time we finish eating – then you can keep them. I will tell you a story about my people as well. What do you say, lads? Do we have a bargain?" Athelstan had a gentle look. A chorus of 'sure!' 'Wow!' and 'thanks!' followed his offer.

"Now would one of you stout lads run in and tell your father we will both need a hot meal. I will pay with silver." Both boys frowned at each other then, deliberately left. Their actions left Athelstan puzzled.

He unpacked the sturdy beast with a gentle pat and began to brush away the water streaming off the white coat. "If you want to go in and get comfortable – Connie, I will be along directly," he looked at her new and improved disguise and nodded in satisfaction. She had just fooled the toughest audience possible – country boys.

A few minutes later as Athelstan placed a disk of silver into the innkeeper's palm, the man's eyes narrowed. It was stamped with Oghams and other strange symbols. He eyed the giant Celt up and down.

"I want no trouble here," he said cautiously.

Athelstan looked at the smaller man. He was stout and had a hard look. "I do not either good sir. The boy and I are looking for food only and perhaps a place to rest for an hour, or so. Then we will be on our way."

The Innkeeper looked past Athelstan at Connie. "Him?" he asked curtly gesturing in Connie's direction.

He nodded slowly. "Yes, why do you ask? Is there a problem with him?"

"Soldiers have been here today asking after a huge fair–haired Barbarian and a pale–skinned boy. Like I say, I want no trouble here," he made a gesture of disgust when he said the word soldier.

Athelstan thought quickly. " A coincidence I'm sure," he dropped another coin into his palm.

The Innkeeper eyed this one as dubiously as the first. He ordered a hot meal for both of them. Connie would not meet his gaze at all, yet the innkeeper's eyes never left their table. Something more was happening here? Clearly, the Spartan army was looking for him and he was trying to find their King before they did. Not a pleasant situation.

The meal arrived and they ate it in silence.

He could see she was utterly exhausted. Her eyelids dipped involuntarily and she stifled a yawn in mid bite. She needed some real sleep.

Something was different about her now. She seemed even more guarded than before as if she had divulged too much information to him for her liking. An idea occurred to him and he paused for a moment to consider it. He watched her eat mechanically.

"Connie, I think I need to tell you something about what I am doing here in Lacedaemon - why I am headed to Sparta."

She looked up at him with expressionless eyes and shrugged. "Do what you want. I will not stop you." She turned her attention back to her meal.

He pressed on.

"You know I am a soldier." She nodded absently.

A dull grunt greeted her apparent disinterest.

"Yes, well," he paused again unsure if he should continue, or not. "What I think you should know is that I am a soldier who commands many men in my country. I am sort of like a... ah... like a Captain of men." He was having trouble finding the correct words in the face of her obstinate silence. I am the man who commands the Senone Multitude. Do you understand what I am trying to tell you? I do not know the proper word in Latin." Silence hung between them for a second before she nodded.

"Yes, I understand. Like a Commander, or a General?"

He seized on the word. "A General! Yes exactly. Thank you."

"I have never heard of this Multitude. What is 'Multitude'?"

"You have never heard of the Multitude?"

She shook her head soundlessly.

"You do lead an insulated life." Her eyes flashed at him and it was like a physical blow.

He regrouped his thoughts and continued. "Hmmm! The Multitude is, in essence, an army made up of many different clans, or families joined together for a single purpose. That purpose is the protection and defense of our homeland in northern Italia. It is just for his reason I am here in Hellas. Our homeland has been taken from us by the Legions of Rome."

"Not much of an army then is it?" she commented idly between bites.

His mouth opened to deliver a harsh retort but he closed it again and drew a deep breath. "Well there is more to that story than we have time for oven dinner, but as it stands, it serves us well enough."

She shrugged again. "If you say so. Why are you telling me this?" she was clearly annoyed.

"I am telling you this because you do not know anything about me. I do not know anything about you either. I must admit I am just a bit curious." "Yes, you said that," she said flatly and her eyes returned to her plate. She continued to eat without further conversation.

"Hrumph," he muttered again. He returned his attention to his plate. "I will shut up now. I just thought we might take some time and get to know each other. Perhaps we might avoid any more misunderstandings. You did kiss me back there you know." He ripped another piece of meat from the bone and popped it into his mouth.

Again, her eyes looked up at him with a look that dripped venom. "I think I will take my meal some place else," she said standing. "I do not think I like the company. And for the record, you kissed me back!"

"Alright, alright, lower your voice, Connie. I meant nothing by it. Please sit down." He sighed and motioned for her to resume her seat.

For long moments, she just stared at him. Nevertheless, after a long painful pause, she sat down stiffly.

There was a long awkward silence. Finally, Athelstan could stand it no longer. "So, why are you here in Hellas so far from home? Do you have family here?"

For long moments, all she did was eat. After awhile she said "No, no I have no family any more. But if you really want to know why I am here I will tell you." She put her spoon down. "I am a daughter to the brother of Rome's ruling family. My father was crucified and my estates were given to another loyal family. I am now a slave owned by my Uncle. I was kidnapped with six other girls by people who look very much like you do and brought to Sparta for reasons I do not understand. I escaped my captors and when you found me, I was trying to steal enough food to feed the other girls and to try to rescue them. Where they are now is anyone's guess. You did not rescue me as much as you doomed them."

He stared at her for several seconds. "I see," he said flatly. "That was quite a tale. OK, I can understand your need to keep your business to yourself. Who am I, after all, to be asking you these things? If you do not want to tell me the truth, it is fine. It is none of my business. You have made that clear. I am not a dullard you know." he said sadly. "What is your family name?"

"Does it matter?" she said still not looking up.

"No, I suppose not." He heaved a huge sigh and then looked up at her. "Yes!" he said suddenly. "Yes, to me it does matter." He even asked himself why it mattered to him, but he could not admit the reason why even to himself yet.

"You are being awfully loud Captain. It is Cursor if you must know, not that any of this matters to a Barba..." she said with a bitter tone.

He frowned at the rebuke but his head snapped up. "It matters. It matters because I like you. Your father's name was...?"

"Marcus."

"Thank you. That is a common name in Rome?"

She nodded mutely and there was genuine fear in her eyes. She was shaking. "Now do you believe that this little guttersnipe is telling the truth?"

"I never said..."

"You didn't have to!" she barked.

He paused and looked at her. There was a twinkle in her eye again. A chuckle rumbled in his chest that almost sounded like a giggle. What was it about this girl that kept him so off balance? "Yes, the little guttersnipe is telling the truth. We have to find these other girls and rescue them as soon as possible. That does bring up a much larger question. Why kidnap slaves and bring them all the way to Hellas. What information do you have that is so important you had to be taken from under the very nose of the Proconsul and brought here?" He was frowning.

"I am sure I do not know," she said shudder.

"THINK!" he almost shouted the question and she flinched at its intensity. Heads turned to look briefly. "I didn't mean to yell," he said in a whisper, "but we need to find out who took you, why you were taken, who you were being sent to and why. We need to find this out quickly if they are going to survive."

"You do believe me?"

"I would like to, yes. There is more to this story you are not telling me."

Connie heaved a sigh of relief and smiled.

"I do know one thing for certain."

"What?"

"I like it when you smile. You are pretty when you smile. Even if the reason for the smile is dire." He mopped at some of the meat juices with a heel of bread and chewed it with a smile of his own.

 Connie's sm

The following day the change in terrain was startling. The once gentle river now raged through a deeply cut canyon. The sandy beaches were now replaced by water-polished rocks. Connie rode as Athelstan led his horse, picking his way carefully around some of the larger obstructions. His attention kept shifting from Connie to the riverbed, to the high canyon walls on the western shore of the river.

It did not take a genius to see the Celt was tense. He felt confined and for the last few hours, he knew in his bones they were being followed. Even Maehadren tossed his head and issued blasts of air from his nostrils. A soft hand on the horse's muzzle helped to quiet the uncomfortable animal.

"Not my imagination then? How many?" he asked in Gaelic. The horse shook its head repeatedly and snorted again. Athelstan got his answer. He decided to call a halt. He had hoped this was not a mistake. Romans could be fiercely determined when the mood was on them and the Gods alone knew he had given them cause for just such a determination.

Both horse and young rider needed to cool down.

"What is wrong?" She had to speak loudly to be heard over the roar of the river.

"Not your concern. Here is a good place for a rest." He had picked a one hundred foot long swirling backwater to stop. There was a sandy beach and a good cover of trees to shield them from prying eyes.

He looked up at the canyon walls above as he helped Connie dismount. He unstrapped the heavy bags from the horse's rump letting the Maehadren drink.

"I thought you might be hungry. Either way, you have earned a rest." Clouds had slowly thickened all day. Sniffing the air, he knew there would be a storm.

"Will we have to ride through the rain?" she asked looking up. He nodded absently. She did not take her eyes off him.

"When are you going to tell me what is wrong?"

He looked at her with some surprise. "We are being followed. I am afraid I may have underestimated a very persistent and dangerous foe. I did not think they could pick up my trail so quickly," he placed a hand on her shoulder. "I am sorry I have wrapped you up in all this."

Connie shrugged. "It is me they are after. Besides what is done is done. How many are there?" she asked. He silently held four fingers to his chest.

He had her look at the canyon rim about a league distant. Small shapes could be seen creeping through the trees high above. He bent over and spoke quietly into her ear.

"They are no danger to us at the moment. It is impossible for them to cross the river here. They will need to cross over to our side at some point, or we over to theirs. I would like to know where they are when that happens. Now, stretch your legs and have something to eat. Once we can get free of this canyon we can have these Romans chasing their own tails in short order," he gave her a warm smile. "After all, they're hunting a wild beast."

"So first I am a little girl and now I am a wild beast?"

"What makes you so certain they hunt you?" he asked and then saw her smile.

"If they do catch us it will be comforting to know that I will have company hanging there on the cross," Connie said, her smile gone.

She nodded then bent to take a sip of river water. He could tell she was worried and a rest would not help. "Shall I catch us some fish?"

She was an amazing girl. Even with unknown, presumably dangerous men within hailing distance, she had found something that would take both their minds off the situation for a few minutes. "Yes, I think that would be fine. Perhaps you might show me how you plan to do that."

Connie stripped off her hat and sandals then waded into an eddy of the swiftly moving river slowly taking a crouching position scanning for fish.

Following her example, he took up a position several feet in front of her then put his hands in the water like he was being shown. In an undignified crouch, he watched Connie and waited. He looked up at her and noticed the shirt did little to cover her chest. He felt a tug in his loins and decided to return his eyes back to the water.

She glanced at him and smiled. She waited until a school of fish to begin to swim between their legs and called. "Now!" and reached forward to grab a fish.

He saw the fish and at her command grabbed the nearest one. A cascade of water erupted from his hands that washed over Connie in a huge wave. No fish appeared at all. The motion pitched the Celt off balance and after a vain struggle to remain standing, disappeared in a massive splash under the water.

Connie, also off balance, tumbled forward and landed on him. He surfaced sputtering and laughing all at the same time.

"Takes some practice I presume," he laughed.

"Apparently so," she giggled.

He sat laughing with water streaming from his moustache and hair. With a playful motion, he splashed her again. "Shall we try again?" he asked offering her his hand.

She splashed him back. "Think you can handle it old man?"

He grinned showing a full set of brilliantly white teeth. "Old man? Oh, you insolent young whelp. Here, just help this old Mongrel to his feet; I will show you what an old man can do."

Connie laughed, splashed him again and dove under the water.

He stood, stumbled and dove in after her. She was a powerful swimmer. Only with a herculean, effort was he able to close the distance between them. He seized a foot yanking her back dunking her under. After a brief struggle, he found her pressed against his chest blinking; her long lashes drooling water. She just kissed him.

It was the last thing Athelstan expected. Yet, when she did, his mind shut down and his body reacted.

Connie's arms came up to encircle his neck; her breasts pressing hard against him. Before he realised it, she had wrapped both her legs around his waist. It was a profoundly passionate embrace.

When the kiss broke he stared at her in stunned silence. He brushed a dripping tangle of hair from her face. She felt so good against him and his heart hammered in his chest. He was quite powerless in her embrace. It was as if his willpower had utterly vanished and the world narrowed to such an extent that only her eyes remained. His grip on her waist tightened and he fought the urge to kiss her again. It was a fight he lost. Their lips met again but now there was a savage hunger in the touch. It was like falling from a very great height - a very great height indeed.

Connie could only stare at him. His lips found hers again and her fingers slipped deep into the strands of his hair. Her grip was strong and hard; her legs tightened around him; her body ground against him. He responded to her touch, her taste and her fingers in his hair. She felt like pure clean water in a pool of clinging muck. His tongue sought out hers and his eyes closed. He drifted on a cloud buoyed up by his rising passion. His breath came faster and faster and his hands began to slide down her back. He cupped her buttocks and pulled her closer. He could scarcely think about what he was doing, he just let the animal within him run free.

Connie looked into his eyes and shook her head. "Stop!"

He blinked twice and reality crashed back into his brain. He let her sink back into the water. "I do not know… I mean it was not my intention to… I mean," he stammered.

She pushed away from him and began to back away. "Do not do that ever again. Never again!" Connie swam away disappearing upstream.

He was embarrassed at the rebuke and was instantly furious with himself. He had broken his word to her already. First telling her, he had no interest in children and now, to do this was beyond dishonourable. She was quite right of course. Yet, where she had touched him still felt like he had been burned. Somewhere deep inside he knew he would never forget that burning touch or those soft lips.

It seemed to take all his efforts to wade ashore. Should he say something to her? He felt that nothing would help repair her trust in him.

Athelstan sat on a large flat rock and buried his face in his hands. He felt miserable. He had wanted her so intensely that all other thoughts fled. No other woman had ever done that to him and she was just a girl. He had no right to do what he had done and she was right to push him away. For all his life, he was convinced he was in total control of his actions but this girl had proved this belief wrong in only a few seconds. Did he actually kiss her? Did she kiss him? He could not remember.

His morose reverie ended sharply as he remembered the men following them. He had to find Connie and quickly. He found her a few hundred yards downstream. She was crying and it drove home the fullness of his deceit.

He walked up to her and said. "Connie, I am sorry. That was not my intent. I cannot explain my actions except to say they will not be repeated. We have to go now." He scanned the cliffs across the river but could see no sign of their pursuers.

Connie did not look at him. She could not look at him. "But it was – alright," she said softly.

"I just need you to know this. I will be here for you when you need an ear or a kind word. You understand? No matter what."

She never looked at him but allowed him to lead her back to Maehadren. This quiet acceptance only added to his guilt.

They continued their journey in silence; each wrapped in their own thoughts. A spattering of rain began to fall and Athelstan finally climbed aboard Maehadren behind Connie. He wrapped her in the white fur and they picked their way out of the canyon. The river valley swung away to the southwest but he continued the journey north crossing a wide grassy plain. The land descended and as expected a rough narrow bridge spanned the river two miles further upstream. The wide curve on the western side of the river added over ten miles to their enemy's route.

The sound of rain and the roar of the rushing water deadened the hollow sound of Maehadren's hooves on the boards and the pair rode towards the town. She had not said a word since leaving the river and he feared she might never speak to him again.

Night had fallen an hour ago and only now did he begin to see the outlying homes and farms of a small village. The sky had finally opened and a heavy cold rain fell. They had been in the saddle for a long time taking only one other short rest around mid-afternoon. They travelled north and concealing their tracks in the river. They followed the main road. There was no other choice. Now they were travelling directly towards Sparta and hopefully the salvation of his people.

Connie, now cocooned in the white bearskin, had rested her head against his shoulder not long after dark and was dozing now. Lights of a small farming village began to twinkle in the distance and a few minutes later Athelstan turned Maehadren out of the rain and into a warm, dry, common stable.

Two stable boys, brothers by the look of them, craned their necks looking down from the upper hayloft to see who had arrived. When it was not someone from the area, they scrambled down a sturdy wall ladder and ran to grab Maehadren's reins.

"STOP!" Athelstan boomed and the pair skidded to a halt, still several feet from the reach of Maehadren's deadly hooves. "He's a bit touchy lads, I will see to him if you do not mind."

He climbed wearily from the saddle and pulled Connie off as well. "Sit here," he indicated a low mound of hay and she did.

"Say that is a real shiner you have there!" offered the younger brother looking at Connie's swollen cheek and eye. It had turned an ugly shade of purple. "How–ja get that?" The pair cast a dubious eye at Athelstan. Brutality was all too common here. Yet in spite of that, the pair seemed eager to talk – any stranger was a welcome distraction from the plodding monotony of life in rural Hellas.

"I'm Mitzu and this is my brother Athios. What is your name? You guys are from a different country are you not? Hey, look at how pale his hands are. You should get out in the sun more."

Connie looked up at the two boys and smiled softly.

"Mitzu and Athios right?" Athelstan inquired.

The boys looked back up at the giant Celt in wonder and nodded. "My friend Connie here has been through a lot today and he really needs some sleep. I have an idea, now stay right there. My horse IS dangerous. I mean it," he glared at the boys and received grave nods in response.

He opened a saddlebag and rummaged about. He removed two copper disks the size of their palms. One side was covered with brightly coloured enamel and the other side had a Celtic Ogham letter engraved onto it. He handed one to each boy and watched their glittering eyes as they examined the shiny prizes. The copper alone would seem like a fortune to them.

"You boys can keep these for awhile. Look at them closely, see how they were made; dream about them, make up stories about them if you must. If you can tell ME what I am and where I am from by the time we finish eating – then you can keep them. I will tell you a story about my people as well. What do you say, lads? Do we have a bargain?" Athelstan had a gentle look. A chorus of 'sure!' 'Wow!' and 'thanks!' followed his offer.

"Now would one of you stout lads run in and tell your father we will both need a hot meal. I will pay with silver." Both boys frowned at each other then, deliberately left. Their actions left Athelstan puzzled.

He unpacked the sturdy beast with a gentle pat and began to brush away the water streaming off the white coat. "If you want to go in and get comfortable – Connie, I will be along directly," he looked at her new and improved disguise and nodded in satisfaction. She had just fooled the toughest audience possible – country boys.

A few minutes later as Athelstan placed a disk of silver into the innkeeper's palm, the man's eyes narrowed. It was stamped with Oghams and other strange symbols. He eyed the giant Celt up and down.

"I want no trouble here," he said cautiously.

Athelstan looked at the smaller man. He was stout and had a hard look. "I do not either good sir. The boy and I are looking for food only and perhaps a place to rest for an hour, or so. Then we will be on our way."

The Innkeeper looked past Athelstan at Connie. "Him?" he asked curtly gesturing in Connie's direction.

He nodded slowly. "Yes, why do you ask? Is there a problem with him?"

"Soldiers have been here today asking after a huge fair-haired Barbarian and a pale–skinned boy. Like I say, I want no trouble here," he made a gesture of disgust when he said the word soldier.

Athelstan thought quickly. " A coincidence I'm sure," he dropped another coin into his palm.

The Innkeeper eyed this one as dubiously as the first. He ordered a hot meal for both of them and they ate it in silence. Connie would not meet his gaze at all, yet the innkeeper's eyes never left their table. Something more was happening here? Clearly, the Spartan army was looking for him and he was trying to find their King before they did. Not a pleasant situation.

The meal arrived and they ate it in silence.

He could see she was utterly exhausted. Her eyelids dipped involuntarily and she stifled a yawn in mid-bite. She needed some real sleep.

Something was different about her now. She seemed even more guarded than before as if she had divulged too much information to him for her liking. An idea occurred to him and he paused for a moment to consider it. He watched her eat mechanically.

"Connie, I think I need to tell you something about what I am doing here in Lacedaemon - why I am headed to Sparta."

She looked up at him with expressionless eyes and shrugged. "Do what you want. I will not stop you." She turned her attention back to her meal.

He pressed on.

"You know I am a soldier."

She nodded absently.

A dull grunt greeted her apparent disinterest.

"Yes, well," he paused again unsure if he should continue, or not. "What I think you should know is that I am a soldier who commands many men in my country. I am sort of like a… ah… like a Captain of men." He was having trouble finding the correct words in the face of her obstinate silence. I am the man who commands the Senone Multitude'. Do you understand what I am trying to tell you? I do not know the proper word in Latin." Silence hung between them for a second before she nodded.

"Yes, I understand. Like a Commander, or a General?"

He seized on the word. "A General! Yes exactly. Thank you."

"I have never heard of this Multitude. What is 'Multitude'?"

"You have never heard of the Multitude?"

She shook her head soundlessly.

"You do lead an insulated life." Her eyes flashed at him and it was a physical blow.

He regrouped his thoughts and continued. "Hmmm! The Multitude is, in essence, an army made up of many different clans, or families joined together for a single purpose. That purpose is the protection and defence of our homeland in northern Italia. It is just for this reason I am here in Hellas. Our homeland has been taken from us by the Legions of Rome."

"Not much of an army then is it?" she commented idly between bites.

His mouth opened to deliver a harsh retort but he closed it again and drew a deep breath. "Well there is more to that story than we have time for oven dinner, but as it stands, it serves us well enough."

She shrugged again. "If you say so. Why are you telling me this?" she was clearly annoyed.

"I am telling you this because you do not know anything about me. I do not know anything about you either. I must admit I am just a bit curious. "Yes, you said that," she said flatly and her eyes returned to her plate. She continued to eat without further conversation.

"Hrumph," he muttered again. He returned his attention to his plate. "I will shut up now. I just thought we might take some time and get to know each other. Perhaps we might avoid any more misunderstandings. You did kiss me back there you know." He ripped another piece of meat from the bone and popped it into his mouth.

Again, her eyes looked up at him with a look that dripped venom. "I think I will take my meal elsewhere," she said standing. "I do not think I like the company. And for the record, you kissed me back!"

"Alright, alright, lower your voice, Connie. I meant nothing by it. Please sit down." He sighed and motioned for her to resume her seat.

For long moments, she just stared at him. Nevertheless, after a long painful pause, she sat down stiffly.

There was a long awkward silence and some people were wondering what these two Romans were arguing about. Latin was scarcely ever heard this close to Sparta. Finally, Athelstan could stand it no longer. "So, why are you here in Hellas so far from home? Do you have family here?"

For long moments, all she did was eat. After a while, she said "No, no I have no family anymore. But if you really want to know why I am here I will tell you." she put her spoon down. "I am a daughter of the brother of Rome's ruling family. My father was crucified and my estates were given to another loyal family. I am now a slave owned by my Uncle. I was kidnapped with six other girls by people who look very much like you do and brought to Sparta for reasons I do not understand. I escaped my captors and when you found me, I was trying to steal enough food to feed the other girls and to try to rescue them. Where they are now is anyone's guess. You did not rescue me as much as you doomed them."

He stared at her for several seconds. "I see, he said flatly. "That was quite a tale. OK, I can understand your need to keep your business to yourself. Who am I, after all, to be asking you these things? If you do not want to tell me the truth, it is fine. It is none of my business. You have made that clear. I am not a dullard you know." he said sadly. "What is your family name?"

"Does it matter?" she said still not looking up.

"No, I suppose not." He heaved a huge sigh and then looked up at her. "Yes!" he said suddenly. "Yes, to me it does matter." He even asked himself why it mattered to him, but he could not admit the reason why even to himself yet.

"You are being awfully loud Captain. It is Cursor if you must know, not that any of this matters to a Barba..." she said with a bitter tone.

He frowned at the rebuke but his head snapped up. "It matters. It matters because I like you. Your father's name was...?"

"Marcus."

"Thank you. That is a common name in Rome?"

She nodded mutely and there was genuine fear in her eyes. She was shaking. "Now do you believe that this little guttersnipe is telling the truth?"

"I never said..."

"You didn't have to!" she barked.

He paused and looked at her. There was a twinkle in her eye again. A chuckle rumbled in his chest that almost sounded like a giggle. What was it about this girl that kept him so off balance? "Yes, the little guttersnipe is telling the truth. We have to find these other girls and rescue them as soon as possible. That does bring up a much larger question. Why kidnap slaves and bring her all the way to Hellas. What information do you have that is so important you had to be taken from under the very nose of the Proconsul and brought here?" He was frowning.

"I am sure I do not know," she said shudder.

"THINK!" he almost shouted the question and she flinched at its intensity. Heads turned to look briefly. "I didn't mean to yell," he said in a whisper, "but we need to find out who took you, why you were taken, who you were being sent to and why. We need to find this out quickly if they are going to survive."

"You do believe me?"

"I would like to, yes. There is more to this story you are not telling me."

Connie heaved a sigh of relief and smiled.

"I do know one thing for certain."

"What?"

"I like it when you smile. You are pretty when you smile. Even if the reason for the smile is dire.? He mopped at some of the meat juices with a heel of bread and chewed it with a smile of his own.

Connie's smile slowly faded. A blush tinted her cheeks and she lowered face her quickly so he would not see it. Biting her lower lip, she said, "I am not really hungry anymore. I believe I will go upstairs to retire. You did secure me a room." It was not a question.

"No. It will be too dangerous to stay here. We will be leaving here very soon.

I am now certain we are being hunted. I think it is for the best if you stay by my side."

She said nothing but the look on her face showed uncertainty. "Oh come on Connie, we were just finding common ground. Surely, you can stand to be around me for a few more moments longer," he said raising his bushy brows. "There is more I need to know."

She chuckled. She could not help herself.

"I have told you everything. I told you who I am. I do not know why I am here. All I want to do is go home. You still think I am a liar," she said sitting.

"I did not say that."

"You have all but implied it, however," she said nodding with a smile.

"Ah yes, that is right, You are niece and slave to Papirius and someone seems to think you are worth kidnapping upon pain of death, yet you do not know who it is, or why they want you? You must think me a colossal idiot."

"Quite right, I do. Not your fault, though. Most men are," she smiled.

He nodded but smirked to himself as he looked back at his bowl to finish off the last of his meal. He did not tell her this time that he liked her smile. For some reason, that simple admission set her off last time and he had no idea why.

Chapter Thirteen

Sometime later, a deep satisfied sigh escaped Athelstan as he pushed his board away and leaned back in his chair. He watched Connie set down her cup of sweet wine and lick her lips. His heart jumped at the sensuousness of this unconscious act. Even with her floppy hat and ragged clothes, she was common and exotic all at the same time. She was the most closed and frightened young girl he had ever met. Mysterious hardly covered it.

Out of the corner of his eye, he saw Mitzu and Athios approaching his table, both beaming with triumph. They stopped at a respectful distance away until he motioned for them to approach.

He switched to Greek.

"So, you young men seem overly pleased with yourselves. What have you to report?" He spoke in a deep resonant voice that carried to the farthest corners of the room.

"We know where you are from!" Mitzu smiled.

"We know what you are," said Athios

"Do you now? Very well then, before you tell me and everyone else in the Inn where I come from, first tell me what did you do to find out?" He was looking at the boys seriously.

"We did not do anything wrong! " Athios blurted out, worried he was in trouble.

Athelstan looked up at their father and received a blank expression.

"Oh, I have no doubt on that score. You and your brother here are honourable men – like your father and his father before him." The two boys glanced at each other and Athios elbowed Mitzu with a frown and a shake of his head. Mitzu nodded at his brother and they returned their attention to Athelstan. Athelstan risked a glance at the Innkeeper and his wife. The Innkeeper held his wife's arm tightly and bore a stern expression totally devoid of any pride, or love for his 'family'.

'So,' Athelstan concluded silently, 'not the boy's father. Who then?'

"I know you did nothing wrong," Athelstan continued without pause. "I would rather die than utter such foolish words. I placed no conditions on how you discovered the truth. Now, if you please, tell us. How did you do it?" He was smiling now and encouraged the boys to press on.

"Well…" Athios looked at his younger brother and he nodded. "Well, we did not know what to do at first. We asked some of our friends and neighbours at the Inn here if they knew. No one did. Then Mitzu had an idea. Tell them, Mitz!"

Athelstan liked Athios already. He was ready to hand credit to his younger brother without jealousy, or envy.

Mitzu was shy, but when Athelstan nodded at him he admitted in a rush, "I told Athios to check and see what kind of money you used to pay for your meal," he beamed at his cleverness.

Athelstan's bushy eyebrows lifted in surprise and he laughed a rich infectious laugh. Chairs were being turned towards their table as everyone knew some kind of entertainment was coming. He clapped a massive paw on the boy's slender shoulder.

"Did you now? Very good indeed! Even I would not have thought of doing that. How did you get so clever?"

The boy blushed from the bottoms of his feet to the tips of his hair at the unexpected compliment. He shook his head with a shrug, but his proud smile lit up the entire room.

"So then, if you would be so kind, please tell the fine folk gathered here as well as your mother and - father, what am I and where am I from?"

"You are a Senone Celt from the Po Valley in Italia across the Ægean sea to the west!" Mitzu announced.

Athelstan stood and bowed to the two boys.

"You are quite correct young masters, on all counts. I am impressed." He reached out and formally clasped arms with the two boys. "I am called Athelstan. Can you say that? Athelstan."

"Affelstam," they tried. He laughed again.

"Show everyone your prizes for being so clever."

They each produced their copper amulet that covered their palms. They held them up and passed them around for all the people to see.

"These are magical protective amulets of great power. White-bearded Druids made these and to own one is a rare thing indeed. I would venture to say they are the only two of their kind in all Hellas," he nodded gravely.

"Keep them safe and close to your hearts boys and they will keep you from harm," he glanced up and winked at their mother. She nodded back, but she was also standing stiffly somehow. Something was clearly troubling her.

"If I am not mistaken, there was a second condition to our wager, was there not?"

"A story!" Athios blurted out.

"Yes, that was it, I promised a story and I will not disappoint." The boys nodded.

"Well, here I must consult with your mother, our gracious and lovely hostess this evening. You see boys, I have been a soldier all my life and I know many stories. Most of them are hardly suitable for gentle ladies like your mother or for young boys like yourselves."

He stood and bowed to the hostess. Townsfolk loved this and they strained to see and hear better.

"I thank you for your hospitality, My Lady. I beg your permission to tell a tale that is, in fact, suitable for both gentle ladies and fine strapping young men."

She inclined her head at the polite compliments, shook her arm free of her husband's grip. She settled into a chair in the back to listen. The innkeeper frowned and then disappeared into the back rooms. Athelstan knew he would have to be wary of this man.

"Pull up your chairs boys, this story is for you. Indeed, this story is for all."

He reached into his tunic and under shiny rings of chainmail withdrew an old wooden flute. He wet his lips and blew a few short notes before holding it up for all to see.

"You two boys like music, right?" he asked seriously. They nodded. He turned towards Connie.

"I know you like music," he secretly recalled the song from their first night.

Athelstan swept the crowd with his eyes. "How about all of you fine honest folk; do you like music too?" An affirmative murmur swept the long common room. He smiled. An audience was born.

He returned his attention to the young lads. "Do you boys know what this is?"

"It's a flute," Athios stated.

"That is right. I hold in my hand a simple wooden flute. It is hollow and has a place to blow into and there are a bunch of finger holes, can you see them?" They nodded their heads.

"Have you ever wondered who made the very first flute? No?" The boys were smiling.

"Well then, I will tell you."

Placing the flute up to his lips, he blew a simple tune that was both tender and haunting. He looked at Mitzu, Athios, and Connie; then began.

"Once upon a long time ago…"

Smiles bloomed even on the oldest faces and he could see the patrons settle into their chairs and refill their mugs. He paused a moment until the room was quiet and began again.

"Once upon a long time ago… there was a great Celtic King named Vestorix and he ruled all of the Celts from Gaul to Persia and from Rome to Hibernia – a very long way from here," he whispered this last phrase conspiratorially as an aside for all to hear.

"His castle was in Italia and one stormy day, Good King Vestorix was walking alone along the seashore. The sea was high and the wind chased the clouds across the sky in an unearthly hunt. Huge waves crashed upon the rocks of the shore. It was a perfectly wild day."

"As he walked, he began to imagine he was hearing an odd sort of music. It would rise and fall in pitch and volume and he had never heard such wonderful music in all his life. But try as he might, he could not find what made those sweet and sad sounds." Athelstan raised the flute played a tune like a soft wind moaning through the willows. It was the same tune as before and it was sweet and sad.

"Good King Vestorix just had to find the source of this wondrous music and hurried further along the shore; further than he had ever walked from his castle. As he walked the sounds of the music grew louder and louder and louder still. It whistled, warbled, rose and fell in pitch and tone. The King felt a tear run down his cheek. The music had enchanted him – bewitched him in fact," Athelstan said ominously. An expectant hush fell over the Inn. Even the local greybeards were leaning forward so not to miss a single word.

Athelstan blew his flute again mimicking the rising and falling of the beautiful wind music, the tune remained the same but it became more complex each time he played it.

"Vexed!" Athelstan boomed suddenly and everyone jumped.

"Good King Vestorix was vexed but continued his search and in time he finally came upon the source of the divine sound. Wouldn't you know, but he stood before the skeleton of a great whale half buried in the sand. Its bones were white and they rose skyward in long curving arches. The music was made as the wind blew through holes worn into its huge ribs. The King sat down with a THUMP in the sand and listened as the wind and the sea sang to each other. He was enthralled." Athelstan returned to the flute and played a new and even more haunting tune for several minutes. You could almost hear the gulls and smell the sea.

"So enchanted was the Good King Vestorix that he sat there for the rest of the day. He sat there all through that night and all the next day. He just sat, listening. Finally, a search party from the Palace found him sitting in the sand not moving and they were very concerned indeed. They all gathered about him and asked what he was doing. He told them to sit and listen to the wind in the bones and they did. They all agreed they had never heard such beautiful music in all their lives."

He winked at Connie, put the flute to lips and played. Now there was a rich happy lilt to the song and many a head swayed. Since his story began, the Inn had filled up. News travels fast in a small town. The Innkeeper's wife was doing a great business. Yet, throughout, his attention was focused entirely on the two brothers and their round unblinking eyes.

"The next day the Good King Vestorix called all his best craftsmen, architects and musicians together and told them to go to the whale bones and listen to the music. Then he told them to build an instrument that could play this lovely music. So, they went to the bones and like the others, they were enthralled by the sound of the wind in the whalebones." Athelstan's tune had changed again and one could almost see the jutting white bones and the wide sea reflected in Mitzu and Athio's eyes. Even Connie's eyes had closed as she listened.

"Well, the craftsmen, architects, and musicians all put their heads together and stroked their long white beards. They talked and discussed and argued, planned and argued, conflicted and argued, calculated and argued again but, in the end, they came up with a grand design for an instrument they all said would work. Once they returned to the palace they all got to work and the next day told the King it was ready. He followed them out onto the courtyard and there stood a marvellous construction. It was made of wood, stone, canvas and ivory. It resembled the curving ribs of the whale and it towered over everyone. As the wind blew, it made music," he played but now there was a discord to the tune – something not quite right.

"No! No! No!" the King said. "That is not right! It is all wrong! The sound hurts my ears, besides it is too big to get into the palace and there is not any wind in there. One man suggested placing it outside the drawing salon and letting the music come in through the open windows."

"No!" stated the King, it would be too windy and cold in the Hall with all the windows open and the music could not be heard with them closed. They were commanded to try again. It was then that a clever young lad, just about your age Mitzu, peeked around the leg of his father and said, "I can make the instrument Sire, would you let me try?" He was the son of the head Musician and had heard the music as well."

"The King agreed and the boy went off to make his instrument." Athelstan played the same tune as always but now it was simple, innocent and gay.

"The next day the boy returned to the King with his invention and the craftsmen, architects and the musicians all gathered around to see what he had done. The boy was shy – a bit like you Mitzu, but he did not let fear stop him. He pulled out a long goose bone with tiny holes drilled into it. He placed one end against his lips, put his fingers over the holes, took a deep breath and blew into it. He played this very tune." Athelstan played the tune again and it was a sweet joyous sound.

"The sound of the goose bone was even richer than that of the whalebones and King Vestorix proclaimed that the search for his instrument was over. A rich glorious music filled the Hall." Now Athelstan's simple flute took on a full resonant quality and the sound of his playing filled the Inn.

"Good King Vestorix jumped to his feet and clapped his hands in glee. 'What do you call it, you clever boy?" He asked the young Musician's son, at which point the boy sneezed into the goose bone and it made this very sound," he blew a single note and everyone gasped.

Fluuute

"'So be it!' proclaimed the King, 'Flute it is!' The young musician's son was proclaimed the smartest lad in all the land and he played his music for the King until the end of his days," he concluded with a soft refrain on the flute and finally put it up. He was greeted by a deafening roar approval.

The boys were smiling, laughing and clapping with glee. This clearly had far exceeded their expectations. As the sound of excitement flowed over then, he bent down and had a few private words with the two boys. They were suddenly very serious and shook their heads in negation then nodded seriously. Athelstan handed his flute to a totally stunned Mitzu and tousled both boys hair. "Now off to bed with you both, or your mother will be truly and rightly angry with me," he looked up at the balcony where the guest rooms were and the boy's mother stood at the railing looking down. He nodded at her and she nodded back at him. Everything was in readiness.

"Thank you, sir." They bowed to him and ran off in a rush.

He whispered conspiratorially in Connie's ear. "We have trouble. The Innkeeper knows about you. I do not like his look." Connie stiffened. "Here take this. Keep it close to hand." He handed her the long knife again. She slipped it under her shirt.

"Stay clear of the Innkeeper. He is not what he appears to be. The soldiers already have a good description of a large fair-haired Celt and a pale–skinned boy. You have got to change out of this disguise and into a dress, tonight," he counselled. "The Innkeeper's wife is going to help. No arguments! If you need to flee, go out a window and head for the stables. Maehadren will defend you. Repeat this to him. Sabaid Maehadren." She repeated it. He looked at her and gestured with his head that she should join Thea, the innkeeper's wife, in the rooms upstairs. The portly woman had been quietly ferrying bundles upstairs throughout Athelstan's story. The Innkeeper was nowhere in sight.

Connie nodded nervously and joined the innkeeper's wife in a room upstairs. The door to the upper room had just closed when a large troop of silver and bronze clad soldiers stormed in. Their red-plumed helmets indicated they were the elite cavalry. The mood of the common room changed instantly from one of happy ease to nervous tension. With a quick glance around, a grim-faced Spartan Commander came to stand in front of a seated Athelstan.

"You! Stand up!" the Spartan demanded.

Athelstan ignored him.

"Up!" He commanded again.

Athelstan barely glanced at him. "No. Go away," he growled and waved his hand at him in a rude and dismissive manner. The crowd gasped at his refusal. No Greek would dare speak to a Spartan military commander in such a disrespectful way.

"I said get up barbarian, or I will kill you where you sit. You are under arrest!" He repeated.

"What you mean to say is get up 'Sir'. You will kill me where I sit 'Sir'. You are under arrest 'Sir'. I am commander of the Senone multitude of Italia. You may address me as General, or Sir, or preferably not at all. Now go away, you annoying little man, while you are still capable of doing so under your own power," he returned his gaze back to his cup.

The commander dragged the table away from the Celt spilling wooden dishes and crude metal flagons onto the floor. He stepped forward to haul Athelstan from his chair. It would not be necessary. The Celt stood up.

A truly surprised Spartan looked up at him. Moreover, Athelstan had levelled a look at him that caused the Greek to lower his eyes and drop his head involuntarily. Few people had the kind of personal aura that Athelstan possessed. It was one of absolute authority. It had the quality of thunder and lightning and of a howling storm seething just below the surface. More than a dozen soldiers, hands on weapons, now surrounded Athelstan's table but they stood well clear of the big man's reach. Confronting this giant was the Commander's job – they hoped.

"Under arrest, am I? Give me your name and tell me why am I under arrest

– exactly?" His intense gaze bore into that of the smaller Spartan and he was clearly intimidated.

"I am Ptolemarch Demetrios of the Ninth Spartan Army Group. Now Celt, give me your name."

"Wild is my name! Any other would be but a pale description. I am widely known as General Athelstan on business in Hellas from my King.

"Alright," he said slowly, "Then be it known General Athelstan that you are under arrest for murder. Four men were beheaded in Yithion. You fit the description of the killer."

"Murder?" his bushy eyebrows rose in mock surprise. "That does sound serious, but I do not kill without just cause. I assume you have brought proof – witnesses perhaps! Show me your proof Ptolemarch Demetrios of the Ninth Spartan Army Group; bring forth your witnesses, or go away. I have no time for prattle!" Athelstan bristled at the stocky Spartan in his red-caped, black and bronze armour.

His armed soldiers now tightly surrounded the Celt but it was their leader that was shifting from foot to foot under Athelstan's intense scowl. The patrons of the Inn sat in mute witness to this intense battle of wills. The Spartan licked suddenly dry lips. Athelstan knew he had him.

"We tracked you from Yithion and your trail led us right through that door," he lied pointing behind him. "Do you deny you killed and beheaded four men in Yithion? That is the barbarian way is it not?" Demetrios countered. Athelstan knew by the title that this was one of ten Ptolemarchs that made up as many Spartan Army groups, totalling some three thousand men.

"I never kill without just cause, Ptolemarch Demetrios as I have already said. I am sent by the Senone King to beg an audience with the Spartan King. I have travelled here from Italia fresh from a war with Rome, all of which lies to the west, not the south. What then, do you think, would prompt me to journey so far out of my way to kill four dogs in a city I have never heard of and know nothing about? Answer me that if you can. I do not fear you, or your men, but if I am lying let one of your Gods strike me dead. Go ahead Ptolemarch Demetrios - pick one. Hera, Poseidon, Hades, Athena, Zeus. Choose one, I have not got all day." The Celt stood feet wide apart with his arms folded across his chest. People were moving out of the way.

When nothing happened the Celt smiled. "See?"

"You Barbarians do not even fear the Gods." He shook his head.

"Of course I fear the Gods. I just do not fear YOUR Gods."

Another pair of soldiers entered dripping wet from the rain outside, concern etched across their faces.

"What have you found?" the Commander demanded.

"Nothing sir… we cannot get close enough to search his gear. His horse will not let us near any of it." The soldiers were clearly not pleased… neither was Ptolemarch Demetrios.

"His horse – will not let you…? Find the boy! Search the Inn and the rooms upstairs," he ordered. Four of his men turned towards the stairs and two others headed towards the back. "He will tell us the truth even if this one will not!"

"Stop!" Athelstan commanded and the four soldiers froze. "I have been very patient with you Commander, but like everything under the sky, it has its limits. My companion and I mean to speak to your King and no one else. You may accompany us, with our thanks, or hinder us at your own bloody peril. I believe the time has now come for you to choose – which course of action you prefer."

"You are unarmed so your threat is an empty one. Get the boy! I'll not issue another order twice," he boomed at his men. The nervous-looking soldiers immediately headed for the stairs, a second pair fled to the kitchens. Athelstan liked this Commander. He ruled with an iron hand.

Bushy eyebrows rose at this and a grim smile crept over the Celt's face. "I have no need of weapons for this – this rabble of yours." He waggled a casual finger in their direction. "They have brought all the weapons I will ever need. Give the order Commander and be amazed how quickly I send you and all your men to visit Hades. I understand it is quite warm this time of year."

Hesitation flickered behind the Spartan Commander's eyes as he assessed the Celt's resolve. It was clear to Athelstan that Demetrios was not used to being openly defied like this. The tension had built to a painful level as these two men faced off. Eight guards partially drew their Machaira – the long Greek Cavalry swords. Four others mounted the stairs slowly, staring intently at the scene below. Silence fell and time ticked by, one agonizing second after the next.

The door at the far end of the upper balcony suddenly opened and a stunningly beautiful woman stepped out. She was dressed in an emerald green peasant's dress that fell to her ankles. It was trimmed in gold and cinched at the waist by a deep sapphire cord. Long blonde curls cascaded over her shoulders and down her back. Her eyes were lined with coal and some colour had been added to her cheeks and lips masking the bruises. The Spartan guards looked up and those at the top of the stairs froze in open-mouthed amazement. She calmly walked up to the four men who stepped aside for her to pass. They followed her slowly down the stairs like a 'Royal' procession.

"Where is the boy?"

"There is no boy. He lied. He was only after money. That foul mercen…" a soldier began but shut his mouth at a look from Demetrios.

Constantina gracefully swept up to Athelstan seemingly without a single care in the world and took him by his left arm. She smiled sweetly at Demetrios.

"Is there a problem here Captain?" she asked looking up at Athelstan. He winced inwardly at the title.

"No my lady, I am sorry your rest was disturbed." He faced Spartan again.

"So then, Ptolemarch Demetrios of the Ninth Army Group, this does not look like any boy I have ever seen. If it does to you, I might suggest you get away from the barracks a little more often." Demetrio's eyes jerked towards the soft chuckles coming from the townsfolk at the inn before they swept over Connie's willowy form again. Clearly, this was not the 'boy' he had expected.

"Very well, Captain is it now? I shall take you to Sparta, but you will not get an audience with the King," he grumbled.

The Celt ignored the sarcasm. "You seem quite – certain of that Commander, why?" Athelstan queried.

"He is dead." Demetrios countered flatly.

A frown creased Athelstan's brow. "Dead? King Cleomenes II is dead? When did this happen?" Athelstan openly showed his surprise. He had hoped to talk to this elderly King and use existing alliances to request his help against Rome. Now, with this news, his mission might well have been in vain.

"Two months ago; he died in his sleep," Demetrios answered.

"I had heard no one in Sparta ever dies in their sleep. Who now sits upon the Throne of Sparta then?" he asked.

"Queen Leonida former Priestess of the Goddess Athena and daughter of King Cleomenes II. She is the first Queen of the Aglad line."

"You are joking! A Spartan Queen?" Athelstan sounded aghast.

"I NEVER JOKE! EVER! Demetrios announced bristling with indignation.

"No, I don't suppose you do. Peace Ptolemarch Demetrios, I meant neither insult nor disrespect. Although, it is a sorry world where women rule over men, is it not?" He clapped a hand on Demetrio's shoulder. He missed the wide-eyed look outrage that bloomed on Connie's face. It was gone as quickly as it appeared.

"It is."

"Then I will request an audience with this Priestess Queen Leonida," he stated finally.

"She will not see you either. She has more pressing matters on her mind."

"What? Why not? What pressing matters?" Athelstan had a bad feeling begin to build in his belly.

"We are at war. She marches to Athens' defence even now. Gather your gear General, we leave in five minutes!" Demetrios stated.

"We leave when my companion and I have had a proper rest. I suggest you either billet your men here for the night or go on to Sparta without us." It was a statement of fact and the Celt's tone ended the matter right there. He raised an arm for the Innkeeper.

"Who are you at war with if I might ask?"

"Macedonia!" growled Demetrios as he turned to leave.

Athelstan's heart sank and he sat back down with a thump. This changed everything. Western Macedonia was where his entire nation was heading when he came in search of Spartan aid. That was two moons ago. Did his nation still exist? Was he the last Senone? Worse than that, he looked at Connie and clenched his jaw. He was taking this girl into a war zone and he did not like it. Not one little bit.

"I think we're going to need that room."

Chapter Fourteen

He shut the door behind them and scanned the small room. There was a rough table with a bowl, a pitcher of water and several candles on it. A small chair sat at the table and across the room, a low, narrow bed was crammed in the corner to the right of the window. The window was large, leaded and shuttered from the outside. It looked out over the roof of the stables. A steady rain fell outside and somehow the sound of it striking the shake roof was soothing. "You can have the bed," he said casually tossing the bear cloak on the floor beside it.

Connie looked into a tiny polished metal mirror above the table when he noticed her expression.

"What?" he asked innocently.

Her eyes were shot with fire. "Get out," she said coldly.

He looked at her and blinked. He looked behind at the closed door then back at her.

"Why," he said softly and continued to struggle with his leather vest of chainrings.

Her voice never raised but there was a tone in it that brokered no argument. "Just do it."

Turning slowly, Connie stepped away from the table. She went to stand at the open window to watch the rainfall. She was clearly furious.

"I do not understand Connie, what is wrong." He took a few steps forward.

"Stay right there. Not another step," a raised finger halted him in his tracks.

His hands clenched, but he came no further. "You know full well I cannot leave you alone until you are safe. I do not trust the Innkeeper. You have already been told, you have nothing to fear from me. I will sleep on the floor over here by the door."

"I do not care! You can sleep in the stable with your horse, or hang from a tree in the rain for all I care but you will not be sleeping in here. At

110

least you and that creature have something in common – stupidity. Male stupidity," Connie said in a deathly quiet voice.

He was tired and her tone and her attitude were beginning to annoy him. He understood that things between them had been stressed since the incident in the river, but he had vowed never to let it happen again. Why was she acting like this?

"Connie…"

"You will call me Constantina. No, actually henceforth, you will address me as 'Highness'." she interrupted.

Athelstan rolled his eyes. "Highness? You are joking. I know we are still getting to know each other, but this is a bit much. You are no more a Princess than I am a duck. Listen to me, when I guard someone, it is not for a few hours and then it is over. I mean to see you come to no harm and I mean to do that right bloody here. Now either tell me what it is that is wrong or lie down and try to get some sleep."

"You listen to me you lumbering..."

"…Mongrel?" he helped.

"Silence!" she shrieked. "You are nothing to me! You are not my father; you are not my husband, nor my personal confessor. You are not my master. You may command men. You may command the sun, the moon and the stars for all I care, but you do not command me! 'A sad world where women rule over men?' What absolute rubbish! I will have you know, that if women ruled this world, there would be no need for war, or bloodlust, or all the other ridiculous nonsense that men like you force upon the innocent. I have never been so insulted – ever! Now if you want to get even a single moment of peace tonight, I would advise you to get out of here, now! OUT!"

His bushy eyebrows were raised in abject astonishment. "Ha!" he snorted. "That is why you are angry? For Epona's sake, you took offence to that?" he shook his head perplexed. He tried another argument.

"Perhaps Your Highness has failed to notice the squad of armed Spartan soldiers down below. They are not here to pay a casual social call on this lonely little Inn. They are dangerous men – more dangerous than you could ever imagine and the only thing that stands between them and you is me! Now since you need your rest and frankly so do I, I would advise you to shut up, lie down and go to sleep," he was fighting with a buckle on his chain mail vest. It was on the side where he was injured and frustration was setting in.

"Get into that bed!" he thundered his patience now at an end.

This silly waif could scarcely comprehend the peril sitting below and here she demands that he be gone because of an idle comment? This unfortified Inn could scarcely keep out a herd of cows let alone a determined assault. No! He was staying and that was that. "I will not tell you again. BED!"

Just then, Connie let out a blood–curdling scream. She turned quickly and threw the candle and iron holder that sat on the table at him. Before he could recover, she backed up, threw the other candle and continued to throw one thing after another, some hitting him and others hitting the wall.

"Stop you, crazy Roman!" He tried to dodge the sudden barrage of missiles.

She stopped briefly then to glare at him. "Now get out! Out! Out! Out!" She picked up another missile and raised it over her head.

He backed into the door with a boom. "Have you lost your mind? Enough of this!" he bellowed at her.

"Get out, get out, get out!" she shrieked.

She was fighting him at every turn and there seemed no way of convincing her to stop. He would be glad to be finally free of this wildcat. He turned finally, scooped up his shirt and pulled it back over his head.

"Very well then – have it YOUR way – Little Princess! I will be with my horse – he is not half as dangerous, or a tenth as bloody crazy as you are! Clearly, fatigue has you overreacting. I will be back once your annoying little tantrum has ended." He tore open the door and slammed it shut behind him with a resounding boom that shook the entire inn.

A cat-like yowl of sheer frustration came through the door and he heard the bolt thrown shut with a sharp bang. He stood outside rigid with fury. He had pledged to protect her from all perils – including him! He would rather cut off his own head than harm a single hair on hers. How could she not see that? He stood at the long balcony rail gripping it with whitening knuckles. A dozen pairs of eyes looked up at him. Clearly, they had all heard the yelling match.

"Ha! That was awfully quick, Barbarian. Does she not fancy the taste of wild meat tonight?" an amused Spartan called up from below.

The Celt's eyes narrowed at the cackles of laughter from the Spartan soldiers now at their ease waiting for morning.

"Silence!" hollered an unseen Demetrios. "The next man who speaks like that to visiting dignitaries will suffer unit punishment! Am I clear?" He had stepped forward from a table under the long balcony. They replied. "Sir!" He could hear the contrition in the scolded soldier's voices. Athelstan headed down the stairs.

Demetrios scowled at his men and from Athelstan's perspective; this was the way a proper leader should behave. He commanded his men with absolute authority.

"I apologize for my men, General. Is it General, or Captain?"

"General," he replied. "I know something about soldiers Commander and I thank you – it is of no consequence," he finally came up to Demetrios and clasped forearms with him.

"Why does she call you Captain?"

"How in all black Tartarus and Hades should I know? Perhaps because it amuses her." Demetrios nodded grimly.

"She is fiery to be sure. Would you join me in a flask of wine?" Demetrios looked up at the Celt.

"In a few moments. I had planned to check on Maehadren…"

"Your horse?" the Spartan queried.

He nodded. "You are welcome to join me. You did want to look through my belongings. I believe you have now earned that right. I can think of no better time. Maybe after seeing him, you will think better of those men you sent to the stables. Had they persisted, he would have killed them all. Afterward, I will be honoured to raise a flask with you and your fine men." Demetrios nodded graciously and motioned for Athelstan to lead the way. With a jerk of Demetrios' head, two Spartan soldiers fell into step behind them. They almost made it to the door.

A chilling, heart-stopping shriek of terror and outrage echoed down from the upper rooms. Everyone looked at the door Athelstan had just left and a second of stunned silence followed.

"Noooooooooo!" echoed through the Inn.

When the second terrified shriek ripped the air, Athelstan was already moving.

"Form up," Demetrios ordered. Tables and chairs went flying and crashing and Spartan blades were drawn.

He ploughed a path through the chairs, tables, and people like they were chaff in the wind, before taking the stairs three at a time. He pushed the door but it did not move. She had locked it behind him. A terrible fight could be heard behind the locked door. Demetrios and many of his men followed in hot pursuit skidding to a stop before the door.

He launched his eighteen stone frame against the door and it splintered inward on twisted hinges. A dark masked shape flew out the door colliding with Athelstan. His eyes blinked in astonishment before he slumped to the ground gurgling blood from a nasty throat wound. Athelstan looked up at a grim sight. Three other armed and masked men had cornered Connie on the bed and one was moving in for the kill. She slashed and jabbed at them with one of the long–bladed Celtic knife he had left given her. She was valiantly and rather skillfully, keeping them at bay.

An unarmed Athelstan let out a bellow of fury and charged.

One of the assassins turned towards the Celt. He held his leaf-shaped Xiphos low and took one shuffling step forward then lunged forward in an elegant move designed to disembowel. This was a highly trained professional. Yet, it presupposes that his enemy was afraid of him and is on a defensive footing. However, confronted by an enraged Celt for who fear was an alien concept and retreat was never an option, the assassin had little chance.

Athelstan pressed forward his own attack and casually slapped the flat blade aside with his left hand and struck. His right hand closed on the wrist of the assassin's and with a violent twist snapped both arm bones. His left hand took hold of the sword; deftly reversed it and he drove it completely through his exposed belly. Athelstan released his grip on the sword and the dying man's wrist like so much rubbish. The assassin crumpled to the ground. The deadly manoeuvre took no more than a heartbeat.

A third killer noticed his comrade fall and glanced away from Connie for the briefest of seconds. It was the only opening she needed. Lightning fast, she lunged at him with her knife and drove it deeply into his eye socket. A very brief howl of agony ripped through the room and he twisted away twitching as the razor–sharp blade sliced into his brain. She pulled the knife free.

The remaining attacker used her lunge to press home his final attack, but Athelstan had closed the distance between them as the Spartan soldiers swarmed into the room. The killer's blade was raised high over his head and had started its murderous downward arc when he was violently yanked backwards by his cloak. A massive paw closed on the killer's throat and Athelstan drove his head against the far wall with a hollow crash. He roared into the killer's face with feral rage and shook him like a dog shaking a rabbit. There was a sickening crunch of neck bones and the Xiphos clattered harmlessly to the floor. He flung the dead man aside and the corpse came to rest hanging half in, half out of a shattered window. No more than five seconds had passed between Athelstan's breaking down the door and him gathering up a trembling but stalwart Connie into his arms.

Demetrios and two of his men had enough time to enter the room when the fight was suddenly, decisively over. The Spartan looked around at the dead assassins with naked amazement and a newfound respect for this Celtic warrior and his young companion. Unarmed he had dispatched two highly trained killers and used their own weapons to do so. No small feat. His men began removing the bodies.

Demetrios was blinking in surprise. "I see what you meant earlier about sending my men and I to the next life, even if you were not armed," he said grudgingly. "If I had given that order, how many of my men would you have killed like that?" The look he directed at Demetrios was answer enough. "I see," the Spartan said nodding his head grimly.

"It is all over," he whispered into her ear, holding her close to him and rocking her slightly. "It is alright now. Are you hurt?"

He brushed back her hair and looked into her eyes. She blinked at him and he caught himself falling into those bottomless eyes of hers again. He gave his head a shake.

"Are you hurt?" he repeated

"No, I am fine," she said softly. She started to tremble and slumped against him.

Athelstan looked her over carefully and he found what he hoped he would not. What he found was a large and rapidly growing wet spot spreading across the fabric of her dress under the hand and arm she was using to hide it. His eyes went wide and his face lined with worry. Some of the blood soaking her hands and arms was her own. She had a nasty cut on her left side just below the ribs. He clapped his hand over the ugly slice.

"She has been wounded! Get help! Now!" This was no request and several men began to yell for water and bandages. Athelstan tore a chunk of bed sheet and bundled it up. He replaced his bare hand with this crude bandage. It reddened much too quickly for his liking.

"Awww that is not so bad, it is just a bit of a scratch. Just sit here with me for a minute and we will get that all cleaned up," he held the bandage tightly against her side with one hand and stroked her hair with his other. Her rich caramel complexion had turned ashen.

"This is my fault, Connie. I should have been in here," he whispered.

"Yes it is," she whispered back and winced at the pain. "If you had not been such a…"

"Mongrel. Yes, I know."

"That's right a Mongrel."

"I know, just stay still. Help is coming," he put steady pressure on the wound but the bleeding was not stopping.

"You are just agreeing with me because I am hurt." Connie tried to smile up at the man who was holding her but winced when she did.

"Yes that is right," he muttered in a distracted tone.

"Well stop it. I am fine," she said.

"I know you are. Where are those bandages?" he asked forcefully. He looked under the bandage briefly.

"Stop patronizing me!" her eyes blazed with frustration again.

He raised a finger to her chin and turned her head so he could look directly into her eyes. "How little you know of us – of me. When a Celt promises a thing, you may depend upon it. No power save that of a God will prevent it from taking place." His look was kind and gentle and she blinked back up at him. In that moment, that single space between heartbeats, her eyes shot their arrows into his heart. He was falling in love with her. Now he was afraid she might be dying.

"I did not want you to stay because I was angry. You just make me so angry! What is wrong with a woman ruling? What makes you think one can not," she winced again. Athelstan frowned and groaned inwardly.

"Cannot what? Rule? I never said a woman could not rule. What I said was something to build a bond between Demetrios and myself where none existed. How little you understand men, Men of my world. In our culture, it is a common thing that a woman rules. Caileigh is a Druidess and her word is law even to my King. I am also beginning to discover there very little you cannot do either. If only you were not so… so bloody stubborn."

"What is a Drui…" Connie began. Thea, the innkeeper's wife, shouldered her way into the room.

"Out! Everyone out!" Even Demetrios retreated before her commanding tone. She sat beside as he. "Alright my dear let me have a look at that." Athelstan removed the bandage and to her credit, Thea showed no emotion.

She looked at Thea contritely. "I am sorry about the room. I will pay for the damage." Thea shushed her.

"Forget about the room for now. It is fine. We can worry about that later." Thea probed the wound and sniffed the bloody shirt.

"At least it is not poisoned. I need more room to work. Bring her downstairs," she commanded.

"Gently mind you – she is not a bag of beets you can just sling over a shoulder, you know."

Athelstan looked at Connie and slid an arm under her long slender legs. "I'm going to carry you now." He said softly. "We will get that cleaned up." Athelstan kept his massive paw pressed tightly against her side.

"Downstairs? No! I can not let anyone see me like this." Constantina's brow furrowed with concern.

Athelstan looked over his shoulder and saw Demetrios standing just outside the door.

"Commander Demetrios, if you would be so kind as to clear the common room. We do not need a crowd of the curious in our way." Demetrios nodded and disappeared.

"No one will see you as anything but the strong beautiful girl that you are. I did not realise I had upset you so much, Connie. It was not my intent."

He replaced his blood-soaked shirt back over her wound and listened as soldiers efficiently removed patrons from the Inn.

"Ready?" He gently lifted her into his arms. She groaned but quickly stifled it. He supposed she did not want to appear weak to him either. He was inwardly proud of her. She was one tough little girl.

Constantina looked at him sharply.

"If anyone sees me like this, I swear I will be an even worse Harpy than I was earlier," she said with a weak smile. His heart missed a beat.

"Worse?" he asked wearily. "That hardly seems possible," he said in mock gravity. She graced him with a thin smile. "What is a Harpy?"

The common room was empty and showed signs of having been hastily cleared. A lone cup still rolled along the floor leaving a trail of red wine behind. These Spartans were ruthlessly efficient. He followed Thea down the steps and turned towards the back rooms. He gently placed Connie onto a long table before Thea ordered him out.

"I'm staying," he announced flatly. He still held his shirt firmly over Connie's wound. "It is my fault she is laying here now; I will not leave her alone again."

She smiled weakly at the argument between the two. Thea placed her fists on her ample hips. "What are you going to do? What can you do with those chubby fat fingers of yours?" He looked at his fingers – they were not chubby.

"Get out," Thea insisted again.

He thought about it as the two women glared at him. "So we are back to that now?" He frowned unable to offer anything helpful. "I am still staying," he growled trying to look intimidating.

Constantina looked at Thea and sighed. "Be patient with him, he is a bit slow and very stubborn."

"Just tell me what to do. I am not slow!" he offered. Thea smiled and nodded kindly before pointing towards the door.

"I have something for you to do." Athelstan's face brightened for a moment before falling again. "Get out of here and let me do my work – and take those horrible dead men with you. I run a clean Inn." She handed him a mop. He sighed and looked down at Connie. He still held her hand.

"As you wish, Gentle Mother. I will be just outside – if you need me."

"He is getting better. I had to throw things at him to get him to leave the last time," Connie seemed reluctant to let his hand go. "Thank you for coming to my rescue Athelstan. I am glad you were there," he held her hand for a moment longer before gently laying it down.

He nodded and gave her a worried smile. His voice almost broke. "I will see you in a few minutes. You will be fine," he stroked her hair one last time before turning and ducking out.

The ladies looked at each other. "Men!" he heard them say in unison.

He immediately ran into a very concerned looking Demetrios.

"She is alright?" the Spartan asked tentatively.

"Fine. The cut is long but shallow and clean. We have both seen much worse in our day have we not?" Demetrios nodded gravely and the Celt wondered if he ever smiled. Since he was a Spartan, he suspected not. "I want to have a look at those Romans, Ptolemarch."

"I brought them to the stables… Romans?" Demetrio's eyes went wide as he realised what Athelstan had said. "They don't look like any Romans I have ever seen."

"My people are at war with Rome. Who else would launch such an attack on me? Who else knows I have come to Hellas? Who else would have a reason?" he asked.

"The families of the men you killed in Yithion?" He prompted. Athelstan ignored the probing comment. Undaunted Demetrios continued, "But you were not the one attacked, she was. You were not even in the room."

"No, but I should have been, had she not kicked me out. If that slip of a girl was the target, why send four men when one would do? No Demetrios, they were after me – do not be fooled. Rome has deep pockets and very long arms. I will need your men to guard the Inn tonight. I must speak with your new Queen as soon as it is possible."

"I am still not convinced these assassins were Roman," Demetrios muttered dubiously.

"Anything is possible as I am beginning to discover," the Celt admitted. With a last backward glance at the door to the back rooms, he followed the Spartan outside.

The bodies had been brought to the stables and dumped in the straw beside the carriages in the back. Mitzu and Athios watched from their supposed concealment in the loft above. Athelstan examined the dead men. Their clothing and weapons, everything they carried in fact, was of Greek manufacture. From their Xiphos to their sandals; everything had been made locally. Where were their Gladius, those short Roman swords? The men were an even bigger puzzle. They seemed to look like members of the Northern Hill Tribes. They were swarthy and tattooed like Goths. This didn't make any sense at all –, or did it? If Rome wanted to kill him here and still remain anonymous, captured Goths would be a perfect way of throwing off suspicion. Yet, Rome rarely used mercenaries. They were too unreliable. A leather pouch of coins was located. Demetrios poured a few into his palm and Athelstan growled like an animal at the sight of them.

"It would seem that you are correct after all General." Athelstan took one of the coins and peered at it in the dim light. His face darkened further as other, all too familiar images leered up at him from the surface of a Roman trireme warship. It was an image often used on Roman coins to convey their superior naval might. The other side bore the face of a tyrant, Papirius himself.

"Whoever they are, they have been paid in Roman silver."

Athelstan led Demetrios to the stall that housed Maehadren. A soft pat on the chargers rump caused a shiver of delight to ripple across his whitish–grey coat. He gathered up his horse's packs and opened one.

"You wanted to search me. Time to have a look." The Spartan barely glanced at the open packs then at Athelstan. Without so much as a glance inside, he handed them back to the Celt.

"I have seen all that I need to see General. I know a man of honour when I see one."

"So do I Ptolemarch, so do I!" The men exchanged a moment none but them could completely comprehend. A powerful friendship had just been forged. Neither man doubted it would be lifelong.

Later they returned still discussing the attack only to find Thea helping support Connie as they headed for the stairs.

"Well do not just stand there. Lend a hand for pity sake." Athelstan took Connie and lifted the nearly weightless girl into his arms. Demetrios brought up his packs. She wrapped her arms around his neck. Tired eyes blinked up at him. He headed up the stairs slowly. She winced at the pain but uttered no sound.

"Take her to the third room on the right," Thea instructed. He did as he was told and laid Connie carefully on the bed, then removed the remains of her bloody dress. She uttered a small protest at this treatment but he just wrapped her up in his white fur cloak and carefully tucked her in.

She watched past pain–shrouded eyes as he settled down on the wooden floor beside the bed.

"Oh Athelstan, do not sleep there. Use the bed." Even as she spoke these words sleep stole over her.

"I will be fine right here." An unintelligible murmur was his only answer.

"Who are you running from I wonder?" he asked the sleeping girl.

"Axum," she breathed. She was talking in her sleep. Athelstan had never seen such a thing before.

"Who is this Axum?

"My doom."

"He will not find you. I will not allow it."

"Axum eyes are everywhere," she whispered before falling into a deep sleep."

Athelstan found this statement profoundly disturbing. His honour stopped him from asking anything else of her. This journey had been hard for her. It was not fair to use her this way. He leaned back again to ponder what he had just learned. He reached out and opened the covers to examine her wound. He briefly chewed a long narrow leaf from his medicines and laid it on her cut before replacing the tight bandage. He covered her back up and took her tiny hand in his. He fell asleep wondering if this Axum person could actually find her here. If he did, it would not go well for him, Athelstan vowed silently. Not well at all.

Constantina awoke slowly and groaned at the tenderness in her side. She was naked under white furs and was unsure of where she was at first. She stretched and then turned to see the Celt slumped uncomfortably on the floor beside her bed. Her hand and wrist rested gently in one of his giant paws. His head wedged awkwardly between the thin straw-filled mattress pad and the wall. Memories of the previous night flooded back into her suddenly and she touched her bandaged side gingerly.

Carefully extracting her arm, she reached to brush his hair away from his face. As she touched him, she remembered how he helped her. "Athelstan," she said and leaned over to gently brush his forehead.

"Thank you." A contented groan greeted the soft caress but he did not stir. His head moved a bit before letting out a long sigh.

She stood stiffly and stepped up to the table to wash off the dirt, sweat, and blood. She probed her wound and winced again as she touched it. Gently peeling back the bandage to look at the cut, she was surprised to find a long green leaf pressed against the wound. She looked back at the sleeping man and smiled.

This was his doing. It was probably something to stop the pain. He was so gentle at heart it made him almost seem childlike to her. However, neither could she forget the speed and savage brutality of this man as he confronted her attackers the previous evening. A shiver ran up her spine. He was a big, lovable, positively ferocious animal. She rummaged through his belongings, curious at what sort of things he carried, then pulled one of his fine linen shirts over her head. It hung almost to her knees.

After a few minutes, his eyes opened slowly. He yawned, stretched and looked at the bed. She was gone! Panic gripped him and he sat straight up suddenly, quickly scanning the room with bleary eyes.

"Oh thank Epona," he breathed when he saw her standing by the window. He leapt to his feet and very nearly swept her up in a tight hug. An upraised hand stopped him.

"I was afraid you were gone. I mean, I did not expect to see you up so soon," he stepped back abashed. "How do you feel this morning?" He resisted bending to probe her wound. He learned from his mistakes.

She turned to him, "I am fine, a bit sore is all. How are you? Did you sleep well?"

"I am relieved if you must know. I honestly believed I was going to lose you last night," she looked down. His fiery intense gaze was disconcerting. Profound emotions warred within him. "I failed you yesterday. I am sorry," he said finally.

Connie reached up and touched his face. "You have saved my life – twice now. I was angry with you and my actions nearly got me killed. I will go get you some breakfast," he watched her walk to the door. His shirt was far too big for her slender body. His loins tightened watching her slender legs and the seductive sway of her hips when she walked.

"I will come with you," he offered.

"No," she said. "You wash up. I will get breakfast and bring it to you. It is the least I can do."

He nodded, knowing armed soldiers guarded the Inn.

"You look beautiful," he said honestly. He immediately regretted doing so.

She glanced over her shoulder and blushed at his words. "Get washed." Connie turned left the room.

He turned, stripped off his shirt and began to wash.

Humming softly, she made her way down the stairs. The tune was that of Athelstan's little ditty from a few days ago in the Orange orchard. Athelstan's shirt hung on her like a sheet.

"Good morning Thea," she called out cheerily seeing the innkeeper's wife.

"Good morning child, what are you doing out of bed? Here, sit down," she looked Connie over critically and grinned at the long voluminous shirt. The sleeves were rolled halfway up her arms and despite the amount of material; its simple cut did little to hide her body. "Are you hungry?" Thea asked smoothly in Latin.

"I thought I dreamed you could speak Latin. Yes, actually I am famished. It is amazing what a brush with death does for the appetite. However, I am here to get Athelstan something to break his fast. I owe him that small kindness after what I did to him and what in turn he did so selflessly for me. I am ashamed of myself for being such a... such a... I do not know what."

"He is an enigma is he not? Men often are. As for food, you first! You are the one in need of hearty food. You were wounded after all. He can survive for a few more minutes on his stored up fat!" Thea giggled like a young girl and winked at Connie conspiratorially. From what either could see, he was far from fat.

"I think we can find something more suitable for you to wear than one of his shirts too. Let me fix you some plates while you have a look through some of my old dresses; you know when I was less round," she giggled again.

She led Connie to the back and opened a deep chest. "Have your pick, I will not be passing any of these down to my sons now will I?"

Connie giggled. "Let's hope not."

Thea went back to her cooking and Connie began to rummage. She found a lovely blue dress that she felt would look good on her and idly wondered if Athelstan would like it. She caught herself. Why did she wonder that? She should not care what Athelstan thought. She must not care, but she did care. Why did she care? Her people and his were at war if he could be believed.

Her people. She suddenly realised, she had no people. She had no one at all. Her father was dead. Her uncle was a monster and revelled in having his way with her at night. Was it Roman soldiers who attacked her last night trying to bring her back as a runaway slave? Was it the monsters that kidnapped her trying to recover their merchandise? Was it... them?

She shuddered at the thought of them and went cold. She remembered those men with the dark skin and the jet–black hair and eyes; the ones who showed no mercy to her father when he was killed. Killed slowly. Killed in front of her. She remembered his eyes when her father's as he died screaming. She never knew where these animals came from. Tears were running down her cheeks at the memory. Her appetite abandoned her. Thea returned with a plate of baked eggs and warm bread.

"What child?" Thea asked. "Has he done something to upset you again?"

Connie shook her head, buried her face in Thea's shoulder and cried.

"There, there. You just let it all come out. Everything will work out. You will see." She stroked Connie's hair and let her cry.

Minutes ticked by and a pacing Athelstan resisted running down to check on her, but since there was no hew and cry of danger or disaster, he waited – albeit uncomfortably. Why was he feeling like this? She was so incredibly pretty, so perfectly innocent and so obviously vulnerable but he could not shake the fact that she still was just a little girl. He felt his heart race at the thought of her. He had no business thinking about her that way. He had no business thinking about her at all, but he found he could concentrate on nothing else. She was a thief, a proficient knife–fighter and who knows what else. Who was this girl?

The door opened and he let out a silent breath. Then it caught in his throat. Connie stepped in just as the sunlight entered the room. It bathed her in a golden light and in the blue dress; she was stunning. It was as if the Gods ordered the sun to shine only upon her. He very nearly fell down. Her eyes were rimmed red with melancholy. Somehow, it made her all the more lovely.

She bore a tray in both hands and his shirt was draped over one arm. He must have just stood and stared at her open-mouthed until she looked down shyly.

He looked at the tray and blinked. "Oh, I did not mean to... It smells good."

"Tell that to Thea, she cooked it not me."

He shook his head amazed. What a staggering transformation from the grubby waif he had met just three days ago. He set the tray down, sat and took a bite of warmed cheese. He could not take his eyes off her.

"Please stop looking at me like that," she said seeing his stare and turned away to straighten the bed.

"Like what?" He continued to eat.

Connie seemed flustered; he could tell by the self–conscious way she walked and held her arms and tossed her full head of curls. His gaze was piercing and intense. He did not so much look at you as he looked into you – through you. He looked into your heart and soul. It was unsettling to some. An impish grin tugged at his moustaches.

"You are very pretty in that dress. Did you put that on for me?" he teased.

Even with her back to him, he could feel her blush.

"No," she lied very badly.

A playful grin tugged at the corners of his mouth.

"Of course you did. You wanted me to see how pretty you really are. and you are – very pretty."

"I did not." She shook her head realizing she kept repeating that phrase as if it would become more truthful with repetition. It did not.

"I am not pretty. Stop saying that," She redoubled her efforts at smoothing out the blankets and spent some time fluffing the pillow but said nothing more. She did not turn around but she could still feel his eyes on her.

"I see, very well, he said between bites. "I just wanted you to know that. Connie, all my life I have studied people. I watch what they do and why they do it. I know what drives one man to greatness and another to despair. I know what drives one woman to love and another to hate. Instinct, primal animal instinct is what drives us all, you, me – everyone. I am a man and when I look at you, I see a very attractive young lady. I hope when I look at you, I make you feel like a very attractive young lady, why? Because that is just what you are."

"Oh really?" she countered smoothly.

"Yes, really."

"You are being foolish. I picked this dress because it was the first one Thea showed me. Do not flatter yourself barbarian. Get dressed we have to get riding soon." In a huff, she stalked towards the door. She had to get out of this room.

He moved to intercept her and caught her arm. His look captured hers.

"Connie, thank you for the breakfast."

His thumb brushed her cheek and he released her.

Connie sighed softly. Her eyes fluttered closed and then opened. Suddenly, she slapped his face hard. "You take dangerous liberties, sir."

A slow smile crossed his face. "Of course I take dangerous liberties. I am a dangerous man. I am a Mongrel remember? I do like that dress; especially from this angle," he commented at her retreating back. A smile curled his moustache when she stiffened at his obvious comment about her backside. The door closed. What was the matter with him, she was a child!

Chapter Fifteen

Connie left the inn and stepped into the sunshine. The air smelled fresh and clean. She nodded briefly at the four guards lounging by the front door. Every step she took hurt. When she reached the stables, she kept clear of Maehadren, but the great warhorse whinnied a joyous greeting at her. She needed a horse – any horse. She sat on a bale of straw to rest and to scribble a hasty note to Thea. She supposed she should leave Athelstan one as well and needed someone to give it to. Thank goodness for the boys.

"Salve (Hello,)" she said in Latin to the stable boys when they appeared suddenly.

"Hey Athios, look, it is Connie!" Mitsu said in Greek. He immediately began to speak Latin, but with a thick accent.

"You look different. Hey, why are you wearing that dress?" Mitzu skidded to a stop in front of her. "Wait!" he exclaimed wide-eyed. "Up close, you are a girl!"

Connie smiled. "I am a girl far away too. Can you forgive me for my deception?"

"Yea, I guess we can." The younger boy admitted dubiously. "Why were you pretending to be a boy? We heard there was a fight and you got wounded. Can we see it?"

Connie smiled again. "That is a lot of questions. Yes, there was a fight and yes, I was wounded and yes, you can see it if you like. It is pretty gruesome, are you sure you want to see it?" Mitzu nodded they did. She looked around conspiratorially. "First you must promise me that you cannot tell anyone I dressed like boy especially those soldiers."

"Alright, we promise. Hey Athios, come here. She is going to show her sword wound." When she was sure no one was around, she lifted the side of her dress and pulled up the bandage showing the long jagged cut on her side. Mitzu let out a low whistle and it was clear he was impressed. "Does it hurt?"

Connie smiled at their reaction. "Yes, it hurts, bad. It almost killed me. If it were not for Athelstan and your mother, I would have died."

"Wow! Really? You almost died?" Connie nodded.

"What is that leaf under there anyway?"

"The leaf is to keep it from hurting as much."

His eyes were wide in wonder and he touched the edge of the leaf. "That stuff grows all over the place here. We have to dig it out of Mothers garden all the time."

"Sooo," began Mitzu conspiratorially. He glanced around making sure they were alone. "You want to see the dead guys?"

"Dead guys? Yes," she said before she could think. The question caught her off guard.

Mitzu took her hand and led her to the back of the stables and with a flourish; he pulled back an oiled sailcloth to reveal the four 'dead guys'. One had a ghastly wound across his neck; a second was missing his left eye. A third had blood on the front his tunic and the fourth had no wounds at all but his head was looking the wrong way. Their skin was blackening and flies buzzed and crawled around all the bloody surfaces.

Connie shook as she stared at them. These were the men who nearly took her life, twice over. There were markings on their hands that she recognized; a stylized black rose. It was the markings of the enemy. She had to get home; now more than ever.

"Cover them up," she said. "I do not think your parents would like you seeing this."

"Ma said she would give us a good thrashing if we did, but I thought it was alright to show you."

"Where are you from anyway? We only see ordinary people here."

"Ordinary people?" Connie chuckled. "I am Roman and you two are so sweet," she tousled his hair.

She took the boys by the hands and led them away from the dead men.

"Now if you can help me. I need a horse, a fast and sturdy one."

An all too familiar voice rang out. "Maehadren, trobhad (come here). The Lady needs a fast horse." Athelstan casually leaned on a stall door.

Connie stiffened at the voice. She had not expected it. Swallowing, she looked down at the boys.

"Your mother needs you. You go help her and I will keep up my end of our deal," she said with a wink and nod. "It was nice to meet you both. Now off with you."

Maehadren backed out. The horse's hooves boomed on the wooden planks of the stable floor.

"Going somewhere little Princess? I thought we were getting along so well. This is quite a note you wrote," he said waving it idly. There was absolutely no amusement in his tone. "Did you really think I would just let you ride off –, or that those soldiers would let you just – ride off?" Two Spartans stood at the stable entrance at attention. "I swear that bump you took on the head must have been worse than I thought." His frown was one of concern, not anger.

Connie sighed and her expression became steadfast and determined. "I knew you would not let me 'just ride off', which is why I had no intention of telling you. As for the soldiers, they have no reason to detain me," she said walking past him.

He glanced over his shoulder and spoke softly so only Connie could hear. "Oh, I do not know – thievery - murder? For Epona's sake, do you think I just fell off a turnip wagon? I am trying to keep you from doing something that will get you killed and all you can think of is running away. When will you get it through that thick stubborn head of yours that I am on your side? Epona give me breath, I care about what happens to you." He let out an exasperated sigh. "Or did last night not teach you anything?"

She stood in front of him, hands folded in her lap. "Of course it did. You saved my life, which is why I am leaving you. It is the only way I can repay you. If I stay with you, you will be killed as surely as you stand there. Besides, I have never murdered anyone and never pretended to be anything but what I am. I have never told you I was a Princess. Why do you think I am?" she peered at him.

"Last night. How did you put it? Oh yes, 'henceforth you will address me as Highness', but, if you are a real Highness then where is your Royal Guard and personal entourage? I do not see anyone." he glanced around the empty stable. "Anywhere."

"So, I am forced to wonder; why does a visiting dignitary from Rome need to dress like a peasant boy in order to steal food? Especially when you have coins in your purse? I can only assume that you are not the person you pretend to be. I am also forced to believe that you stole those figs and the coin purse in the marketplace because that is what you do. So, if you want to pretend that you are someone you are not, fine. Just know that I have no interest in your childish little world of make-believe. I can tell you, however, that you are playing a very dangerous game indeed in this land if you persist with this fantasy. My bet is you have stolen something very valuable from either someone like Papirius person or whoever this Axum fellow is and he wants it back. Small wonder too. I want to believe you but you have to tell me the truth. Either way, you are not riding out of here without protection – and that is final."

She stiffened when she heard the name, Papirius. "You fancy you are a smart man Captain?"

"Fancy yourself smarter, my Little Roman Princess? Then for Epona's sake tell me the truth."

She smiled. "I am nothing but a simple slave girl only capable of pleasing the lusts of stupid men," she snapped. "That is why I was pretending to be a boy. I wanted to keep my virtue intact because I have already been used by a man who thinks I am a thief and a traitor."

Connie turned away from him and went to the stall with the horse she had chosen. "This discussion is over. I am leaving and that is final and nothing you can say will change my mind," Connie said opening the stall.

"So now your answer is to leave here on a stolen horse? Would you like me to tell you what Spartans do to horse thieves?" He put his hand on the stall door and looked at her. "You simply cannot leave alone Constantina. You know it is not safe. Why are you doing this? I know you do not want to die – last night taught me that at least. Honestly, I do not care what you are, or what kind of trouble you are in. Just tell me what is going on. I can help you if you would only trust me. But trust does not come easily to you does it?" His voice was stern but it still held a real hint of sadness.

"Why should I trust someone who thinks so ill of me? Who thinks everything out my mouth is a lie? Who thinks he knows so much when he knows nothing? You are right. I have something someone wants. Axum wants me dead. Did it not occur to you that I am leaving to save all of you? And what makes you think Thea has not given me this horse?" she said glaring at him. "What makes you think the concubine has not worked off the money for this horse from one of the many Spartan soldiers who look at me with lust in their eyes. We have been separated for a time. How long do you think it takes for a girl to earn the price of a horse?" she said pushing past him. "And what makes you think I have not gotten the money that is due to me for killing those men who attack me? It matters not. I am leaving and I will walk if I have to," she said.

"I do not think ill of you. I could never think ill of you," he said in a rush. He meant it. He looked at her for a long time without speaking. Then he nodded slowly. "But neither will I stand here and be lied to by someone who does it so badly. Thea does not own a horse. I asked her if I could buy one for you. I have the Roman money from the dead assassins that tried to kill ME. Spartan soldiers prefer boys not girls and you just lied again about being a slave girl and concubine so pardon me little Princess if I have over-stepped my bounds. By the Gods, you have no idea how lucky you are wounded lest I take you across my knee."

"I am not a 'little Princess I am a grown woman!" she barked. "So save it!" she could feel something in her chest constricting... something that made her want to stay with him.

He closed the stall door. With a determined stride, he walked into Maehadrens' stall. He heaved his heavy packs over the horse's rump and secured them. "Fine, but until you give me the truth, you can face this chilling reality. I will keep you safe and you will do as you are told. So mount up Princess, we must not keep our Spartan brethren waiting. I will meet you outside," he finished with a snort.

She looked at him with fury in her eyes. She huffed and then climbed aboard Maehadren and rode out to join the Spartans.

In the quiet of the stables, Athelstan stood and poked around. "Something I can do for you – innkeeper - if that is what you are?"

"How did you know I was here?" said a voice from one of the empty stalls.

"You smell," replied Athelstan. "You were responsible for the attack last night. To leave you dogging my steps beyond here would be folly indeed. Would you not agree?"

The older man appeared carrying a short sword. "I would. But, you will not be travelling beyond here. Better men than you now lay mouldering in their graves for testing me and suspecting far less than you know. I see you do not carry a blade barbarian. How… unfortunate." Athelstan stood perfectly still and said nothing.

126

"I do not think you will be joining Demetrios this day…, or any other day barbarian. Your path ends here." He advanced cautiously and Athelstan's eyes narrowed slightly. His sword was held high. This man knew his business.

"You killed the innkeeper."

"I do not respond to speculation from the dead." The killer swung his sword in a murderous stroke. Athelstan ducked and where once there was a Celtic head, the sword found nothing but air. In that same instant, Athelstan charged unarmed and caught the Greek entirely by surprise. He drove his head into the killer's midsection. The air rushed from the killer's lungs. Over-balanced, he scrambled to keep his feet. The sword was sent spinning away and landed in the straw of one of the stalls.

Now, inside the killer's guard, Athelstan wrapped his arms around the Greek and began to squeeze. He bent the man backwards and the killer tried to squirm free while punching Athelstan in the head. Their faces were inches apart and Athelstan growled menacingly. He could smell the killer's breath and it stank of fish.

Slowly the man's ability to breathe diminished as the Celt applied more and more pressure. There were audible cracking sounds as ribs broke one by one. The Greeks' face turned a bright red, then purple, slowly deepening to black. His arms slid down to his sides and his eyes rolled back in their sockets. Blood welled up and trickled past the Greek's lips. Slowly, relentlessly, life left the man's body and after a few moments more, Athelstan let the body slump to the ground. He searched the body then dragged the lifeless man over to the pile of dead men at the back of the stables and tossed him on top.

He found a purse filled with silver and one gold drachma. They bore the likeness of a Pegasus on one side and a helmeted head with curls on the reverse. These were Greek coins, not Roman. When he discovered the source of these coins, he would have some more answers concerning who was hunting him. A small noise from above caused him to blink.

"I knew last night he was not your father, boys," he stated turning around looking up. Mitzu and Athios watched from their perch above.

"How did you know?" they asked.

"You told me. Your look, when I mentioned your father, was not one of pride it was one of fear and loathing. He killed your father?"

"Yes," answered Athios.

"He came with the Spartan soldiers?"

"No. He came before."

"Before? Odd, I was certain that… never mind then. The death of your father is avenged. Take care of your mother, she will need you both, now, more than ever." They nodded.

"I go now and I will probably not return. Remember this day and remember my story. Live your life with honour like your father would have wanted you to. Make him proud and you will make me proud as well."

"We will – General," Mitzu said formally.

"Epona be with you both, now and always." He joined the Spartan troupe outside and noted the astonished but clearly pleased expression on Demetrio's face.

"Any trouble Athelstan?" Demetrios looked into the dark stable.

"None at all," he stated casually. "Why do you ask?"

"Oh, no reason. The blood on your jerkin and cheek perhaps," he said with a sly wink and a grim smile.

"Oh that. It is nothing. Nothing at all." The Spartan took one last look at the stable.

"Shall we be off then?"

He mounted Maehadren behind a glowering Connie. "Lead on sir."

Chapter Sixteen

The Spartan Queen craned her neck looking for any signs of the Carthaginians. These would be the first of the allies to join her and she was sure that Bomilcar would have things in good order.

It had taken some time for the army to exit Sparta. Glancing back over the heads of her men. The players had placed their wagers and now, all that remained was war. Talk was over.

Beside her rode Queen Kratesipolis of Corinth, radiating confidence atop her bay horse. Leonida hoped she also looked the part.

"My Queen!" Two heads turned in his direction. A red-faced Spartan captain wove his way between the mounts and trotted alongside her. It was hardly dignified, but the man would not have dared disturb her if his message were not urgent. Perhaps word had come from Bomilcar at last?

"Yes, Captain," Leonida acknowledged.

"My apologies, I have come from the city," he explained. "A barbarian ambassador has arrived, seeking an audience with you…"

"What sort of barbarian?" Leonida asked.

The Captain shrugged, no mean feat whilst trotting alongside wearing armour. "I don't know," he admitted. "They all look the same - Long haired, scruffy looking. His words are odd to listen to. He says his name is 'Apple-stand' or something. He says he is a Senone, whatever that is. He looks like a Gaul." There was a sneer on his face. Clearly, he did not believe such a creature was worthy of his Queen's notice.

"Apple-stand? That is an odd name, but then Gauls are an odd people I am told. You've made sure his retinue is comfortable within my sphere of influence?"

"That's just it Majesty, he doesn't have a retinue, he's on his own and travels with but a single slave. He sleeps on the ground like an animal." The Captain paused. "I didn't want to interrupt the march for one man and his slave…"

"You have acted correctly, Captain, I cannot hold up the march. This Athelstan may follow on and meet us all in good time. Please convey my apologies– but we are at war. I will receive him in the White City."

"He has also made a request."

"A request? What kind of request?"

"Suitable clothing for his attendant to wear during their audience with you." Both Queens exchanged unreadable glances.

Kratesipolis smiled. "He seeks to make a good impression. That is unusual from what I know of them. Suddenly, I am anxious to see this 'Gaul'. Speak to my servants in the palace and have them select something," she issued an amused chuckle, "suitable." The Captain stopped, saluted and sped off towards the city.

"Senone?" Kratesipolis mused and arched a perfect eyebrow. "I have heard of these creatures. In truth, I have never seen a Gaul before. I wonder what they're like," her eyes grew distant.

"More to the point, what does he want?" Leonida resisted the urge to glance back again.

"What does any man want?' she cast a lecherous look at her friend who blushed at the thought.

"Probably a mercenary of some kind," Kratesipolis forecasted. "War attracts them, you know. In the end, let a Ptolemarch deal with him. These Senones once marched with Alexander. If he is a delegate from Cassander, he could be an enemy. He should be disarmed in our presence." Leonida nodded but said nothing.

†

"Your people have failed me Gudron - again. I ask so little of you. Bring me 'The Other', I say, but, I see her not. She and her animal creature have defeated you again. Even vith their disguises your, 'trusted operatives' failed. Vhy do I put my faith in you Greeks?" A skeletal hand waved absently in the air. Its effect was like a physical blow to the prostrate man. The man shivered in terror. He had been told not to utter a sound or even to look up, but he felt if he did not say something, his death would be upon him. He opened his arms in supplication and began.

"Exalted One, in any campaign a simple foray to gauge the strength... of... the enemy is necess..." He looked up but the hooded figure was already gone. With a sigh, he began to rise. The spear sliced through the back of his neck and out his throat with sudden ferocity. His death was not swift.

†

It had taken four days ride from the Inn to catch up with Sparta's military. In all that time, Constantina had not spoken a single word to him. He slept on the ground near her. When the Rear Guard of the Spartan army came into view, it was impressive. Ten armies arrayed in orderly camps southwest of the brilliant white walls of Corinth. True to his word, the Spartan captain returned and delivered Leonida's missive. He also brought clothing befitting a Corinthian lady for Connie. Having always worn a simple cotton sleeveless toga, she had little reference for some of the items delivered. Still, with some time and patience, she managed to don each item correctly. Athelstan pressed another of the copper disks into the palm of the captain and thanked him for his generosity and courtesy. Ptolemarch Demetrios was clearly taken aback by the barbarian's manners and civility and so it was that Athelstan and Connie remounted Maehadren and were escorted into the city of Corinth.

To the Spartans, they were a fresh curiosity and news of their arrival travelled quickly through the ranks. Corinth was clean if a bit crowded. Demetrios and his select band of twenty led the pair through the streets to a gleaming white marble palace. A groom dashed up to take the reins of Maehadren from Athelstan but the great beast cast a wild eye on him. The Celt held up his hand and as fortune would have it, the groom skidded to a stop just outside the horse's kill zone. "I fear good sir, that my animal will not tolerate being handled by another. If you would direct me to the tether lines I will take care of him myself. The groom simply retreated several steps and pointed."

After seeing to his horse, Athelstan allowed himself to be escorted by a troop of Royal guards into the presence of the Spartan Queen. Athelstan, with some grumbling, was disarmed as they entered. He surrendered each of his knives and his long sword with a snarl that spoke volumes concerning what would happen if even a single scratch were to mar their finely polished surfaces. Connie was also searched.

"Be careful," Athelstan whispered in Latin to her as they strode in. "We cannot tell yet what kind of reception we will get here."

They came to a stop before grand, lavishly carved double doors, depicting the Pegasus inlaid in gold and mother of pearl. A page struck the doors with a sceptre and they were opened from the inside.

"Lord Athelstan of Senone and companion," the page announced. Athelstansqueezed Connie's shoulder and began to walk forward. The room was filled with Corinthian and Spartan nobles, government officials, servants, soldiers, and slaves. All eyes fell on this odd pair as they entered. They approached a wide dais.

Sprawling on long divans were a young woman and several older men. The younger woman stood and the pair came to a stop. Athelstan descended onto his knee. "Your Majesty."

"Greetings Lord, um, Apple...?"

"Athelstan, your Majesty."

"Lord Athelstan. Please accept our apologies for mispronouncing your name."

The Celt stood. "No apologies are necessary. Many Greek names do not roll off my tongue as easily as mine rolled off yours."

"You are very gracious Lord Athelstan, I am Queen Leonida of Sparta. Welcome to Hellas." It was a sweet voice but one used to command.

"Thank you, Majesty. It is my pleasure to present..." Connie interrupted him with a dismissive wave of her hand and began to speak.

"Thank you, Captain, that will be all." She began in Latin. "Your Majesty, it is a pleasure to meet you. I am Constantina Aurelius of Rome."

A collective gasp echoed through the room. Leonida looked at her aides in puzzlement

Athelstan did not flinch but he sure wanted to. Queen Leonida's eyes widened in surprise. "What?" she exclaimed. "Aurelius as in Papirius Aurelius?"

"The same."

"Is he not the Proconsul?"

"He is. I was kidnapped and brought here. I have been on my own until I met the Captain here."

"So then Papirius is your father?"

Athelstan interjected, "I believe he is her... Master," he said.

"Husband actually," she contradicted smoothly and without even a sideways glance.

'Husband?' Athelstan stiffened noticeably. Even as he inwardly winced at the term Captain, his mind tried to process this sudden turn of events.

"I see, so Lord Athelstan is your..."

"He is my cap..." Connie started.

It was Athelstan's turn to interrupt.

"I am her cap..." he stopped and looked at her with a hard expression.

"Captain?" Leonida helped with upswept brows.

"Cap - tor your Majesty. I am her captor. The sovereign nation of Senone and the Republic of Rome are at war. She is my prisoner..."

Now it was Constantina's turn to stiffen and look at Athelstan with horror.

"Prisoner?" she gasped.

He glared down at her. "Prisoner of War. Yes!" Her mouth dropped open in shock.

He found Leonida's dark eyes upon him and almost squirmed under their steady gaze.

"Is this true Captain Athelstan?" she asked.

"First General actually and yes it is, your Majesty. Had it not been for Ptolemarch Demetrio's swift intervention some days ago all would surely have been lost. My prisoner would be dead and my bargaining position with Papirius - gone. Now I have the leverage to strike a deal with Rome. She is the pawn I shall use to achieve that end." He bowed and knew only Constantina would hear the sarcasm. "Demetrios alone helped defeat those assassins that would have robbed me of my prize. I owe him a great debt of gratitude. It is a debt I will not easily repay."

"Truly?"

"We are alive today because of this man's bravery." He pointed at Demetrios.s

"Ptolemarch Demetrios. Come forward," Queen Leonida commanded. He did so sharply and stopped shoulder to shoulder with Athelstan.

"Your Queen thanks you for your bravery and upholding our laws as they pertain to visiting dignitaries. Your devotion to the protection of our honoured ambassador needs to be rewarded. I elevate you to the rank of General of the Expeditionary Armed forces of Sparta. Kneel!"

He did so. An aide handed the Queen a scarlet sash and she placed it over his head across one shoulder.

Demetrios looked a bit stunned as he rose and resumed his place. He glanced at Athelstan but the Celt might have been carved out of stone. He betrayed no expression at all.

"Prepare rooms for Lord Athelstan and conduct his prisoner to the dungeons." Two guards took Constantina by the arms and began to march her towards a side door. She looked over her shoulder with naked fear spread over her face like a brand.

"If I might ask a favour of your Majesty."

"Surely, name it General."

"I would prefer if my prisoner remained in full view of me at all times. Once jailed, one never knows who might be bribed to open a lock or a door, is that not so.

Constantina seemed surprised by this. Leonida nodded, "Corinth conceals many hazards Lord Athelstan – it is true. I would urge you to reconsider. Even a small child can wield a sharp blade when the need is upon them." A slight shake of his head was her only answer. "Very well sir. We shall leave her in your custody. Accommodations will be found for you both at once. Will you need slaves and hand-maidens to attend you?" Leonida asked Athelstan.

Athelstan smiled and took the Spartans Queen's hand. "Just one to help her bathe and dress, good food and a comfortable bed to lay her head upon. She might be my prisoner but she is also a lady of rank. I would ask that she be treated as such."

Leonida barely gestured and two guards released a badly shaken Constantina.

"I think there are still proper apartments in the west wing of the palace. Arrange for food and drink. See to our new Ambassador and his prisoner's needs. By your lives," commanded Leonida. The two men saluted and said nothing. Both sharply turned and came to attention. Blank expressions covered their faces. "We shall dine at sundown." Leonida continued. "It would please us if you both could attend the feast."

Constantina stared in shock and disbelief. Athelstan inclined his head. "We would be honoured to do so Queen Leonida. I am humbled and wish to extend equal kindness if you ever find yourself in my homeland. Will the Corinthian Queen Kratesipolis be in attendance as well?"

A sharp look from Leonida said much about the two monarchs relationship. "She will." With that, Athelstan bent kissed the woman's hand and stepped down from the dais.

"That is good. I can now keep my promise to Admiral Piros. Until this evening."

Athelstan bowed one last time to the Spartan Queen and fell into step behind the guards. He propelled Constantina before him like he would drive cattle. General Demetrios remained behind and quietly spoke to his Queen.

Athelstan retrieved his weapons after the double doors closed. They were then escorted to the west wing.

The two guards bowed as they closed the doors to the suites they had been given in this massive temple. Athelstan stood fairly trembling with fury and he leaned his back against the doors.

"Captain! Captain!" he asked. There was a deadly quiet in his voice. "Have you any idea at all what you are doing – what you almost did?"

"Prisoner, am I? I see," she said sitting down on the bed.

"Wife, also, it would seem."

"Guards," she called. "Can you please show the Captain to his quarters?" They looked at each other with confusion.

"Ah, these are his quarters," one stammered.

"I am not leaving and neither are you. So settle in, you are here to stay. Thank you," he said to the guards, "That will be all," The two guards very nearly fled.

"What am I going to do with you?" he asked and suddenly his anger was gone. He began to examine the complete absurdity of his situation and the humour of it overwhelmed him. He began to laugh.

"I was actually beginning to…"

"Believe me? That's a laugh."

"No never that. Your story is getting more outlandish as we go. So, now you are his wife? What's next? Perhaps you are soon to become his mother and suckle him at your breast?"

She slapped him hard.

"I was beginning to like you," he said." Little danger of that now, thank Epona."

He shook his head and spread his arms in mock surrender. He was beaten and he knew it; all that was left was laughter.

Constantina was not at all amused and found nothing funny in any of this.

"That Queen actually thinks our people are at war with each other. What happens when she discovers the truth?"

"Our peoples ARE at war, you stupid little girl. If you paid more attention the conversations swirling around you and less to the state of your fingernails, you would know it. This is no game! You just met one of the most powerful women on earth, and you spoke to her like she was your handmaiden." He was furious.

"I am NOT stupid!"

"How can you Tell?"

She screamed in outrage and launched herself at him with a withering assault of fists. He withstood the onslaught stoically until he felt her tiring and then grabbed her by the waist. She continued to beat him but her strength was waning. She finally shook free of his grasp and stormed towards the door. He caught her arm.

"Neither one of us will be leaving this room. Do not make me tie you up!" She said nothing and just looked into his eyes. He gazed back just as intently.

"Do you remember what happened the last time you tried this? Be mad if you want, but I will not make the mistake again of denying what it is we are feeling. So, answer me truthfully. Are you married to Papirius?"

"Yes!"

"He does not love you and you do not love him." It was not a question.

"No," she whispered. Tears trickled down her cheeks.

"Will you continue to fight me?"

"Yes always. No aspect of your life is going to be safe from me. We are enemies remember?"

Athelstan smiled. "Good. I think I would be wildly disappointed if you did not."

"Will you abandon me when it suits you?" she asked

"No. I am a man of honour. Would you go back to him if given that chance?"

"Never. He had my family killed."

"I am sorry."

"So am I." Neither spoke for a few moments.

"He is your enemy too."

"Yes." He stared at her for several moments and nodded once. A long silence followed.

"Twenty–one winters," she blurted out.

"What?"

"I have seen twenty–one winters not fifteen."

"I believe you." She said nothing more, took his hand and led him to the bed. He simply sat with her until she dozed. Sunset glowed on the horizon and she was fast asleep when finally he departed.

Chapter Seventeen

It was fully dark when Athelstan arrived at the banquet hall. He wore his best clothes and left his armour and weapons in his room. A page formally announced his arrival.

"Captain Athelstan…"

Athelstan touched his shoulder and the Page paused. "If you please, that is General Athelstan." The man nodded without expression.

"General Athelstan, Lord of the Senone Gauls of Milan Italia!"

"My dear Ambassador! Leonida greeted him as he strode into the banquet hall. "Come sit. Where is your captive? I had hoped to talk with her tonight." Leonida looked past him half expecting the Roman to make an entrance.

Athelstan bowed low before her and tried to compose himself as he did. He had noted Leonida's beauty during their first meeting, but there, she was a soldier in her bright bronze armour. Now, in an azure gown spun with gold and lapis lazuli jewellery, she was transformed into a lovely young woman. There is a big difference between being told about cold water and actually being plunged into it. No matter how complete the warning, the shock can still be intense. It was such with Leonida. Demetrios had told him about her beauty but seeing her in person was something else again. He reclined in the indicated divan and locked eyes with hers. He was silent for a moment and drew a slow deep breath to settle his hammering heart.

In his soft baritone voice, he spoke. "Majesty! To Queen Leonida 1 of Sparta, I bring greetings and best wishes from Trahearn–Livy, King of the Senone Tribe of Italia. He deeply regrets not being able to come personally but the dogs of Rome nip at his heels and he is busy scratching at their fleas." Although the language he spoke was Greek, his phrasing was odd to the ear and some effort was needed to decipher his meaning. Celts tended to speak in metaphors and rhyme among themselves, or during formal situations like this.

"It pleases me to hear your King's gracious words and we welcome you Lord Athelstan in his place. Please sit and be at your ease. You may address me as Leonida, I never liked Majesty," she smiled sweetly. "Is Constantina Aurelius not joining us tonight?"

"I am honoured Leonida. Sadly no, Constantina sends her regrets, but her journey to get this far has been perilous and she begs your forgiveness and has taken to her bed," he sat and looked at the Royal Corinthian court. All eyes were on the oddly dressed Celt.

"If it pleases your Maj… er Leonida, I would like to correct a small matter concerning my title. I am Athelstan, First General of the Senone army. At my command stands the ten-fold ten–thousand. It is more often referred to as the Multitude!" It was a simple statement of fact that took many listening by surprise. Surely, he had used the wrong words to describe the famous Celtic army. Athelstan took note of the reaction.

"Yes, I know, General Demetrios corrected that mistake with us earlier. I would beg your pardon General, your phrasing is strange to our ears. You speak of the ten-fold ten–thousand. Is that the name given to your army, or is it a measure of actual numbers?

"It is an actual tally of soldiers. I do not know the Greek for this number."

"One hundred–thousand?"

Athelstan nodded. "Just so." Leonida sat back with an inaudible gasp.

"I command the largest army on earth next to Persia. General Demetrios informs me you are at war with Macedonia and good fortune, it would seem, has brought me here in a most timely manner. I bring an offer of a continued alliance between our two peoples, such as existed with the Great Alexander of Macedonia and your late father, King Eudamidas 1 of Sparta. Might I now offer you the sympathies of King Livy Trahearn and all of the Senone for your recent loss." Leonida inclined her head at this honorific. Athelstan paused and scanned the people in the room. He laid his pale blue eyes on them, they returned his gaze calmly and with great pride. These were people the Senones could fight with.

"It may interest you to know, that as we speak the Multitude along with that many again women and children close on Macedonia from the northwest." At this, several jaws dropped and at once all eyes went to Leonida. To her great credit, she regarded Athelstan passively and betrayed nothing of her thoughts. She let him continue.

"It is my understanding that you and several Helenic city-states wish to join together to form a Hellenic nation. It is an admirable idea, even if Macedonia disapproves. If you command it, we shall be the Anvil to your Hammer. We have no love for King Cassander and his new policies. Too often, of late, we have had to urge them back to their own lands. Illyria, sadly, is no more. They chose to block our way through their lands. We swept them from existence. Pella sits a short march from our lances and chariots. At a word from you, we shall turn it to dust as well. We shall leave no stone there but those placed there by the will of the Gods. In return, we ask for ten Spartan military advisors and strategists to aid us. Rome has taken our homeland. I mean to take it back." He lounged uncomfortably before the Spartan Queen. "My pledge of friendship and alliance lays before you, how say you, Leonida–Queen of Sparta?" he said no more.

Athelstan drew another long, slow, breath in an effort to bring his hammering heart under control. He was not a nervous man, but this was the first time he had dabbled in politics and he wondered if his simple words would be sufficient.

Leonida started at the words of the barbarian and did her best not to let it show. She wished once again that she had the poise and savvy of Kratesipolis – she would never have allowed her thoughts to be so transparent. It was not easy, given that the strange, lyrical way that the Celt phrased his Hellenic was somehow disarming.

The truth of the matter was clear in her mind. If Athelstan was true to his word – and she had no reason to believe he was not – then the war was won. She felt sudden warmth in her heart; Sparta – little Sparta faded from the world stage – was suddenly thrust into a position that would bring the greatest power in the world to its knees. She would be insane not to take this opportunity.

"I thank you and your King Trahearn for your kind words. This," she said, "is a most generous proposal…" She opened her mouth to speak again, but as she did so, the entrance doors to the hall swung open with fanfare and a raven-haired beauty stepped in – glided in would be apter in this case. Leonida looked a bit sour at the interruption. Her surliness was melted, however as the newcomer threw her a surreptitious wink.

She was wearing Corinthian armour clearly designed to accentuate her narrow waist and ample breasts, yet no dust and grime coated her; indeed, she bore with her the smell of crushed rose petals. Athelstan stood as she swept up to the tables and watched Leonida's expression as this newcomer arrived. There was more to this relationship than met the eye.

The newcomer made murmuring sounds, not unlike a cat and circled the barbarian, her fingers lightly trailing across his chest as she passed. His whole body stiffened involuntarily. "A Gaul," she said. "We are honoured, General did I hear? Please accept my apologies for my lateness. I was… indisposed. I am Kratesipolis," she added almost as an afterthought. "Queen of Corinth," she held out the same graceful hand that just jolted his loins and raised goose bumps on his exposed skin.

Athelstan bowed graciously and took the extended fingers offered, gently in his massive paw. "I am honoured Majesty. Not a Gaul however. I am a Celt. Gauls are quite - different. I would thank you on behalf of Constantina and myself for your gracious hospitality and your kind invitation to dine with you," he remained standing.

Queen Kratesipolis looked up and down the table before returning to stand very close to the towering Celt. She looked up at him with long lashes and a slight pout on her lips.

"Are you the Celt we have been hearing so much about?" she asked almost as an aside.

"Without a doubt, Majesty. I have met your Admiral Piros. It was he, who told me of your wish for an audience. I await your pleasure."

Kratesipolis smiled and clapped her hands. "Grand! I hear you are travelling with a beautiful companion. Where is she, I had so wanted to speak to our sister from the west," her hand traced a line down his chest and her eyes followed it even farther. "I do hope you have not worn out the poor dear while you were… holding her prisoner?" The tone and the look dripped with innuendo. Here was a woman who got exactly what she wanted and knew exactly how to get it.

A smile unbidden tugged at the corners of his lips. "I can assure your Majesties, her flight from her homeland and journey here was sufficiently tiring; she had no need of any additional –, guarding by me."

Chuckles greeted his statement. He gave Kratesipolis a knowing smile. Her eyebrows rose. She smiled delightfully.

"No? And you with all that pent up… energy," her long graceful fingers traced an erotic trail across his chest and down his stomach. His gaze did not waver and his calm expression seemed to unnerve her. Kratesipolis pouted before turning away. "Perhaps we can discuss it later."

"I look forward to it."

A coy backwards glance ended the discussion. "But I interrupted, you were saying?"

By her look, Leonida must have believed that Athelstan would lose his temper at having to repeat himself, but he showed no signs of irritation as he once again went through his proposal.

Kratesipolis poured him a large cup of wine, not bothering to water it, before artfully arranging her lithe body on a cushioned divan next to him – an impressive feat given her armour. As he repeated his offer, Leonida felt rather than saw Kratesipolis glance at her and Athelstan instantly knew the Corinthian was against the idea. Leonida pressed her lips into a thin line; she was clearly irritated.

She looked over at the beautiful Queen of Corinth, Kratesipolis crinkled her brow slightly and Leonida realised that they both were expecting her to speak.

"A most generous offer," she said again, floundering a little. "Please, sir, have some wine. It has been aged to perfection," she gestured to the wine on the banquet table. He did so and had a clear view of Kratesipolis listening and watching Leonida.

"A most generous offer indeed, but it is one I cannot accept at this time." A collective gasp filled the room. "Please do not feel that this is a rejection of you, of your worthy King Trahearn –, or your people. I am sure that they are honourable indeed. However – and I will speak plainly to you – I know neither you nor your kin. I appreciate that you have no love for the Macedonians – neither do I. That is all that binds our two peoples at this time."

Leonida glanced again at Kratesipolis and the Corinthian Queen lowered her eyes ever so slightly in agreement. Leonida continued.

"I offer you this counter-proposal; that the land of Senone and the free poleis of Hellas extend the hands of friendship and non–aggression towards each other. Further, that the tribes of Senone may – should they desire it – join our trading alliance. Our cartel extends far over sea and lands. All nations that are part of it have – and will continue to – prosper."

"Allow me to be honest," she went on. "It is, after all, the Spartan way. This is not a war of conquest, General, but one of liberation. It is not my intention to wipe Macedonia from the face of the earth – although some might say they deserve it. I merely wish to drive them from Hellas and back to their own borders. Consider – your fathers were allies of Alexander were they not? He was a Macedonian and a great one – the son of a God they say. It is not the people of Macedon with whom I have an issue, but rather their current leadership. In time, I do not doubt our two countries will become fast friends."

She glanced quickly at Kratesipolis, whose own gaze was hooded but pleased – her eyes brimmed with approval and he watched the flood of elation wash over the Spartan Queen. If not for the presence of the Corinthian, Leonida might very well have accepted his offer.

Athelstan had listened intently to Leonida's words and watched her mannerisms just as carefully. Many unspoken truths were revealed to him during this brief exchange, not the least of which was the personal relationship between these two Queens. He smiled inwardly.

As was his way, Athelstan sat perfectly still as Leonida posed her question and he allowed the silence inside the room to build to an intolerable level. All eyes in the room rested on him as they awaited his response. Murmuring began in soft hushed tones and slowly swept the hall. His expression was that of a calm sea before a violent storm.

He stood and faced the assembly. The hall stilled again and every soul leaned forward. In a loud booming voice that might have been heard as far away as Athens, he said. "I can accept your proposal!" His eyes flickered to Kratesipolis and read her reaction. A slight smile tugged at his moustaches. There was palpable relief at his words and he allowed the moment to build until he uttered one last word. "Provisionally!" he concluded. It was like a bucket of ice water had been tossed on everyone.

Leonida and Kratesipolis both seemed stunned and echoed his last word as a question. "Provisionally?"

He faced the two monarchs but now his uncomfortable expressionless gaze rested solely upon the Corinthian Queen. He watched her stiffen but to her credit, she did not squirm under the penetrating ice–blue stare.

He withdrew a long bone tube from his linen shirt and extracted several old documents. He handed them to Leonida but kept his eyes firmly fastened on Kratesipolis. She returned his stare.

"Since my arrival was unannounced, I can appreciate that your ministers have not had the opportunity to acquaint you with the mutual defence treaties already in place between us. Therefore, I accept your proposal with two provisions. One, that this trade alliance between us must be extended to include, Argos, Marathon, Athens, Corinth as well as all their satellite states," his head nodded slightly toward Kratesipolis and an impish grin tugged at his lip. Leonida was now a bit flustered and looked at Kratesipolis for guidance. The Corinthian Queen took the documents from Leonida and examined the agreements.

"These documents are in order, we were unaware of them. What is your second provision General?" Kratesipolis asked looking back up at him.

"It is that you permit me to accompany you into battle against Macedonia. Whether it is a war of conquest or liberation, I realise the distinction becomes meaningless once the armies clash. I am honour–bound by this treaty signed by your father and my former king, to lend my sword in your defence and so, with your blessings, I shall."

He finally transferred his attention back to Leonida. Very slowly and very deliberately, he leaned in towards Leonida. He could feel the soldiers in the room tense and several reached for their swords involuntarily. Her nostrils filled with the scent of him, of Sage and Lavender. He leaned in almost close enough to kiss her. Her mouth opened in anticipation. In a barely audible whisper, so carefully practised, he spoke to the Spartan Queen so none but she could hear and asked simply. "Can I trust you?" He waited only long enough to read the expression that flashed across her face.

"Can you trust me…?"

Leonida rose abruptly to her feet, startling everyone in the room, even Kratesipolis, who had the look of cat that had been tipped off a couch during a nap. She drew a guards' sword. "Trust," she said her gaze on the iron "is like the blade of this sword, Senone! It has two edges." She turned her gaze to the giant barbarian. "You ask to accompany us to battle, a request I am pleased to grant. But can you trust me?"

She cocked her head to one side. "I will show you that I trust you and you alone at least. I ask you to fight at my side, to guard my life with your own. In this way, I may see how well you fight and you will see how well you can trust me."

"I will happily honour your request, Leonida–Queen. I already know I can trust you. I am a Celt and I have read your heart. Had I not read trust in your eyes, I would not still be standing in your halls, or drinking your wines." His wine had remained untouched. He stroked his moustache again, an action Leonida would become very familiar with over the next few weeks

"You are correct in your belief that the Senone are people of honour. Clearly, you are reluctant to deal with us because you do not know anything about us and that is fairly spoken. I now take responsibility for this grievous oversight. I stand ready to remedy that omission. It might interest you to know that among my people I am considered rather – small." The last was a lie but Kratesipolis' eyes glanced down to his crotch. He crossed his muscled arms over his barrel chest smiling and said no more.

He was testing them both, Kratesipolis knew it and because she did, she would not look away. It was not in her blood to do so; generation upon generation of Corinthians had looked such challenges in the face and she was a scion of that line. He had captured her undivided attention.

"Who are the members of this Hellenic alliance? Corinth? Perhaps Rome?"

Kratesipolis grinned at him and then returned her attention to her wine cup. At Athelstan's addendum, she spoke. "Corinth is indeed part of this cartel, good Athelstan," she said. Leonida wondered at her ability to make the object of her gaze feel as though he or she were the only person in the world. Athelstan was an interesting creature, but she wondered if anyone could resist a full–scale charm assault from Kratesipolis for long. "As is Ptolemy's Egypt, Taras…" she paused for effect, "As Leonida said – all parties benefit from this arrangement.

Rome turned us down."

"Your second provision is that you accompany us into battle," she glanced at Leonida for a moment and the two women exchanged a look.

Leonida stood. "We accept your offer with our thanks. Once your guardianship of your Roman captive is discharged, you will be assigned to aid General Demetrios as you can. He shall decide where you shall best serve."

A white-toothed smile slowly crossed Athelstan's face and he began to chuckle. The chuckle rose to a booming laugh. It was the kind of laugh that was infectious and it clearly came from deep within that great Celt's heart. His whole body shook when he laughed and the enamel disks he had braided into his long shiny mane jingled like a thousand tiny bells.

"Handsomely put Majesty! Majesties!" He said with a bow once he regained control of his mirth. "I had heard Corinthians and Spartans speak plainly and I am pleased to find I was not deceived," he looked at Leonida again and stroked his long moustache several times now cocking his head to one side.

"So be it," he said suddenly. "Hear then my pledge, Leonida, Queen of Sparta!" He pulled himself up to his full height and squared his shoulders. A fierce and savage look transformed Athelstan's features; he fairly dripped with menace. The aura he now projected fled to every corner of the marble audience chamber and filled those assembled with dread.

"I, Athelstan of the Senone nation shall, from this moment forth, protect you from all perils so long as I draw breath. I shall fight by your side. I shall vanquish your foes wherever they may be found. I shall defend your life with my own so long as war exists between you and the Kingdom of Macedon. Do you now accept my pledge?" He stood before her, hands upon his hips and legs slightly apart. His head was held high, a look of ferocious pride etched on his face. A nearly unseen smile tugged at his lip and was that perhaps a mischievous twinkle in his eye?

"I DO!"

"I believe we have begun well and if I might be allowed I would raise a cup to the success of the Hellenic League of City States and to the continued health of your majesties. I give you a united Hellas!" He raised his cup and the others followed suit. Although the purpose of his trip seemed a failure since he would not get the experts he had hoped for, he still felt that the agreement reached here would ultimately benefit all his people. He would have to find the help his King needed, elsewhere.

The feast went on for a long time and by the time it ended, Athelstan was drained. He had been forced to answer a stream of questions concerning Constantina and his involvement with her. He stood at the vortex of many dozens of curious dignitaries. He told a riveting tale of their battle at the Inn with Roman assassins. He explained that Constantina was the unfortunate victim of their attack on him. Her wounds alone would have kept her from this feast. When Demetrios confirmed his story, Leonida and Kratesipolis were deeply concerned, that Rome might arrive in force to find him.

"Was it you who beheaded those four men in Yithion?" The Spartan Queen asked suddenly.

"It was," he stated flatly.

Demetrios looked at him with vindication. "I knew it," he whispered to himself.

"Might I ask why?" the Queen continued.

"You are the only one - Magesty, who may ask why. I will not – I cannot – I must never tolerate the abuse of the helpless if it is in my power to prevent it. Had I done so, Constantina would now lie dead in a shallow grave, lost and forgotten. Her fate would have remained unknown. I dispensed justice upon rapists, murderers, and brazen cowards according to the laws of my people and the terms set down in the treaties you now hold in your hand. I would do so again if similar circumstances presented themselves. Of that, you can be absolutely certain."

The decisive moment was upon him. Would they check his story, or condemn him as a killer outright and have him summarily executed.

Leonida was frowning and it only made her look even more beautiful. Kratesipolis had an entirely different look on her face. Was it hunger? Athelstan knew when a woman wanted him and this Queen definitely had that look. Her every gesture and intonation also spoke volumes concerning the love affair between these two women. Leonida looked up to Kratesipolis for strength, guidance, and approval. Kratesipolis looked across at Leonida as a means to an end. What end? He had no answer to that… yet.

Leonida spoke. "It is my belief that you acted correctly and in doing so you saved an innocent," again she glanced at Kratesipolis and there was that ever–so–slight nod. "It is also my belief that Constantina is your prisoner in name only. Will you confirm that opinion My Lord Ambassador?"

"I do so confirm it Leonida Queen. I protect her only. She is free to leave me at any time and I will make no move and plead that you also make no move to prevent it should that become her wish."

"General Athelstan of Senone Nation of Celts, you are truly a man of honour and I state it for the record now. I absolve you of all guilt in this matter. I will warn you now, have a care sir; murder is a very serious crime here. I trust you take my meaning."

"I do Leonida Queen. Killing, when unnecessary, is unacceptable in my land as well. The destiny of a soul is something that cannot be foreseen even by the wise. Only the Gods can dictate the course of a life with impunity. I will take a life only when I am commanded to do so by my King, by you, or when I am morally offered no other choice." His gaze fell on Demetrios. "I never kill without good reason."

"A philosopher too," mused Kratesipolis. "Be welcome in Corinth Athelstan of Senone. I name you a friend of this city. Let no door be closed to you here and I mean NO door." Her meaning was very clear and Leonida fairly bristled at the sexually charged comment.

The evening proceeded to its inevitable conclusion. In time, he took his leave and was conscious that smouldering hungry eyes followed him out.

He approached the rooms in the Palace and saw the two Spartan guards stationed outside. He walked up to the men who snapped to attention. News of the barbarian General's temper had spread quickly. They moved to open doors but he stopped them. "She is still inside?" he asked simply.

"Yes General," he put his hand on the wood for a moment then stepped back.

"Thank you. Carry on," he followed a guard to a small room hastily emptied for his use. Inside he wearily stripped off his tooled leather vest and white shirt. His muscles creaked as he stretched and stepped up to a marble vanity. A large shallow dish of water sat beside a bowl of scented flower petals. He took the time to wash his face and neck. A cool night breeze blew in through the open arched windows. He stripped naked and stood looking out over the sleeping city of Corinth. His mind went again to Constantina. What was so special about her that in these few short days she was all that filled his mind?

A new scent touched his nose and his brow furrowed as he sniffed. It was of roses and something else. His skin jumped as cold fingers ran up his back and over his shoulders. A feminine purring began. He turned around and Kratesipolis wrapped her arms around his neck and pulled herself into a hungry, passionate kiss. Stunned, he allowed it to continue for a moment before pulling her back. She looked at him with undisguised lust and her hand closed on his manhood.

"Mmmmm, you unconscionable liar. You are not small at all," she firm squeeze. With a shrug of her shoulders, her long indigo cape dropped to the floor revealing a gossamer thin white gown. Her pale skin was flawless beneath it and she stepped back for him to admire her. He had no personal, or national policy, or instructions whatsoever concerning the bedding of foreign Monarchs. Since he expected them all to be men, it had never come up. Her hot scent did not help either. He responded as any man would. She looked him over and bit her lower lip.

"I did not come all this way to bed every Queen that I encounter. Besides, it has..." She stopped him with a finger on his lips.

"Is it not your station in life as General to provide a service to your King?" she asked spreading herself onto his bed like a cat.

"It is," he said, still naked.

"And as a guest of Corinth is it usual to expect you to provide a service in return for our hospitality," he smiled and nodded.

"It is, but within reason," he tried.

"Yes, it is! Then come here you gorgeous bull of a man, your hostess has not been properly serviced in a very, very long time," her voice was husky with desire. He stooped and collected her cloak. Walking over, he reached out for her outstretched hand. He was going to pull her up but she grabbed his wrist and yanked hard. He pitched forward atop her. Instantly her legs and arms coiled around him and she kissed him deeply. He attempted to disentangle himself from her. "Now wait just a minute," he was trying to do three things and he was doing them all badly. Not hurt her, not insult her and most especially not 'service' her. He raised himself up with her legs still locked around him and the door opened. Athelstan looked up in horror, Kratesipolis looked at the doorway in rapt victory. There, wide-eyed with shock, stood Constantina. A gasp of pure despair escaped her. She turned to flee but was frozen in place.

"No! Connie, stop!" he called out. Standing, he set the Corinthian Queen on her feet and wrapped her robe around her shoulders. "Queen Kratesipolis was just leaving." There was an undeniable sense of finality to his statement. He walked her to the open doors past Constantina. "Guards, please see that the Queen returns to her rooms safely. Our discussions are now at an end."

Kratesipolis smiled at Athelstan and gave Constantina a looked that screamed victory. "Hmm, it would seem that our barbarian fancies a different travelling of meat tonight. Pity. I too wonder how sweet she might taste," she said teasing Constantina, "Umm, we could make this a very interesting evening, but you strike me as far too shy for that my dear. What a shame. Good luck getting any warmth out of this one Athelstan. I look forward to you calling for me when she leaves you teased, hard, and wanting."

"I am sure that will not be necessary Kratesipolis. Have a pleasant evening," he said smoothly.

Constantina bristled at the woman's words. She heard the laughter as the woman walked away. That infuriated her so much so, that she took a step towards the Queen.

He placed a firm hand on Constantina's shoulder and pulled her back into the room.

"Steady," and with that, he swung the doors closed. A long sigh escaped him. "That was not what it looked like Connie," he could find nothing else to say and stood naked looking down at her.

She frowned at him "I am nothing to you, Athelstan. You have nothing to explain," she said turning her back to him. "Feel free to pleasure yourself as you see fit."

He turned her around. "I have no interest in women who use sex to achieve their ends. That is why I am far more attracted to someone like.." he stopped speaking. He was tired and it showed. He very nearly slipped. "Come in and sit. Let me get you some wine."

"I do not want any wine," she said pulling away from him. "What does it matter," she said with a sigh. "I came here to apologize. Now I realise there is no need. Good night Captain."

"Constantina, you are wrong. You mean a great deal to me. Do not go," he did not try to stop her. His voice was almost a whisper. What was happening? Why did her approval mean so much to him? He ached to explain the encounter with Kratesipolis. His whole being wanted to make her understand what it was to be a Celt. He had no words and it would seem she would not hear them even if she would. It saddened him to the core of his being, so he simply stood staring at her back.

"And for what it's worth, I am not shy. I am after all a runaway wife, am I not." Constantina stepped out, shaking with fury.

"No! No, you are not anything of the sort! I know that now." He pushed the door closed she remained facing it. "You are a lady! You are a lady who I am proud to know. I realise you do not believe me; I have given you no reason to. It is the truth nonetheless," he walked up behind her. "Constantina, stay a while. I would like to explain. If you are going angry with me, let it be because I was wrong about you, but not for this. Above everything else, I am a man of honour. You need to believe that is the truth. Please stay."

"You have nothing to explain to me," she said with her back to him. "You are your own man, Athelstan. You do not answer to me."

"If that were true, you would already be gone," he held out his hand to her, "Connie?" he asked wearily.

With a sigh, she placed her hand in his and turned to face him.

He fought to resist the sudden urge to take her in his arms and kiss her. He shook himself mentally once again. He led her to a chair before turning away from her. She did not sit.

"I find myself thinking about you all the time. I cannot explain why that is," he shook his head. He was getting very tired. "I do not have an interest in any of the Kratesipolis' of this world. It is important to me that you believe that."

"I believe you. Thank you for being so honest. I appreciate it."

He followed her and stopped beside the doorway. He bent to grab the handle for her but in doing so came down to eye level. Their eyes locked and before he could prevent it, he kissed her. It came as a shock to them both. There was a frozen moment before he gathered her against his naked body and kissed her again long and deep.

Constantina's arms went around his neck. Her body pressed tight to his. Her lips yielded to his passions and her own. Connie's fingers intertwined in his hair and she moaned against his lips, parting her own to lead him deeper to her mouth.

Even as his passion rose, an inner voice shrieked at him to stop. This was wrong! He ignored it. She was like water to a man dying of thirst and he drank her in. His arousal for her was profound and so obvious that he no longer cared.

He pulled back and looked at her. "I do not know what came over me, but maybe now…" He stopped and nodded. "Maybe now you understand," he put a gentle hand on her cheek. The flimsy nightshirt was no match for his hardness. Not thinking, her hands began to make their downward descent. Her fingers wrapped around him and he winced at how cold they were. Given half a chance he would happily warm them for her and anything else that she might need warming. His hands caressed her cheek as she learned about him.

Constantina pushed away from him as if his skin had just burned her. "I really must go," she gasped and this time she turned, lifted her skirts, and ran from the room.

He let her go and the pain of her leaving was a physical blow. When the reality of what he had done sank in, he was saddened. What must she think now? Exhaustion swam over him like a wave. It had been a long trying day. When he finally collapsed into the soft mattress, he was asleep in seconds.

"That," Kratesipolis purred, "was inspired." She rolled across the bed, coming closer to Leonida.

"I'm glad you think so," Leonida grinned.

"What made you do it? A barbarian bodyguard, eh? Even Alexander didn't have one of those; had he, he might still live." Kratesipolis circled her fingers on Leonida's stomach, moving downwards in spirals.

"He seems to prize honour; I don't know how I knew that – I just did. Why didn't you want an alliance," she lowered her voice. Athelstan had been insistent that he sleep at the foot of her bed and it was only after some hours of arguing and then wheedling that she had managed to convince the giant barbarian that it was not seemly.

Kratesipolis' fingers stopped, just above the dark mound of Leonida's pubis and she looked up at her. "You have to think ahead," she said seriously. "I am sure that Athelstan is trustworthy, but I cannot speak for all the other tribal leaders in Gaul – and neither can he. Do you really want an army of barbarians on our northern borders? The war with Macedon will end – for better, or worse. But make no mistake, Leonida – we will be weakened by it and the victor will be easy prey for a while. Better to keep our civil wars civil. These barbarians are known to migrate, to seek new lands…"

"They could do that anyway," Leonida said.

"They could, but not now with your mandate. Think, Leonida. If we defeat Cassander, Hellas will be restored to somewhat of its former glory. This will be thanks to you – as would its destruction if we invited thousands of their troops to mass within striking distance of our lands."

"I didn't think of that."

"No," Kratesipolis continuing her downward journey with her fingers. "You didn't. Lucky for you that I am here."

"Yes," Leonida breathed, "Very lucky."

"Did you go to him tonight? I missed you after the banquet."

"Would you be angry with me if I had?" Her fingers explored urgently, more intimately.

"Yes… No, not really. But why do you feel the need for such creatures?" Kratesipolis' fingers were damp now and Leonidas' thighs parted even wider.

"I will show you why my pet… I will show you."

Chapter Eighteen

Athelstan had been awakened very early. Darkness still clung to the city. A fresh aromatic breeze was wafting out of the northwest and with it came the telltale hint of rain. Yes, morning found Athelstan in a singular mood. It was a physical impossibility for Athelstan to be in a blacker mood. His first waking thought was of Constantina. When the events of the previous night bloomed in his mind, he simply could not believe the ghastly turn they took. He had also been tasked the night before with guarding Queen Leonida. Time to get busy.

He dressed, pulled on a jerkin of iron rings, strapped on longsword and knives before donning the white skin cloak held in place by the bejewelled golden torque given to him by the twins. He marched out of the tiny room and headed for the Queens bedchamber. The halls were virtually empty save for servants preparing breakfasts and finishing off last minute cleaning tasks. They all scattered at his approach and gawked wide-eyed at his passing. He spoke not a word.

Two Corinthian Royal Guards lounged casually before the golden doors. Their eyes were red-rimmed by drink and it took them several seconds to even notice the Celt's approach. They hurriedly straightened and one even managed to get his spear from where it had been left leaning against the wall.

He swept the two guards aside like he was walking through a doorway of beads, took a position in front of the doors turned. He placed one hand on his hip and the other on the pommel of the sword. "You are relieved," he whispered.

"Who are you? What do you think you are doing? If we leave our post we will be flogged. Get away from those doors," one of the guards demanded.

"I am the bodyguard for the Spartan Queen and you two are sick. Go to your barracks at once, or would you fare better being caught drunk on duty?" The pair looked at him, then at each other. Neither decision seemed appropriate.

"I will tell your commanders I found you both here and very ill. Sick as you were, you refused to leave your posts until I just happened along and offered to replace you. Does that satisfy the conditions?"

Each shrugged at the other. Then they turned and departed. Athelstan knew, full well, one would stay within earshot while the other ran for help. So it was, that a disgruntled troop of Royal Guard arrived and found Athelstan rooted in place by the door with his eyes closed. When they managed to approach to within ten feet of the doors, his eyes shot open and a low growl rumbled. General Demetrios arrived, took one look at the situation, and adopted a stoic expression.

"Lord Athelstan, what are you doing?"

"I am fulfilling my pledge to your Queen."

"The Royal Guard can guard her Majestys' rooms."

"I know that."

"Then, why won't you let them?"

"I am. They are guarding their Queens from over there. I, am guarding them from here." Demetrios was fighting not to laugh. The two men engaged in another of their, soon to be famous, staring matches. After a few minutes, Demetrios nodded slowly.

"May I... umm," he half turned towards the growing throng, "May I go now?"

"Of course, General Demetrios. I have nothing more for you."

The Greek snorted, took a military stance and marched away.

In the distance, some disturbance was approaching. A pinched and high–pitched voice could be heard over the hushed murmuring of the crowd. By now it seemed half the household staff was packed into the normally spacious hallway.

"Excuse me! Pardon me! I am sorry, coming through! What is going on? What are all you people doing here? Coming through! Official business! Make way!" All of a sudden, a curious little man appeared. He was short and barely 5 stone in weight. He had big feet, big ears, a prominent nose, and bulging bug eyes. He finally popped free of the throng and kept walking towards the doors while looking back over his shoulder at the mass of people.

"What are you all doing here at this hour?" When he did turn back around to see where he was going, he very nearly collided with Athelstan. He stopped short with an audible squeak. His eyebrows shot up in surprise and his eyes bugged out even more. He took one look at Athelstan and his feet instantly reversed direction. The scroll he was carrying tumbled out of his hands so it unrolled while it still hung draped over his outstretched arms. He shuffled as quickly as he could back to the relative safety of the crowd.

"What is that?" he asked pointing at the Celt. "Is it real? Is it alive?" He was looking at the Athelstan in absolute disbelief.

One of the doors behind Athelstan cracked open and someone peeked out. It closed again quickly. Kratesipolis turned with a giggle and whispered. "Get dressed quickly love. You have got to come see this. Leonida grabbed a robe and dashed to the doors.

Athelstan slowly pointed at the odd little man as he finished re-rolling the scroll and motioned him forward. The scribe very slowly advanced shuffling almost sideways while constantly judging the distance between him and the safety of the soldiers. He was, no doubt calculating the time it would take to run for his life.

Athelstan held out his hand and the scribe quickly placed the document in the outstretched paw. Athelstan opened it and began to read. After a moment, or two, the scroll ever–so–slowly, moved to the right and Athelstan's head moved left so he could peer past it. The little man had remained rooted in place wide-eyed and trembling. The Celt twitched a single finger at him twice, dismissing him and the scribe dropped the other scrolls on the floor and fled at a full run. Athelstan finished reading the document. Behind him, the door had reopened just wide enough so the two women could watch this scene unfold. They each had a hand over their mouths and were struggling not to laugh out loud. It was a battle they lost.

They peered out at the nervous pack of servants, handmaidens, advisors and army commanders standing crammed in the hallway facing the royal bedchambers. They stood arrayed at a very respectable distance away from the opening too. Not one person dared make a noise as the rugged Barbarian stood as a mute sentinel – well almost mute, he was growling! In one hand, he held the scabbard of his long sword; in the other, the scroll. Even though the shiny weapon was not drawn and none within eyesight of this savage doubted their peril was extraordinarily real.

Upon seeing their Queen, a great cacophony of indignant outrage burst forth from a dozen or more throats. A raised hand and a snarl silenced them again. He led the Royals out of their rooms and the crowd parted before him. The Queens fell into step behind the Celt. The rest fell into step behind them all. Leonida silently noticed the Celt was bathed and his hair had been freshly washed. The air in his wake smelled of rosemary and lemon. This was certainly not the 'filthy unwashed animal' she had assumed all Gauls to be. Celts did seem to be quite different. It would seem Athelstan might prove to be a very interesting companion indeed.

Once clear of the main cluster of people, Athelstan stepped to one side, allowed the ladies to pass him, and walked slightly behind Leonida's right shoulder. He scanned every face he saw. He read of a lot of people that morning and he was somewhat confused by what he saw. He would think on this for a time, but he was not sure he would like where those thoughts might lead.

Athelstan was paranoid; that much was apparent, Leonida thought as the giant bodyguard "escorted" her and Kratesipolis through the corridors. The Senone maintained a sour expression, glowering and growling at anyone that came closer than a few feet of them.

This, she thought, would have to stop. It was one thing have a bodyguard, but quite another having a keeper. There was nothing to be done about it, at the moment though. She had made her bed and now she must lay in it.

The news for the day was unsettling; Bomilcar had signed an agreement with Cassander. Carthage was now in the enemy camp. Atop that,

Cassander had made what appeared to be a clever tactical move. He had split his army and a portion of it now blocked the Isthmus of Corinth. As it was, their arrival fits nicely into Leonida's plans – but – she would have preferred to dictate matters. The more of the enemy that could be pinned down here, the better were their chances in Athens. She was quite sure they would not expect to find Sparta's might neatly tucked behind the white walls.

The news of the Macedonian blockade of the Isthmus of Corinth came as a surprise to Athelstan. Clearly, the armies of Sparta, Argos and Corinth would march out to counter the threat. Athelstan was advised that it might take several days to dislodge Macedonia from the narrow strip of land. Athelstan immediately prepared to march out as, but Queen Leonida had already forbidden it. She proclaimed that his sole duty was to Constantina. Nothing else was to concern him. Besides, Athens could not wait several days.

Athelstan went in search of the Spartan commander. Ptolemarch Demetrios bore a black expression. He stood atop the gleaming white walls of Corinth looking east over the flat plain that formed the Isthmus of Corinth. It was a mile–wide strip of grassy hills that separated Peloponnesia from Hellas proper. The Macedonian King had sent a force to keep Sparta and Corinth out of the fight for Athens. Cassander knew Sparta would rush to Athens aid so he split his army. It was a masterful ploy and Demetrios knew it – hence the black expression. Athelstan stood shoulder to shoulder with the seething Spartan.

Away to the east, the grassy strip was covered with soldiers. In the centre was the sixteen–pointed gold and red sunburst standard of King Cassander's Macedonian army. Roughly three thousand in number, they were armed with fourteen–foot long spears and the Xiphos, the Greek short sword. They were heavily armoured and were drawn up in four separate blocks. This was the anchor. Mercenaries and sell–swords joined them from Thessaloniki, Epirus, Aetolia, Odrysia, Cyrene, Epirus and others. They formed into loose associations and were widely scattered across the field. It appeared to be an army hastily thrown together and force–marched to Corinth.

Each army group had a commander dressed in elaborate metal armour and full–face helmets. Most of the others wore cuirasses of boiled leather or scaled iron depending on their status and wealth. Greaves covered their lower legs and they bore elaborate round helmets with cheek and neck guards. Most helmets sported towering feathered plumes or horsehair crests in a riot of colour. Some had shields with colourful embossed designs and carried spears and Xiphos. Some lesser soldiers wore the simple chiton, a flowing robe that left the left arm bare. They either carried bows or slings. Aside from the commanders, very few had horses.

"I should be out there," Demetrios sputtered impotently. "Instead here I stand protecting the women and the old. I am waiting t go to Athelns with too few soldiers." he glanced up at Athelstan. "No offence intended Celt. It is not your fault you are old."

"None taken my friend, I understand completely and I am not old." Demetrios appeared not to have heard. They watched as the bulk of Corinth's army marched out of the city. They took a central position with Argos to their left and Sparta to the right. The Spartan snorted his derision. It was an impressive sight. Sparta with their shields in gold and black with the inverted 'V' design in white, Corinth with their blue and white wave standards and Argos beneath the horned bull approached the Macedonian invaders with supreme confidence.

"Look at those Corinthian dogs. They are as pathetic an excuse for an army as I have ever seen. We Spartans will have to save them from themselves – again. They are strutting like young cocks marching into a house full of laying hens. Mark my words well, Celt, it is Sparta that will rout this Macedonian rabble, not these swaggering fops," he was apoplectic. This was the most emotion he had ever seen come from the stoic Demetrios since they had met.

"I formally requested that I be given the honour of leading our troops against this – this abomination," indicating the Macedonians with a contemptuous wave of his hand.

"But our divine Priestess-Queen, with her many long days of experience to guide her, denied me – ME! After everything I have done for the glory of Sparta in the service of her father, the great King Eudamidas l, I am consigned to stand here and watch these imbeciles strut about pretending to be warriors. It makes me sick. Give me two army groups and I would happily sweep this vermin away like so much smoke and have no fear of missing the evening meal."

"Your day will come soon enough Demetrios. Did it not occur to you that your Queen realises your worth very well indeed? She is sending you to Athens where your experience, bravery and skill will be of the most use. If my King were to send me to certain death as your Queen has done to you, I would comply with a great sense of honour. It is time these 'imbeciles' as you call them, learn how to fight their own battles." Athelstan found little humour in the irony.

Seemingly unfazed by the Celt's words he whirled to face Athelstan and poked him in the chest." and you General, you lied to me!" He slowly glanced down at the offending digit with a frown.

"I? How do you reason that?"

"You told me you did not kill those men in Yithion, but you admitted to my Queen that you had," he poked Athelstan a second time and the Celt seized the finger and bent it backwards.

"I told you nothing of the sort, my friend. While it is true, I did not confirm your suspicions back at the Inn, if you recall, I did not deny them either. Instead, I asked you to produce your proof. I told you I do not kill without just cause and that is the simple truth. As it turned out, you had no proof and I did have just cause. I chose not to elaborate at that time for obvious reasons. You would have had the right to dispense justice on the spot and I could not risk that at the time, since Constantina's safety was paramount – it was an act of omission perhaps, but it was not a lie. You may be assured sir, I never lie."

Demetrios freed his finger with a yank. "You are splitting hairs, sir."

"I think not. Hair splitting is a useless endeavour and one that is beneath such men as us. I used language as a weapon, an endeavour that *is* worthy of men such as us. I trust you have learned something, General. Now that I am acquitted of these killings, I believe the matter is settled."

"You could have told me your reasons back at the Inn."

"Then let me ask you this. If I had you would have had no choice but to kill me, correct?"

He thought about it for a moment. "Yes, by law, I would have had no choice."

"And you would have had to arrest Constantina and have her hand removed as a thief, correct?"

"Yes, but…"

"And if you had removed her hand for theft, then what do you suppose would have happened to your promotion?"

"Well…" he stammered.

Athelstan was smiling. "So things worked out well for both of us, would you not agree?"

"Yes, I suppose it did. Stop smiling! I am still angry with you." Athelstan made a vain effort to comply.

"And so you should be. So stop poking me, or I will remove the offending finger at the shoulder and smack you stupid with it."

Moments later both men were laughing.

Word came by way of a runner. It had been decided that Queen Kratesipolis of Corinth would command the combined forces of Sparta, Argos and Corinth in this battle for her city-state. Leonida and Constantina would immediately travel by sea, with two hundred Priestess archers from the temple of Athena and as many mounted Spartan cavalry, in defence of Athens and the fledgeling Hellenic League. The bulk of the forces would make their way overland once this Macedonian threat was eliminated. Demetrios would lead the expedition to Athens and Athelstan would provide protection to both Queens. To Athelstan's way of thinking, it seemed far more important for Kratesipolis to defend Corinth than it was for the Hellenic League to fulfil its pledge to defend Athens. What irked him the most was Constantina's situation was not considered at all. If she was Papirius' wife, sending her from one war zone to another was madness.

"Come along Demetrios, we must not keep your Queen waiting."

At the dock, all was in readiness.

"Is Constantina aboard already?", Athelstan asked of Piros.

"I do not know, I haven't seen her. Maybe she is aboard one of the other ships."

"Maybe? Let's find out." Runners were sent in all directions. Leonida held the launch until all the ships were searched. Word came that a woman matching her description had been seen leaving the city early that morning in

153

the company of two men.

"Was she being taken against her will?"

"It did not seem so. These men looked like you."

"Like me?"

"Ahhh, yes like foreigners."

"Like Roman foreigners?"

"No, like barbarians."

"What direction did they go?"

"South."

"Did anyone question them? Did anyone ask who these men were?"

"M'Lord, nothing seemed amiss so they were allowed to leave peacefully."

"I see…"

"Did you own this girl? We could send a squad after them."

There was a long pause while Athelstan thought.

"M'Lord?"

"No, that will not be necessary. Thank you." Tide and time could be ignored no longer. He boarded his ship and they set sail.

Chapter Nineteen

Athelstan found something laughable in an unfunny way. Athens was three days from Corinth by sea, or a one–day walk overland. A fast horse could cover the distance around the Saronikos Kolpos in hours. By blocking the isthmus, Cassander had masterfully removed the overland route.

By mid-morning, thirteen ships set sail in an easterly direction, carrying Leonida, Athelstan, Demetrios and his token four hundred Spartan cavalry, two hundred female archers from the temple of Athena and half a thousand Corinthian infantrymen to Athens.

Athelstan was in a sullen mood. Constantina had left. He could not blame her. Kratesipolis was masterful. She created an impossible situation for Consrtantina to deal with. In the end, she chose to flee. He thought back to Caileigh and her admonishment to 'Stay out of business that does not concern you.' It would seem he was going to be able to follow her instructions after all.

Their day at sea turned into a race. The coming of dawn revealed the black sails of the Carthaginian fleet stretching in an unbroken line across the western horizon behind them. A flurry of activity ensued. The twin decks of oars were double manned with Spartan soldiers lending their strength to that of the Corinthian sailors. The single sail was raised and angled to make the best use of the light breeze. The aft catapult was in place and manned. All that was left to do aboard the Aphrodite was to watch those black sails grow steadily larger.

Nothing would be left to chance. At Admiral Piro's order, the four trailing Greek ships turned around and headed directly towards the approaching enemy. They would try to disrupt the enemies approach and give the remaining Greek vessels time to reach their destination safely. Queen Leonida appeared on deck offering a prayer to Poseidon for the brave men who would die today. She committed their souls to the deep even as they closed on the Carthaginians. These ships grew smaller and smaller until they were just dark specks in the distance. The men aboard were never seen again.

Corinth's remaining warships rounded a final spit of land and the massive white walls surrounding a sheltered harbour came into view. Leonida stood beside Athelstan at the forward rail.

"Is this Athens?" asked Athelstan.

"No, this is the port city of Piraeus. This is the home of the Athenian Navy.

Athens is still over ten miles inland," Leonida explained. The huge white towers protecting the harbour entrance loomed over them ominously as they slipped under their watchful gaze. Hundreds of armed men lined the walls staring mutely as the nine Corinthian vessels entered the wide sheltered bay. A long line of Athenian warships sailing out to counter the approaching Carthaginian fleet was passing them.

She made a point of not showing any outward interest towards Athelstan yet she shot odd glances at him when she thought he wasn't watching. The mood between them had changed somehow. Although it was different – and quieter, it felt odd. Time, like always, would tell.

"We will be docking soon, I should see to the horses." He could not stop looking at her.

"Leonida–Queen, try to be of good cheer today. We will win. Cassander will not stay long once he realises his peril at home. You will triumph."

All she did was nod.

They both watched as the long docks grew larger. Thousands of people covered the wharves waiting to board the Athenian warships as rowers. Athelstan had heard tales of this but to see it unfold before him was impressive. They boarded ships to face a danger all too real and immediate. Many would not see hearth and home again. What dangers would they face here? Only the Gods knew and they were all too predictably silent on the matter.

Thirty minutes later he led a resplendent Queen Leonida, seated regally aboard Maehadren, down the gangplank into crowded Piraeus. White on white. They followed the red-cloaked Spartans through a jostling throng of onlookers. Behind Athelstan came the Spartan Royal Guard in their gold and black. Four hundred heavy cavalry and two hundred Athenian Priestess archers followed by the meagre infantry disembarked the nine ships and formed a double column behind the guard.

Ptolemarch Demetrios with his red sash led the procession through the cacophony of the port, with all its exotic smells and stinks and into the half-mile wide space between Athen's famous Long Walls. From this distance, they looked quite small, even though each stood nearly twenty feet high and thirty feet wide at the top. Soldiers, chariots, carriages and siege engines could quickly travel along these elevated highways. The Spartans marched along the wide boulevard between them.

Athelstan saw Leonida's nose wrinkle at the overwhelming stench of the boulevard as they left Piraeus. Thousands of peasants huddled in loose groups on the ground to either side of the paved roadway. These were the poor, the destitute, the old, the infirm, the women and the children of Athens. All those with no status in Athenian society crouched here for good, or ill as the city came under siege. They gathered inside these walls for protection and came from the farms and land holdings beyond the walls. They were dusty, dirty, ragged and tattered mops of human refuse. Athelstan's nose also wrinkled but not at the smells rather at the unconscionable misery surrounding him. In his world, this festering mass of humanity would not – could not exist. The Celtic nobility would never allow it. His, was an ordered society where every man woman and child had value and a place. Life had value to him. Here it had none.

He shook his head in frustration and muttered into his moustache. "And they call themselves civilized."

Leonida's eyes swept the human wasteland surrounding them, her hands clenched in her lap. Unknown to Athelstan, she was still a priestess of Athena. What she was witnessing was appalling to her. These people had no food, no water, no shelter… no hope. It showed in their eyes.

All eyes were on the foreign army. A small child dressed in a dirty sleeveless shift tottered out onto the boulevard and sat down with her back to the column of warhorses and riders. She began to trace the paving stones in front of her, oblivious to her peril. Athelstan released Maehadrens reins, sprang forward past the lead horses and scooped the infant up just before she was trampled. A shrill scream of terror ripped through the air as the child's mother realised her baby was gone. Demetrio's raised hand called an immediate halt.

The little girl was giggling and had a firm grip on Athelstan's moustache. Her face was covered in dirt save for where tears or snot had washed it away.

"He is trying to steal my baby! Give me back my baby!" she howled.

"Calm yourself, madam, he is not trying to steal your baby. He saved her from being trampled." Leonida's voice held a tone that calmed the woman immediately. She slid off Maehadren's back.

"We are so sorry to cause you such a fright." The mother looked at the barbarian with open suspicion The small child kissed Athelstan's cheek suddenly then playfully slapped his cheek. The Celt laughed heartily at this and his amulets tinkled. Children all over the world were the same. He kissed her back and the child collapsed in a fit of giggling. Leonida took the girl from Athelstan and handed her to the very relieved woman.

She threw a few last looks at Athelstan, bundled her baby up in her arms and melted back into the crowd to be comforted by her own people.

The Celt bowed to Leonida and walked back towards Maehadren. He pulled the lashings of his food bag and water skins and returned to Demetrios.

"General, order your men to leave what food and water they now carry to these people. They have nothing. What use is being safe from a war if only to die of thirst and starvation?" The Spartans eyebrows lifted in surprise. He was about to refuse but his Queen nodded her consent. He gave the order. Athelstan handed his food and skins to the mother and her daughter and the Corinthians did the same. It was not enough but he had given these people back some hope. The starving people rushed forward to receive the offerings. Some scuffles broke out among them.

"SHARE THE FOOD!" he bellowed. The crowd froze and went strangely quiet. "Share amongst yourselves as we have shared with you. At least pretend to behave like civilized people even if it is clear you are not." Anger flashed over the Celts face briefly.

"This war will not last long. Sparta and Corinth march to your defence even as I speak. Besides gentle sirs and madams – I HAVE COME! No power under the eyes of any of the Gods known by man, nor beast can resist the force of nature that I command." He bowed to the peasants with a flourish and nodded at Demetrio's odd expression.

"I did not know you were so skilled at foreign relations," Leonida said with no small amount of surprise. Athelstan looked up with a questioning look.

"I do not know about foreign relations. I know people. I look at them not past them. I do know what is right. This was right," he concluded.

The column of knights and archers continued and he saw Demetrios chuckling with his Queen.

"So you have come have you?" Demetrios asked over his shoulder. "Look at them. Look at how relieved they are to hear that. I suppose that is a good thing"

"That is right, friend Demetrios, it is a very good thing. You will see."

The boulevard stretched ten miles from Piraeus to Athens but the crush of peasants dwindled after a mile, or so. After what should have been a pleasant ride, they finally arrived in a city under siege. Representatives from the ruling 'Council of Two–Hundred' were present to meet the incoming army, once a hated enemy, now grudgingly a friend. Their disappointment was evident in Sparta's small numbers, coupled with the fact that nearly half of them were women. They were greeted with cool politeness only.

They continued into Athens proper. They rode past Temples to every God in their Pantheon, past statues of those Gods, Goddesses and heroes. They rode through Doric–columned roads and past government buildings and sprawling estates beyond count. They approached the Athenian Agora with its colourful awnings and amphitheatre. This was the place where Aristocrats and Tyrants enforced their rule on their Athenian subjects; where philosophy was born and where the concept of "direct democracy" was first discussed. The Agora was the physical place where every Athenian citizen gathered to conduct their business, participate in their city's governance, decide judicial matters, express their opinion for all who cared to listen and elect their city officials. For every free Athenian citizen, participating in such "common" activities was not merely a duty, it was a privilege and an honour.

A page lifted a bronze horn and blew a long note. "Queen Leonida 1 of Sparta!" The chant was taken up and a massive roar erupted from the citizens packing the Agora. They were quickly conducted in a closed, oval building, unroofed, with a central space for the presentation of public events. Tiers of seats for spectators surround the central space. The Athenian army was closely guarding it and all who tried to enter were carefully searched.

The Leaders of the Council of 200 sat stoically watching the Spartan delegation file in. There was much whispering behind hands. There was a certainty that Queen Leonida had arrived without the Spartan Army and none seemed at all pleased by this. She swept into the amphitheatre with her odd entourage and walked towards an ornate table littered with maps. Advisors and strategists argued and gestured wildly.

A trumpet sounded and Queen Leonida was announced. Few even bothered to look up from their squabbling. Athelstan took several quick steps and shouldered two of the loudest men aside, placed two ham-sized hands on the table and hollered, "Quiet!"

The reaction was immediate. They stumbled over each other to get away from the unexpected newcomer and blinked at him with a mixture of surprise and fear. He stepped back away from the table and Leonida seamlessly took his place with a simple nod.

"I bring greetings to all the august gentlemen in the council of 200 as well as to all these fine personages gathered here today. I thank you for such a gracious welcome." The sarcasm was obvious.

A single corpulent man dressed in the finest of Athenian armour stood.

"Welcome Queen of Sparta. To spíti mas eínai to spíti sas. (Our home is your home.) He bowed as best he could.

"Thank you My Lord Cliethenes, you look resplendent today. Would that my soldiers dressed as well." He tried to indicate it was nothing but his expression betrayed him as a vain man.

Athelstan was paranoid; that much was apparent. He managed a sour expression, glowering and growling at anyone, including Cliethenes, that came closer than a few feet from them.

The news for the day was unexpected; the Athenian militia had already arrived – unscheduled. Formed into ranks from the farmers, cobblers, fishermen and cutpurses of the area, they were a ragged bunch and as far removed from being soldiers as any group could be. Here they were busy drilling with seasoned warriors on the use of the unfamiliar tools of war and death. If there was one thing that was unnerving, it was changes to a set schedule. As it was, their arrival fit nicely into the plans as Athelstan knew them, but he would have preferred to dictate matters. He stood silently and watched the proceedings unfold

The rotund Athenian, Cliethenes looked rather comical in his cuirass and greaves, but the criss-cross cuts on his forearm showed that the orator had not shirked his duties when it came to the fighting. Evidently, he had been successful.

As they convened, he regaled them with the story of the fight to liberate Athens and it sounded like a desperate affair. Street to street fighting was hardly the province of the hoplite, or phalangites for that matter. No tactics of use could be employed in the narrow alleyways of the city – it had been a gutter war, the outcome decided by who wanted it most.

"I raised the militia and the wall fortified," he finished. "We are free, yes – but I fear it will not be long before Macedon responds." He mopped his brow and glanced at the massive, silent presence of Athelstan.

"My bodyguard," Leonida said by way of explanation, "and you are right, the blow will fall hardest here. It will be heavy and it will be soon."

Athelstan stood silently and listened carefully. He also scanned the crowd anticipating danger. Save for the council, dignitaries and soldiers the open–air structure was clear.

"What shall we do?" Cliethenes asked and as he did so, the weight of responsibility landed on Leonida hard. She was Spartan, the famed warriors of Hellas and now, they would look to her to lead them. "Our walls are strong," he went on. "We can hold them off…"

"No." Leonida interrupted. "A protracted siege is not the answer. I appreciate that the ships could keep Athens well supplied as they did in Pericles' time, but this is not Pericles's time. We can no longer trust to the sea for succour. We face the same issues he did – Athens is large, yes. Its walls are tall and strong, yes; but this time we have many thousands of men. We cannot risk disease." She got to her feet, all too aware of Athelstan's eyes upon her. "The attacker can break off the siege at any time, retreat and return as he pleases. In this instance, HE has the advantage of the time to resupply while he waits for us to starve and weaken. There is no victory for Hellas in this," she stated flatly, "We must meet Macedon on the plains of Attica and defeat him outright. We must cripple his war effort with one decisive blow."

"How do you know he will face us? He may hold back – we could be in the field for some time." Cliethenes was probably thinking with his stomach, but he raised a valid point.

"He will face us," she said confidently. "This is an army lead by two Queens."

"Your pardon Leonida, but I see only one Queen and her with no army at all."

"They are coming overland but are slightly delayed dealing with a branch of Cassander's forces that attempt to blockade Corinth. I am assured they will be on the march by daybreak tomorrow. Cassander's honour will demand that he beat us both outright, I am sure. If he holds back or attempts anything other than a military victory, his leadership and perhaps even his manhood will be questioned. I would hazard that his throne depends on this." There was a chuckle sweep through the assembly at the manhood comment.

Athelstan looked around and sitting high up on the very last seat of the amphitheatre was a solitary man. His complexion was dark and he sat with an easy bearing. When they locked eyes, the odd man tilted his head and gave Athelstan a simple nod. Athelstan stared at the man for a moment but the man did not move. He was small and thin. His dark hair was short on top with long ringlets hanging down on either side of his head. A shadowy beard clung to his chin and he sported a stiff dark hat. Athelstan quickly swept the rest of the theatre for others but there were none. This took only seconds but when he looked back the seat was empty and the odd little man was gone. A cold chill went up his spine.

"Demetrios," Athelstan whispered. Demetrios looked at the Celt and then followed his upward. A moment later the Spartan marched in the direction of the nearest stairway up towards this strange man. He took four guards with him.

Cliethenes was speaking, "…perhaps it does and I'd say you are right; Cassander will fight. Now, we come to the crux of the matter, Leonida. Many times the hoplite has faced the Sarissophoroi and always, the Sarissophoroi has walked away victorious. I lay a damnable curse upon their long spears. We need a plan." He spat.

"Spies," whispered Athelstan again.

Leonida smiled sweetly and gave him a slight nod. "I have a plan," Leonida began.

"History teaches us that these previous battles have been waged with the advantages going to the Macedonian – either in numbers, or political stability – the exception being the battle of Chaeronea. This defeat, however, was at the hands of Philip, when the Hellene armies were led by Demosthenes – hardly a strategist. Macedonia employs and trains their army to the exclusion of all other occupations. They do not have Soldier–farmers or soldier–potters. They have professional soldiers, period and so they are devoted to the art of war."

"A danger to be sure," Cliethenes put forward.

"Of course," Leonida acknowledged. "In any event – Philip was a military genius – and we were still unfortunate to lose. Now, things are different. Cassander is no Philip and certainly no Alexander. Furthermore, he is facing a confederacy united in purpose and under one leader." Her eyes flicked to Athelstan with a questioning look. His lips twisted into a grin of acknowledgement and his eyes flickered towards the now empty seat. To her credit, she did not follow his gaze.

"I had not," she went on, "expected your army to meet us here. But, that is for the better. In a day we will be a full compliment."

"But as strong as we are, we cannot expect to stand toe to toe with Cassander in the old ways and expect to win. Even if we did, we would be finished as a fighting force. We need, therefore, to be flexible and not play to his strengths. His strength is in horsemen. We cannot match the companion cavalry, so the key to this battle is nullifying them. Force them into a fight they cannot win."

"But what of the phalanx?" Cliethenes wanted to know.

"Athelstan here is a General of a great Celtic army and if my research is correct, his army consists almost entirely horsemen. Is that correct General?"

He was surprised to be drawn into this discussion.

"It is, Leonida–Queen. Horseman and chariots."

"Can we beat their cavalry outnumbered as we are with our Horsemen?"

"No, Leonida–Queen." He watched her face fall.

"However…" every eye was on the Celt.

"We can beat them easily with our horsemen and well-placed archers."

Leonida smiled and took a step back. "Like this." He stepped forward and sketched out a triangle facing a square on a piece of parchment. He drew a straight line from the point of the triangle towards the front of the square. As it neared the facing line of the square, he bent his line so it touched the square at a thirty-degree angle

"Never attack cavalry, especially one as well trained as Cassander's, head on. Make them chase you." He stepped back so everyone could see.

"This pattern shows our cavalry in a spear point pattern. By that, I mean a heavily armoured lead horse followed by two and then three and so on. It will act the same way a thrown spear acts, piercing a tiny hole and widening it with each successive rank of cavalry. It charges against the Sarissophoroi formation and at the last minute, it wheels striking the spear wall at this angle. The formation cannot react fast enough to cause much harm." A murmur ran through the advisors and Cliethenes nodded his understanding. "The real threat will come from the ranks of javelin throwers in the rear."

"Do as much damage as you can with fifty strokes of your sword, no more and then retreat back the way you came in."

"What about the javelin throwers you mentioned?"

"That is actually a very good question. Don't let them hit you with one. Javelins are really dangerous. Especially the pointy tip." He let that comment just hang. Some of the men chuckled while others frowned and nodded sagely. Leonida was quietly scanning the upper seats.

"We will suffer a few losses. It is war after all, not a pleasant stroll through the Agora. But, we will do cataclysmic damage to the formation. Their pikes are useless in very close quarters. Retreat, reform and repeat as ordered. In time, their cavalry will be forced to respond. We must never turn the same way over and over. We will set a random pattern we must all memorize. That is when we turn and retreat to the walls and let those priestess archers decimate their cavalry from above. Hit the horses, not the soldiers. These are specialized troops and cavalry soldiers make poor foot soldiers. What we have on our side is that Cassander and his professional army is predictable. We use that weakness to our advantage and we can rout them in a day."

"That," Leonida said, "is beautiful."

"I rather thought so too," Athelstan sounded dry and matter of fact.

"Can you do this?" she asked.

"Yes."

"We don't have to deal with them on an equal footing. If matters go as I suspect, we can mop the cavalry up once their phalanx is broken."

"And Achilles?" Cliethenes asked. Leonida sipped her wine.

"If he is good to his word, then the battle will be over in an hour. I will not count on Thessaly. If they betray Cassander as I hope, this is good. However, I do not plan our battle plans on the mindset of others. We can beat Cassander – with this plan – we can beat him. We must march out soon. Are there any questions?"

Cliethenes did his best to look like the experienced commander he wished to be. The sad truth was, he was not. The revolt in Athens was the only real battle he had ever witnessed in his life and there was not that much in the way of tactics involved. He kept his dignity and composure and continued to speak with his typical Athenian tone.

"Are there any mercenaries that we can rely on?" His eyes rested on Athelstan briefly. "Our lack of cavalry concerns me and since Cassander has the experienced companions under his control, I fear we will not be able to hold them off. Perhaps Bomilcar of Carthage would consider stirring up trouble in Thrace. This may distract Cassander while we quickly advance closer to his homeland."

An advisor spoke, "My lord Cliethenes, we have heard rumours that Bomilcar has declared that he is an ally of Cassander. It would be unwise to contact them!"

Leonida nodded, "I have heard the same news. Indeed the Carthaginian navy currently blockades Piraeus." Demetrios reappeared in the long corridor under the seats and shook his head at Athelstan. The Celt made no indication he had seen the Greek.

Cliethenes was slightly embarrassed, but he shook that off and continued to speak. He hoped to find a way to save many Greek lives and to try to guarantee victory.

"In that case, we must be wary. We cannot be certain that Antigonas is actually allied to the Macedonians and even if he were, would he be willing to send aid? Maybe we could stir up trouble in the east and provoke lord Seleucus and Antigonas to fight one another? Their relationship is famously tense, meaning that we could take advantage of this."

"Just like Nicaea in the west who can't send help because he fears the Romans will invade his land, we can make Antigonas nervous that the Seleucids will invade. Clever use of diplomacy can give us the edge without the need of more bloodshed."

Leonida allowed Cliethenes to finish speaking.

"What you say has merit," she said. "But what we lack is time. Antigonas's involvement, or lack thereof – is not something we can base our campaign on, Cliethenes. Consider you only have a small army, a hoplite militia and a troop, or two of cavalry to defend Athens. Even as we speak, Cassander will be preparing to or indeed has commenced, to march this way. We cannot tarry, considering move and counter-move."

"Leonida–Queen is right," Athelstan gave Cliethenes a sage look. "As she says, your plan is worthy. I propose that we march now, with all haste to the fields. We dig in and prepare for Cassander to declare his intent. It is my guess that he will expect you to hide behind the walls and will be unprepared for a formal assault on the open field. In the meantime," he smiled at Cliethenes, "perhaps we should put your plans into operation. They will never be in place in time for this battle. Still, any dissent you can stir up in the East will keep prying eyes away from our concerns here."

Cliethenes looked somewhat mollified by this and Leonida wished that she could have phrased things better.

"What about the cavalry," the Athenian pressed, breaking her moment of pique.

"As Athelstan has outlined," Leonida said as lightly as she could. "We can beat them using guile instead of force." The Celt leaned over and whispered in Leonida's ear and she showed her agreement with a blink. Demetrios came and stood by her side.

The confederation moved out soon after. Athelstan left by another exit alone. He wanted to see if he could find this swarthy man. Not for generations had Athenian and Spartan marched side by side. It had taken a threat to the freedom of Hellas to bring them together once before and now, in modern times, the same threat from a different foe had served to reignite the flame of unity once again.

Athelstan knew that win, or lose, Leonida would have to work as never before to keep that flame burning. Still, the Corinthian Queen's underlying motives bothered him for some reason. That little voice in his head was screaming at him. It was rarely wrong.

Chapter Twenty

Athelstan was very concerned about the identity of that mysterious man sitting in the top row of the amphitheatre. How did he get past the guards? Did they see him there? Why was he there? Was he a spy? Was he watching the meeting, or was he looking at Athelstan? He had many questions for this stranger. He made his way to the Agora and began to look at faces. Athenians all dressed and looked alike. They all gestured wildly and yelled at each other. It was a wonder there were any of them left.

The Agora was a riot of colour. From the street beggars to the merchants to the wealthy patrons it was a living breathing chaotic riot of humanity. He knew that finding that man here was slim. Still, he felt he needed to start somewhere. If this had been a spy, he was likely long gone and giving damning intelligence to the enemy.

"Find what ewe are looking for Keltoi?" It was a melodious yet oddly accented voice that addressed him from behind and Athelstan knew in an instant the man he sought had found him instead. He was small and had a round head. His ears were prominent if a bit small. On his closely cropped head, he wore a strange circle of a cap that did nothing to block the sun. His beard was long and he wore his sideburns in equally long curls. The beard told him that this was the same man seen from a distance in the Amphitheatre. Colourful but dusty robes swaddled his gaunt frame and the sandals on his feet were well worn. He carried a staff and beneath his robes was an oddly curved sword.

"Yes, it would seem I have, or more correctly you have found me." Athelstan turned.

"Aye am fla–tard sir that you would seek out so low a creature such as Aye. Surely more important matters trouble ewe, than my humble self, Saul from Jeru–Salam, City of the Jews." He bowed low bearing a smile of straight white teeth. He also boasted shrewd eyes and a remarkably easy way about him.

"What were you doing in the Amphitheatre today?"

"Why, Aye was watching ewe of course. It is not often Aye get to see one of your race and when Aye heard ewe had arrived, Aye was curious. Aye hope you did nut mind. Aye meant no harm."

"You know there is a war about to start here?"

"Yas, Aye have heard something about it. Nasty business - war. Aye should avoid it if Aye were ewe. God would nut approve."

"You mean 'The Gods' would not approve.

"Aye mean nothing of the sort Keltoi. There is only one God."

"Only one? Isn't he lonely?" A rich and genuine laughter rang out.

"Aye have nevah thought about it that way. Aye suppose he is, but he is lucky. He has Jews to worship him. He might be lonely, but he has a lot of us to talk to."

"You are a spy?" Athelstan never shied away from the brutal questions.

"Yas, Aye am – as are ewe. We are just nut spies for Macedonia. Aye am also a pilgrim and a musician and a fathah. What are ewe Keltoi? A warrior certainly, but are ewe a husband, a fathah, a son? Are ewe even aware of what ewe are? Aye ask again Keltoi; think carefully now on your answer; what are ewe?"

"WILD!" The odd little man with the serene face did not jump. He didn't even blink and a slow smile blossomed on his face.

"Yas ewe are. Aye think ewe will make an interesting travelling companion 'WILD' man. Have ewe a name?"

"Athelstan. What makes you think we are going to be travelling companions?" Saul ignored the question. He pondered the name and mouthed it silently for a moment.

"What a curious name. Ath, of the House that Stands Firm. That is the translation from Arabic. It suits ewe Aye think. What makes ewe think we will nut be travelling companions?"

"I choose my friends very carefully."

"Very wise of ewe - yes. So do Aye. Aye think Aye am quite good at it too."

"Where is it you think we are going Saul from Jeru–Salam?"

"Aye hardly care Ath–al–Stan. The destination is of no consequence. It is the quest for the destination that is filled with wonder – is it nut?" He opened his hands like a flower blooming in the spring. "Aye simply seek, that is all. "

"What do you seek Saul of Jeru–Salam?"

A shrug was the only reply he received.

"What if I refuse to travel with you?"

Saul waved a hand absently. "Another matter of no consequence. Aye must come with ewe, or ewe will come with me. If this does nut happen, ewe will die. My God has spoken to me of this. He is never wrong. The matter has been decided months ago."

"Months ago? How do you know of me?"

"Aye do nut know of ewe, but my God does, whether you believe that or nut."

"I am going to die? How? Why has no one told me?"

"Aye just did tell ewe. Besides, Aye must come with ewe if only to keep ewe from being robbed blind." He reached into his robes and offered Athelstan his own boot knives, handles first with a formal bow. Athelstan took them and looked at them with suspicion.

"Where did you get these?"

"From the thief who stole them from ewe, while ewe walked through the Agora of course. Ewe might as well wear a bell around your neck and a sign that reads 'rob me' in nine different languages." Athelstan looked around with no a small amount of paranoia.

"You were following me."

"Yass. Since ewe were looking for me, Aye thought it was only polite."

"It would seem that you are coming with me whether I like it, or 'nut'."

"So it would seem Ath of the House that Stands Firm, yas." Again that brilliant smile. "Shall we go or are there other items ewe would like to have stolen?"

His steps took him atop the city walls. Saul joined him there. He needed to feel the wind on his face and survey the forces arrayed against this fortress city. King Cassander had planned this operation well. Thessalonians and Macedonians formed ten distinct Army groups of six thousand men each, facing the three thousand Athenians. That was sixty thousand professional troops facing a conscripted rabble. The forces from Attica, Marathon and Piraeus reinforced them but combined they added two thousand at most. Hope for victory was still looked for from the west. It was a terrible mismatch. The force left to liberate the Isthmus of Corinth effectively took Sparta, Corinth and Argos out of the fight. It would take days to remove that threat, only to have to fight their way through the bulk Macedonian Army again, just to get into the city. By then siege engines will have pounded half the city flat. A grim smile formed on his lips. It was just the sort of thing he would do in Cassander's place. It was a brilliant strategy. They were in very grave danger.

Turning he saw the bright sparkle of the Mediterranean. Its surface was covered with masts and sails by the thousands. The great navy of Carthage had effectively closed the port, but they kept a safe distance from the high fortifications around Athens harbour. Great catapults could fire a flaming missile nearly a mile with surprising accuracy. Two hundred pounds of burning pitch and oil was not something any captain wanted landing on his deck. There was no way to get anywhere near the horseshoe-shaped harbour, safely.

From this vantage point, he watched as the Athenian allies bravely marched out to confront King Cassander. They formed up and seemed utterly insignificant. All that could be hoped was that word of his people's arrival in Gwennderion Glade would be enough to break the siege and force Cassander to confront the more immediate threat at home. When the King realises that the Senones are there for a religious celebration and not war, it will be too late in the year to remount their campaign for Athens. Even as he pondered this, the Thessalian infantry was moving south to flank the Athenians.

The wall was covered in people; many were Queen Leonida's Priestess archers. Each was dressed in a simple white toga and each had several baskets of arrows at their disposal. Their bow arms were bare except for the leather guard lashed to their inner forearms. As he walked along, he spoke to several of the archers and although they were not the most talkative women, he had ever met, they were polite.

Saul remarked, "She is very beautiful, no?"

"Who?" Saul simply pointed.

He spotted the Spartan Queen talking with a few of her archers.

"Excuse me, Saul. I must speak with her." Saul tilted his head in understanding.

"Your Majesty, I will now discharge my pledge of duty to you. I present myself for duty in defence of this city."

"I thank you, Lord Athelstan, for your service. Who is your friend?"

"Oh, him? He looked over his shoulder only to find Saul had followed him and was standing right behind him grinning.

"Your Majesty, may I present Saul, a pilgrim from Jeru–Salam."

She smiled graciously and began to speak to Saul in a language Athelstan could not understand. After a moment, Leonida laughed and Saul bowed low.

"I see you have found your spy."

"He is nut… not a spy."

Still chuckling she agreed, "No he is definitely not a spy. You have made a rare friend today. Keep him in your council, Athelstan. He will prove most valuable. So, you wish to fight that?" Her arm swept the formations of Macedon.

"We are wild, Leonida–Queen and that is what I do." The intensity of which he said this caused her to jump. "When the need is upon us, we are predators of the highest order. Those men in Ythion should have realised what I was. Yet, they did not and they died never knowing. That is why I offered you the chance to know us… to understand what we really are. Allow me to join Demetrios and show you what it is to have a single Senone fighting by your side, then imagine what one hundred thousand might mean to your place in history." He let these words sink in.

"Since the dawn of time, we have been Kingmakers. We can be Queen–makers just as easily. Remember this as you watch and learn young Priestess–Queen; I do not know fear. Not even the Gods can do this for you," she looked at him with serene calm but he knew this was something she craved. She bit her lip unconsciously as she thought about his offer.

A slow nodding replaced her ill-concealed indecision. "Very well Lord Athelstan. If that is your decision then let it be so. I shall watch and learn. Report to General Demetrios and place yourself under his command. I shall watch from here and then we can discuss your offer in more detail later." He turned to watch as the combined allied Hellenic forces clashed with the Macedonians and a bloodbath ensued. He left the walls to join the Spartan cavalry.

Now that the sun had reached its zenith, Athelstan sat aboard Maehadren alongside Demetrios and his one hundred and fifty very determined–looking Spartan knights. The Spartan was surprised when the Celt informed him that he would obey his orders, or die in the attempt. He smiled wickedly when he was informed this arrangement was by Royal Decree.

"So now we will both find out if you are really as tough as you believe you are," Demetrios commented idly.

"So we shall. Pay careful attention Commander. Just try not to cut off any of your more important bits with that – thing," he gestured at his Machaira; the long–bladed sword favoured by Greek Cavalry. It had a far greater reach than the shorter utilitarian Xiphos. The men chortled at the comment and Demetrios winked at the Celt.

Demetrios led his armoured knights and the Senone onto the field through the West Gate. They turned towards the retreating Athenians and drew their long Machaira. Both noticed the Atticans wheel, attack and effectively disrupt the Macedonian pursuit. This served to separate the two forces somewhat but they paid an immediate and heavy price. Hundreds fell to the invaders' long spears.

Athelstan pointed a spot where the separation between the two armies was the narrowest and with a curt nod, Demetrios agreed that was where they would have the biggest impact.

At a signal from Demetrios, the troop deftly transformed from a column into a solid wedge and then to a pair of 'V' shapes – one behind the other. As they approached the Macedonians, they picked up speed. The first companies of Athenians were running past them in the opposite direction as they raced for the safety of the city walls. The Spartan Cavalry held formation and closed the distance with the enemy. By the time, they came abreast of last of the Athenians the red cloaks of the Spartans whipped wildly behind them and they galloped headlong toward the lead units of Macedonian infantry.

The initial clash with the Atticans had scattered and broken the pristine Macedonian lines and there was a great melee underway on one flank. Athelstan and Demetrios approached the same formation from the other side and thundered towards a bristling wall of shields and rank upon rank of braced fourteen–foot long spears.

Unlike Spartan steeds, Maehadren's chest and face were armoured with overlapping plates of brightly enamelled banded iron. His hooves were shod with iron and he ate up the ground like a vengeful wind – Athelstan finally drew his long sword and held it high over his head. He whispered a prayer of protection to Epona. The White Horse Goddess suddenly took over Maehadren's spirit and with a mighty surge of power he felt his horse pull forward of Demetrios's mount forcing Athelstan to lead the charge.

In every cavalry charge, there is a magical moment just before the collision. Time slows and every detail is crisp and clear. Every movement is briefly frozen. Expressions are fixed and expectant. Bodies are clenched awaiting impact. Insects hang motionless in the air. Every sound is muted. So it was now. Athelstan took a last deep breath wheeled Maehadren sharply to the left and screamed a savage whinny at those who were about to fall.

CRASH!

Time resumed apace.

Athelstan swung his sword and swept away the spear points in front of him just as his steed leapt into the tightly massed soldiers. Maehadren descended on the first rank of soldiers with bared teeth and flailing hooves. It was a prolonged collision. The first 'V' struck a bare heartbeat before the second and five ranks of soldiers suddenly died under the horse's hooves. A wide gash had been opened in the tightly massed ranks of infantry.

The Spartan knights swept away fifty feet of shield wall and plunged deep into the tightly bunched Macedonian infantry. Over a dozen Spartan horses fell, impaled by their long barbed spears and those knights who fell were left afoot to fight and die as best they could. The rest pounded on. Dozens then scores of Macedonians fell to thrashing and flailing hooves alone and many more fell to the Spartan javelins, spears and swords. Maehadren cut a bloody path towards the centre of the formation; Athelstan had been unable to break him of this dreadful habit. Simply along for the ride, the Celt was left to swing his six-foot sword in wide glittering circles.

Crimson dots trailed like fairy dust from the tip of the sword as it whirled up and down. He sang and laughed maniacally as he slew and soon there was a large clear area around Maehadren that few seemed willing to enter. The Macedonian pursuit faltered and the Athenians placed more distance between themselves and the invading hoard.

Maehadren turned in a full circle, reared and shrieked his challenge causing those closest soldiers to back up another step. This was a practised and polished manoeuvre – one Maehadren loved. As the beast turned, Athelstan scanned the immediate battlefield quickly. His eyes fixed on what he sought and he turned Maehadren toward the unit Commander. The man was screaming for his troops to regroup and counter-attack and horns trumpeted his commands for all to hear. If Athelstan had his way, this would be his final set of orders. He dug in his heels and his wild-eyed blood-soaked beast leapt forward and plunged back into the massed troops. Many were trampled as they tried to get clear of the lethal slashing hooves. These professional soldiers launched immediate counter-attacks.

He had only travelled a few dozen paces when an expertly hurled javelin sliced through Athelstan's banded leather shield and drove deep into his left forearm. He roared in fury and pain as he pitched backwards off Maehadren and slammed to the ground. It took a moment for him to regain his wind before hacking the javelins long shaft from the face of the shield. He struggled to his feet and tried to keep his arm up. Little by little he was receiving annoying nicks and cuts from the expert and determined Macedonian regulars. Maehadren stepped in front of Athelstan and ground another soldier to death with his hooves. It gave Athelstan the time to regain his saddle and once aboard Maehadren again, the odds changed in the Celt's favour.

Maehadren drooled blood from numerous slices and punctures of his own but he pressed on resolutely towards the mounted Macedonian Lord. The enemy pointed, gestured and bellowed instructions red-faced and wide-eyed. He drew his sword and a small vanguard of soldiers formed a square around him. Then there was only open ground between them and Maehadren began his final charge.

These few soldiers were like chaff upon the wind as they collided with Maehadren's deadly hooves and Athelstan's razor-sharp sword. The fourteen hundred pound warhorse raked and slashed at the Commander's hastily assembled guard. Chests and skulls alike were crushed under Maehadren's savage assault.

Then it was only Athelstan and the enemy commander. They engaged the other with masterful skill and relentless ferocity. Each strove to gain an advantage over the other in this whirling ballet of horse, rider, sword and shield. Great bloody gashes appeared on Athelstan's unprotected arms and thighs as the Macedonian wielded his sword with precision. Soon these two simple soldiers were locked in a brutal mounted combat to the death... and Athelstan was losing.

It was quickly apparent to Athelstan that this Macedonian Commander was not some flabby spoiled Greek Lord more concerned with table and bed then the practice yards – no indeed. Here was a professional warrior, skilled, cunning and deadly. There was no fear, or anger in his eyes. There was no doubt or confusion in his mind. He was a highly trained killer performing his craft in the service of his King and he bore that cold calculating determined look a man gets when he is certain he cannot loose.

It was a blur of iron and a rhythmic ringing as these two fought for advantage. Athelstan ducked a brutal decapitating blow almost too late. His left arm was now numb and he could no longer hold it up. He could feel the steel javelin tip grinding against the bones near his left elbow and the pain was blinding with every blow he blocked. Fate, however, cast the last die in this deadly game.

Maehadren also fought hard. He bit and kicked anything that came within reach. His iron-shod hooves had ripped the enemy horse's neck in several places. The Macedonian's horse began to succumb to blood loss and toppled over backwards onto his rump. This sudden drop caused the General to windmill his arms for balance as he fought to stay aboard and it was now that a downward slash from Athelstan's sword took him fully in the belly. Both he and his brave mount fell and died as one, the rider beneath his horse. Athelstan saw the man smile as he fell. Such a team should be together in the next world. It was only proper. He saluted his fallen foe for the great warrior he had been.

There was an open area of ground surrounding Athelstan now and as he turned, he suddenly saw why. Nearly sixty Spartan Knights were still a–horse and had progressively widened the path carved by Maehadren. A full third of the leading vanguard of Macedonian infantry had been cut off from the rest. They seemed ready to break and run when Demetrios ordered disengagement. He saw that the enemy cavalry was being ordered to reinforce this infantry unit.

The task they had been ordered to accomplish was successful. The army group pursuing the Athenians had been slowed to a stop. There was wide separation between the two armies now. It was clear the reckless, ineffective Athenians would gain the city gates safely. The mounted Spartans fell in behind their leader for their final flight back to Athens walls and Athelstan fell in smartly at the rear. There was little resistance on the return ride except for five Spartan knights that were felled by javelins just getting free of the melee. He saw cavalry moving in from the rear to intercept Demetrios' men.

As the Spartans neared the walls, Leonida's Holy Athenian Priestess archers began their deadly work. Head Priestess Appolonia stood among them in her violet gown and veil. White-robed and veiled priestesses stood with her. They were armed with decorative bows and at Appolonia's command, loosed their arrows. The shafts high–pitched whistling flew overhead then faded behind and Athelstan grimaced with wild glee as the sky darkened briefly with the first volley of divine arrows. Then he howled his delight as he heard the screams of those skewered behind him. This was a magnificent day with a proper delaying action successfully accomplished.

He sang and wept as he rode. He began to slump in his saddle from the pain in his arm and loss of blood. His shield was still firmly nailed to his forearm by the barbed iron lance head. Every jarring stride his horse took, sent another lightning bolt of pain from his fingertips to his shoulder.

Looking up at the battlements he saw Queen Leonida bathed in the afternoon light like some Goddess incarnate. An odd dwarf of a man stood nearby. It was Saul and he held a bow. He pulled back his bow and lowered it in his direction. Athelstan's vision wavered. He shook his head to clear it but it did not help. A wave of dizziness washed over him. He could hear hooves approaching hard from behind. The Macedonian cavalry had given chase as he knew they would and Maehadren was tiring. This was a race Athelstan might very well lose. Saul loosed his arrow and it screamed by his ear like an angry hornet. A solid thud ended the sound and seconds later a riderless horse charged past Maehadren. Athelstan slumped oven Maehadren's neck and tried to hold on. Saul felled a good number of Thessalians before Maehadren finally found the safety of the Athenian gates. They closed with a mighty boom behind the Celt and as he toppled to the ground, he could hear watery cheering.

Suddenly out of the blur of hands and faces, came someone he knew. It was Leonida and fear was etched on her face. Her hands went into his hair and beard. She wiped blood from his face.

"Leonida–Queen, it is not safe here," he said weakly trying to stand.

"Athelstan, do not try to talk," she smiled but there was heavy concern on her face. Saul stood behind her. Athelstan reached up and placed a bloody hand on her cheek.

"Saul, get her away from here." War was so random and senseless. A life was there, vibrant one moment - gone the next.

"Come away now, he will be tended by Athenian surgeons." Saul took her by the arm.

"NO! Bring him to my villa. I will tend him there."

These were the last words Athelstan heard.

Chapter Twenty One

The Spartan Queen Leonida had Athelstan brought to rooms in her villa and Saul immediately took over. Athelstan's arm wound was bloody and ragged. The tip of the spear was still lodged deeply within. The Athenian surgeons had wanted to cut off the arm at the elbow. Ridiculous! It made Saul realise who the barbarians really were. Saul would not let the surgeons near Athelstan at all. Leonida immediately took charge and with Saul's help personally removed the barbed javelin head. It was a wicked looking weapon that left an ugly jagged wound. Saul assisted as Leonida performed the surgery needed to save his arm and help save the nerves to his left hand. She used needle and thread to sew the bloody bits of his arm together. Each stitch was a separate thing

She bathed him. When he was clean and dry, they wrestled him onto a bed to rest.

"Aye can tend him now. Ewe go and Aye thank you for your concern for him. Ewe might not know this but history revolves around him, like the end of a knife on the tip of a sword. He stands where two forces meet, ours and theirs. Do ewe understand?"

"Yes I think I do. Will he survive?"

He nodded. "For now, it is in our best interests that he does. We need someone our enemies can focus their attention on. He will do nicely" Saul took a position on a bench by his bed rocked gently back and forth. He produced a scroll and opened it. He began to read out loud from the Holy Torah.

After a time, he stood and examined Athelstan's hand. To his great relief, he felt it was warm. There he sat, hour after hour reading from his ornate scroll. He had used a poultice of aromatic herbs and honey. He re-wrapped it carefully for two days. Leonida saw to it that Saul was brought food and allowed to sleep. Together they tended the unconscious Celt night and day.

Outside the white walls of Athens, the war with Macedon raged on.

A low groan and creaking of the cot told Saul he was waking up. Athelstan fought the medicine making him sleep and he groaned again. His eyes opened and for a moment, he blinked to focus. He looked over at his left arm and it was heavily bandaged. It throbbed unmercifully.

'What?' he wondered. Beyond the white linen sat that profoundly odd looking man. He was smiling with straight white teeth. "Mmmm," Athelstan grunted. "You are still here. I thought you left to go seek."

"Yas Aye am still here and a good thing Aye am too."

"You might be one of two people in this room that believes that is true."

"These Greek butchers that proclaim themselves doctors would have cut off your arm had Aye nut stopped them."

"Nut stopped them?" Athelstan was trying hard to shake the cobwebs from his brain. "Why would they want to cut off my arm?"

"Ewe were wounded in the battle. Do ewe nut remember?"

"Nut remember? What are you talking about? You are the spy." He blinked and tried to sit up. Pain ripped through his left arm and memory returned all at once. He groaned and slumped back into his pillows.

"It is pronounced not," Athelstan corrected.

"Yas, I am the spy. That's what Aye said 'nut'."

Demetrios arrived in the middle of this exchange.

"No, say it with me, Not."

"Nut."

"NOT."

"NUT."

And so it went.

"Friend Demetrios," Saul began, "Welcome again."

"Get it through your head, Jew, I am not your friend."

"Nut?"

"Not!"

"Stop it both of you," Athelstan winced, "I am giving myself a headache. Maehadren?" He croaked. Saul gave him a sideways look.

"Oh, I am just fine… thank you for your overwhelming sense of concern," he sniffed as if hurt but his wide smile belied his true feelings.

"Yas." Saul put a hand up to his mouth as though is would hide his words from Demetrios' ears.

"He does nut think we are friends. Aye know we are but he is still resistant. Aye will work on him."

"WE ARE NOT FRIENDS!" the Spartan bellowed.

"See? Aye will give him time."

"Is everything you say and do some divine vision from your one God?" Demetrios asked.

"Yas, it is! Why do ewe not find that a comfort in that as does my friend Ath of the House that Stands Strong?"

"It is Athelstan," the Celt said, "and I am still not sure we are friends either."

"Yas. Aye know ewe do nut see it either. Aye will work on ewe too." He patted the Celt's shoulder.

"I swear by all the Gods, Athelstan I am going to do him an injury," Demetrios growled.

"There is only one God, friend Demetrios," Saul reminded Demetrios probably for the hundredth time.

"What?" Demetrios looked at Saul like the Jew had just eaten a bug.

It was all too much for Athelstan and he began to chortle. Saul joined in and with open arms invited Demetrios to join in. The dour Spartan snorted twice and that seemed to be what passed for laughter in him.

"We have much work to do with this one Ath, do we nut?"

"NOT!" Demetrios corrected again. "It is pronounced NOT!"

"Yas that is what Aye said nut. Nut! That is how Aye always pronounce it ever since Aye was just a leetle baby jew–boy."

"Ahhh, you are hopeless!" he dismissed Saul with a wave of his hand. "Queen Leonida asked me to come and see how you are doing."

"Tell her I died and she needs to come and breathe life back into me." Saul hid his face so the others would not see him laughing. Demetrios looked at them both with contempt.

"Are you two insane?"

"Very possibly. Yas."

"I can't tell her that. I will say you are awake and sitting up." Athelstan sat up straight.

"Yes and tell her I am also firm."

He looked at both men with a derisive snort and stormed out.

Once he had gone, Saul stuck his tongue out at the closed door and said, "NAUGHT!" It was very funny sounding coming from him.

"You don't suppose he will actually tell her that do you?"

Saul's silent wide-eyed expression of uncertainty caused them both to burst out laughing again. "Aye hope she knows as leetle about the world as he does, or she might have ewe executed."

BOOM! Neither man jumped.

"I see Cassander has come knocking again, get that for me will you?"

"Catapults. Aye am surprised it has not woken ewe before now. That stunt ewe pulled with the cavalry has angered him mightily. He lost a great many seasoned troops.

The ground shuddered again. It was a vicious onslaught. Macedonia had brought their siege engines to bear and had begun to pound the city. Athelstan had employed catapults himself in the past and he knew how quickly they could quickly reduce a city to rubble.

BOOM!

This was much closer now. Athelstan looked around. He had no idea where he was.

"Saul, what I need is to get up and go back out there. I must fight to defend the city. I cannot watch this city fall while lying on my back. Help me up," he tried again to sit up.

Saul poked Athelstan's arm with a stiff finger. It sent him back into his pillows numb with agony.

"Ewe are nut invincible and there are others who are capable of fighting in your place. Aye can see that we have perhaps answered one of your questions. Aye may be saving your life right now. My God is seldom wrong."

"What sort of man would I be if I let others fight and die in my place?"

"An intelligent one!"

BOOM!

Athelstan's head turned to the other side of his bed. "Where is my armour?" he asked. A wave of dizziness caused him to slump back onto the cot. He saw Saul smirk. Saul knew he was too weak to sit up let alone ride into battle.

"You are enjoying this?" Athelstan stated with a snort.

"Yas... yas, Aye believe Aye am," he crossed his arms.

"Well then if you will not let me get up and you will not let me fight, then what is left for me? Fetch me a courtesan." Leonida had quietly entered the room and stood silently listening. Demetrios closed the door behind her and remained outside.

"Still 'firm' then are we?" she asked dryly.

His face looked puzzled for a moment as he turned to look at her. Then his eyes widened and his mouth dropped open. "Oh, no, I can assure you that I am... not... umm..."

"Nut," corrected Saul in a whisper. Athelstan shot him a withering look. Saul shrugged and offered Leonida his chair.

"You are a wicked old man is what you are." She sat.

"As for what you propose, we surely cannot do anything of the sort. Besides, just firm would hardly do. You are injured." She paused.

"I am younger than you. I would just hate to kill you. At least not without a proper trial."

Saul was about to correct her usage of the word not but a look from Athelstan stopped him. He poured a flagon of wine and stood in the background.

Leonida's face was stoic but there was a mischievous twinkle in her eye.

Athelstan nodded sadly. "Yes, but how else am I expected to regain my strength? He will not let me fight." There was an exaggerated head jerk in Saul's direction. "You would not want me weakening any further would you? What if we are overrun and killed? You would hate yourself for missing this opportunity," he sighed sadly but his smile was intact. She shook her head and blushed again.

"I will risk it." She asked Saul, "Has he always been like this?"

"Ewe have known him longer than Aye have Your Majesty, but in all probability – yas, he has very likely always been this way."

"Truly? You seem to have known each other all your lives. When did you first meet?"

"Three days past, in the Agora but Aye first saw him in the Amphitheatre during your meeting."

"You're the spy?"

"Yas, Aye am the spy," he said with a sigh. "He really is a bad judge of character is he nut?"

"Not."

"Nut."

"Stop it both of you!" she commanded.

"I am not a bad judge of character!" Athelstan muttered with feigned indignant.

"Saul is not just a spy either, he is an..." Saul lightly touched her arm and shook his head. "Now, is nut the time."

Athelstan looked back and forth at them with suspicion. "... Nut the time? Well, if all you two are going to do is malign my good character and keep secrets from me, then I think I would like a drink. Talking to this one is very thirsty business," he looked at his arm again. "I want to see how bad it is. Help me take this off?"

BOOM!

Leonida jumped.

"No," Saul and Leonida said in unison.

Leonida reached for the pitcher on the table. She poured some water into a cup and held it to Athelstan's lips. He greedily slurped the water.

"I was hoping for something stronger."

"Water is all ewe are getting."

"That wound needs to stay bandaged," Saul continued. "Aye can remove the bandages in a week. Ewe will stay here in bed for three days." He showed him three fingers.

"Three days? We will all be nothing but butchered meat by then." He was aghast. "Are you sure you do not want to taste something more wild than Spartans Leonida-Queen?"

"Quite sure, yes, thank you. Perhaps you might settle for dancing. I like dancing," Leonida replied.

"No, it is not the same. Let me fight! It is what I do."

"Please General, do not make this more difficult than it already is. I know you are a soldier, but you cannot fight today." Leonida came over to him with a pot. She took the lid away and it was a soup, still warm.

"I made some soup earlier in hopes that it would still be warm when you awoke."

"You made it? That smells wonderful. I did not know you could cook."

"There is much about me you do not know and I think I should keep it that way for the time being," she sat on the bed. "Shall I feed you?"

"No, I think I can sit up." He tried. He was wrong. "Well maybe a mouthful, or two – until I can get my strength back you understand," he tasted the first warm bite and his eyes widened. "This is very good," he took another bite and shook his head.

BOOM!

Leonida jumped again.

"I will never get used to that noise," Leonida muttered.

"Aye helped," Saul stated feebly.

"With the noise?" Athelstan asked.

"No with the soup," said Saul.

"I swear I am beginning to think there is nothing you two cannot do. You both can shoot a bow like a warrior, you can repair spear wounds like a healer." He looked at Leonida. "And you can cook like an Innkeeper's wife. I think if both you put your minds to it you could repair broken clouds and cure a hangover."

"Aye can do all those things and," he raised a finger in punctuation. "Aye seek."

"And I rule!"

"So you do Leonida–Queen."

She knew he was a prideful man so to help him she placed all the pillows she could find behind him. She picked the pot off the floor and sat it on his lap. After the first two mouthfuls, she placed the pot in his hand.

"In a few minutes ewe will sleep again."

"How do you know that?" he asked past mouthfuls of broth and chicken. "I am actually feeling a lot better."

"Aye fetched the water for the soup and Aye have drugged the soup as well… so, ewe will sleep."

He looked into the pot with suspicion. "Drugged?" Already he could feel his limbs growing heavy. "Now that is not fair."

"Ewe need your sleep, friend Ath of the House that Stands Strong. Fair, does nut matter. Sleep matters." Saul took the soup from his failing hands and set the pot on the floor.

"Then let me say this now. I am grateful to you both for saving my arm and my life. It is a debt I shall repay someday."

"Ewe are welcome, now go to sleep."

BOOM!

He had a faraway look. "We will talk about this… this drugging of… this um…" His eyes closed and moments later he was fast asleep.

BOOM!

Leonida and Saul withdrew to the door.

"Why did you not want me to tell him who and what you really are?" Leonida asked.

"Now is nut a good time for him to know this. For now, Aye must remain the simple pilgrim – the one who seeks. Aye will be a friend who he can count on. He is very intelligent. In time, he will discover the truth."

"What do you suppose he will do then?"

"He will be angry and feel betrayed. By then, we will be friends. Aye just hope that will be enough."

"And what will you do if you 'find' what you seek?"

"Aye will do what Aye must. No one man is more important than he who bears the task given to him by my God. Aye am no exception."

"But he has no interest in your quest. What end would his death serve?" Leonida queried.

"Ewe do nut understand Leonida Queen. He must NUT die; God commands it," Saul responded with a grim look.

Leonida sighed and looked over at the bed. "He will not die? Then why are you here? Promise me he will not die!" It was a command.

Saul had a wide smile. "Aye do so promise ewe. He will live," he said with a bow.

Leonida watched him sleep for a few moments. Demetrios had stood by the door listening. His expression showed his concern. He waited on Leonida and finally escorted her to her section of the villa.

BOOM!

The floor shook with the force of the impact.

Chapter Twenty Two

It was early morning on the fourth day after Athelstan's now famous charge, and the second day after their talk, when Saul finally declared him fit to leave Leonida's estate. A dozen stinging cuts and bruises still vexed the Celt and while he showed no outward sign of distress, his left arm ached. He worked with the healers for most of the morning. After a brief reunion with Maehadren, he helped carry the wounded to the surgeries. Screams filled the air. They were the screams of the living and screams of the dying. Each had its own uniquely chilling sound. It was always like this after a war. Athelstan hated war, and this was the part of war Athelstan hated the most.

That the war was at an end. There was no army of occupation, no executions and no rounding up of slaves. Only the dead and the wounded still littered the battlefield. The populations tended the wounded and robbed the dead. Wagons, chariots and siege engines sat abandoned. Hundreds of horses and oxen grazed among the human and inhuman carnage. Clouds of crows, ravens, magpies, and gulls feasted on the dead with ravenous abandon. Some so fat they could not fly. Children ran after them trying to catch them. It was as if the entire Macedonian army had simply evaporated during the night. It was completely inexplicable.

Macedonian siege engines had tried to pound parts of Athen's walls to rubble for three straight days, but those walls stood firm. The armies of Sparta and Corinth never came and Leonida was heard wondering if their armies had gotten lost. Now, on the morning of the fourth day, Macedonia had quit the field. Carthage had also ended its blockade of the harbour. The Athenian Council hailed it as a great victory. They claimed victory without the help of Sparta, or Corinth. Still, no one could understand how, or why the two powers had left.

A single wounded Celt knew why. No one bothered to ask Athelstan his opinion concerning the departure of the enemy. Neither did he offer one.

He had asked what was going on but Saul refused to tell him, or even give him a hint. When Saul did finally allow him to get up, the bombardment was over.

As Athelstan helped carry litters from the courtyard into the surgeries, his mind was occupied entirely with what might have become of Constantina.

Theophrastus the Healer glanced up briefly as Athelstan helped set down another wounded soldier and casually remarked. "Lord Athelstan, do you realise you are losing humour."

He blinked at the surgeon in confusion. "What? Losing humour? Small wonder I am not in a good mood."

"You are bleeding. Maybe we should have another look at your arm."

The Senone glanced down at his forearm drooling crimson and just as casually replied. "Doctor, I do not have time to bleed. There are still hundreds, of men waiting outside your surgeries and ten times that many still a–field dying of exposure." His left arm throbbed.

"Then at least sit over there and let someone wrap that up again. You are dripping blood all over the wounded and it slowing up the work."

Athelstan blinked again, not quite grasping the Greek word for blood was humour. Once he thought about it, he smiled and sat with a thud. The big man was still dizzy from his own wound. A young apprentice in a white toga completely soaked in blood examined his arm. He unwrapped the bandages and both men's eyes rose in surprise when he saw the three–dozen knotted threads holding the skin together. He wiped the excess blood and dirt away and watched as it welled up. One of the knots had torn free. The apprentice clamped a cloth down hard on the wound and looked up at the barbarian with some trepidation.

Athelstan scowled down at the young man and said softly. "I do not care how bad you think that looks. If you somehow manage to cut it off without me beating you to death, then I will beat you to death with the stump." The young surgeon blanched and his eyes widened to small round moons. In a high-pitched stammer, he quickly assured Athelstan that he could most assuredly keep the arm, but could cauterise it to stop the bleeding. Athelstan nodded and Theophrastus the senior physician returned with a glowing iron and a block of wood.

"Here bite down on this," he thrust the block at Athelstan's mouth but the Celt scowled and pulled away.

"Would you put that thing in your mouth given a choice?'

The healer looked at it with a frown.

"But Milord, this is going to hurt. The block is for the pain." Theophrastus explained patiently.

"Well if you think it will help; you bite down on it for me. Just get on with it. That way you can get back to your work and I can get back to mine." Athelstan stiffened and clenched his teeth as the burning rod hissed and smoked against his left forearm. When he blinked the tears from his eyes, the surgeon briefly examined the stitching and knots with great interest. He then re-bandaged the wound.

The old Athenian was right. It did hurt. A lot!

It was at this inopportune moment, that a grimy, smelly Goth found Athelstan. The smell of burning flesh still rose from his arm. He spoke in low Gaelic with a distinctive accent from the Danube region. One thing was certain the instant he spoke. He had no manners whatsoever.

"You that Senone Athelstan I be lookin' all over for?" The Goth asked with an impertinent smile. Athelstan's brow furrowed as even more waves of pain coursed up his arm. He raised and lowered his chin once very slowly at the Goth. The young surgeon worked faster to bandage Athelstan's wound.

"We have 'em'. They are safe an', I've got'em all stashed just west of the city. I left 'em there cause ya' never know the lay of the land in a city after a big battle ya' know," he winked with a black-toothed smile to somehow punctuate this insane babble. Athelstan did not have to affect a pained look; his arm throbbed like all Tartarus was pounding on it. With a slowly deepening scowl, he cocked his head to one side like a dog, trying to make some sense of this gibberish.

The smelly ill-mannered Goth continued. "So if you'll jist give me the 50 silver ya owe us, you can have 'em an' I be on me way." He offered another phoney smile and held out his hand expecting money. The young surgeon had finished bandaging his arm and Athelstan tousled his hair thanking him. He got a curt nod before the man scurried away. He took a moment to examine the bandage before rising somewhat unsteadily to his feet.

The Goth hand slowly dropped as the Celt rose to his full height and the massive Senone fixed him with a very uncomfortable glare.

"You are ranting, so tell me once again with some clarity. Who are you and what do you want? Now I warn you, I am tired and wounded and damn cranky, so tread very carefully." The Goth suddenly felt very much like a mouse caught in the gaze of an owl.

"I be Gargarus of Goth. I have women." Gargarus said simply.

"Women? What are you talking about? I do not want any women. Now go away." The Celt was rapidly wearying of this Goth.

"I have yer women. The Roman women – you know, King Trahearn's plan." Gargarus looked like he was going to vomit.

"My women? Roman women? What plan? What are you talking about? What exactly have you done?" Athelstan's total disinterest in the Goth had suddenly transformed to a narrow and intense focus as a ghastly, absolutely unthinkable impossibility suddenly occurred to him.

"Aargh! What are ye simple man? Me 'n' me men were hired t'go t'Rome t' kidnap members of wealthy merchant families an' bring 'em here t' you. Girls mind ya. Yer King said you'd take 'em the rest o'the way t' yer Glade an' you'd give us our 50 gold when we delivered 'em to ya." Gargarus held out his hand once again somewhat hopeful.

"What?" He mouthed in breathless incredulity. Athelstan was flabbergasted. Roman hostages? Girls? What was King Trahearn thinking? However, he was not thinking; he was quite insane. His King had brought dishonour down upon them all. An absolutely stunned Athelstan let out a held breath very slowly and sat down to think.

"Don't tell me ya didn't know nothi…" Athelstan held up a finger for silence and the Goth stopped talking. There was a long silence before he finally stood again.

"Come with me," Athelstan said slowly. Athelstan and the Goth took their leave of the surgeons and went in search of Ptolemarch Demetrios. He spoke to him briefly in Greek that left Gargarus blinking in confusion. Demetrios looked at Gargarus.

"I understand General. I will see to everything," he nodded at Athelstan, turned and left. Athelstan led Gargarus to the stables and strapped his riding harness and long sword onto Maehadren. The horse was excited to see his master, so this took time.

Gargarus led Athelstan out of the city. Athelstan just hoped Demetrios understood what he wanted. Gargarus led Athelstan some three miles to the north-west and into a forest clearing where EIGHT tired and frightened girls were huddled. They were wet and shivering and being guarded by five sinister looking, heavily armed Goths. One face stood out. Constantina sat in the centre of the small band. Athelstan's heart turned to ice as he looked at this wretched sight. A black rage began to build in him. She did not leave willingly and he did nothing to find her – NOTHING!

He dismounted then waved the Goths away from the 'women'. He discovered to his shock that these girls were just children. There were seven of them; the oldest looked no older than sixteen. They shrank away from him when he appeared and several let out piteous cries. One defiant girl did not seem as frightened. Her, he knew.

He looked at Constantina and in flawless Latin whispered, "You are safe now, just do not move. Keep the little ones down." Her quick eyes looked him up and she slapped him hard across the face.

Athelstan returned to the huddled kidnappers clapping Gargarus on the shoulder. "This will truly bring Rome to its knees, will it not?" Athelstan beamed a wide smile at Gargarus and the Goth returned it somewhat tentatively. His five men crowded around as Athelstan produced a heavy purse of coins from Maehadren's pack and hefted it in his palm. He handed it to Gargarus and then separated himself from the Goth rabble as each fought for their share. He walked toward the frightened Roman girls and silently motioned with his hand to keep down. Shading his eyes, he scanned the surrounding tree line for any sign of movement but there was none. Perhaps Demetrios had not understood.

He stopped and turned to face the knot of kidnappers. In a loud voice, he said. "My dear Gargarus, in appreciation for all your hard work and that of your fine men I have a special gift for you." As one, they turned, greed and anticipation etched on their faces. "A final payment for what you have done. Are you ready to receive it?" A chorus of affirmation erupted from the rough kidnappers.

"Very well, I urge you all to look way up there. It is coming from the Gods. Can you see it there?" He pointed up into the sky and the Goths, as well as the girls, looked up.

Gargarus said absently. "I see nothing. What ya got fer us then?"

"Fire!" commanded Athelstan. The air suddenly filled with Spartan arrows and a second later, not a single living Goth was left standing in the glade. Shrieks of absolute horror erupted from the children. Many were now crying.

"Hurry!" Athelstan bellowed and beckoned a score of Spartan Priestess archers rushed to the aid of the girls. The Celt even tried to carry the girl in the worst shape, but Constantina began to scratch and punch and scream at him to leave her alone. He was forced to retreat under this girl's withering assault. Three carriages arrived with other Spartan Priestesses driving them. Demetrios was with them.

The priestesses began to treat the many cuts and scrapes borne by his seven new 'hostages'. Helena, the Archer's commander, came to speak with the Celt.

"Milord, despite what these girls must have endured they are in surprisingly good condition. One girl does not look good and should probably be taken to the infirmary," she was a striking woman of 40 winters and had a no nonsense way about her.

"Fine... yes by all means. Get her the help she needs" His concern was obvious.

"What about the others? Where do you want us to take your new slaves?" she asked an honest question but it caught Athelstan off guard.

"My what? Take them to Queen Leonida. She will see to them," The priestess nodded curtly and left issuing orders as she went.

The girls were given a hot meal, allowed to bathe and rest. Their injuries were treated and re-bandaged. One girl was badly dehydrated and had a high fever. She remained in the infirmary overnight. The physicians were not optimistic about her chances but Athelstan knew she would receive constant care.

Finally, as night fell, the others were conveyed to a large room in a local estate where Constantina and her fellow Romans could sleep and begin to recover from their ordeal.

Morning found Athelstan at the doors to Leonida's suites. She was already up with the Roman girls, He could hear giggling and laughing from behind the doors to their suites.

His arm ached! He ached. He ached both in body and soul. His mind was constantly fleeing back to the welfare of his new charges and the sick girl. Instead of entering Leonida's rooms, he hurried to the infirmary to see if the sick girl had survived the night. Athelstan girded himself for bad news before he entered, but was shocked and delighted to see her sitting up on the cot and talking with one of the physicians. She was eating hot soup from a bowl and sipping delicately from a cup of water. Her colour looked good and as she spoke to the healer, she managed a sweet smile that further wrenched at his heart. The physician was the first to notice the arrival of the Celt.

"Ah, Lord Athelstan! There you are. I have someone here who would like to meet you," he beckoned Athelstan to come closer. The girl turned her dark-eyed gaze on the 'Wildman' and she seemed astonished but not frightened by what she saw.

"Lord Athelstan, may I present Sabine. Sabine, this is the man I told you about. He is the one who rescued you and your friends from those evil men." The physician nodded quickly at the Senone in response to his questioning look. "Yes, her fever broke during the night and she is hungry; a very good sign."

"I... thought you were a dream," she blurted out and the Celt smiled. "I am grateful to you Lord Athelstan for my life. Had it not been for you I would have surely perished," her soft voice and wide bright eyes tugged at his heart. He gritted his teeth as hot fury at his King rose in him again. Trahearn had put this sweet girl through an unspeakable nightmare and here she was thanking him. It was almost too much for him to bear.

"We are your slaves now? What are you going to do with us?" A simple innocent question, but it caught the huge warrior by surprise.

"What?" He repeated; a confused frown crossed his face. How did he answer such an absurd question? "Slaves? Do with you? Ah… as in doing something to you without so much as a 'by your leave'?" Athelstan smiled kindly at Sabrine.

"How old are you?"

"I am ten."

"Ten. You are clever for your years. What am I going to do with you? Nothing dear girl. Please try to understand me. You are not slaves, mine, or anyone else. You are free to recover and rejoin your friends. I am going to do something for you, however," he paused letting some measure of relief to sink into Sabine.

"I am going to make sure you get the finest accommodations in all Athens for the duration of your stay here. I will make every effort to return you home as soon as I can. Until then, you are under my protection. No one will harm you again, or they will answer to me." It was a statement of fact delivered in such a way that no argument seemed possible.

"I am not your slave?" she asked.

"No Sabine. You are not my slave. You are my friend. Is she well enough to leave?" Theophrastus nodded with a smile but admitted he would like her to stay for a little while yet and admonished Sabrine from overexertion. "Your friends are staying at an Estate not far from here. You will be able to join them there in a little while."

Sabine smiled innocently.

"Tell me, your friends, what are their names?"

"The oldest is Constantina, she is in charge." Athelstan winced at the name.

"Then there is Alessandra and Caterina. She is the same age as I am. Simone and Nicola are almost ten. Alfio is eight and little Paola is seven. She's pretty shy until she gets to know you."

A plan was formulating in Athelstan's mind all night and now seemed the perfect time to put it into operation. "I see. Thank you, Sabine."

"You're welcome sir."

"Sabine, before I take you to them, I would like you to do me a favour. Can you write? I will tell you what to say," she nodded. They sat for a few minutes as Athelstan dictated a simple letter for Sabine to write.

It began, "Dear Mother and Father. I am alive."

Chapter Twenty Three

Athelstan returned to Leonida's suites and stepped through the doors. He requested that the Queen and her men leave for a few moments. Even Saul was asked to depart. He distributed paper and quills and had each girl write a very carefully worded letter. He paced and snarled showing his white teeth. An occasional feral growl would rip from his throat as he dictated what they were to write.

'Dear mother and father,

I have been taken prisoner by the Senone nation of Celts. General Athelstan in Sparta is holding us. He has two simple demands of the Senate of Rome.

First, all hostilities against the Senone people will cease immediately and your legions will retreat to a line south of Bologne. (He spelt this word for them)

Second, the architect of those atrocities inflicted upon the Senone people of the Po river valley will travel here in person. He will trade places with me and the other girls and stand trial for crimes against the Senone people. Athelstan names him, Papirius Aurelius Cursor, Proconsul of the Senate of Rome.

Once these two conditions are met, we will be released. Fail to comply and we will be killed and eaten, in accordance with the ancient customs of the Senone. He says you have a fortnight to comply.'

"Now sign the letter in your own hand."

He watched as five terrified girls wrote truly heartfelt pleas to their families for salvation. He already had one note from Sabine. Drawing his shiny knife, he cut a lock of hair from each child and these would be included with the letters.

When he had collected all but one of the missives he forced them to write, he left without another word to the horror-stricken girls. He ripped open the doors to their rooms with a boom. He found a tight group of very angry looking people. Queen Leonida was foremost amongst them. She stood hands on hips trembling with naked fury. He was brought up short.

"What?" He growled still acting the part of a wild savage barbarian.

"You cruel heartless bastard! I thought better of you." She slapped him hard. It left a perfect red handprint across his cheek. It caught him by surprise and he blinked in astonishment.

"What was that for? What did I do?" Her expression was shot with fire and anger but was tinged with deep disappointment. "I cannot believe what you just did in there to those poor frightened children. I thought you were an honourable man. You disgust me. You are nothing but an unfeeling, uncaring, insensitive brute."

Athelstan was perplexed. "I am an honourable man! Can someone please tell me what she is talking about? I have already…" he looked over his shoulder. The door was still open and the girls were listening intently. He pulled them closed with a great boom. "I have already had the monsters responsible for this outrage killed. I am trying to salvage something useful from this impossible situation. What else do you want of me?"

Demetrios smirked, Saul sighed and looked truly worried. Leonida's voice was deadly calm with her hands clenched at her sides, her face serene, but her words were caustic.

"And the sad thing is you think you have done nothing wrong. Classic arrogance! Well, I hope you are proud of yourself, Captain. You have changed the course of our relationship forever! You will get no advisors or help of any kind from Sparta – or from me!"

He shook his head in absolute confusion. "What are you talking about? You do not say a word to me for three days and now you decide to take exception to this?" He jerked his thumb over his shoulder.

"Do you honestly think what I just did was anything more than an act? Above everything else, I love children, Leonida. By the Gods – what kind of monster do you take me for? What I am doing with those girls in there is critical for their safety. Of course, they are scared, they are supposed to be scared. What has happened to them is absolutely appalling and I simply cannot believe MY own king ordered this, but he did. So, what would you have me do – stay here and just hand them over when Rome comes for them – and they are coming, or is it your council that I take them to my king as ordered? I will do neither! An affront of this magnitude will not go unanswered not by me and certainly not by Rome," he shook his head in abject frustration.

"I do the only thing I can possibly do, politically, to salvage this situation and turn it to my advantage. If I might be blunt, this is really none of your concern. I know you think I am a simple bumpkin, who cannot find his own feet without help from civilized people. Remember this too, Majesty; I have been at this a very long time; I never do anything without a good cause, or without careful consideration and I never lose! Moreover, I do this so that Rome does not descend on Sparta like a swarm of angry hornets. You now have deniability about this whole affair."

"You arrogant son of a…" she slapped him again and he did not make a move to avoid it. "Everything is always about you; about what you know, because you are always so right, nobody else matters. What you have just done is to traumatize these girls for the rest of their lives simply for political gain. I will not apologize for that concern, or the fact that the minute those children set foot in here they became my concern, you narrow sighted peacock." When he opened his mouth to speak Constantina's hand rose in a regal gesture, effectively silencing him.

"Enough, I cannot stomach the sound of your voice and your ridiculously selfish explanations. From this day forth, you will stay away from those girls, or I will see you hanging from a cross!" her voice was a venomous whisper. She was acrimonious. Without another word turned on her heel and stormed off. Her two royal guardsmen formed up behind her and followed her at a safe distance.

"You should learn when to duck, barbarian." Demetrios chuckled.

He watched her back disappear and stood mute. Pat, pat, pat. A soft sound could be heard. Large drops of blood dripped from the fingers of his left hand and were forming a pool by his foot. He looked at Demetrios and Saul.

"Sometimes, gentlemen, it is knowing when not to duck. Is she always like that?" he asked.

"Like what? "Demetrios had amusement bubbling in his voice.

"Like, oh never mind. They say the measure of a true man is how he treats children and animals. She should watch and learn instead of pronouncing sentence and then running away."

He asked the Spartan Commander, "Demetrios, would you see that these letters get on a ship bound for Rome as soon as can be arranged and advise me when they leave. The timing for this will be crucial," he handed the notes to the Spartan and the Greek nodded silently. He wiped the back of his bloody hand on his tunic absently. "Maybe if I confided in you men, at least you will see what I do is the best thing for these girls. Then maybe one of can explain it to her."

"Aye thought women were also included in that saying." Saul said with a smirk. The Celt frowned.

"They are! Anyone who abuses a woman is a madman. Do I look like a madman to you?"

"Aye do nut know ewe well enough to give ewe an answer, but ewe are a barbarian. Aye have learned you, as a people, can be ruthless. Moreover, just because the word insane has not been used to describe the Celts, it does nut necessarily make it untrue."

"When you do decide if I am one, I trust you will let me know."

"Count on it!" The two men locked eyes and neither blinked until Demetrios swatted them both.

"Your Queen is so… It is just that she can be so maddening sometimes I just want to…" Athelstan's hands made a throttling motion. The Greek smiled. He was enjoying Athelstan's torment far more than even he expected he would.

"Why did she run, is it because she is afraid of me?" he asked.

"Oh she did nut run," Saul said seriously.

"She quit the field – retreated to the rear as you say and after what we heard in there you are lucky she did not kill you and eat you herself," Demetrios said smiling a bit. Athelstan winced at him.

"Ewe paint an absurd picture sometimes do ewe know that my mighty friend?" Saul asked Demetrios.

"I do and I am not your friend. I will tell you when that changes as well."

Saul frowned. "What ewe do nut know is, there is nothing more amusing than when a Queen unleashes that wretched temper of hers, especially on helpless barbarians." Athelstan sighed and looked at Saul. "Do you think she meant that whole cross thing?"

"Yas!" Saul confirmed.

"Would she actually execute me over a small matter like this? It might create an international incident." Saul advised sagely.

Saul pulled a face and sighed. "Fine, no probably nut," he said to Athelstan. The Celt nodded.

"So there is a reason for your apparent madness? Perhaps you might enlighten us. I assure you I will not run and would have no problem cleaving you asunder if the explanation is not to my liking."

"Of course there is a reason. There is a well-considered reason. Why does everyone think I am such an idiot?" Demetrios opened his mouth to respond. "Do not answer that. But, here it is. I follow Druidic law. It is explicit and harsh but it serves us well. I believe that anyone who mistreats women, or children is a coward – do I seem like a coward to any of you?"

"To her you do," Demetrios said rubbing it in.

"Why? I have given her no cause for such an opinion."

"She has been out here the whole time. She heard everything that went on inside and, in truth Athelstan, Aye very nearly put a stop to that myself. She prevented me. But no…" Saul said. "You do nut strike me as a coward."

"She should have stayed for the second half of my mummers play."

"Would you care to join me inside?" They agreed wholeheartedly.

He pushed open the doors and stepped back into the room still trailing drops of blood in his wake. The girls were gathered in a tight knot. They stiffened when they saw him again.

With a soft voice, he addressed them in Latin. "Ladies, these men are friends of Queen Leonida who will be taking care of you during your stay here. This man is called Demetrios and this is Saul. If you need anything at all, just ask one of these two men." The girls were still huddled together but they looked the two warriors over closely.

"First, I want to apologize for earlier, but I needed you to absolutely believe what you wrote in those letters. I want to assure you that I do not eat people, especially not pretty little girls," he smiled. "I know you are scared but as soon as we can arrange it, you will be placed aboard a clean ship for your return trip home. What you have been through has been appalling and I am very sorry about what happened. For the remainder of your stay, you will be guest of Queen Leonida. You need only ask and your needs will be met," he nodded. The girls were not sure yet so they looked at him dubiously.

"One of you did not write a letter, may I ask why?" He did not ask whom; it was not necessary since several pairs of eyes rested on the same girl. "You are called Constantina?"

"Yes," she said flatly her voice dripping with defiance. Athelstan inwardly groaned. "You know very well what my name is," she said in clipped tones.

"Yes I do."

He pondered this for a moment – no one in this room would have defied him earlier, so there must be a compelling reason for her not to write. He continued reciting the girl's names.

"You are Alessandra. Sabine I already know. Caterina." He looked back and forth at two of the girls. You are Simonea and you are Nicola?" Both girls smiled and giggled.

"Alfio and Paola. I am pleased to meet you all." His eyes suddenly fixed on Constantina.

"You have no family to write to, do you?" Her eyes widened and she shook her head. "No matter," he said. "You will also be returning to Rome with the others.

"Let one of us know if you require anything. Please try and relax – no one will hurt you again, or they answer to him," he pointed at Saul. The Hebrew's eyebrows lifted at this.

The doors suddenly burst open. Heads turned to see a somewhat battered– looking Guardsman stumble into the room puffing heavily.

"Queen Leonida! She is gone!"

"Let her go. She could probably use a good sulk." Athelstan sighed without looking up.

The guardsman was out of breath, panting and bloody. He had a swollen spot above his left eye, his shirt was covered in flecks of blood and his knuckles bled.

Only Demetrios looked concerned. "Gone? Gone where? Where are the other guardsmen?"

"Dead! All dead." Athelstan and Saul suddenly looked at the lone guard.

"Kostos, give me your report!" The letters fell from Demetrios' hand.

"They have taken her." Kostos blurted out.

"They? Who?" Demetrios asked. "Speak up man."

"Men ambushed us with nets, knives and cudgels. I do not know who. They stabbed Nikos and they threw the Queen into a wagon. She is gone."

Saul's eyes widened. Athelstan stood. "What men?"

"I do not know My Lord. We fought them. They used weighted nets. They clubbed her and threw her in a wagon. She fought them like a demon. So did I but Nikos fell and there were too many of them."

"What??" Demetrios thundered. "Men? How many?" Athelstan was already heading through the door.

"Seven, or eight maybe nine."

"Walk with us Guardsman. Wagon? How big?"

"A hay wagon." Kostos gasped.

"How many wheels?"

"Four, I think. Yes four."

"How many horses?"

"Two hitched to the wagon, another seven, or eight for riding." "Which gate did they use?"

"North to the Gate of Dipylon."

"North?" Saul blurted out. "Ewe are sure? They should be headed south towards the harbour and home."

"Why south?"

"Axum took her," Saul stated; his voice dripped with fury.

"Axum? Why? What is Axum?" Athelstan demanded.

"She is important to their plans."

"GUARDS!" Demetrios bellowed.

Athelstan knew precisely what was going on. Roman operatives had captured Leonida as a bargaining chip for these girls. They had reacted quickly to the kidnappings and would force the Greeks to hand him and the girls over to them in ransom for the Queen. It is exactly what he would have done in their place. It left Athelstan no time to think the situation through and formulate a plan of defence. It was a bold move indeed. They had to get her back. The success of his fledgeling plan depended on it. He shook his head savagely as he remembered it was Leonida that was of the greatest importance; not his plan, not his mission.

Saul followed Demetrios and Athelstan. The Greek General was barking orders to Athenian and Spartan guardsmen as they rushed up. "You are certain about the number of men Kostos?"

"Yes. About seven, or eight ambushed us in the stables; another drove the wagon and there was one more who was their leader. So there were ten in all. We fought our way to the front of the stables. I told her to run here. They threw a net on her and then on me. Nikos did not have a chance. She tried to fight, but they beat her unconscious and threw her in the back of a wagon covering her over with hay. They headed toward the Forum and Dipylon Gate dressed like farmers - peasants."

A pair of Athenian sentries dashed up. "Lord Athelstan?"

"Queen Leonida has been kidnapped! I want ten men armed, mounted and ready fight. Inform the council of 200 and Cliethenes. Mount search teams. Look for a four-wheeled hay wagon drawn by a two–horse team with eight, maybe nine mounted men dressed like farmers. They are going to be heavily armed. They left may have left by one of the gates north of the Forum, but check all the gates. That might have been a ruse. They may be hiding in the city too. Move!" He stopped an Athenian soldier.

"Our young guests in there; make sure they do not wander off unless they have an escort."

"M'Lord." The man bowed. Athelstan left the Athenian in his wake and ran out of the Estate towards the stables. "We will catch them," Athelstan shouted as he ran. "They cannot hide from me, not here, but men, I am in no condition to fight. So it will be up to you to do that once we find her." They reached the stables at a full run and mounted horses bareback.

"You should stay here," Saul said as he mounted a horse.

"You can ride bareback too?" Athelstan asked.

"Like Aye was born to it friend Ath."

Demetrios stopped Athelstan with a hand on his chest. "This is our job, Athelstan. She is my Queen, not yours. You stay here with the girls. We will be back shortly."

"Can you track them through brambles, thickets, fens, bogs, spinneys, Heaven, and if necessary - Hades?" No one answered. "I thought not. I am trained for this. I am coming. He handed his scabbard to the groom. "In case I am tempted.

†

"Lord Athelstan, General, we just want…" Demetrios tried.

"Thank you for caring about her, sir. You are a man of honour. You might also be a madman, however." Demetrios said smoothly. Saul nodded mutely.

Tracking one wagon among many along a busy roadway was a daunting challenge. To the men following, it seemed that Athelstan relied on his nose as much as his eyes to follow the wagon. Then he reined Maehadren to a complete stop and examined the road carefully. He paced slowly up and back along the wide highway; his nose inches from the ground and when he straightened, he had a grim look about him.

"I have lost their trail. They have turned off this road. We need to backtrack and find that cart," he then issued another deep growl. It was a feral sound.

Demetrios was growing ever more impatient. "They are getting away at speed. They know where they are going. We will never find her like this."

Saul spoke to Demetrios quietly. "Let him do what, for him, is a natural ability. Nut even a brace of dogs with their noses can track a quarry with greater ease than can a wild man of the north. He will find her friend Demetrios. Of that fact, ewe can be certain."

A mile back down the road Athelstan found what he was looking for. The wagon had turned west off the main road and headed along a narrow lane running between the endless rows of pale leafed olive trees. Great care had been taken to obscure the tracks but Athelstan's keen eyes were not fooled. A few stray stalks of hay lay partially obscured where there should have been none.

The thirteen raced along the lane at speed not bothering to dodge the well–spaced branches and the globes of fruit dangling from them. Yet they knew they were making up much lost ground. Side lanes branched off this one but the wagon tracks in the dusty earthen road were now clear to everyone. It was not long before the faint shape of a horse-drawn wagon came into view in the distance.

Almost at once, his companions disappeared into the trees on either side of the road and began to outflank the captors. Maehadren kept to the lane and closed the distance between them like a storm. The great beast knew somehow he was charging into battle and the feeling was infectious to the Celtic warrior.

Athelstan reached for his sword only to find it missing. He remembered Saul insisting he leave it behind so he would not be tempted to fight. He was right to do so, Athelstan admitted grudgingly. Instead, he drew his knife as Maehadren pounded on. The warhorse fought Athelstan's commands to stop. Without reins, the great beast had a mind of his own and he let out a tremendous whinny of protest. Three of the captors turned at the sound and two immediately grabbed curved longbows and in rapid succession fired two arrows each at Athelstan.

192

He ducked as the first two shafts whistled over his back. He just managed to turn Maehadren off the road in time to prevent him from being shot out from under him. Once under cover of the trees, he slowed Maehadren. Now, he had to place his trust in Queen Leonida's men. From here on, he followed at a discreet distance. He was simply not equipped to deal with skilled archers.

Shouts erupted suddenly and he knew the Greeks had struck. Battle was joined. Three against ten were not good odds. Still, these were Spartans. Odds did not matter.

Screams of pain accompanied the shouting but he was too far behind to see what was happening. The fight lasted some time, which he took as a good sign. If his comrades were all dead, their enemies would stop fighting. He eased forward to get a glimpse of the battle and as he approached the spot, he could tell the screams of pain grew louder and the shouting grew more frantic. Then all sounds stopped.

No more shouting. No more screams. He could taste copper as his heart rose into his mouth. He spat.

Finally, the motionless wagon came into view and he approached it with care. Dead men littered the road and lay slumped across the wagon. Both the wagon and men were covered in blood. His heart started to beat again as he saw the men inspecting the dead. Saul carefully inspected the dead men's hands growled the word 'Axum'. He had been correct all along. These men were not Romans.

"Axum! They are beginning to vex me mightily. What do they want with the Spartan Queen? What are they?"

"They are many things." He held up one of the enemies hands. "It is a place and people with a tyrant to drive them. See? They bear the sign of the Black Rose." This was not the first time a black rose had been seen.

"That is not helping. Real explanations will have to wait," Demetrios said.

Someone lay struggling under a mountain of straw in the back of the wagon.

Demetrios moved the straw, untangled the net and lifted his Queen from the wagon. He held her face in his hands. "I do not know what we would do if..."

"Well that did not happen – so there is no reason to – to even think about it," she was spitting bits of hay from her mouth. Athelstan came to her side frowning. Saul also stood there with a tear or two of relief in his eyes. The guard dragged the rest of the bodies aside and turned the wagon around.

"I am sorry, my Queen I failed you," Kostos sputtered.

"You did no such thing Kostos. There were too many men who attempted to take me. You had no chance against so many. I saw Nikos fall. He will be honoured." All he did was nod his agreement. It was then that she turned and saw Athelstan. She frowned turning her back on him.

He was suddenly keenly aware that she wanted no part of him, so he simply stood and watched. He was not easily impressed, but these men had just astonished him. They had been ruthlessly efficient. They had a lot at stake; it was their future they were fighting for after all. Saul's place in all this was less clear.

Maehadren's left shoulder glistened red with fresh blood from Athelstan's arm wound. Leonida felt him staring at her so she whirled to face him. Her eyes fastened on Athelstan and she pointed an accusing finger at him.

"So not only do you kill and eat children and you ruin all of our hard work by fighting when I commanded you not to until your arm healed."

"No I do not kill children, I only eat them remember. Atop that, I never eat Roman children. When you eavesdrop you should at least pay attention," he growled back.

Leonida's mouth opened. "What? You don't eat Roman Children? Why not?"

"Because they taste funny, why else?"

"Did you split open your stitches fighting?" She was cross and fought not to smile at his jest.

"I didn't fight anyone, I can assure you and for your information, they came undone on their own. Someone should teach you how to tie a knot."

"Tie a knot? Well! Then do not expect me to fix them. I will not do it," she said simply standing angrily behind the wagon.

He glanced wryly at the men while glaring down at her. They rolled their eyes at him in warning.

He glared at them. "Do not trouble yourself. I would hate for you to worry about me at all. I am just a filthy ignorant uncivilized Barbarian after all who eats children."

"I will not then. Why did you come after me?" She pouted.

"Me? Come after you? Perish the thought. I am just out for a quiet ride in the country. You are the one constantly running off with strange men in wagons."

"RUNNING OFF? Indeed!" she spat.

"Indeed!" he countered.

"Very well then I will not worry about you one little bit, Keltoi," she stepped over a dead man, trying not to show a small barely perceptible shake to her body.

"Fine Leonida–Queen and you owe your thanks to Kostos, not to me." Suddenly she turned on her heel and reached up grabbing full handfuls of his shaggy mane. She pulled him down towards her and boldly kissed him in front of all to see. He lifted her off the ground and held her tightly against his chest. Still, she kissed him – without pause. He raised a bloody left hand to caress her cheek. When they did part, her eyes sparkled and had a soft dreamy quality. She struck him playfully on the shoulder with a deep gasp for breath.

"You take too many liberties, Captain," she panted softly.

He passed a bloody thumb across her cheek, leaving a pink smear. He still held the petite Queen in his arms as easily as he would a child. A mischievous grin tugged at his moustaches. "Yes, Leonida–Queen. Some men dare take liberties when necessary, I am such a man." He kissed her again just as deeply as before.

"I should have you flayed alive for such effrontery."

"That will be just fine... if you have the time... later, now do shut up – Majesty!" She did.

"I have never done this before," she whispered.

"High time then," he whispered back. "You do know that those children are as safe with me as they are with you, don't you?"

"Yes," she whispered back. "I know."

"Never doubt me again, just have me crucified next time. It is kinder and more efficient," he set her down and looked sheepishly at Demetrios and Saul.

He cleared his throat self–consciously. "I believe you gentlemen have a Queen to escort back to Athens. I think she has had quite enough excitement for one day."

Demetrios was looking at Athelstan with an odd expression. "You would have charged after these men alone if we had not gone with you."

"Is that a question Demetrios?"

"No – sir, I don't think it is. How is it that you would rather die than perform a selfish act. How many men would do what you tried to do without fear?" he asked with a grave expression. "Until today I would have thought none. I believe I have finally met one. I do respect you. I do not think I can honestly say that about any another man."

To that, Saul laughed. "Oh ewe respect him now do ewe, friend Demetrios."

"Shut up. I was not talking to you. We are not friends."

Athelstan tightened his grip on Demetrio's shoulder. "Respect, or not, friendship, or not, you men have opened my eyes today," he looked at Kostos and Saul.

"Our Druids have a saying, 'Measure your successes and failures from within for the only opinion of yourself that really matters is your own. Believe in yourself and those around you, will have no choice but to do the same.' Vestorix taught me those words when I was very young. You have just taught me what those words actually mean. You men live these words with your every action and your every breath. I need to learn from that and strive to be more like you." He leaned against the wagon wearily.

"Kostos, you said you failed your Queen earlier, but you did not fail her. Quite the opposite in fact." He placed a bloody hand on his shoulder. "You alone saved her. Without your keen eye for detail while under attack, plus our firm belief in you and your descriptions of her attackers; the wagon, their horses, their number, we might surely have lost her. You are a brave and honourable man. I believe my Gods have placed me here in your company so I might learn these things from you. I shall never again question your motives, or your methods, strange though they may seem to me. I would stand proudly with you in battle and call you friend at my table," he clasped arms with Kostos.

His eyes settled on Saul "I would ask a question of you." Saul nodded.

"You say you seek. You seek this Axum don't you?" Saul did not answer.

"Get up here and let me look at that, or do you plan to chit–chat until you bleed to death?" Leonida interrupted from her sheave seat in the back of the wagon. Kostos climbed into the driver seat and Demetrios helped Athelstan up into the wagon beside Leonida. Saul sat on the other side of the wounded warrior.

"Tell me where you learned to shoot a bow like that." Saul's face was grim as he looked at Athelstan's charred and oozing wound.

"My mother taught me to shoot if ewe must know. She said to me it is all in the thumbs." Saul looked at Athelstan with a profoundly serious expression on his face.

Leonida stifled a snort of laughter then set aside his bloody bandages and examined his arm. Athelstan was frowned and looked at his thumbs. Not for the last time either.

Chapter Twenty-Four

There was a muffled hum of conversation in the dining hall as Athelstan entered and the instant he did so, that conversation abruptly halted. The servants froze in their place staring wide-eyed at the strange newcomers. So did the seven hostages, some in mid-bite. He wore a bright chainmail vest and simple shapeless drawstring pants. His bare arms and shoulders were corded ropes of muscle. A shock of wild blonde hair and moustache were braided and woven with dozens of brightly coloured enamel disks. It cascaded over his blue shoulder tattoos and hung to his belt. A neat white bandage on his left arm now replaced the bloody one. Queen Leonida insisted he be shaved again; an action she performed herself. Saul had expertly replaced the four ripped and burned stitches. The trio now stood side by side.

Leonida was startled to see that Constantina Cursor was among the other prisoners.

The Celt looked at each girl in turn then motioned the servants to resume their duties. Their expressions contained a mixture of both wonder and fear. They stared at him like he was some fairytale come to life. Athelstan suddenly realised that he was scowling at them. Constantina returned his gaze cautiously. He cleared his throat and began to speak in flawless Latin.

"Good afternoon ladies; call me Athelstan, I do not stand on titles. Welcome to Athens. I have someone here I think you know," he reached out his hand and Sabrine suddenly appeared from behind the door frame smiling wickedly and giggling. A joyous reunion took place. The girls buzzed around Sabrine like bees and squealed their delight until Athelstan's ears hurt. He pulled a chair over for Leonida to sit, heaved a sigh, and sat beside her at the far end of the table from Constantina's hungry charges. He waited for the tumult to subside. The sight made him smile but Constantina still shot him venomous looks.

"Girls, I must confess your arrival here has come as quite a surprise to me. I was not expecting you. I want to assure you that the men who did this will never join their ancestors. I have seen to that in proper fashion. They will never harm you, or anyone else again throughout time and unto the last incarnation of men!" This last was said with a slight growl. It still infuriated him when he visualized those Goths driving innocent girls like cattle into a war zone for money. Athelstan paused for a moment.

He looked at Constantina directly for some time before he spoke. "You are now under Queen Leonida's direct protection but despite what you have been told; despite what I have told you, you are neither my prisoners nor my slaves. The owning of people is simply wrong," he shuddered inwardly at the thought of owning children.

"You will not be confined, or censured in any fashion. You will have complete access to this estate and its grounds. However, I would urge you not to roam about the city; it is not safe yet. I will be taking my leave of Athens in a few days at which time you will be placed aboard a ship bound for Rome. You are going home to your families and I can assure you under far finer conditions than you just experienced."

"You Pig!" Constantina shrieked at him. "We have been ripped from our homes, our families murdered. We were locked up in a filthy hole for seven days, fed on stale bread and rancid cheese and given sewer water to drink. Two of us died and they were thrown into the sea like so much garbage. Are we now to believe this was some kind of mistake, that you have no knowledge of all this? Are we to believe we are now free to go? Liar!" She spat and turned away from the table.

"But Constantina, they are treating us so wonderfully now and he just said we were under the Queen's protection! Why do not you trust him?" Sabrine chimed in, though there was some hesitation in her voice as she looked at Constantina. The older girl frowned, deep in thought for a moment, before arching a slender brow higher than the other.

"Because I… because he is a Barbarian. They are the sworn enemies of Rome. Of course, he will treat us this way. He will try to gain our trust. That is when he will betray us. They all do."

Constantina gave a laugh and glared at Athelstan again.

"Neither your prisoner nor slave?" she sneered, "Is that what you said? I have heard you say the opposite. So which statement is true I wonder? Was it not your King who ordered us to be taken?"

He nodded. "It was he who ordered this operation, yes."

She shook her head, continuing to softly chuckle aloud. The other girls fell silent, turning their gazes toward her, real fear beginning to show in their eyes.

"So it was his responsibility that Cordelia and Amalea were thrown into the sea alive and screaming?"

"It was upon his command that these actions happened, yes?"

Her gaze went sharply, dangerously toward another girl who made to silence her.

"You say we are not your prisoners or slaves; what are we then? You say we will not be confined, or censured, however, we are only allowed access to this villa and its grounds. In other words, we are allowed to go anywhere you want us to go as long as it is in this place?" Constantina glanced about the villa with a look of disgust, her voice strong and full of outrage.

"You will arrange for our families to retrieve us here in Athens when? After we are sold and made harem slaves? When we are no longer your problem? Or is that just to appease us before you bring us in chains before your monstrous, faithless, honourless King?" She was screaming now.

Athelstan locked his pale blue eyes with those of Constantina as she spoke and he winced at the talk of slavery, faithlessness and honourlessness. He nodded softly and listened to this frightened girl's outburst. He knew she had every right to feel angry and scared. He knew she had every right to hate his King, his people and especially him now that many truths had emerged.

She stopped speaking and struck as defiant a pose as she could. Athelstan waited, his eyes never leaving hers until he could detect a slight trembling steal over her.

Athelstan began to speak, only this time it was in those soft whispers he used to focus his audience's attention. "Constantina of Rome you are the wife and niece of the Proconsul Papirius. We have met. Tell me this then, do you always blame the messenger for the bad news contained in a letter written by another? Do you always blame the Gods for a rainy day that has spoiled your plans for a picnic? Do not blame me for the actions of another. Blame me for MY actions only. In the time we travelled together, did I ever once prove faithless to you? Did I ever tell you something that was ever proven to be a lie? Perhaps in time, you can bring your grievances to King Trahearn personally. Perhaps in time, you will have the opportunity to yell at him and ask him why you and your friends were treated so dishonourably. Now is NOT that time." He inclined his head as she blushed crimson.

"Please recall, my words were, 'I urge you not to roam the city alone', dear girl, but I do not command it. As for your friends who were lost, I am sorry. Sadly, at the time, I had no knowledge of you, them, or the plan hatched by my king that brought you all to me. I was busy fighting a war with Macedonia. Fighting, I might add, so you would have a safe and secure place here to rest and recover instead of being summarily butchered like cattle, or sold as 'harem slaves as you so decoratively put it."

"You think this world was created simply to offer you kindnesses? It is not. This is an unkind world filled with merciless, faithless and dishonourable men and so long as you are in our care; so long as you are in MY care, you will do as you are told! You have no conception of the dangers that lie beyond those doors and until you do, Constantina, Princess of Rome, Queen Leonida and I will be your guardians. If you choose not to listen to me, that is your choice. Listen to her." His eyes finally broke from Constantina's and he looked at the other girls still cloaked in their own mantles of silence.

"I had you to all compose letters to your families detailing your ordeal and advising them that you are currently captives of the Senone Army. I had you tell them I have two demands for your collective ransom. Failure to comply and you would be eaten." He smiled at the horrified looks.

"I did this for very specific reasons. Reasons I will not go into now. I am sorry I frightened you, but you have nothing to fear from me. I have no intention of harming any of you and I do not eat people."

"If any of you wish to see the city we will arrange for that to happen safely. That is all for now." Athelstan stood and made to leave.

"Then you take us! You show us this so-called city." Constantina demanded.

"Very well, in a day, or two we go to the market. There is no better place to see the city and its people than where they gather for food, entertainment, politics and philosophy." Athelstan said.

"Could I have a private word with you, Constantina?" It was not a request and Athelstan led her to a common atrium with a deep balcony overlooking the Estates compound and the surrounding city. She walked over to the railing, turned and faced away from him.

"You did not run away from Corinth, did you? You were taken by force by those men weren't you?"

"What does it matter now?"

"Had I known about this when we first met, I might have saved you and your friends a lot of misery. It is sad you did not trust me. You did not write a letter to your family because you have no family. Yet, not even a note to your husband? It is he that I most want to contact." There was no recrimination, or malice in the question. She spun to face him and all the explanation he needed swam in her large blue eyes.

"Very well," Athelstan said softly. "Yes – to answer your unasked question. Yes, you will be travelling back to Rome with the others in a few days time. You said it took you seven days to travel here. Now that the letters have been sent, it will take another seven days to return, a day to get them to Rome, another two days for the Senate to decide what to do and set that plan in motion and a final seven days to arrive in Ythion. If my count is right that makes at least sixteen days before your husband arrives to fetch you back. I think you and your friends will be here for eight more days." he indicated a long stone bench along the terrace's rail and motioned for her sit. Enjoy your stay.

Deep concern etched his countenance as he stood beside Constantina and he let out an audible sigh. He absently tried to stroke his nonexistent moustache. It was an unconscious action he did when he was faced with a dilemma. Now that it was gone, he felt at a loss.

"I am sorry I was harsh with you," he paused. "Is there some way I can make up for what happened? None of you has anything to fear from me. I know you do not believe that now, but one day I hope you will." A pained expression crossed his face.

"Can I tell you a something? This – all of this – was not my idea and until yesterday, I knew nothing of your ordeal, or of your kidnapping. That is the truth. I know you were trying to tell me, but you must understand, I am at war with Rome. I am in a perilous position. I can trust very few people and I must trust nothing strangers say to me. Gargarus and his men are dead for what they did to you. Were any of the children – did they – ah…?" He could not utter the words for above all things, he feared her answer to this one question. His voice trailed off. This time, the expression on his face was all too easy to read and all too genuine.

"No. They knew better. We were to be delivered in a pure condition," she trailed off, not quite sure what to say beyond that.

Very well," he said and turned to go.

The silence lasted a few more moments before she cleared her throat hesitantly.

"I wanted to apologize too. I should have realised... I was just so afraid of you – I am still afraid of you." Hot tears streamed slowly down her flushed cheeks. A warm genuine smile lit the Celt's face and he took both of her hands.

"I am so sorry." She sniffed and dragged a sleeve across her nose again. She turned her face away once again slightly embarrassed. "You must think terribly of me. I assure you, not all Romans are as selfish and ungrateful as I have been." He sat beside her.

"Do not apologize. You had every right to fear those men, they were dangerous unpredictable animals and the world is well rid of them. Honestly, you have every right to be afraid of me as well," he absently blotted at her tears and smoothed her hair before he continued. "Still, to stand up to them for as long as you did; to stand up to me the way you just did, shows bravery – you are perilous in your own way. You live in a very dangerous and uncertain world my dear, in even more dangerous and uncertain times. Yet, the fates have conspired to bring you here to me and you may not realise it yet, but that was a very good thing. For it is entirely possible that I am the most dangerous person you will ever meet in your lifetime and I will die before I will allow any of you to be harmed again. That is my pledge to you Constantina of Rome." There was a fire burning in his eyes as he spoke and his grip on her hands tightened slightly.

"I believe you," she whispered

"I do not know many Romans. Most of the Romans I have met, I have done so with a sword in my hand. I would be willing to bet my life on the fact that there is not a single selfish, ungrateful bone in your entire body. I did notice you asked for nothing for yourself. Is that a sign of selfishness? No. Above all else, remember this. Never apologize to me because something was done to you against your will. You are one of the bravest people, warriors included, that I have ever met. It is an honour to know you." He looked down and found he still held Constantina's hands in his and he released his grip and looked around. He saw Leonida had brought the other girls close enough to hear their conversation. She was smiling.

He quickly stood and loudly cleared his throat. "For now, know you are safe. You will have several days to rest and recover before you begin your journey home," he made to leave her in peace but something stopped him and as he looked deeply into her eyes again he shook his head sadly.

"Constantina, I can think of a thousand reasons for you all to hate, fear and distrust me for what I am and what I intend to do to your entire country. You are Roman, I am Senone and we are enemies and have been for a very long time. Our countries are at war. In a few minutes, you could easily find many reasons not to trust me and in a dozen lifetimes, I could not find one single reason for you to change that opinion. In fact, even I would advise you never to believe a single word I say to you. That would be the prudent thing to do." He could not hide the pain in his voice and did not try.

"Trust me anyway! Believe what I tell you. I would rather die than lie to you. I am absolutely what I appear to be, barbaric, savage and profoundly dangerous – yes, but I will never lie to you. You have nothing to fear from me and that is the absolute truth."

He straightened and smiled at the other girls. "Ladies," he walked over to Leonida who was still smiling softly. Obviously, she had heard every word he had told Constantina.

"Do you begin to understand me a little better yet?" He whispered to Leonida. She nodded silently.

Constantina got up slowly and just as slowly followed after him. Her bare feet soundlessly touching the floors as she went and she called after him one last time.

"Thank you for that. I do believe you!" The girl shook her head, her hair bouncing and tumbling across her shoulders. He looked back at her. "I do not know you yet. Not really." Still shaking her head, she laughed lightly as if thinking back on some fond memory. Looking around a moment, she nodded her head at him this time, smiling wholeheartedly. "But I know now I could never hate you."

He was tired as he entered his rooms with Leonida. He had lost a lot of blood chasing after her and once she had him back in bed, he heaved a sigh and looked at her. "Am I doing the right thing with these girls?" he asked.

"You are. I am proud of what you are doing and frankly astonished at the depth of your concern. I would be careful with Constantina however."

"Why? She is no threat."

"I have seen the way she looks at you. It is the same way I look at you."

"You?"

"Are all men so blind?" She sat on the bed. "Ever since I became a priestess I have only known the touch of a woman. Now that I am Queen, I am being urged to produce an heir. Who do I select for this? If I take a husband, he becomes King and that is something I cannot allow. You, on the other hand, would sire a strong child…"

"Just a moment. Has Kratesipolis put you up to this?"

"No. I come to you of my own free will."

He looked hard into her eyes but they were devoid of deception. Her gaze held his steadily. "Then I thank you very much. You would not be the first Royal I have met interested in...."

She reddened at his comment but Athelstan was smiling. "No in truth Leonida–Queen, I am most flattered and if times were different I might just take you up on that interesting honour. But I must not." He cupped her cheek.

Leonida smiled and reached out to touch his face, "Times are different now. You came to me to ask for help and now I might have to come to you to ask for your help. It would serve me right if you turned me down. I cannot seduce you either. I have had no practice in this."

He felt pity for her. Was she seeing at last how she had been manipulated? "I wish that I could abandon my mission to my people and stay here with you. I cannot. They are my world and pretty as all this is," his hand swept the room, This is not. If I asked you, would you come north with me?"

"I cannot answer a question like that. I keep asking myself the same question and get no answer."

"I leave in a few days and I leave perhaps forever," he took her hand and kissed her palm. His left arm still ached terribly but its pain was dwarfed by the ache in his chest. Every breath was a struggle. He realised suddenly that he had feelings for her. He also finally admitted they began when first they met.

"I could ask you to come and talk to the Senone King. I know he will help you, but I also know that when you set your mind on something, nothing will deflect you. The Helenic League is too important to abandon isn't it?" She nodded.

He shook his head again with a thin smile. He wrapped an arm around her. "Well at least we have this last day and you have no need to seduce me Leonida–Queen. I am here. Tonight I am not leaving."

She returned the same thin smile. "This will last me forever," she whispered.

"It will have to." Athelstan turned her face towards him. The sun shone orange and her smooth skin glowed with the deepest gold.

He kissed her and a terrible hunger came over him. He caressed her face and neck with his lips and slipped the gown from her shoulders. She was warm and the scent of her skin and hair was delicate and intoxicating. A soft growl rumbled deep in his chest as he nibbled her ears, neck and shoulder. His hands began their own exploration of her and she willingly responded to him. He let her curiosity have full reign as he gently encouraged her. Another rumble of rising passion ripped from him as she stoked his flame.

Leonida gasped as the cool air kissed her skin. Her hands went to the hem of his tunic pulling and tugging so that it rose over his head. Her hands went to first his chest and then his arms. Learning, exploring. "Your arm…" He shook his head.

The taste of her was blinding him to everything but her. The world faded away until all that remained was her. A fine soft down covered her shoulders, arms and breasts. His hands brushed them gently at first but with a growing urgency. She drew him in as he suckled her and a long soft sigh escaped her. He nuzzled and nipped her ears and the back of her neck. He explored her flat belly and the gentle sweep of her hips; still, he went until he cupped her moist warmth in his hand. He raised her chin and kissed her lips. It was strong almost feral in its intensity. His other arm encircled her waist and he pulled her close.

Leonida whimpered. Her hands went to his trousers, slipping inside the fabric, to take him in her hands. She exhaled passionately with one word on her lips.

"Now."

He pulled her down atop him and locked lips with her in a breathless kiss. His whole body clenched as her cool fingers wrapped around him. He felt her enshroud to him like a fog. Firm hands roamed her naked body, his soft fingers tracing her. He caressed her back, waist and the soft curve of her hips and legs. His manhood grew larger with every heartbeat and so did his need for her. Like a blacksmiths forge, his desire blazed white–hot utterly consuming him. His fingers playfully tormented her body until she could stand it no more.

Soon she was moaning, whimpering and groaning in delight, in pleasure, in need, in urgency. She kissed him. Her body moulded onto his and she needed him. Her body needed him now. She descended with a cry and danced rhythmically upon him.

She leaned forward to kiss him her. She stared at him. "I will never forget these eyes," she said to him. "Or this hair, or this mouth," she said kissing him hard with desire and lust.

"You do not have to," he said breathlessly. No other woman had ever possessed him like this. He kissed her. "You could come with me. You are not safe here, you know." he kissed her again. "I could protect you," he whispered into her ear. In one fluid motion, he rolled her under him. His eyes filled with fire. She was so beautiful, so delicate, so impossible to resist. He lowered to kiss her lips and his breath was like a blast from an oven.

"Shhh, do not talk of that, not now. Please," she said kissing him touching him, tasting him. "Please."

He took her gently, softly at first and he groaned as her warmth engulfed him. Slowly, a deep passion overtook him. A profound connection swept over them and he matched her need with his own. The depth of her need was revealed as she demanded more and more of him. A delicate sheen of sweat blossomed across her lip and brow as she grew more insistent. He let her take what she needed from him and he, in turn, took from her.

Her grip on him tightened and it drove him to wild abandon. He took her with power, strength and ferocity. His muscles flexed and hardened as he unleashed himself. She was so tiny and delicate yet she had the strength to endure him and to match him. He turned primal and showed her the depth of his yearning for her. Sweat poured from him in rivers and his breath came in gasps. She clawed at his chest and shoulders. Her fingers twined in his hair and she bit his neck. Hoarse howls of passion tore from her throat. The sound was sweeter sounding than the clearest bell.

Teeth closed again on his wrist and she arched her back with a soul-rending cry of rapture. She gripped him like a powerful vice and he could hold himself no longer. His love for her poured out of him and he howled with each shuddering release. With a giggle of pure joy, she stroked his face and lips.

Finally sated – utterly exhausted he slumped to his elbows and kissed her like his very life depended on it. She clutched at him and kissed him back.

"Is it always thus with men?" she asked innocently. He nodded and brushed back her hair.

They stayed entangled in each other's arms until well past sunset. Neither spoke again – no other words could recapture this magic they shared. He knew then he could not leave her here, if he did, he might regret it forever.

"You must promise to write me. Long letters filled with all the details of your day and I shall do the same; promise me!" she whispered.

"I promise my love, long letters," he looked down at her in the darkness. He stroked her hair.

A tear trickled down her cheek. "I shall never see you again, Athelstan. Oh, we will write a few letters showing a cheerfulness neither of us feels. It will be a futile attempt to reclaim what we have here, but the truth is, no matter what we say, or do, I shall never see you again. Today your laughter is the sweetest music I have ever heard, but I shall never hear that music again. Your scent, your taste, and your feel – all will be lost to me after this moment. I cannot come to your rooms after tonight and I shall never see you – be with you again."

"In time you will forget about me Leonida-Queen."

"Forget about you? Are you serious?" she sniffed. "How is that possible? You are the only Barbarian I know." Her expression caused them both the burst out laughing.

Chapter Twenty-Five

It was an arrival filled with all the pomp and circumstance befitting a Royal procession. The heralds announced the Corinthian army had arrived at last. At its head, swaddled in her Royal Palanquin, sat Queen Kratesipolis. The covered chair was being borne by eight slaves. The curtains were drawn back and a resplendent Queen waved graciously at the crowd that swarmed out to greet her. Rank after rank of Corinthian soldiers flowed through the western gate and lined the road, Spartan soldiers were nowhere in sight. Leonida stood atop the walls stiff with fury. Athelstan and Demetrios stood a few paces away and watched her rage build.

"I am sure the army is fine Leonida–Queen."

"I did not ask you. My instructions to them were all too clear. Attend me here! I may not be able to ask them but I will certainly ask her!"

"That may not be wise. I have a feeling about her Leonida. The time has come for you to play the innocent with her. I will dispatch riders to as certain your armies' fate for good, or ill, we will have the truth. Until then, hold your tongue. Promise me" Her headshake was all too non–committal.

Athelstan walked away as the procession filed into the city. Demetrios was even angrier than his Queen if that could be believed.

"What has that Witch done with MY men?" he growled.

"Send a few companies to find out. Send them by different routes in case the roads are watched. Send others by sea. If it is as I suspect, ambushes await them." Athelstan commented.

"Exactly my plan Barbarian. You show real promise."

"I am glad you believe so." The Spartan turned on his heel and headed south to the barracks.

Athelstan headed for his rooms in the Estate. As he drew nearer he saw Saul standing some distance away in a garden talking to a man he did not recognize. Both were deep in conversation but a moment, or two later Saul nodded once and the strange man left. This left an uneasy feeling in Athelstan's gut.

"Friend Ath," Saul exclaimed, "How fares your morning?"

"Fine, friend Saul. Who was that you were talking to just now?"

"Oh, Aye am sorry ewe missed him. He is my younger Brother Esau and even now, he journeys home with news of our father. We met here quite by chance. A happy coincidence is it nut?"

"You never mentioned you had a brother."

"Aye have three, friend Ath. We all seek. One is south in Egypt, another east in Persia and Esau seeks west in Iberia. Aye seek north."

"So what news of your father?"

"Sad news, Aye am afraid. He has died. Abraham travels home to tell mother and my fathers' brothers. Shiva will be performed there."

"I offer my sympathies to you and your family."

"That is kind of you, Ath of the House that Stands Firm. Aye believe we have ladies to escort shopping?"

Athelstan inclined his head, "Aye, believe ewe are correct friend Saul," he said mimicking Saul's odd inflexions.

"Ewe might make a fine Jew after all my enormous companion. That is only if ewe can choke down the terrible food of course."

"It surely cannot be that bad."

"It tastes like ewe have died and gone to Gehinnom. And Sama'el cooked!"

"Gehinnom, Sama'el? Is he a friend of your family?" Saul burst out laughing,

"He certainly is if ewe believe everything my mother says." Both men laughed and headed towards the estate.

True to his word, Athelstan let it be known to the roman girls that the trip to the Agora would proceed. They squealed with delight and Athelstan passed out coins of Athenian copper and silver. The purse strings were to be managed by Constantina, who snatched the pouch from his hands once she was satisfied sufficient coins rested within.

"Perhaps I should hang on to the money." The look he received from Constantina froze his blood and led him to firmly believe his war wound pale in the extreme if he tried to wrestle one bent copper from her hands. "Or not…" Her smile was sly.

"Watch and learn old man." With a swing of her hips, she was off and a chatter of young Roman girls were hot on her heels. "Try to keep up," she called back over her shoulder and the two men hurried after them.

For a visitor to the city, the market square of Athens provided an excellent focal point from which to explore. Situated below the Acropolis and the hill of Areopagus, many roads radiated outward from its central hub, several ending in other wondrous places.

The Agora of Athens was something that could be heard, felt and smelled long before it came into view. Their villa was in Limnae, south of Athens, they approached from the south and before them, dominating everything, sat the gleaming white Acropolis. At the top sat the Parthenon with line upon line of brilliant white columns sharply defined against a rich blue sky. Their first glimpse of the Agora proper was not until they passed the long rectangular Vespasianae (public latrines).

He smiled as he remembered being inside one earlier. It was accessible from one of the narrow ends and contained a wide anteroom in front of a square hall with benches containing holes on all four sides. A sewage pipe ran beneath effectively flushing the waste away. The inside was lavishly decorated with statues of Zeus and Athena as well as frescoes and bas-reliefs of every mythological creature imaginable. The floor was covered with inlaid tiles of bright colours and everything was immaculately clean.

Statues of Heros and Gods lined the roads; alters to the Twelve Gods, the Royal Stoa, the Stoa of Zeus, the Bouleuterion and the circular Tholos. It was here in the Tholos, that, the chairman of the ruling council of 200 (Boule), dined and spent the night. He lived, ate and slept here twenty–four hours a day. It seemed important to The Athenians that someone is on duty day and night. A standard set of weights and measures could be found here as well. It was in the Bouleuterion that the council met.

The Stoa of Zeus and the Bouleterion framed the wide steps leading up to the Temple of Hephaestus, the Greek God of fire and metalworking. No trip to the Agora was considered complete without paying homage to Hephaestus.

Athelstan and company bypassed all this and continued north into the heart of the Agora.

As it was most mornings, the Athenian Agora was teeming with people. It was a garish blaze of coloured awnings, tents and pavilions. Exotic scents filled the air. Strains of lively music and dancing girls drew crowds to the many troops of performers. Jugglers and acrobats performed amazing acts of skill and flexibility. It was a riotous feast for the senses at every turn. Athelstan followed the riot of excited girls that scampered around Constantina like little fox kits.

The arrow–straight road led them first to the SW Fountain House (public access to water was free) tucked neatly in front of Heliaea containing the law courts. Also on the right was the Middle and South Stoa. It was a long two–storey building made almost entirely of alabaster columns. The Stoa was open to the air on all four sides. The lower floor contained dry goods of every imaginable kind from the length and breadth of the known world. Here bedding and clothing were acquired for the girls including heavy furs from the Northern territories.

He always amazed at the number of people here and how festive the atmosphere was. Even this soon after the war, life had a remarkable way of returning back to normal. Saul would ensure the girls remained safe and Athelstan would watch from a distance to see who was watching. A large gang of children followed by the extraordinarily tall Celt – at a very discreet distance. Many had never seen a giant before and he was the most interesting thing in all the Agora for young boys. Athelstan stayed back twenty paces watching as Constantina laughed and pointed at all the splendid sights and sounds with the same wide-eyed amazement as the children.

He was also very careful to pay in person and use only Senone silver. He meant to leave a trail even the dead could follow. Papirius would have little trouble. Athelstan made sure that enough supplies were purchased for a twenty–day journey in rough terrain for ten people. The number was specific for Papirius – nine girls and one Celt. The fact that this number would likely be comprised of seven girls and three trained killers was entirely beside the point. He needed to maintain the illusion that nine hostages (including the two who didn't survive the journey) were alive and well and presumably eating and drinking.

He had little to worry about – for who in all of Athens could forget an encounter with these seven girls. They spoke Greek with a delightful singsong Roman accent and bartered like merciless pirates. Constantina was a force of nature in her own right. She did not shop – exactly; she more accurately launched a withering financial assault on the merchants. Constantina had a good eye and was a superb bargainer. Small wonder. He had never met a more determined woman in all his days. Haggling over price seemed second nature to her. Once she had fixed a fair price for an item in her mind, she was doggedly unmoving. Inevitably, the merchant was manoeuvred, coerced, or browbeaten into agreeing to her price and only then did she part with a coin, or two. She was a singularly remarkable lady. He strolled along and was aware he had attracted a small crowd of his own.

He paused and turned around. The children stopped. Athelstan grinned, winked and motioned it was alright for them to approach. He asked each their names and told them his.

"Boys, I am known as Athelstan. Can you say that?" he asked one of the younger lads.

"Affelstam!" he announced proudly and had his hair tousled for his efforts. He had always liked children – they were honest to a fault and great judges of character. At home, they often surrounded him. Today, in this strange place, it seemed no different.

Constantina moved through the Agora with practised ease. It was just like any other marketplace in any city. People out early to do their business, people walking, people rushing. She smiled at the girls as they moved from one wonder to another. Constantina had been a big help to him recently. The young ones were such a handful and she managed to keep them from getting underfoot.

"Can we go off on our own?" Allesandra asked.

She was one of the older girls about ten years old. "Only if you promise to take one of the younger girls with you and look after her. If you make sure she behaves, then yes you can," Allesandra smiled and nodded her head profusely. "I promise Connie. I promise."

She placed a few coins in Allesandra's hand. "Then have fun."

Allesandra smiled and took off at a run with two of the younger girls hot on her heels.

Athelstan's gaze kept returning to the Roman. She shepherded her exuberant group like a mother goose with her goslings. It occurred to him she would make an excellent mother. He turned his attention back to his audience.

"Alright boys, gather around and I will show you something you have never seen before. Have you ever heard of magic?" His tone spoke of ancient secrets he was going to show only to them. Parents gathered around as well. Adults and children alike were all hooked. Many in the Agora also paused to watch what was about to happen. He picked up a smooth pebble from the ground and held it up. "You can all see this rock?" Heads nodded. He took one of the boy's hands and placed the stone in his palm closing his fingers over it then placed his own hand over the boy's tiny fist.

"Now I want you to squeeze that pebble just as hard as you can and when I tell you, look inside."

The lad squeezed really hard. You could tell by his protruding tongue and his brow furrowed in concentration.

"Alright," he tapped the boy's hand with a finger. "Open your hand and have a look," he did and his hand was empty. The boys gasped and even Athelstan's eyes rose in surprise.

"Hmmm. Where did the stone go?" The boy blinked and looked around. Athelstan looked at his hand dubiously.

"Yes, something must be wrong. How did you do that?" he asked the boy.

"I don't know. Maybe I squeezed too hard. I am really strong you know." The lad admitted.

"I can see that. Let us try again," he closed the boy's empty hand and once again closed his hand over the boy's clenched fist.

"Now this time really squeeze hard." His expression told everyone he did.

"Yes, open your hand," he did and everyone cried out in surprise. Lying in his palm were two shiny silver coins. Gasps of astonishment and surprise echoed around the small crowd of boys. Those parents who had come over to watch murmured and clapped at the curious magic trick.

He smiled and tousled the lad's hair. "Go get everyone something to eat with that and bring the rest of the money back to your mother. You are good boys, now off with you." They howled with excitement and dashed off. He looked back at Constantina and her brood. They were engaged in a fearsome negotiation that had a Greek olive vendor wide-eyed and howling for mercy. She gave him none.

A lady shook and kissed his hand in thanks and headed after her children. "You are welcome, gentle mother."

Athelstan came upon a man in the square talking, speaking aloud. Although he did not stop, he listened to as much of the speech as he could. The Greek was prattling on about some nonsensical notion about the people governing themselves. He referred to a term Democracy. The idea was laughable and Athelstan stifled a smirk.

Athelstan strode through the crowd easily, few stood in his way. He was offered everything under the sun, from apples to armour; moldivite to mead, sex to slaves – all were available if enough coin rested inside his purse. He declined each offer. He kept a sharp eye on Allesandra and her two young charges. A sweets stand had captured their attention and final negotiations were underway. He laughed as this stalwart Roman girl demanded he lower his prices. She had learned quickly from Constantina that every price was negotiable.

Athelstan waved a hand catching the merchant's attention. He held up a coin and put a finger to his lips nodding. "Alright young lady," he said finally. "You strike a hard bargain" He handed a bag of sugarplums to Allesandra and she handed him some money, before triumphantly dashing off to find Constantina and the others. The sugar–plums were shared evenly and everyone got a sweet treat.

After the pair had gone, Athelstan handed the second coin to the man and thanked him. "Yours?" he asked. Athelstan nodded with a smile. "She is a tough one," he commented.

"Yes she is," agreed Athelstan but he was looking at Constantina again. "Very pretty."

Constantina had finally caught up with the merchant with the doll cart. Paola could barely contain her excitement. "I want that one," she squealed and reached for the doll with stubby hands and fingers.

"Let us see," Constantina turned to the merchant who gasped when he saw her. Even the merchant was not immune to the Roman's stunning beauty.

"How much for the doll?"

"Three coppers," he sputtered handing the girl the doll.

"Come now sir, it is but one doll. Three coppers would get us two dolls and some pretty bobbles for our neck and hair in any other stand in the Agora. Surely you can do better than that." Her smile was disarming.

He looked closely at the little Roman girl. "Four coppers and two dolls it is – plus a pretty hair clip for you both. Have your pick" he said.

"Three and a half coppers for two dolls and four clips and I promise to send more business your way," he looked at Constantina closely and a slow smile began to grow.

"Done then," he attached two more hair clips on the dolls before handing them over. "I thank you Lady and I thank you little one," he smiled at Paola.

Paola squealed with delight at the dolls.

"You must share one with Alfio," Constantina instructed. Paola pouted once. "Then you do not want one, let me give it back."

"I do. I will share," the girl said.

"Good girl," Constantina said. She winked and smiled at the man at the cart. She handed him the three and a half coppers and began to look for another cart she had seen. It took her no time to spy the jewellery cart. Something was transpiring here but Athelstan could not see what.

Athelstan had kept his distance this morning for two reasons. One, he wanted Constantina to have a special time with the girls; she had developed a strong bond with them in such a short time. Two, he needed to discover who, if anyone, was watching them. He knew if they were here, he would know it and he scanned the crowd constantly.

It all stemmed from an offhand comment by Saul. Athelstan was convinced the kidnappers were Romans. The first band of assassins at the Inn carried Roman silver, so it followed that this second kidnapping attempt was by them as well. However, Saul had not been as certain.

'Rome does not strike me as a nation that uses deception to achieve their goals.' he had said.

"They announce their intentions, pass some law to back it up, then go and get it. Constantina's and Leonida's enemies seem to work from the shadows and use guile and subterfuge to achieve their aims. They hide like rats and pay others to do their dirty work.' Athelstan had to admit, Saul was right and his words gnawed at him. Axum he called them is a place and people and a person.

It was frustrating. He scanned the sea of faces once more and wondered who could remain unseen amid this sea of humanity. Saul was being kept busy helping Constantina keep the excited girls in a manageable group. He strolled with a casual ease through the market keeping Constantina and the girls in sight.

"Alms kind sir." Aa annoying tug at his pant leg, from another one of the hundreds of beggars, was shaken off absently as he continued to look from face to face. What was he missing? It should not be this difficult for someone like him. He took several more steps and stopped as something suddenly occurred to him. Who is invisible in a crowded Agora? Who could hide in plain sight? He suddenly spun on his heel and looked back at the man who had touched him. He was plying other market patrons who similarly ignored him but he kept glancing at Athelstan. Beggars could hide in plain sight. They were invisible. Beggars saw everything but no one ever saw them.

Athelstan began to look more carefully and discovered that beggars and cripples blanketed the Agora as they did throughout Athens. Nothing happened without them seeing it. As he looked at this layer of Greek society with fresh eyes, he realised that all of them were all keeping very careful track of where he, Constantina, the girls and Saul went.

Athelstan returned and stared down at the crippled beggar who had touched him. His gaze was expressionless. The cripple looked up and shaded his eyes, squinting to see who stood over him.

"Alms kind sir," he repeated hopefully and held out his hand. Athelstan showed him a silver coin. The beggar reached out for it but the Celt snatched it away and squatted. He brought his nose within an inch of the beggar's face. The man reeked of alcohol and faeces.

"You can have the coin if you deliver a message to your masters," he showed the coin again.

"Masters? I do not know what you are talking abo…" The Celt grabbed the man's misshapen nose between his thumb and forefinger and twisted it. He yelped and struggled to break the Celt's iron grip.

"I am in no mood. Do you understand? You will deliver this message, or I will rip your nose clean off and eat it. Do – you – understand?" he asked with a growl.

"Yes! Yes! I will deliver your message, just let go. Let go!" He cried. Athelstan twisted it again and then let it go. His hands went to his face and he glared at the Senone.

"Tell the Axum this. I now know who they are now. Tell them, I will come for them, one by one until they are but a memory. No matter what they do, no matter where they go, I will find each one of them. They can no longer hide from me." His expression was intense and the beggar leaned back as Athelstan gave him the message.

"You want me to tell them that? All right barbarian; I will tell them. You must want to die really bad."

He stabbed the beggar's forehead with a stiff finger. "Just tell Axum, their world will soon be ashes. The Multitude has come." He dropped the silver coin on the ground, stood up and walked away.

A grim smile tugged at his lips. He learned a lot. Now he understood how these people were getting their information. Romans would never use tactics like this. These were Constantina's enemies and Leonida's enemies. He also knew this would get their attention. He would make them focus on him. He could wait and let them come to him. Now the only bit of information left was the answer to a simple question. What do they want? It was just the kind of puzzle he liked. He had an advantage now. He was surprised to discover that he could not wait to tell Saul the news.

At long last, however, they were finished and a veritable train of bearers loaded with gear followed Athelstan, Constantina and her giggling, jabbering entourage. They recovered their carriages and finally turned for home.

Once there, Constantina intercepted him.

"Lord Athelstan, may I have a private word with you?" He was reminded of Constantina's warning to tread lightly with her.

"Of course?" She steered him towards the long balcony and stood looking out over the city for a long time in silence.

"I do not want to go back to Rome," she said simply. This came as a surprise to the Celt.

"Why not? It is your home," she would not look at him.

"I have nothing to go back to. My father was declared an enemy of the state and they killed him. My family's holdings were seized. I am homeless, penniless and without any family. I will not go back," she seemed adamant.

"I see. What will you do?"

"I can get work here as a nanny, or I could teach Greek children Latin and numbers." Constantina had already given this a lot of thought. Now it was his turn to gaze out over the city in silence. She will not go home and he could not leave her here alone. He had only one option and it was not a good one.

"I will not leave you here. You will only wind up someone's slave, or worse."

"I am not going back there. I would rather be a slave." There was a fire in her voice.

"Are you still afraid of me?" he asked softly.

She looked up at him. "No."

"Do you think I will eat you?"

She giggled, "no, of course not."

"As clan chief, I could adopt you into my family. You would become a sister to me and, as such, subject to my protection. I know this was not something you expected so I will let you think it over."

"Sister?" She breathed the word as if trying it out. "Are you serious?"

He nodded silently and let her ponder his offer. She followed him with her eyes as he turned to leave. She mouthed the word again. Astonishment was plastered across her face.

"I accept," she blurted out.

He levelled a shrewd look at her. "Sleep on it. Think about the offer. I do not make it lightly so you should not accept it lightly. I come from a very different world than you do and you may not like it. There will be no servants, or fine silk dresses, no fragrant oils for your skin, or pretty combs for your hair. You would have to learn a new language and a new culture. I will not lie to you; this will be a very difficult time."

"Everyone lies to me. People have lied to me my entire life. The only person that has ever told me the plain honest truth, without apology, has been you. I do not need to think about this overnight. You are a strange man Athelstan of Senone. You honestly care about the people around you. I have never met anyone like you before. I would like to be more like you. Nothing could make me prouder than to call you my brother. I accept your offer with my heartfelt thanks."

"Constantina, you must be certain about this. You will be my sister forever. Be certain you do this for the right reasons," he had taken her by the shoulders and looked at her hard.

"I am doing this for the right reasons. I have never had a family like you describe. I want to be apart of something bigger than just me," her voice was steady and firm.

"Welcome to the clan of Epona, Constantina. I hope you are not disappointed by this decision," he took her and hugged her. He bent his head and pointed at one of the amulets.

"Unbraid this and weave it into your hair. It is our clan crest and it will tell anyone who knows that you are part of that clan," her nimble fingers made quick work of the task and she took a moment to examine it.

"It looks like a white horse," she said.

"Epona is the white horse Goddess. She is our clan's guardian. Now your name is Constantina Epona."

"Constantina Epona. It sounds much better than my old name," she was genuinely happy and it showed in her voice.

"What was your old name?" he asked in an offhand way. Her eyes dropped.

"I told you before. It is Cursor," she whispered. "When I was kidnapped I was a slave already in the Senate. Papirius had me running errands and…"

"Papirius? Your husband," he prompted.

"Yes. He is also my uncle," she suddenly feared he would take back his offer. He was silent for a long time. He sat beside her and watched the sun set.

Athelstan was flabbergasted. "Your Uncle? I mean to kill him you know," he said softly.

"I know. Make sure he suffers a very, very long time for what he did to my father," her voice was just a whisper. He patted her hand.

"What does this Axum want?"

"It could be, he has mistaken me for my sister."

"Sister?" He queried surprised. She nodded.

"We look alike, but we are very different. I have not seen her in many years. I think she works for him."

"Doing what?"

"I have no idea. I seem to remember something about illegal trade. Someone came to me before I was kidnapped and asked me if I had seen Octavia. I told them no."

"What do they want with Queen Leonida?"

"I don't know."

"I see. Get something to eat. You did very well today helping with the little ones. I am very proud of you. You have given me a great deal to think about."

†

In near total darkness, a cloaked and hooded man listened to the beggar as he relayed this information. His arms were bent back painfully and one of the darkly robed guards held his face to the floor with his sandal. Following a sharp hiss, there was prolonged silence once the man stopped speaking.

"You are certain that vas exactly its vords? It knows who ve are? It is coming for US?"

"Yes Exalted One – those were the Barbarian's exact words. I think it is a…"

A guard kicked the beggar to silence. "The Exalted One is not interested in your thoughts filthy cur. Answer only when spoken to and pray I do not beat you into a bloody paste.

A choking, sputtering cackle began to issue from the Hooded Man. "It thinks it knows vhat it has done. It is powerless to resist us now that ve know The Other is here. My plans for The Other have now changed." There was a casual wave of his skeletal hand and as the Hooded Man turned, the guards broke the beggars neck and let his ruined form go limp.

"Your orders Master?" one of the guards asked.

"The Creature has vexed me for the final time. Let the creature come, if it vishes. I vill make an example of it. Yes, let it come. Ve shall give it a varm velcome indeed. Varm as its own blood. Vhen they leave Athens, Acaph, The One and a capture team vill follow and track them into the vild. There ve can replace The Other at our convenience. Bring The Other to me in chains. Leave the rest alive. Do not inform Acaph his brother is vith them. I vant this to be a surprise. Inform the Corinth-Cow she needs to find another plaything. Kill the Spartan Queen. Send vord to Prince Mikonos Arios. He vill assume the Spartan throne immediately. Have him receive our operative ven he arrives. Have him follow the operatives instructions precisely."

"Ve vill now take Sparta. Ve vill soon take Rome. Ve vill have Athens."

"Exalted One, are you sure The Other is leaving with the Barbarian?"

"Do you doubt me?" he asked as he slowly turned to face the now prostrate guards. Spittle bubbled out of the darkness of his cowl. "Do you doubt that I have foreseen vut The Other is about to do?"

"No Exalted One. If you say it, then the Gods will hear your words and make it so. There can be no doubt."

"So they shall," he whispered with great self–satisfaction. "So they have always done. I speak and they make it so. Yes, I have foreseen The Other vill travel north vith those pitiful little guard dogs. They, of course, vill not know vut has happened until it is far too late. The Other vill come before me on bended knee. I am to be her master now. The Other vill be made to see that. Then I shall own the vorld. Invincible! Then I vill be a God and grant my own vishes," he cackled again. "I vill grant my own vishes – yes."

During this soliloquy, the guards backed out of the room.

Chapter Twenty-Six

Athelstan was awoken early by a royal summons. It was Demetrios. There was a haunted look on his face. There was no need to ask the question of him. The Spartan Army was no more.

At first, he thought it was Kratesipolis who issued the summons but found it was the Spartan Queen. It seemed they were going to revisit his request for military advisors. He dressed and followed the page to the Queen's apartments. Inside he found exactly what he expected. Kratesipolis and Leonida awaited him with a sumptuous breakfast. The former was smiling the latter was not.

"Lord Athelstan, so good of you to attend us at such short notice. We have been discussing your request for our help. Please sit and join us." Kratesipolis purred seductively. He sat, but waived off the servants who brought him food. He kept his face tranquil but one look at Leonida and rage flared in him.

"What have you decided?" he asked bluntly.

"All in good time, General. First, we have some additional questions," the Corinthian Queen turned towards Leonida and smiled ingenuously.

"Athelstan, this war with Macedonia ended rather curiously. They simply left. Athens has declared this 'victory' was due to their superior skill at arms and their intimidation of Cassander. This troubles us greatly. Macedonia should have won. It puts our Hellenic league in grave jeopardy. The Athenians and others no longer believe they need our alliance to help defend them. We have reason to believe you might be able to cast some light on Cassander's sudden departure." Leonida stopped speaking.

"Who is asking the question?" he asked quietly.

"I am," Leonida responded hotly. She glanced at Kratesipolis with some uncertainty.

"No Leonida–Queen, you are not." His head slowly swivelled and he stared at Kratesipolis. "She is."

"How does who asks the question change the answer?" Kratesipolis asked. Her smile faded.

"Oh it does not change the answer; it only changes my interest in answering it. I have already told you what Cassander–King would do and why he would do it. Why are you so surprised when you discover he did exactly that? Do my wild look and strange accent make my words carry less value? I am very curious, why Macedonia's defeat puts the Helenic League in 'grave jeopardy?' Could it be there is another player in this game that only you know about? " He spoke softly. Queen Kratesipolis began to speak but a raised finger from the Celt silenced her. He addressed Leonida.

"Everything I have told you from the moment we met, has been the truth. Everything I have said I will do, I have done. Everything I have said would happen has happened. But you have chosen to treat my simple request with blatant disdain; not because the request has no merit, but because of your fear and because of your motives and because of your highly questionable advice to your sister Queen and another as yet, un-named player." he shook his head sadly.

"I would understand if the idea came from you, Leonida. It could be argued that you are still young and lack seasoning, but these ideas do not come from you. Our first meeting in Corinth taught me that. It seems that helping us does not fit into Corinth's plans. I doubt that my bedding her would have changed anything, so I am glad I did not. Ask yourself this, Queen of Sparta, what happens when the Hellenic league no longer fits into her plans or his? What happens when you no longer fit in her bed? Produce an heir, or this dream will die with you."

"Are you quite finished?" Kratesipolis snapped.

"No, not quite. My arm is fine, thank you for asking. I formally withdraw my request for your help. If this Hellenic league cannot see the danger presented by Rome, then no words from me will make that reality any clearer. If Rome manages to fights past us, they will march over the entire world and create an empire that will last a thousand years. Should I just stand idly by and let Rome convince you where I cannot? No. I will not. I will continue to fight them as best I can. If I do not, they will burn your world to the ground while you try to plot and seduce your way to an empty throne and a paper league." he looked directly at Kratesipolis.

"I will not be spoken to in this manner." Kratesipolis was embarrassed and outraged.

"You have already been spoken to in that manner and it is high time someone did too. You are lucky I do not take you over my knee and tan your backside for what you are doing here. You are being manipulated by a very dangerous and intelligent entity. She is promising you power and you are just greedy enough to believe she will honour those promises." Kratesipolis had turned white with fear. "Yes, I know far more than you or even Leonida thinks. I will deal with Cassander all in good time. She killed your army on purpose. One more thing before I take my leave of you both," he stood and tore an amulet from his hair and removed a note, handwritten in Latin, from his tunic. He placed them both in front of the Spartan Queen.

"These are for you. Proconsul Papirius Cursor will be coming and he will be none too happy either with this turn of events either. Give him this note. It will do what can be done to deflect his anger from you towards me. He and you should be clear that you had nothing whatsoever to do with any of this. I am sure you will be quite believable concerning your outrage in this matter," his eyes were full of concern.

"When you are in need of a true friend, send it back to me and I will come. Scratch the back with an X and I will arrive," he levelled a chilling glance at Kratesipolis, "with the multitude. These are MY words. These are the only words you can count on when all other words sour on the tongue and fester in the ear. These words are TRUE words where all others words are false. They will endure to the end of your days, Leonida–Queen."

"I know what you…" His eyes snapped over to rest upon Kratesipolis, "…are thinking."

"If you believe you can do to MY army what YOU have done to hers," he leaned closer, "I urge you to try. It will be a lesson that you and history will never forget. Corinth will be a forgotten pile of rocks." A long pause followed as the pair stared at each other. Kratesipolis was the first to blink.

"Thank you, both for breakfast. Goodbye!" he turned and left without a backward glance. The last thing he heard was a screech of rage and impotent frustration emanating from the Corinthian Queen. He wore a grim smile knowing he had created an enemy this day.

Later he did break his fast with Saul and related the meeting with the two monarchs as well as his encounter with the beggar from the previous day. As he did so, Demetrios burst into the room bristling with anger.

"What have you done?"

"I have done many things. Some I am quite proud of while others..." You will need to be more specific."

"Queen Leonida! She is furious. What did you tell her."

"I told them both the truth, perhaps for the first time in their lives."

"You NEVER tell an angry Queen the truth. You tell them what they want to hear. Everyone knows this. I am banished from her side and told to join you on your journey home." Demetrios barked.

"Ewe do seem to have a way of angering foreign Queens and just infuriating people in general. Are ewe the same with your own King?"

Athelstan looked at Saul and nodded. "Yes. The last time I saw my own King I tried to beat him to death… so… yes, I am the same with my own King," he smirked sadly. It was a sad memory.

"I am banished from her side and told to join you on your journey home," Demetrios repeated sputtering with rage.

"Ahhh," Athelstan exclaimed. He clapped Demetrios on the shoulder. "This is excellent news."

"It is NOT excellent news. I don't want to journey home with you. I am a soldier. Our army is all but gone."

"But mine isn't," Athelstan stated softly.

"What?"

"My army is fully intact. It is one hundred thousand strong. I came for help from the Sparta military. You are a General in the Spartan Military. I am offering you a job if you have the wit to accept it," he turned his head and asked Saul, "Are all Spartans this slow?"

Saul looked up with a mouthful of bread and cheese. "Yas."

"A job? Doing what?"

"I want you to create the most dangerous army on earth, that's all."

"Well, I could do that I suppose. Are they all as bull-headed as you?"

"Yes."

"I see. When do I start?"

"You just did." He clasped forearms with both Athelstan and Saul. "Sit down, Commander, your breakfast awaits."

"What did ewe hope to gain by telling that beggar what ewe did? Ewe have antagonised a very deadly enemy friend Ath. For what? We will be gone and headed back home tomorrow and we will quite likely take the threat with us." Saul said.

"That IS exactly the plan. I appealed to their greatest fear on purpose. I threaten them with exposure to the light of day. If what you tell me about them is true, it is something they cannot afford to let happen. Now, someone will have to be sent to deal with me. I plan to learn quite a lot from that someone."

"Like ewe, Aye came here seeking and like ewe Kratesipolis turned me down but offered herself up to me like a cheap harlot as well," Saul commented. "Aye would not bed her either. Maybe we start a trend? Or should we both go to her and make all her wildest dreams come true. That might soften her up some. What do you say, friend?" For some reason, Athelstan found this uncontrollably funny. He exploded in laughter; tears rolled down his cheeks. The other two found his laughter infectious.

"Mercy!" He finally managed. "Please no more." Athelstan was wiping his eyes and attempting to get control of his laughter. Another chuckle escaped him. He looked down sadly.

"Your idea has merit friend, let us go to her now, but I might have to use a stick because I fear I am not sufficiently equipped to…" He looked down at his lap, his hands opened in mock defeat. The three men collapsed laughing again. It had been a long time since he had laughed like this. It was a poignant moment because it had been with his friend and King Trahearn. He doubted if he would ever share a moment like that with him again. In fact, he meant not to.

A strange look came over the Celt.

He was about to say something but before they could continue their discussion, Constantina arrived and announced that a picnic with the girls had been planned. All that remained was their attendance at the festivities. They carried their meal to the seaside. The girls took to the water like fish.

Constantina sat smiling watching the kids at their play. It was a wonderful sight to watch children play. The girls were even able to get Saul into the mix. He was chasing them and they were laughing and squealing as he tried to pinch the little one's backsides. Instead, they were pinching his bottom when his back was turned. Everyone was having a good time. They spent the day swimming, laughing, and playing. It was over far to quickly

Sighing softly, Constantina turned to look out at the orange sun reflecting on the water. It was sinking lower in the sky and cast a reddish glow on the western shoreline. Athelstan stood nearby watching the sun sink lower. He walked over to where she sat and beamed a bright smile at her. Saul had quietly gathered the girls and headed back to the temple. Athelstan sat.

"It was a nice day was it not? One to treasure."

"Always," she said with a smile. She looked up then to see that it was only the two of them. "Everyone is gone? Yes, you said Saul took the girls back." Constantina stood then. "I guess we should get going."

He placed a gentle hand on her shoulder. "Let us just sit awhile," he looked at her face bathed in a soft glow and smiled. "You have given more thought to coming with us?"

"I have. I will miss Rome. It really is a wonderful place."

"I too have been in Rome, Connie, what makes it wonderful is that it is your home. Can I infer your decision to come with us is final?"

"Final, yes."

"Very well Little Princess, let me show you where paradise really lies." They walked back to the Estate arm in arm. This felt right somehow.

Unable to sleep, Athelstan lay awake for some time and listened to the night sounds. Finally, he rose, dressed and slipped a knife into his right boot. He slipped quietly from the estate into the humid night. There was not a hint of breeze yet the air smelled of the sea. He needed to clear his mind and plan his journey northward – home. It was not a trip he looked forward to. It was his arrival home he did not relish.

He padded silently through the darkened streets listening to the night sounds. Even the beggars had deserted the avenues and alleyways. Nothing moved save the occasional produce wagon resupplying one of the many stalls in the Agora. They were only allowed to enter the city at night when the population was asleep to cut down on accidents with citizens.

He entered an unfamiliar part of the city. It was a warren of curving alleys to the south of the Agora. Here the poor had their homes and they were packed tightly together with rooms perched precariously overhanging the streets. A sudden shiver rose up his spine and the hair on the back of his neck stood up. Someone was behind him in the darkness and he was being stalked.

His senses came alive and he opened his mouth like an animal to taste the air around him. His pace did not alter, nor did he turn around but his nose told him there were three men silently closing the distance and hemming him in. The Axum assassins had found him. He would make them wish they had chosen a different profession. He strolled along like he had not a single care in the world but he flexed his left hand to loosen the stiffness in his forearm.

The javelin wound still ached but it had closed and it was no longer in any danger of bleeding.

The track between the buildings narrowed by several feet as it swept around another blind corner and it was here the Celt took his last step. He came to a sudden halt and cocked his head like a curious wolf.

"Only three? I might have hoped your master had more sense than that." He turned slowly. The trio carried wickedly curved, snake-like knives that glittered in the starlight and they advanced as a unit. This was clearly not their first foray into the world of murder. They carried their knives low, herding their prey backwards. Athelstan kept his eyes firmly riveted on the centre assassin. The assassin slowed his advance and let his mates flank him close on either side. Athelstan raised his foot and drew the long Celtic knife from his boot. Sweat had already plastered his linen shirt to his body and it dripped down the back of his neck.

With every step he took backwards, he took a half step to his left until his shoulder brushed the wall of the narrow alleyway. The Axum operatives adjusted their advance so they kept him ringed in between them. Then Athelstan looked past the three and up, changing his expression from focused concentration to one of astonishment. The man on his left followed his gaze with a quick glance and at that moment, Athelstan struck with savage ferocity. He lunged forward, grabbed the man's knife hand with his left and drove the long slender blade into his forearm. In the same motion, he drove his right elbow directly into the man's nose with crushing force. He then yanked hard on the assassin's left arm, dislocating his elbow and pivoted sharply. The other two were caught somewhat off guard by the sudden assault but recovered after a heartbeat. The man on the right charged and stabbed low hoping to take Athelstan in the back but the tuning motion brought his comrade around and the knife tore into his kidney instead. With a backhanded slashing motion, Athelstan opened the second man's throat just above the collarbone. Blood gushed from the throat wound and covered Athelstan's white shirt with crimson gore. Both men collapsed with mortal wounds.

Athelstan casually stepped around the prone pair and returned his cold gaze to the centre man who took a step back. He only took the one step back and lowered into a crouch. Knife fights were often rapid affairs and just as often, it was the smaller, lighter man who tended to prevail. The two combatants began to circle each other and feinted with trial lunges and slashes in an effort to gain an advantage. There were two types of feints, one to attack and one to retreat. They were designed to give the impression that one action would take place while another, unanticipated one, is planned.

Both fighters were skilled but it was the Axum fighter who drew first blood. Athelstan chose wrong based on the man's proficient movements and took a deep cut to the top of his left shoulder, but the attack left the mans side exposed and he hopped back with a long shallow slice to his ribs. They circled again each staring into the other's eyes. Again, both men attacked and retreated in a rhythmic ballet of death. For the first time, Athelstan faced an opponent with more skill and speed than he had. After a few minutes of this, the Celt was bleeding from four irritating nicks and cuts to his face and arms. He was losing the fight and both men knew it.

There was a patient determination emanating from the Axum fighter. He did not press, or rush any of his movements. With him, it was less a fight and more of a dance. For Athelstan, it had become a struggle for survival. Fate can be a fickle mistress. The assassin tried a complex feint once too often and Athelstan finally guessed right. He blocked the thrust and drove his knife deep into the man's right shoulder joint. The Assassin let out a howl of pain and the knife clattered onto the pavers. Athelstan then lashed out with his left fist and caught the man on the temple and he crumpled to the ground stunned.

As predicted, over the next hour, amid howls of agony, he learned a very great deal about the Axum, Lower Egypt and someone called the Hooded Man. Saul met him as he entered the estate. The Jew looked at the Celt and shook his head with disappointment.

"What happened to ewe?"

"I fell down and cut myself."

"Fell down and cut…? How many times? Ewe cannot let Constantina see ewe like this. Take off your shirt." Athelstan pulled the shirt off with some difficulty. Saul tended the Celt's wounds with efficiency.

"I learned that this Axum leader has a real name, Dilip Harichandan and he desires to be a God. I have no idea how he hopes to accomplish that, but Constantina figures into his plans somehow."

"That is true. How did ewe learn this?"

"With some difficulty as I am sure you can see. Are all of those men so skilled at knife fighting?"

"Yes, we are all taught how to fight with knives at a very early age. Ewe are very lucky to be alive and nut floating out to sea in chunks my friend."

"We? You are one of them?"

"NO! I am nut."

"Never mind that for now. Can you show me?"

"How to fight? Perhaps. Show me your hands." Athelstan held out his hands and Saul looked at the front and back of both. He shook his head sadly.

"Well?"

Aye would show ewe, but it is your thumbs General – your thumbs!" Athelstan frowned and looked at his thumbs closely.

"What about them?"

"Ewe do not have a knife fighters thumbs. There is nothing Aye can do for ewe."

He stared at his thumbs for several moments before noticing the mischievous smirk on Saul's face.

"Very well then, stand up. Show me how ewe stand with a knife," Saul demanded of Athelstan. The Celt stood and pulled a knife.

"Hrumph! No wonder ewe were injured."

"What?"

"Take your knife and kill me with it."

"No.

Saul chuckled. "I have lived a very full life Ath of the House that Stands Firm, and my God awaits me with love. It is with respect and sadness that I say, there is little chance of you harming me. Now, do as you are told. Kill me with your knife."

Athelstan raised his eyebrows and shifted his weight in order to step towards Saul with a powerful thrust. In less time than it takes to describe what happened, Saul struck first. Before Athelstan was able to take a single step, the Jew had disarmed him and held the point of Athelstan's own knife at his throat.

"Oye! How did you do that?"

"For this particular demonstration, Aye did it very slowly." Saul reversed the blade and handed it back to Athelstan. "Ewe did everything wrong."

"So it would seem. How did you know I was about to strike?"

"Ewe told me. Ewe showed me. Aye learned everything Aye needed to defeat ewe from your eyes before ewe even moved. Ewe should wear a sign. Now! Again. Pretend ewe mean it this time."

Athelstan took the knife back and lowered to a slight crouch. As he was about to move again, Saul stepped to one side and pushed the Celt onto his backside with one hand, removed the knife from his hand as he was falling and followed him to the ground, again held the knife easily to his throat.

Athelstan blinked in wry astonishment and then laughed nervously. Saul helped him to his feet.

"Oh! I have got to learn how you do that so easily."

"First, ewe are holding the knife incorrectly. Ewe hold it like ewe are throttling a chicken. Does this look like a chicken to ewe? Hold it like this and everything becomes possible. Behold."

He rested the handle of the knife lightly upon the length of the four fingers of his right hand. The blade pointed forward. He kept in place with his thumb. He began a dance using the knife and one hand. His hand flashed over the handle changing grips with lightning speed. The knife twirled and spun seemingly independent of the hand movements until it seemed like the knife simply hung in place in the air. With one final flick, the knife spun high in the air and came down point first into the table. When Athelstan's attention returned to Saul, he was casually cleaning a fingernail with a second knife. It was Athelstan's other boot knife.

"I have never seen anything like that in all my days. I know nothing about knife fighting! What else don't I know?"

It was Saul's turn to blink in surprise. "Ewe will make a good student. Ewe begin to ask the correct questions. Aye will teach ewe what else you do nut know. Your stance is all wrong and ewe incorrectly assume that it is the knife that will kill. It is nut. Ewe kill with your mind first. In both cases ewe ignored my right hand, my feet and my eyes. Aye ignored nothing."

For the next hour, he taught the Celt how to stand with one foot behind the other – toes pointed slightly inward for improved balance. Then he began to train his mind what to look at and what not to ignore.

"Never look at your target's body. The knife knows where it is going. Look at the opponent's eyes only. Do not blink. Show no emotion. Do nut react with anger. Strike and block simultaneously. This is nut a fight with strength, it is a dance - with grace. During our journey north, each night we will practice and ewe will learn."

"I have much to learn. Give me a sword anytime."

"A sword is a tool just like the knife. Each has a different function. One does not use a saw to pound a nail."

"You are a philosopher too?"

"Aye am a philosopher first friend Ath. Everything after that is secondary. My God has taught me this is so.

"Your God is wise."

Over the next five days, the training turned out to be more intensive than anything Athelstan had ever endured and each day, when the lessons ended, he would collapse into an exhausted sleep filled with dreams. The dreams were always the same. He was flying on Raven's wings over a dead landscape. He rushed towards a vast dark army arrayed against him and in the centre of this host was a hooded man. There was no face. There was never a face but he could always hear laughing. The laughing woke him. For the first time in his life, he felt scared.

Chapter Twenty-Seven

Six days had passed since the girl's letters set sail for Rome. They would have to travel around the southern peninsula to avoid the spine of mountains running the length of Italia. Papirius Aurelius Cursor, Proconsul of all Rome, spat out a series of curses that would have made the most hardened sailor cringe. He was apoplectic. He threw down the letters he had just received from the kidnapped girls onto the marble floor and started pacing furiously around his office. The Proconsul wanted to strangle the messenger who had brought them to him.

"Who gave these to you, slave?" he said as he tried to impale the man in front of him with his eyes. The messenger looked around uncomfortably.

"Uh, well, master, huh, you see…"

"SPEAK!"

"I got them from a captain of a Greek freighter! He pressed them into my hands and commanded me to bring them here to you personally. Please do not punish me, my lord!"

"Where was the ship from?"

"I do not know."

"WHERE?"

"Athens I think."

"Athens? The letters say Sparta." Papirius' chest heaved with rage, his fists balled up, knuckles white with pressure. At least the mystery of the disappearances had been solved – but there seemed no solution save to do as the missives bid him to do – follow the girls to Gracia. After a few moments, Papirius grabbed the slave by his neck and threw him out of his room. After landing with a groan, the slave was picked up by two Lictors and dragged off. Papirius motioned Quintus Maximus to approach. He had been standing outside the door, waiting for an audience on an unrelated matter.

"Quintus," said Papirius, "assemble five hundred of your finest Equites and prepare them for a foreign campaign."

"May I ask where?" Papirius gestured at the letters. Quintus picked one up and read it.

"Gracia! We are going to find that Celtic monster – the army commander from Milan that cost us so dearly. This time, I mean to kill the creature myself. He is responsible for the missing girls from the Festival of Lucaria. How long should it take for us to get to Sparta?"

"He took them? That Barbarian General? How? How does he just walk into Rome and take children without being seen? Is there one from your wife?" Quintus hoped the question did not sound desperate. An idle wave of Papirius' hand indicated that now was of no consequence. He checked them all. Based on the number of girls taken there were three letters missing, There was no letter from the Proconsul's wife and two others. Were they dead?

"HOW LONG?" Papirius pressed.

Quintus' heart was hammering in his chest. Quintus shook his head to refocus his mind on the reality at hand. "Well Proconsul, at the quickest, perhaps five, or six days. We will have to resupply at Syracuse, instead of the mainland cities, but that will add another two days to our travel. My opinion is eight days at the most.

"Damn. Fill your transports and biremes with more slaves. They will row night and day, three shifts. We cannot waste time! I want to disembark on Saturn–day. HE WILL NOT ESCAPE ME!"

"Yes Proconsul!" he saluted his master and turned on his heel to comply. Quintus's mind was racing. 'The letters say Athens. Why do we head for Sparta? Papirius has information I do not.'

Unknown to Papirius was that Quintus had a far more personal reason for finding this Celt and his captives. It was the sort of thing that could get him killed if the Proconsul were ever to discover it. Great care was necessary to prevent this, but now a fantastic rage and an even more fantastic hope began to build in the heart of this Legate. He prayed to the Gods that he could keep that rage in check until he could put this Celt and others to the sword and finally claim what had been stolen from him.

That same day Athelstan and Saul prepared for travel. Demetrios attended his Queen. Saul set off to purchase clothing and provisions. Athelstan set off in search of transportation. A carriage and team along with a wagon for provisions were purchased. Athelstan had little sense or knowledge of bartering but his knowledge of horses was vast. He searched several stables while calmly and resolutely ignoring the banter of the merchants selling them. They even tried several languages yet his reaction was the same. He might just as easily have been deaf.

He looked the horses over carefully. He was looking for a specific sort of horse – intelligent, even-tempered and undamaged from abuse. There were some fine specimens and in each case, he looked into the beast's eyes and sang softly in its ear. Only then did he press silver coins into the merchant's hand and led the horse away.

Occasionally a merchant or stable master would argue that the price of the horse was somehow greater than the value of the coin. Athelstan would feign astonishment and look at the horse again. He would then look at the coin in the merchant's palm, then back at the horse. Now Athelstan would look at the merchant – in the eyes with a look that could sour a fresh–dug turnip.

"Are you sure? Perhaps you should look again!" He leaned forward slightly with every word until he towered over the merchant. In every case, there was a hasty re-evaluation and miraculously the silver coin was, in fact, the exact price for the horse.

He settled on riding horses and a wagon with a team.

By late afternoon, a line of nine horses had fallen in behind Maehadren. Athelstan stabled them on the estate and had the wagon brought there as well. Tomorrow, he thought, would be a good day to leave.

They would look to him for guidance and protection – he would not fail them.

Constantina had not fallen asleep until the afternoon, waking only an hour or so later to look up into the face of the girl she'd sang to sleep – Caterina. The faint sound of chatty, girlish voices floated on the air, but it was the girl's voice that filled her ears. It too was faint Caterina called her name, but as Constantina's eyes fluttered open tiredly, all she saw was the girl's lips moving. As she grew more awake, the voice became clearer.

"Constantina, are you awake?"

Constantina replied with a long groan, then swatted her hand and drew her face into a pillow.

"Are you awake?" Caterina chimed again, voice growing a bit louder as she pressed two fingers to Constantina's shoulder and jabbing her ever–so slightly.

For the longest time, Constantina was silent. A groan could be heard here and there with each jab Caterina gave thereafter. She lay there with her face buried deep in the pillow, never moving, leaving Caterina in silent suspense. That is until Constantina threw herself forward and grabbed Caterina about her tiny waist, pulling her closer into a hug, not even a bear could get out of. Constantina laughed,

"I am now!" Their giggles and squeals filled the chamber and the other girls rushed in not sure what to expect, only to find the two wrestling of sorts – lot's of grappling, laughing and tickling going on.

A few more girls joined Constantina and Caterina in their childish game. Nicola and Paola piled on. It went on for some time, even after most of them fell off the mountainous placement of pillows and crashed to the floor. Caterina complaining of their arm, Alfio of her hip, while Constantina begged whoever's hand it was to get off her hair.

"Sorry," Alessandra's hesitant voice sniffed. "Well, I had breakfast for you..." Caterina trailed and nodded to the table that had fallen over with them – fruit, bread and cheese now dashed across the floor.

"Look," Alessandra called from her place at the balcony, urging the girls to come see. A moment later, they were all gathered on the balcony looking down. They looked toward the stables watched as, one by one, ten horses were led inside. A carriage and wagon were brought around and stationed near the stables as well. All the provisions Saul bought earlier were being loaded into the wagons.

There was a smile on each girl's, most of them wide-eyed as they saw each of the beasts, whispering to each other in surprise.

"I wonder what they are for?" Caterina thought aloud. Constantina was quick to answer, her gaze never leaving the horses.

"They're probably for the journey," she paused, finally looking at the younger girl with a grin. "North...To Delphi, remember?"

Paola clapped her hands. "Oh yes! I remember! We are going to Delphi to see the Optical."

Constantina laughed, "The Oracle my sweet – the Oracle."

Constantina searched for Athelstan and found him amidst a crowd of men. She smiled at him, though she was unsure if he noticed. He was going to give her a new life. Who did that she wondered.

However, with the seven excited voices and bodies piled onto the balcony, she wondered who could miss them? How long it would take them to notice. She could hear the girls talking, some about how beautiful the horses were, a few others wishing they could see the steeds closer. Sabine wanted to ride one, despite the fact she had a fear of them; she decided to confide this to them all at that exact moment.

"Constantina, can we ride them?" Alfio asked.

"How should I kno..."

"Go and ask him!"

"What? Me?"

"Yes! Ask Athelstan, please?"

"He likes you."

"No, he doesn't."

Oh yes he does," they chorused. Constantina was smiling.

"Please." They pleaded in unison.

It went on like this for some time, but the last plea from Caterina had Constantina incapable of resisting any longer.

"Alright. Alright! I'll go...But what if he says no?"

Athelstan stood among a small throng of servants, grooms and crimson-cloaked Spartan soldiers. His garish blue-green tartans, white bearskin cape and wild blonde hair made him stand out. His left forearm was bandaged in white linen and as he gestured it was clear it was bothering him. He heard the commotion on the balcony of the villa and briefly glanced up from under his bushy golden eyebrows. A clot of girls seemed to be pressing Constantina for something. He continued with his instructions to the workers. Some repairs were needed to the harnesses before their journey began. When he glanced back up, Constantina was gone, but now the balcony was lined with girls standing cheek to jowl waiting expectantly for something.

Constantina was ushered outside and toward the stables, her eyes downcast in an attempt to block out the suddenly bright sun. Athelstan stood just a few yards away. He was giving instructions on how the goods should be packed. The least used items at the bottom and the most used at the top.

She inclined her head to him, she smiled, "Good day, Lord Athelstan," She spoke softly in her perfect Latin.

"The girls...They were curious about the horses," Constantina stated, giving an awkward sigh.

"Alessandra and Caterina would like to see the horses closer and Sabine would like to pet them? Alfio was hoping she could ride one for a minute." Her voice trailed off for a moment.

"Alfio wants to ride one?"

"Yes."

"For a minute?"

"Yes, and they would also like me to add something to that." There was a long pause. She glanced back at the girls whose faces were filled with hope. Athelstan looked up too then returned his attention to Constantina.

"Yes, something to add?"

Embarrassed and blushing, she blurted out, "They wanted me to tell you that you are looking very handsome today."

"Oh Really? They asked you to say that?"

"Yes. Well, no," she admitted. "I wanted to say that," she said in a rush.

Athelstan paused for a moment and a hush fell on the courtyard. Then he began to chuckle. He took her hand and squeezed it softly.

"You do have a way of brightening my mood and that's a fact!" He was still chortling as he waved at the other girls to come down and see the horses. They vanished from the balcony like magic.

They burst out of the estate in a tumbling, giggling rush. They raced down the rocky path slowing to a respectable walk only after covering three-quarters of the distance to the stables. There was a chorus of 'Lord Athelstan' and he inclined his head to each girl and spoke her name. Each blushed and giggled when he did so. He led them into the stables. Most wore only their soft bedroom slippers and two had forgotten even those. Athelstan called out to Saul.

"Boots?" he was answered by a nod.

"Eight pairs."

They came to a stop at a line of stalls. A huge white horse tossed its head and whinnied as soon as Athelstan opened the gate.

"I would like to introduce you all to Maehadren. Now one by one you will come in, bow your heads to him and wait for him to do the same. Then you may stroke his cheek and breathe directly into his nostrils. He will snort air back at you. When he has done that, it is him saying, 'Hello, I am very pleased to meet you"

One by one they did so and he noted that Sabine was both elated and frightened at the same time.

"Would you like to feed him a handful, or two of oats?" he asked he.

"Can I?"

"Yes, but if you do, it will be your responsibility to feed him oats every day during our journey. Can you do that?"

"Oh yes. I surely can sir."

He had her dip her hand into a feedbag near the stall door and showed her how to offer it to the horse. He showed her how to keep her fingers clear of his teeth. She was hesitant at first and several handfuls fell into the hay as she jerked back. Finally, Athelstan took her delicate wrist and held her hand steady. She giggled and squealed as she felt Maehadrens soft lips tickle her palm.

"Two handfuls only mind you. No more."

"I will remember."

Soon she was stroking his face and neck and whispering secrets to him in Latin. Maehadren liked all this attention of course and the great beast would gently push and nuzzle Sabine. His sweet moist breath filled the air. Athelstan silently stepped out of the stall to let these two have some time together.

By now, the other girls had chosen their mounts. The girls would ride part of the day. The carriage could be used to rest, to sleep in and under at night. The journey would certainly be slower with a wagon. He knew all too well that an afternoon pony ride down the Apian Way was one thing, but negotiating game trails atop a full grown horse for days on end was quite another.

He entered the next stall and found Alessandra and a roan mare becoming fast friends. She was making soft clucking sounds in the horse's ear while carefully braiding the reddish blonde mane.

Athelstan asked quietly with a soft smile. "Have you named her?"

"May I?"Alessandra asked suddenly.

"Of course you can. After all, she is your horse now." The Celt answered.

This news instantly travelled like magic through the stalls and another half dozen voices asked if they too could name a horse. Soon Athelstan was leaning against the far line of stalls and watched as the Roman girls fawned over their new friends. He had a warm feeling as he watched the animals react to these gentle ministrations and allowed the group to socialize for some time. He also noticed Constantina had chosen the only Palomino in the bunch. It was only then he noticed tiny Paola standing at the entrance to the stables.

She was just standing there crying.

He picked up the little one and asked, "Why are you crying Paola, are you frightened?" A wet tearful nod was all he got. She buried her face into his neck and sobbed.

"Well, this will not do at all. I picked out an extra special horse just for you. Would you like to meet her?" another tearful nod. This time the round wet eyes were turned on him with trust and hope.

He walked slowly down the long line of stalls. "Tell me, Paola, what is your favourite girl's name in the whole world?"

"Fiona," she whispered. He wiped her face and nose with his sleeve and came to a stop in front of a stall that held a brown and white dappled pony. The tiny creature was exactly Paola's size and the beast shook with excitement when they arrived.

"What a remarkable coincidence Paola. Do you know what this pony's name is?" Paola shook her head.

"Her name just happens to be Fiona."

"Really?" Paola asked in a bright firm voice.

"Really. Let's go say hello to Fiona and tell her that you and she are going to become very good friends."

"OK!" Paola was trembling with excitement. Together they made the acquaintance of Fiona and soon Paola was telling Fiona the story of her life. The pony couldn't have been happier. She was fed grass and hay and two tiny handfuls of oats. He stepped out of the stall slowly and leaned up against the wooden rail.

A memory returned to him from what seemed a lifetime ago. Two voices that spoke as one and what they said came back to him, "'Oh my! Athelstan, your father is showing me more girls, a great many young girls. They are telling us that they will all come into your possession. Treat them with care and kindness.'"

In an instant, he suddenly had eight girls under his care. His reverie brought back the phrase 'a thrice saved life'. "Constantina!" he blurted out. All was suddenly clear.

Her head appeared from behind a stall door, "Did you call me?"

"No," he shook his head. "Yes!" he corrected himself.

If you would say your good nights to these animals, it is time to go inside." He collected Sabine, who was braiding Maehadren's fetlocks and singing softly to him. He was in rapture. Maehadren was possibly the most dangerous warhorse south of the Alps. Yet here he stood stone still and as gentle as a kitten, as this wisp of a girl circled his giant head with her willowy arms. Athelstan laughed and wagged a finger at Maehadren.

"Belt–up lad! Don't you be getting too used to this kind of treatment, ya great midden ya." Maehadren tossed his head and voiced a none–too–polite reply.

Athelstan smacked his horse's cheek softly and asked, "So, do you like Sabine here?" Maehadren trumpeted his reply and the very rafters shook.

He took collected Paola, Sabine and headed for the stable doors. "You see my dear, nothing to be frightened of at all. If Maehadren likes you, then all horses everywhere will like you as well. Maehadren here will see to that – for you see he is not just a horse, he is also a God!" he ignored her wide questioning eyes.

He, Paola and Sabine waited outside for Constantina to round up the others and together they returned to the villa.

It had been a long stay in this walled city and it was time to leave. Dealing with Queens, horse vendors, a herd of little girls and the Axum assassins had taken its toll.

Once back inside the villa, Constantina followed Athelstan to his apartments, and he shucked off his cloak. His torso was a veritable map of conflict and war. The shoulder tattoos were the only adornments of their kind on him. Other marks had been caused by a sword, a javelin, or a knife. The latest cuts were obvious but for the moment, ignored.

"Did you name your horse?" he asked.

"Iola. I named her after my mother. It means Violet, a flower."

"It is a good name then. I am going to the bathhouse. I should be back soon."

He retrieved a brownish stone of some sort from his packs, slung a clean tunic over his shoulder, and left the apartments.

It took time to unbraid his long hair. In time, there was a pile of copper and silver disks, leather straps, two rings, a pair of bracers made of silver and a green moldivite lying beside the edge of the pool. He swam easily to and fro. Once his stiff arm had loosened up a bit, he stopped swimming, retrieved the brownish rock, wet it, and started to soap up. Soon his entire head and chest were covered with amber bubbles that smelled strongly of Thyme and Roses.

A soft tread told him someone else had entered the baths. Even above the aroma of the soap, he knew exactly who it was. He did not turn but continued to wash and soak.

Some time passed as she examined the mosaic walls and for a little while she simply sat on a bench. A sigh escaped her as she stood.

She watched Athelstan's movement and the soft sounds echoing off the walls of the chamber. His body was half hidden in the water and the pool. His hair hung in wet coils and he had an even more wild than usual. It was the melding of the civilized and the feral combined in equal measures that fascinated her. Those bright disks from his hair lay on the tiled floor at her feet. She stooped and picked one up.

Still, he did not turn or speak to her.

Constantina's dark eyes never strayed from him. She watched his every move. She did not move at all. She did stifle a gasp as she caught sight of his many scars and cuts again. So many – too many looked new.

"I have decided," she said simply.

He did not turn but he did look up. For a time he said nothing.

"Decided? Decided what little Princess?"

"I have decided that I do not want to be your sister."

He ducked completely under the water and reappeared facing her. Water streamed off his body like an ethereal glow.

"Not?" he repeated.

She shook her head. "Not!" With a single motion, she let her toga fall away and stepped into the water. Slowly she approached him, her eyes neither faltered, nor blinked. When she was face to face with him, she gently placed her hands on his chest. Her head shook ever so slightly.

"Not – your sister." Her arms went around his neck and she pulled him down and kissed him ever so softly. It was a ragged exhalation – the lightest flight of a butterfly. It was almost not a touch at all.

"Tell me the truth Athelstan, wouldn't you rather have…" He kissed her back before her question was finished. She clung to him tightly and no other questions were needed. She let out a long shuddering groan.

Her legs wrapped him as she arched her back to wet her hair. Their coupling was simple, tender, and easy. She nibbled and bit his lips and ears. She whispered things into his ear that no woman had ever dared utter to him. It heightened his passions yet curbed his lust. Lovemaking took on a dimension he had never known before. He fell into her eyes and soared with her breath.

When she let out her guttural cry and clenched down on his manhood. She did not pull away but clung to him tightly and panted a single word into his ear. "More."

She urged him slowly relentlessly to the very brink and held him there. Finally, he succumbed and it was an exquisite mixture pleasure and pain in equal measures. Still, she did not release him. They stayed coupled in the water for an eternity – her head on his shoulder, his arms around her. When finally they parted and became two once again, it seemed suddenly lonely being one. Yet, at that moment he realised he would never really be one again.

"It's alright Connie, I already have a sister," he said quietly.

"A sister? What is her name?"

"Simonea."

She looked up. "Simonea. What a lovely name. Is she pretty?" Connie asked.

"Pretty?" Athelstan thought for a minute. "I do not know about pretty. I do know that I am frightened to death of her."

With a sudden gasp of air Connie began to laugh. It was pure and clear and filled with immeasurable joy. Athelstan could not imagine what was so funny.

Chapter Twenty-Eight

Quintus Maximus leaned against the sturdy rail of the bireme, his forearms planted solidly against the smooth wood. He gazed out at the azure blues and deep greys of a rolling sea. The gentle rocking motion of the ship was soothing as a stiff breeze carried the small fleet east towards Greece and a very uncertain future. They had been blessed up to this point in the journey with fair weather and the vessels had made good time, the voyage well beyond the mid-point. Rowing night and day had shortened the journey of seven days to less than four. They would make landfall by late afternoon three days hence.

He watched as the bow of the ship cut through the waves, white foam and spray rolling back along the hull before tapering off past the stern. With a deep breath of the fresh air, he closed his eyes and returned to his thoughts.

His mind had been in turmoil since he had carried out Papirius's order to kill the Senator's family and all his followers. His family and theirs had been close and as a lad, he played with their children. He cut all their throats save two. One throat he could not find, the other he could not cut.

She slept while he did his bloody work. He had done his duty, in that he was confident, he also knew that a refusal on his part would have resulted in his own death. Only one of that family yet lived. He had caused the girl to suffer a terrible grief. He had found himself drawn to her upon his return to Rome from the northern parts of Italy. He was surprised and pleased by the changes she had gone through in her transformation to a young woman. It had not taken him long to develop feelings for her, surprisingly strong feelings at that.

Now, she was the property of Papirius, his third wife. It galled him. He had been certain that she had felt something for him as well, but how could she feel anything for him now with the knowledge that he killed her father, her last remaining family. He sighed deeply. Already, his duty to Rome had cost him dearly, perhaps too dearly.

235

Quintus was on an expedition to retrieve kidnapped girls. Was she among them? He had no proof that she was not. When they had departed Rome, he carried some sort of hope that if he found her and if he could rescue them, she would somehow forgive him his sins against her. Perhaps they could start from where they left off, but he realised it was a fool's hope – a young man's hope. He had been surprised to find that he had any young man's hopes left within him. Surely, the fighting he had done in the north had been enough to bleed him of any of the naive thoughts that borne by youth.

It had not taken him long to dismiss those notions. With the quick, decisive manner of his, that had made him so effective in battle, he dismissed and pushed away any feelings he had. He could not afford to be distracted from this mission. It was his duty to Rome alone that carried him now – nothing else. If he wanted to survive; if he wanted the hostages to survive, he had to become something much simpler. He had to become the wolf again.

With another deep breath, he released all his cares, all his feelings and stared back out at the water, his eyes glinting with a dangerous light. The mighty fleet containing the Legion Equis and its five hundred mounted soldiers sailed on relentlessly towards Greece and the unknown.

It was early and still dark when Athelstan roused his sleepy charges. Within the hour, they were fed, dressed and the young ones, Simona, Nicola, Alfio and Paola, were tucked comfortably into the carriages. They were wrapped in blankets against the damp. The horses had been harnessed to it as well as to the supply wagon – all was in readiness. The four older girls, Allesandra, Sabine, Caterina and Constantina, rode. Athelstan peered through the light fog that had crept in over the city during the night. His journey home began here and he wondered if he would see this land again. 'No matter,' he thought. The fate of that was now in the hands of the Gods.

His thoughts returned to Leonida. He had not expected to see her again, but as he exited the Northern gate, there she was glowing in the morning sun like a goddess high on the walls. Athelstan bowed his head to Leonida as he passed beneath the gatehouse and once clear of the city, he turned to wave one last time. He wondered if he would ever see her again too. He vowed in that instant he would – whatever the cost. He also knew for certain that his 'Little Princess' would shake this world to its very bones one day. In such a short time, she transformed right before his eyes from an uncertain kitten to a Lioness. A savage smile lit Athelstan's face at the thought. None now will resist the Spartan Queen save at their own peril. His job here was done. Her army would be rebuilt. Sparta would be great again.

It was a moment before he saw a mounted soldier patiently waiting by the roadside. It was Demetrios in full Spartan armour.

"Come to bid us, farewell friend?'

"No, I come to join you on your journey. Queen Leonida has commanded me to offer you and your people whatever assistance you require with your conflict with Rome, remember?"

"Truly? Yes, I do think I remember something about that." He turned in his saddle and looked back up on the walls. Leonida waved and nodded her head before she suddenly turned and disappeared. Athelstan raised a hand to an empty wall.

"I am grateful for your company and your help Commander." Demetrios did something odd. He simply smiled. Saul and Athelstan exchanged a brief glance. Neither was sure if they had ever seen the stoic Spartan just smile before.

"Shall we go?" he asked. The smile faded as quickly as it had appeared.

They travelled north through the shattered villages of Peristeri and Petroupoli. Nothing remained of these farming villages save the blackened ruins of farmhouses, livestock barns and storage. The same was true of Archarnes and Fyli.

Signs of the Macedonian army's presence were everywhere. Everything was either trampled flat, or burned black. Bloated corpses of people and animals lay scattered along the side of the road; each supporting swarms of flies, carrion birds and a stench that was an offence to the very Gods. It was a dismal scene and it showed on the faces of his girls.

"This road is depressing, let us finds a more pleasant route north I do not want to always be reminded of war," Athelstan muttered.

Here the road swung north and the party left the roads. They headed west into the dark forests south of Avionas and picked their way down into a long shallow valley. There was a swiftly flowing stream at its base and he picked his way through the trees between rocky defiles. Signs of King Cassander's army had all but vanished. For the next few hours, the ladies were huddled deep in conversation. This left Athelstan deep in thought.

If he had calculated correctly, the letters he had the girls write would have arrived on the coast of Italia two days ago, it would take another day for them to arrive in Rome. Here is where the timing would be critical. It might take two days for the Senate to mount a proper response. Demetrios and the girls would arrive on the coast of Italia in eight days from now. Papirius would sail from Italia a good five days before the girls arrive home. If they do not accidentally meet en route, then count a final eight days by sea and Papirius would be in Greek territory. Athelstan's party should have a nine or ten–day head start at best… and they were faced with a twenty–day journey north if they were lucky. It would be quite a chase.

He knew the Roman response would be a carefully measured one. If the Proconsul were to arrive in Hellas with a Legion, this would seem like an invasion and it would be countered with decisive force. Athelstan surmised that a troop of fifty to eighty men with horses and equipment would be about right. This small force could move quickly and could pretend to act as an Imperial guard allowing Papirius to claim that his arrival in Hellas was diplomatic.

Moreover, he needed to leave enough clues for Papirius to follow once they arrived. The Spartan Queen knew enough of the situation to aim the Proconsul directly at Athelstan, but it was up to him to leave Papirius some crumbs to follow.

Following the water upstream, they came to a heavily wooded trail just after midday. Athelstan made some excuse to water and rest the horses so they dismounted north of the deep woods. "Is anyone hungry?" he asked.

He asked Saul to join him for a brief walk back down the trail to mask their trail. Instead, with Athelstan's instructions, the pair constructed a deadly spring trap out of bent branches and sharpened stakes. They placed it with a well–concealed trip wire across the trail and when Athelstan was satisfied it was sufficiently hidden the pair rejoined the others.

"We should camp here for the night. We have water and good cover," he was proud of the girl. It was a hard ride without a single word of complaint. They were not used to a full day in the saddle and the first day was always the worst. They slipped stiffly from their horses and seemed grateful just to stretch.

"Athelstan? How many days ride is it to this Glade of yours?" Constantina asked wearily.

He frowned. "Hmmm, that is hard to say. Let me see," he pondered the question and muttered phrases like… 'nine days and Papirius will be in Sparta.' 'travel twice as fast we do.' and 'if the weather holds.' He cleared his throat.

"We must arrive in Gwennderion Glade in twenty days, or the Romans will catch us. I hope we can make it in eighteen. I have somebody to attend to the moment I get there and…" He stopped speaking once he realised what he had started to say. The older girls looked absolutely shocked. Did they know what he was planning? How could they?

"What did I say?"

"Twenty days; riding like this? Are you serious?" Caterina asked absently rubbing her numb backside. Constantina swatted her hand away.

He nodded slowly. "Yes, twenty days, but the ride will not be like this. We are going into the very heart of those mountains to the north-west of us. Today was a gentle ride in the country by comparison to what lies ahead. There will be times where you will have to lead your horse and other times where you will have to hold onto her for dear life. We will be sleeping under the trees and in caves. This will not be an easy journey." Their faces were grave. Athelstan looked around. "Remember, though, most of you will be heading home once we reach Delphi."

Constantina nodded at Athelstan's words. She was tired, that was sure. Walking to a flat stretch of ground under a towering maple tree, she spread blankets down for both her and Alessandra to sit on.

Athelstan went to work immediately. Using his great sword he began to lop long branches off nearby trees while the others set up camp. In a few minutes, he had deftly created a solid shelter long and deep enough for the two women to use for the night. It had a low sloping roof with two sides and an open front. Three travel cloaks closed the opening and the smaller branches stripped from the longer poles formed a tight roof. He would make one each night of their journey.

Saul came to speak to him.

"Lord Athelstan, may Aye have a private word?"

He nodded.

"Two things trouble me. First, ewe made efforts to hide our trail earlier. Will not these severed branches give away our route to those who will follow behind?"

"Yes, they will. I mean for Papirius to follow us but I want to make his journey as difficult as possible. If he has to waste manpower locating our trail this will add time to his journey and give us more time to reach our destination safely. What else is troubling you, my friend?"

"Food. Much of what we have will spoil unless eaten quickly. I had not counted on twenty days travel." Athelstan smiled. "Sometimes food can be found along the trail if one has the skill to find it. Let me see your thumbs." Saul groaned and with a wry smile extended both thumbs.

Indeed food was everywhere if you knew what to look for. Saul took to the trees to gather apples and berries. Berries were ripe and were the size of a man's thumb, wild rosehip, mushrooms and fern roots enough to feed hundreds abounded and soon a small feast of fresh produce from the lands had been laid out.

Demetrios worked on gathering dry grasses, small twigs and wood for a fire. He laid his wood in a pyramid shape. Athelstan watched as practised hands adeptly started a small fire that quickly grew into a cheery blaze. He used a method Athelstan had never seen before. It was surprisingly effective.

Saul turned to Athelstan. "So what meats will we find here?"

"Animals abound. Fish do as well. Deer, sheep and goats are perhaps the largest wild game, but smaller creatures live here too; hares, badgers, porcupines, wild cats. Some taste better than others of course, but we can set snares and see what Epona will give to us."

Saul looked at him with confusion "Who is this Epona ewe keep talking about?"

"We have different names for our Gods. Epona is one of the horse Goddesses; Rhiannon is the other. Epona is my clan's guardian. I take my family name from her. She watches over us and provides what we need when we need it most. She gives us life. She grants us sovereignty over the land and protects all who work with horses."

Saul nodded. "Your ways are so different from mine. AYE come originally from Judea near the city of Jeru-Salam, city of the Jews. We worship the one God, Jehovah."

"Yes, you said you had only one God." Athelstan shook his head. "What happened to all the others?"

"There are no others, Athelstan. He encompasses them all."

"Astonishing! That is much to ask of a single God is it not?" he breathed.

"No Athelstan, it is nut. He is a God after all."

"In Greece, we worship Zeus, Aphrodite and Hades. Do you have similar Gods, Athelstan?" Demetrios asked.

"Yes, we do but our notions concerning them are probably quite different. We worship the Earth Mother Goddess Gaia, the passing of the seasons and the God of Nature of which the Sun is a major part. It is the sun in his hand that makes all of this around you possible. All life springs from the womb of The Earth Mother because the God of Nature shines his life-giving light on his beloved Gaia. He waves to her with the sun every summer and we track it back and forth across the sky year after year over a period of…" Athelstan was interrupted.

"Nineteen Years! Yes! Yes, the sun crosses the sky; first one way and then the other way and then back again over a period of nineteen years when he returns to its centre point in the sky. This year is a centre point year is it nut?" Saul said with a curious expression on his face. It was an expression that was mirrored by Athelstan.

"Yes, it is. Every nineteenth year is a Golden Year for us. That is why our people journeyed from Italia to Gwennderion Glade in Macedonia this summer." The Celt was grinning. He turned to Saul. "I would like to learn more about your one God Jehovah as well. I would wager there is much more that is similar than different between us."

"As I said, Epona provides for us all," he stepped over to the huge tree with wide green leaves the men had camped under and gave a branch a mighty shake. Nuts by the thousands rained down on the small band of men. After a moment of surprise, they assisted Athelstan as he bent to collect them. He placed them in piles around the fire to let them roast. They took packages from the wagon and laid them out as well. He looked towards the tree the girls rested under. "Ladies, I believe our dinner is served."

Alessandra continued to stroke Constantina's hair, her eyes closed in exhaustion.

"You should both eat something," he handed them some berries and steaming hot nuts.

Alessandra tapped a sleepy Constantina indicating the fruit and nuts. Saul came and offered the women some fresh cut apples. Constantina ate sparingly. They sat around the fire after and one by one, the girls curled up under the wagon and carriage and fell soundly asleep. That night it began to rain.

"I do not think we are in any danger yet, but we should 'stand watch' each night." The three agreed and Saul offered to take the first and promised to wake Demetrios after a few hours.

The next day he charted a course north-west and still, all remained tranquil and still. Each night a shelter of branches was built with a soft bower of scented cedar boughs upon which the men could sleep in peace. A steady rain was becoming wearing and keeping dry became a struggle. In places, they had to lead the horses pulling the wagon and carriage. At night,

Athelstan took turns with Saul and Demetrios keeping watch during the nights but nothing approached the camps.

On the third day out of Athens, they came out of the dense forestlands. The terrain had been rising steadily ever since they left the north road behind. All traces of the Macedonian army's hewing, slashing and burning was far behind them and they journeyed through wild open grasslands. For all it's openness, these undulating lands were much more difficult to manage. Shallow, deep-sided cuts crossed their path causing them to detour several miles north, or south out of their way. The ground at the bottom of these cuts became wet and boggy. They were filled with clouds of biting insects. Despite the rain, the grasslands were hot and still.

The following several days were little better. The horses could graze and drink their fill of the brackish water, but it was bitter, scummy and unfit for humans. This sixth day out would see the last of the water and soon thirst began to plague them. The mood of the girls began to drop and their pace slowed even more. The sun had finally broken out and beat down on them unmercifully.

"Aye worry that our enemies will overtake us before we reach your homeland, Athelstan," Saul admitted in a low voice.

"These broken lands will not last forever. We are approaching the foothills of those mountains steadily. There is also a river crossing our path no more than a day's march to the west. When we are back in the comfort of the forest at their feet I will breathe easier. There, we will make better time following the low ridges of land yonder. It will also be cooler."

"That may be true General, but our pursuers will also make better time, will they not?"

"Not with the welcome I will leave for them in our wake. They will race to catch us at their own peril and if they persist with haste, they will be charging to their own destruction. One does not catch a Celt born and bred to the mountains unless he permits it. I do not plan to permit it until a time of my own choosing."

"We shall see."

"So we shall."

They had not gone far on the fifth day when the sound of rushing water could be heard. They pressed their way through the thickets and brambles into spinneys of alder and willow. The sound grew steadily louder and the air grew perceptively cooler and moister. A narrow river came into view and Athelstan called a halt. The girls spent a glorious hour splashing in the water while the men saw to their weapons and supplies. They refilled their water skins and when everything again was in readiness, Athelstan told them to mount up. Howls of protest erupted at the news and the scene resembled one of herding cats.

Constantina stood before Athelstan with feet firmly planted and an expression of abject defiance on her face. "My lord, the girls are weary and need time to regain some of their strength," she stated with finality. "I for one, will not move another foot until I am satisfied they are fit to continue."

Sabine stood behind Constantina equally resolute. The rest stared at the Celt in wide-eyed expectation.

"I wish we could spare the time but we are travelling too slowly as it is. Not to continue while there is light may very well prove disastrous if we are set upon in the wilderness."

"That may be well, but rest is needed now. Go on without us if you are scared."

Athelstan sputtered, "Scared?" He harrumphed at the temerity of such a statement. Saul was smirking at his obvious distress and only shrugged his shoulders when Athelstan turned to him for support. After a moment of two, the Celt's shoulders sank and he dropped his head to his chest with a sigh. In the face of her defiance, he had lost the argument – again and he knew it.

"We make camp here for the night. Tomorrow we will meet the road to Delphi" he stated loudly as if saying so loudly might make it his idea. No one was fooled. Cheers of approval greeted the statement. Even Constantina clapped her hands in glee and favoured the general with a quick peck on the cheek. Presently a cheery, smokeless fire blazed in a ring of river rocks. Nuts and roots were placed nearby to roast. The girls played a spirited game of tag while others busied themselves with a lightening–fast hand slapping game to Latin poetry filled with nonsense.

"I am going to have a look around. I want to see if there are any prying eyes about."

"I will come with you," Demetrios announced.

"I would feel better if you two men stayed here with the girls. You never can tell." He glanced over his shoulder. "I will be back within the hour." He strode off with some determination.

He smelled wood smoke on the air and needed to find its source. It could be a simple outlying farm… or a band of soldiers. He followed the scent upwind and it grew stronger.

He crested a steep rise and saw a tumbledown cabin surrounded by sheep. Meat might come in handy with so many mouths to feed. Athelstan watched for some minutes before he stood and approached the cabin. As he drew closer, he saw a man seated next to where the door might have hung.

"Hallow Friend!" Athelstan called out.

"Hallow back,' came the reply. "That is close enough armed as you are. What do you want?"

In response, Athelstan removed his sword and two knives, held them up for the man to see and placed them in the tall grass at his feet. He spread his hands and called, "I mean you no harm sir. May I approach so I may speak without yelling?"

The shepherd waved for him to approach. It was then that the Celt noticed the man had a companion. It was a lolling tongue and a rapidly wagging tail with the effigy of a red-boned hound dog strung loosely between them. The creature let out a half howl, half bark before bounding towards the Celt. The tail wagged even more wildly. He did not so much run, as he wiggled his skinny body back and forth. That, more than anything else, seemed to be what caused his forward momentum. Its gangly legs seemed to trip and stumble along more as an afterthought.

"QUIET!" the shepherd bellowed. The dog let out another of its curious howl/barks. "I said QUIET... oh never mind. That beast does not listen to me much. But then I be not in the habit of talkin' to the beast much either."

The dog raced up to Athelstan with a huge grin on his face and a snout and tongue covered in dirt. The Celt bent to greet the animal and scratched it behind the ears and at the base of the tail. In payment, he received two slobbery muddy kisses. The dog took to circling Athelstan with bounding wild abandon. He proceeded forward to greet the shepherd.

"That's some guard dog you have here sir," commented Athelstan as he extended his hand to the shepherd.

"The man took the offered hand in a strong forearm grip. "Oh, ye think so do ye? What be ye name if I might be so bold as to ask?"

He puzzled at this odd turn of phrase. "Athelstan, and yours sir?"

"Foreigner I see. Eugammon, be my name if it pleases ye. Most folks call me Eu." His nickname sounded very much like the word 'you'.

"Well met Eu, so you say he is NOT much of a guard dog then?"

"Judge for ye–self. Just yesterday, he found his self a fair brace of baby rabbits. I had to rescue him from them."

"Maybe if you fed him more, he might be a better guard dog."

"Maybe if he'd be a better guard dog, I would feed him more. Difficult to know which would be best. Since ye didn't just spring up out of the grass. What brings ye to me door this time of year?"

"I am a traveller and smelled your smokehouse fire. I wonder if I might pay you for some fresh water and a bit of your smoked meat?"

"Spring water be free and I have some smoked Mutton. I might be convinced to part with some should the price cover the costs of it."

"Perhaps you might part with a quarter Sheep for say 10 Drachma?"

"Eu would if this was not the finest smoked Mutton in all Hellas. I would part with a quarter Sheep for 20 Drachma." Athelstan frowned.

"I have eaten in the halls of Kings from here to the Alpine mountains and have never heard of such prices. Why, in the Athenian Agora, a full lamb commands only 8 Drachma. Ten-a-quarter is a kingly price to be sure. I doubt your Mutton is akin to the delicacies served up in such places. I might be able to part with 10 Drachma and not 1 Obol more." (6 Obol = 1 Drachma)

"10 Drachma? PAH!! Then ye best be on yer way sir and let yer hunger argue prices with ye for I shall not. If ye have not the wit to ask yerself, from where the fine meats that all the Kings and Queens from Pella to Alexandria dine upon be raised and cured; then be off with ye – Git! They come from Eu is where! Eu and none other! Eu will not accept any less than 18 Drachmas for a quarter Sheep." Eugammon struck a steadfast pose.

"Well this is a Goddess be praised, luck–filled day for me and that is no lie. Could it be true that I stand in the presence of the one and only Eu? The name Eu is spoken in all those halls and far beyond too if I don't miss my guess. Of that there can be no doubt," Athelstan said with some hint of awe in his voice.

"Alas, I have several young stomachs to fill and like this bony dog of yours, a child's tummy empties so quickly when they are at an age." He sniffed and rubbed his nose in his sleeve. "Would you, with kindness to a traveller sorely put upon, see fit to take pity on these poor orphaned waifs and give us the quarter Sheep for say 15 Drachma? I would even extend to you and your dog a place at our fire for warmth, a bit of conversation, a story, or two as it were and perhaps even…" Athelstan paused secretively. His voice had dropped to a bare whisper and Eu leaned in to hear,

"… a full skin of Mead. Is Eu the pious, God-fearing man that the legends have filled my ears with since leaving the Alpine Halls of Northern Italia? Or do I stand before a different Eu – some lesser man?"

"Well now," Eu began. He too pretended to daub at a stray trickle that coursed down his cheek. "I would disagree with ye if I was a liar and a Mongrel. I is neither. Agamemnon, we have struck a bargain. Tell no one that I stooped to help a foreigner and his brood. I has a reputation to uphold as a shrewd businessman after all."

"Your secret shall be kept behind my lips for all time." He counted out 15 Drachma and passed them to him. Eu went behind his shack and returned with a hind of Mutton, wrapped in cloth. It smelled wonderful.

Athelstan collected his weaponry and led Eu back to the encampment. His red boned dog dancing a circular jig around the pair the entire way.

"What is the dog's name?"

"Shitter," Eu said in his matter of fact way. Sometimes Athelstan had a bit of difficulty with Greek.

"Shitter?" he asked with a puzzled look. "Do you mean…" he pointed to his own backside.

Eu nodded.

"Is that because…"

"… he never stops." Athelstan looked at the dog and chuckled and to emphasize the point, Shitter did as his name suggested. Once done, he hurried to catch up.

Dusk deepened and the meal was over, everyone was nibbling on nuts, 'filling the hollow leg' the girls called it. Their guest was surprised that a Celt, a Pilgrim, a Spartan General and a collection of young Roman girls were travelling through the wilds unaided. A few quiet words from Athelstan in the way of a 'secret for a secret' fit well enough in Eu's mind and he did not press the matter any further.

Eu had regaled the group with stories of the old Greek Empire as well as funny stories of life in southern Hellas. He seemed incapable of calling Athelstan anything besides Agamemnon. Frankly, nobody seemed willing to correct him. Now deep in his cups, he was quite content to listen to others as they shared their stories as well. He had turned out to be an honourable man and a superior dinner guest. Athelstan settled back against a smooth rock and began a story from his childhood.

"Does anyone know why the bear has no tail?" he asked.

"No," some said suddenly intrigued. Others shook their heads silently.

"Bears have no tails?" asked Nicola wide-eyed with innocence as she snuggled close under Constantina's arm.

"No Nicola, they do not and I am going to tell you why."

Saul's head tilted to one side and amused look came over the Jew.

"Do you know why the bear has no tail, friend Saul?" Athelstan asked.

"No General, please enlighten me."

"This story happened many years ago when the world was still very young. It just so happened that back then, bears DID have tails."

"How old were you then... when the world was very young?" Nicola asked. Saul could do nothing to mask the snort of mirth that escaped him. He gave him a withering look.

"Well, I was not much older than you are now sweetheart. Now as I was saying, back then..."

"You mean WAY back then." Saul was clearly enjoying this.

"Yes... Way back then the bear did have a tail. It was long, fluffy and very expressive. It was widely believed to be the most magnificent tail of all the fur-bearing animals, or so the bear thought. It curled high over the bear's back and he would wave it at every creature he met in the forest. His pride in his tail was without equal and he never missed an opportunity to say so and show it off to all his woodland friends. Well one winter day; a very cold winter day, he happened upon a slow-moving river. It was covered with ice and snow except for a small hole, way out in the middle. Now bears are very curious creatures, so he walked out on the ice to look into the hole. And what do you think he saw in the hole in the ice?" he asked.

"Water?" asked Simone in her soft voice.

"A salamander," stated Sabine. Her sister gave her a dig with her elbow.

"Fish?" asked Sabine. Athelstan smiled and pointed at her.

"Fish. That is right Sabine. It was a fish, but not just any fish. It was a salmon, the king of all fish. It was then that without so much as a how do you do, or a by your leave, the bear waved his tail at the salmon and asked, 'Master Salmon, do you not think I have the most beautiful tail in all the land?'

'You have a tail? I had not noticed,' the salmon stated casually. You see the salmon had a tail of his own and it was very colourful and very strong. It helped him to swim upstream in the fall, against the rush of river water. So you can imagine he was not impressed by the vanity of the bear, whose tail did nothing but wave in the breeze.

'Had not noticed? Why of course I have a tail. Can you not see it?' asked the bear who was very put out by the salmon's attitude.

'No, I can not,' answered the salmon flatly, 'show me.'

So, the bear turned around and waved the tail in the air above the hole in this ice, 'see?'

'No I cannot see. Bring it closer.'

The bear held his tail even closer. 'Can you see it now?'

'No I cannot see unless it is underwater.'

"The bear then dipped his tail deep in the cold water and quick as you can say 'Epona Lives' the salmon breathed his icy breath on the water and froze the hole shut tight for you see the salmon king is a magical creature of water and ice. The bear was stuck fast and could not pull his tail out no matter how hard he tried."

"In time the bear had no choice but to leave his tail stuck in the ice and go back into the forest. From that moment on bears were born with no tails. However, the bear learned a valuable lesson that day. Vanity will always cost you what can most ill afford to lose. Now bears go about their business in silence. They walk through the trees without making a sound and avoid contact with all but their own kind. The lesson of the bear's tail is one we can all take to heart." Not a sound was heard after his story as the girls. Even Saul pondered his story nodding at the wisdom.

"That was a good story, my shaggy friend," he said. "I will remember these wise words."

"So will I," breathed Connie under her breath.

Alessandra was regarding Athelstan dubiously. "That can not be true!" she exclaimed suddenly. "What bear would stick his tail into icy water? I mean really Athelstan."

"You do not believe my story, Alessandra ?"

"No."

"Well, when you meet a bear ask him. He will tell you."

"Bears cannot talk."

"You think not?" Alessandra shook her head, her dark curls dancing in the firelight.

Simonea regarded the Celt in horror. "We are not going to meet a bear…" She glanced around at the dark trees. "…are we?"

Athelstan opened his mouth to answer when Connie interrupted him with a shake of her head and a sharp look.

"Of course not Simonea. There are no bears anywhere in these hills, are there Athelstan?" she spoke quietly folding Simonea into her arms.

"Connie is correct. We will not be meeting any bears here."

"I think we have had enough fireside stories for one night. Time for sleep. Gather your blankets." They did as they were bid, but before joining them Connie leaned close to Athelstan's ear and whispered, "The next story you tell better be about a bunny rabbit, or I swear to Pluto you will regret it."

"I only…" he began but Constantina had stormed away from him and joined the girls under the bower of branches.

A low chuckle was heard from Saul. "She means it Ath. Learn and believe."

The next morning, Eu and his dog took his leave and thanked the group for the stories.

They continued south through twisting mountainous lands until they joined a busy road. It bent to the west and to the south of Mount Parnassus. By early afternoon Delphi was finally in sight. Demetrios spoke up.

"Delphi. It is a very sacred spot, indeed. It is considered to be the centre of the world, you know. People come here from the four corners of the earth to consult the oracle."

"Are we going to see him?" Alessandra asked.

"Her. The Oracle is always a priestess of Apollo. It was here that Apollo slew the Dragon guarding the navel of Gaia, Grandmother Earth. It was an earth spirit. Apollo speaks through her."

"What do they want to know from her?"

"They ask her all sorts of things. Is it a good time to marry? Kings might ask if they should go to war. Others will consult her where to build new cities and things like that. Many things are asked of Apollo though her. The answers, however, are not always the ones expected, nor are they always clear. There is quite a ritual surrounding the Oracle. First, the priestess performs various actions of purification such as washing in the nearby river. The one party seeking advice would then offer a pie – before being allowed into the inner temple where the priestess resided and gave her pronouncements."

The road into Delphi was clogged with traffic, both coming and going. Inns and alehouses were plentiful. Dozens of statues and temples dedicated to Zeus and Apollo lined the main thoroughfare and the faithful were everywhere. Street vendors also plied their trade along the cobblestone streets. In the distance, a round temple with Doric columns could be seen and thousands of people were gathered around it.

"I owe you all a look at the Oracle before you leave. This might be the only chance you get." The Celt and seven Roman ladies entered the temple to witness the Oracle at work.

The air smelled like rich perfume. It had a curiously calming effect on Athelstan after a few minutes and the surroundings took on a dream-like quality. He knew to get a personal audience was a time consuming and expensive proposition, so watching from afar was the best they could do. Still, it had its moments. Here in the main audience chamber, a round ewer sat partially embedded in the floor and a fume of some sort rose from its depths. Above, sat the Oracle swathed in white. She swayed to and fro, deep in a trance. A man stepped forward.

"Oracle of Apollo. Long have we struggled in the north against great odds that threaten to overwhelm us. Our enemie's King lay dying and I beseech your guidance. Should we make war upon them, or should we offer a lasting peace." The Oracle raised her hands to the roof that was obscured by a white mist. When she finally spoke, it was loud and shrill.

"Doomed are you of the low streets! Chaos, death and blackness will reign! Can none of you see that? Men will pluck their eyes out of their sockets. Mothers will murder their babies. A thrice–horned cow will give issue to an abomination. With all Hades at its heels, it will scour the land clean at the appointed hour. The earth will crack and split and all the slime and vomit will spew forth, covering the world with stink and ooze and death." She paused to gasp for breath before shrieking. "Pray! Pray now! Pray for your, souls for the hour of your annihilation is at hand!"

The room was deathly silent for a moment. The man, who came to hear her prophesy asked in bewildered astonishment. "Ekrixi orgis?" It was an utterly uncouth Greek expression. He glanced around open-mouthed and helpless – arms outstretched in a vain appeal for someone to explain. Then he turned back to the ewer and bellowed towards the back of the Temple. "EKRIXI ORGIS? DO YOU NOT KNOW WHAT I WENT THROUGH TO GET HERE?" Guards grabbed him and started to drag him away.

"Hey, let me go. YOU BITCH. EXPLAIN YOURSELF! Hey! Take yer hands off me!" He started to thrash and fight. Temple Guards physically escorted out the frothing distraught man as he kicked and shrieked his outrage. He was bludgeoned to unconsciousness. Silence finally fell again on the stunned crowd save for a soft sound near the back. Athelstan was quietly laughing. "Come along now ladies, I think we have seen quite enough." He nodded and Constantina began to herd the rest of the girls out of the temple.

"Wait." It was a softly spoken request and one of the guards laid a hand on Athelstan's arm. He was pointing at the Oracle. The Celt glanced over his shoulder and saw the priestess had stood and was walking down the steps towards him.

"Gentle Mother, are you speaking to me?" He was not answered. She glided up to him and the crowd parted. With a simple gesture, she bade him kneel. The Oracle bent and whispered into his ear for a full minute. Then she straightened.

"You are certain?" The Oracle did not answer. She turned and retraced her path back to her seat. Athelstan stood and glanced around at the crowd. They all stared at him in wonder. Without a word, he turned and followed the girls out.

"What did she tell you?" Demetrios was brimming with curiosity. Athelstan just stared at him. The crowd had followed the Celt out of the Temple and word began to spread.

"Aye assume she does nut do that very often."

"She never does that," Demetrios explained. "Ever. Athelstan, what did she tell you?"

Suddenly shaken out of his reverie Athelstan released a long-held breath. "Not here. We need to get these girls on a ship for home today – now in fact. Can that be arranged?"

Saul nodded. "Ewe and Constantina wait here. Demetrios and Aye will see to it. We will leave the wagon and carriage in the shipyard. The girls can keep their horses Aye think." Athelstan nodded absently. His mind was calculating something grave. "We will be back in one day. Just go. Aye will be able to find ewe then. Ewe know how to leave us a sign. Time to say your goodbyes."

"I will leave you a trail only you will know how to follow. You are familiar with the work of Pythagoras?"

Demetrios nodded.

They quickly bundled the children into the carriage and wagon. Constantina kissed each on the cheek. "You be brave now. Alessandra will be in charge now and you listen to her."

"But we don't want to leave."

"Your parents are very worried about you and the sooner you are home safe the better I will feel."

"This is not how I wanted to say goodbye, Connie," Alessandra said in a shaky voice. "Will we ever see you again?" Connie looked at Athelstan and he gave a small nod.

"Yes. Of course, you will. This war will not last forever." She stroked Alessandra's hair and gave her a hug. The other girls were crying openly. "I will miss each one of you very much." The wagons lurched into motion.

All Athelstan could do was wave. A tear trickled down his cheek. "Now we must move faster. We have spent too long on the road as it is."

"I know we have. I know you will miss them too." Constantina said. He looked at her, nodded curtly and brushed away the tear savagely.

"We need to get out of Delphi quickly. Saul and Demetrios will find us." Athelstan mounted Maehadren and lifted Connie up too. They led her horse. As they left Delphi, they passed a wagon filled with cattle feed. He leaned over and grabbed a handful of straw.

Chapter Twenty-Nine

Constantina and Athelstan turned north off the road with the intention to travel along the west side of Mount Parnassus. Here, he carefully set three pieces of straw on the side of the road. They were arranged in a familiar pattern only Saul and Demetrios would understand. They travelled quickly and easily over the bare land. They skirted scattered areas of dense trees and thorny bushes. Here the land was flat and all but deserted. Then it began to rise. A stream tumbled down little falls and dense copses of trees began to appear in greater numbers again. By early evening, they rode through a lush maple forest that smelled of humus and the recent rain. Once deep in the heart of these trees, he finally called a halt. They had made very good time. They ate sparingly and settled under the thick canopy early. There was little conversation beyond the necessary. After a long time, Connie fell asleep curled up in the white fur and snuggled in the crook of Athelstan's arm.

A watery sun woke the pair. Maehadren and Iola were restless and stamped their hooves on the ground several times. Maehadren's ears were aimed back in the direction they had come.

"This might be Saul and Demetrios returning, but I want you ready to ride out of here if it isn't." She mounted Iola and waited. Athelstan drew his sword. After a short wait it was clear there were more than two horses, there were several as well as something with wheels. He smacked Iola on the rump and the horse headed off at a trot taking Constantina with her.

Athelstan mounted Maehadren and waited. The first glimpse was through the trees and he saw a grim-faced Saul. He was leading Demetrios' horse.

"Ah! There ewe are Athelstan. Aye thought Aye might have missed ewe. Where is Connie?"

"Not far." Where is Demetrios?"

"Aye tried to stop him, but he is a very determined man."

"Where did he go?" the Celt asked in a clipped tone. Iola and Connie returned.

"Corinth." Equally clipped.

"Why?"

He held out a steady hand and handed something to Athelstan. It was a Celtic disk. The one he had given Queen Leonida at their final meeting. He turned it over and there was an X scratched into the soft metal. He stared at it for a moment. "What has happened?"

"One of the former Royal Guardsmen found Demetrios at the harbour and gave him this. Queen Leonida is missing my friend. Aye am sorry."

"Missing?" he whispered.

"She cannot be found. ." Constantina gasped in shock.

"Kratesipolis!" he spat.

"No, Aye think nut. She had no cause. Axum does. Sparta has a new ruler, a man called Arios. Now that Leonida is gone, they are going to hunt ewe." Constantina turned white.

Athelstan nodded. First Rome and now this Axum. At least he knew where one of them was.

Saul looked at Constantina. "Are you all right?" Saul asked

"NO, no I am not fine. Leonida has been taken and I am frightened. There are only three of us now. We are being hunted by who knows how many people. What real chance do we have here in the wilderness?"

"More than you might think."

"Do you think Demetrios will return?"

Saul looked dubious. "He is going to kill the Corinthian Queen if he can."

"Then we cannot afford to wait on him. We need to make up for lost time and my stupidity."

Saul placed a hand on Athelstan's shoulder. "What did that Oracle tell ewe?"

"Papirius is already here, in Sparta. He has come with unexpected numbers."

"How unexpected?"

"Five hundred of the Equites Romani." Connie gave a horrified squeak. She began backing up as if doom was about to descend on them all. "Constantina, please calm down. This is not entirely unexpected."

"He brought his cavalry. Don't you know what this means?" she asked.

"Yes, I do. It means we are going to kill a lot of horsemen."

"They are only days away. You are NOT taking this seriously. They are in Sparta. They will find us."

"How? Think for a moment. They are in Sparta. We were never in Sparta. We went to Corinth instead, then to Athens by sea."

She thought about this. "That's right. We went around didn't we?"

"Yes. No one in Sparta, who knows anything about us, is still there – including Queen Leonida. Her disappearance has bought us some valuable time."

"This means Papirius will talk with King Arios and he knows nothing of this. I suspect his reign will be a very short one. It seems Papirius will do us a favour and throw Axum's plans for Sparta into chaos for a time. Remind me to thank him for that when I see him."

"Demetrios is going to try to eliminate Kratesipolis. Yes?" This question was aimed at Saul. The Jew nodded. "I will not fault him. He is brave to try. If he succeeds, that will buy us more time. Saul and I will be setting traps behind us the likes of which Papirius and his knights will simply not believe. If he catches up to us, there will be a good chance he will be alone, on foot and riding a goat. Remember this Connie; this is my world we stand in now, not his. I know where we are going. He does not. Do you trust me?"

"I…"

"Aye trust him and Aye am a Jew. We do not trust anyone." Connie saw his expression and began a nervous laugh. "Aye would take that as a yes if Aye were ewe."

"So I shall." He put what he hoped was a comforting hand on her shoulder. "Are you ready to ride?"

"Yes," she sniffed. She mounted Iona.

He led them up into the wild lands to the west and as he went, selected several animal trails to set simple snares. They were simple loops of braided vines with one end attached to a tree trunk and a slipknot on the other. The twine formed a loop and was carefully placed over nearly invisible holes in the tall grasses. The snares were quick to make so Athelstan set several. They also took time to construct another deadly trap for Papirius and his men. This was a loose rock–fall with a similar trip line made out of long vines and moss. It could cripple dozens. Each time he left a small hint for Demetrios with the strands of straw. He hoped that the Spartan completed his task and won free, he would heed these warnings. He also hoped Demetrios would find these markings before the Romans did.

For the next five days, they ate and slept in the saddle. They paused only to grab a brief nap, rest the horses and light a fire. Each bore the hardship well but it finally became clear they needed a more prolonged rest.

They had entered into a lush, wild, empty land. Slowly they were entering the vast marches of southern Macedonia and as they travelled northwest, the air grew more fragrant.

They built a hidden camp under the low hanging branches of a massive willow tree. Constantina fell to sleep the moment she lay down on the soft furs. The two men led the three mounts and the horse away so as not to betray her location.

Fern fronds interspersed with mosses, lichens and moulds under the shading arms of smooth–sided larches, red-barked tamarisk, gnarled olive and white–flowering myrtles – all grew in wild tangles. Thyme mantled the tree boles and flourished in deep tapestries among the hidden stones. Interspersed tightly with the thyme were the blue–flowered sages, marjoram and stonecrop sedum. Primroses and anemones carpeted the ground tightly in the hazelnut groves, now swollen with nuts. Deep grasses swayed languidly beside icy pools, where the falling hill streams burst from the ground as artesian wells and paused in cool hollows before gurgling their way downhill. The horses grazed contentedly and drank deeply of these clear waters.

As they walked through bush and herb, sweet odours rose all about them. Athelstan took the time to gather the abundance around them, deftly wrapping the different clusters in leaves, or tying them in bunches with creeping vines. The pair paused at the lip of a natural stone basin covered in mosses and lichens where they drank and washed to refresh themselves. Scattered here and there grew mushrooms in fairy circles where the lords and ladies of the Fairies of Shee might dance and cavort under the light of a full moon. It seemed to be a land where dryads, naiads, sprites and pixies could live and frolic in wild abandon, each in their own fashion.

Saul shaded his eyes and pointed suddenly. The Celt followed his gaze and to his surprise, a ram stood some one hundred and twenty yards away downhill and downwind. Athelstan motioned for Saul to use his bow and his friend's fiery dark eyes sparkled as he looked at the great creature. Carefully he strung and knocked an arrow. Athelstan pointed to Saul's left side; his fist under his arm at the spot on the huge sheep Saul needed to hit. The Jew nodded he understood and took careful steady aim. He watched in amazement as this calm archer took a deep breath before letting loose his arrow. One moment the sheep grazed on succulent fall grasses, the next it sank quietly to the ground – dead.

Standing over the kill the Celt shook his head. He had never seen such accuracy. At that distance, he had hit a spot on the sheep no bigger than his own eyeball.

"You have really got to show me how you do that."

"Remember Aye have looked at your hands. Ewe do not have the thumbs for it." Saul said sadly. Athelstan frowned and looked at his thumbs again but out of the corner of his eye saw Saul smirking.

"Thumbs, my backside." He hoisted the Ram onto his shoulders. "Let us go see if we are being remembered with reverence."

"Aye certainly will be," Saul stated smoothly. "Aye believe Aye should make a bow for Constantina as we travel. It might prove useful to her at some point."

Athelstan agreed and waited as Saul selected a suitable ash bough for the purpose. He lopped it off cleanly with the short oddly shaped weapon of his. There was no hesitation in any of the strokes. Athelstan nodded with hooded eyes.

Returning the way they had come, they found three snared rabbits, which Athelstan took with tender stroking. He said a prayer of thanks in Gaelic over each for the abundance. He took great pains to remove all the snares, even the ones that caught nothing. Along the way, he collected plant leaves and dug up a root, or two.

"What a treasure you must be to your God, but Saul, you are not just a good archer. I am beginning to see there is a lot more to you than meets the eye. You will tell me one day."

Saul chuckled. "Ewe think so? Perhaps. That is if there were something to tell."

"What are you trying to hide from me?"

Saul levelled a narrow gaze at Athelstan. "What makes ewe think Aye am hiding something?"

"My thumbs told me." Saul laughed.

"What is it ewe think Aye am hiding? Speak your mind to me Celt."

"I am not sure. For one thing, at the Agora you showed no fear of me. That is not usual. Most people fear me, but you did not."

"Why should Aye fear ewe? Are ewe dangerous somehow?"

"Dangerous? Yes I am the most dangerous…"

Saul was smiling and shaking his head.

"What? Why are you smiling? That you can even ask and answer that question so definitively, makes me wonder what you are, that fear is no longer part of you. Seldom do I find such a lack of fear in anyone who is not Celtic. That started me thinking."

"Could it nut be, we share that same lack of fear? Do ewe know so much about Jews that ewe can make such a wild assumption?"

"That may be one explanation, but then only an hour later and again just now, you made a bow shot that few would ever have attempted and none would have any reasonable expectation of making. You barely aimed."

"Do ewe nut think that it might have been my God who guided those arrows? Do yours nut favour ewe also, in your Celtic world?"

"I believe that they do, but my belief is that the Gods only guide those arrows that are shot true beforehand."

"Do ewe indeed? Is that curious concept also Celtic, or is just your belief?"

"It is only my belief, but still, with a bow, I have never seen your like before." Saul dipped his head slightly as if in thanks for the unintended compliment.

"Do ewe think it might help if ewe got out more and visited the wider world where such things might be commonplace?"

Now it was Athelstan's turn to laugh. "Perhaps it would."

"What other evidence do ewe have that Aye am hiding something?" Saul asked now clearly intrigued.

"You can fight with a knife as though you were born to it."

"Is it nut possible that Aye WAS born to it?"

"You notice everything without seeming to notice anything. I was watching you in the Agora. You knew thieves stole my knives from me, but now I am beginning to think it was you who took them."

"Do ewe really? It is a mystery is it nut?" he winked at the Celt.

"You know very well It was you and I know very well you did notice me watching you."

"So why should Aye nut watch ewe? Do you suggest Aye should roam aimlessly through a strange world with my eyes shut?"

"I doubt it would make much difference whether your eyes were open or not. Your eyes are never at rest whether open or closed. You kept careful track of everything, the girls, Demetrios and me in that order. It would not surprise me if you could accurately describe every person you saw in the Agora that day."

"Are ewe nut exaggerating just a little bit? Did Aye nut fail to notice the beggars, or The Hooded man's assassin hiding in their midst?"

"You tell me."

Again, Saul's head dipped, but this time there was a hard edge to his eyes.

"Do ewe have more?"

"I do. There is the matter of your advice to me with regard to knife fighting. I had wondered who taught you to fight with a knife like that and why. I believe that mystery will remain."

"Are ewe nut making some more wild assumptions friend Ath-el-Stan? Would it nut be more likely being a Jew is a dangerous thing in this world? Persecuted for centuries. Is it nut more likely that Aye need to know how to fight so Aye can survive and seek?"

"I do not think so, but I will have to concede that possibility does exist. I will end for now with this. I have to mention the ease with which you harvested those ash staves for Connie's bow just now. You used your sword…"

"You mean my Scimitar?"

"Yes, your Scimitar. You used it without hesitation and with it you can kill with pure finesse. Tell me, was that accidental too?"

"Would ewe believe me if Aye did?"

"No, I would not."

"Then why should Aye deny it?"

"I am glad to see you did not and please do not think I have not noticed that during our little chat just now, every word you have said to me has been in the form of a question. You have confirmed nothing and in doing so you have confirmed everything. You, sir, are skilled to the point of mastery, shrewd to a fault and probably damned dangerous both awake and asleep. So yes, to return to my original assumption about you, I do believe you are hiding something, perhaps many things. Of that, there can be no doubt now. The questions that remain are not ifs, but have now become whats and perhaps even whys. Yes, Saul, there is much more to you than meets the eye my friend. Perhaps you will tell me one day."

Saul pursed his lips and gave the Celt a penetrating look. "Perhaps Aye will friend Ath–el–stan," he said after a moment. He leaned in conspiratorially with a wide smile, "but nut today." The Jew straightened his black-rimmed hat and walked away.

Athelstan hoisted the ram onto the spare horse and quickened his pace. "Yes, friend Saul. Nut today."

Chapter Thirty

Both men stiffened when they returned. A dark shape was studying the ground adjacent to the Willow tree where Connie was fast asleep. Saul nocked an arrow but did not raise his bow. The newcomer looked around as if puzzled by what he was seeing. Presently he scratched his chin in a very familiar way and turned around. A moment of elation flashed across Demetrios' face before the stoic Spartan mask returned. He waved at the approaching men and waited for them to arrive.

"You might have left me my horse somewhere along the trail," he quipped.

"And let him run the risk of finding a more pleasant owner? That hardly seems fair to the horse, does it?" Saul shook his head.

"Nut fair at all." The beast nuzzled his master.

"So?"

"Two Greek city-states are now in need Kings. The dream of a united Hellas is as dead as Kratesipolis. My Queen is missing. I fear for her." The three men embraced and Connie emerged into the fading light rubbing her eyes and backside. She looked puzzled. She peered at the three men oddly.

"Demetrios has returned. Now we can make better time." Athelstan stated.

"Demetrios? You are alive." She nodded at the Greek. "I have prayed for the Gods to protect you."

"Yours, or his?" Saul asked.

Her eyes flashed at Saul. "Mine!" she barked. Her tone softened. "Mine, of course."

"It would seem that they have listened to you," Demetrios countered.

Iona backed away from Constantina as she approached the animal and it took no small amount of coaxing before the beast would let her mount. There was growing frustration in Constantina's demeanour.

At the end of each day of riding, Connie would slip off her horse, eat sparingly and curl up into her blankets. There was little or no conversation from her. While Saul crafted a short bow for Connie, the men would share jokes, stories and songs, each in their own tongues. In a short time, they all came to have a rudimentary knowledge of Gaelic, Hebrew and Greek. Each tale would be told, translated and memorized. Constantina would not take part. A change had come over her. She was quieter and distant. She was not wearing the Epona clan badge in her hair. Perhaps she had just lost it.

This night would be no different and Athelstan began a simple folk song in Gaelic.

I speak the truth of the forest and gentle streams.
I speak the truth and follow the path.
I speak the truth of the seasons.
The truth that I speak,
The truth that I speak, it shall always remain.

You feed the light of the Gods and of mortal men.
You feed the light of the power of life.
You feed the light of the ages.
Feed you the light,
Feed you the light – you will never know pain.

We sing the songs that will guide us through night and day.
We sing the songs of the circle of time.
We sing the songs for the fallen.
The songs that we sing,
The songs that we sing, are the truthful refrain.

Later in the evening, soft breathing from under the Willow on the far side of the fire told the weary men that the girl was already asleep.

"How much farther is this glade? I do not know how much more of this she can take. She has barely spoken a word in days." Saul was genuinely concerned and rightly so. The girl looked exhausted.

"I still see another eight days ahead of us at least."

"Aye do not think she will make it another eight days. Is there anything more we can do to delay the Romans? Is there an easier path to follow?"

"I have been thinking of nothing else for some time now. What you do not realise is I AM taking the easiest route for her sake. If my estimation of Papirius is correct, he and his men will overtake us in two days, or less no matter what we do. We will not make it to the Glade if we stay on this path. Our only other option is to go up and over the spine of this mountain range. It should cut our remaining journey in half, but it is much harder." 'If we survive,' he thought grimly. He stared into his lap.

"Why is it so important that you encounter Papirius now rather then later?"

"Politically, we as a nation, need to remove him from the control of the Roman Senate. He is the single most dangerous man in all of Rome. Now is not the best time to encounter him, but now is when it will happen, so I must adapt as my wise friend Saul keeps telling me. I had hoped to face him in the spring on the field of battle. If we try to go around this mountain range, he will catch us. If we go over the mountains, we will catch him. I do not see that we have a choice."

"You do realise you have his wife. She can intervene on your behalf." Saul was always the voice of reason. Athelstan shook his head.

"I would never put her in that position. She has nothing he wants. Papirius would make her a slave in the blink of an eye. You men would not live to see that however since you will be left here to enjoy the lovely view of the countryside nailed to a ten-foot cross," he looked at the men.

"I should never have brought you with me. I should never have brought her with me. What is the matter with me?" He was worried to the core of his being for them all.

"Ewe love her, so there is nothing wrong with ewe. Just remember, it was her choice to come with ewe, Athelstan, not yours." Saul was smiling.

"She is still his wife. He will not harm her." Demetrios countered.

"I am sure you are right Demetrios, but you do not know Papirius as I do. I will not put the matter to the test. He is not a reasonable man. I would have little hesitation letting her negotiate with his successor, but not with him. I will not risk her life in that way." Saul had a grim look.

"You look unhappy my friend. What troubles you?" Athelstan asked.

"We are being followed," Saul stated flatly.

Athelstan looked up but did not move. "Oh, so you know about our shadows. They have been with us since we left Delphi. Do you think I struck a nerve with that beggar?" He settled back on his elbows and looked up at the carpet of stars overhead.

"Probably. Ewe seem to have a gift. We are in terrible danger."

"Those who attacked us at the Inn were Roman. They carried these." Athelstan produced several coins with Latin on one side and a portrait of Papirius on the other.

"Aye wonder about that. It is like the Axum to use just this sort of deception. They were certainly well disciplined regardless of who they were," Saul assured them.

"Our shadows are professionals, but they are not Romans. Their orders would be to kill me and they have had many opportunities to do just that. It is my opinion that whoever is directing them, they have been told to follow us and report back for more instructions," he looked back down at the men. "I have been wrong before. What do you think we should do? Should we hunt them ourselves and put an end to the matter now? It is a simple thing to turn the predator into the prey."

"No," Saul began. "They have been told to take her. Why? Aye cannut say, but that is what they truly want. If we leave her to hunt them, they will take her. They are waiting for us to make a mistake. Aye say we continue as we do now, but pay close attention to 'our shadows' in the moonlight."

Athelstan nodded. "I think your idea is sound. We will set watches from now on. Two hours each? They will notice the change of course. How do you suppose they will react to that? It will tell them we know they are following us. At the moment they think they have the advantage of stealth."

"Let them keep their perceived advantage. We know they are there. It really gives us the advantage does it not?"

"I hate this inaction." Demetrios growled. "I say we face them and send them all to Hades, but that would tip our hand. I agree, we do as we have done."

"It is settled then. We continue as before and pretend we are ignorant of them. It may lure them in closer, so we must be ready to turn and attack at a moments notice. If they approach the camp, our horses will tell us long before they get here. We should remain vigilant. I will wake you in two hours."

Saul said still looking out at the night. "Ewe will take first watch then?"

"Yes, I have some things to think about before I will be able to sleep. The best route over these mountains, for instance, go get some rest," he leaned back again and looked back at the stars.

After some time he stood and stretched.

Constantina was exhausted but sleep would not come. She sat staring into the darkness.

"Shhh. I am just checking on you. Everything is fine sweetheart, just go back to sleep," he watched her for a moment. He had not touched her since leaving Athens, not even by accident and he ached for her.

"Sweetheart?" she half asked, "Do you have time to talk M'Lord?"

"Of course Connie, what is it?"

Her eyes narrowed briefly.

"How much farther is it?"

Taking her hands in his, he looked at her in the gloom. "It will not be much longer, we will be home soon."

"Home? You are taking me back to Rome?" she asked flatly.

"Rome? No, I meant my home. It is on the other side of these mountains. You will finally be able to rest properly. Then you can decide what you will do next."

She watched him as he kissed her hands. "I have missed you," he said.

"I have – missed you too. I am very tired of all this riding. I should get some sleep."

"I understand. Regardless of what the future holds, know this. I can never let you go."

He was not certain if he had spoken out loud.

The remainder of the watch progressed slowly until he woke Saul. Sleep, this night, would not come easily.

Fifty-three of his five hundred horsemen lay dead along the trail from Sparta to Athens. He had found the Athenian villa where the girls had stayed and after interrogating the owners and their slaves, he locked them inside and burned the building to the ground. He smiled as he rode away to the sounds of their dying shrieks.

Now four days hard ride north of Athens and a day away from Delphi, Papirius wrenched his gladius from a sausage maker's chest. The man fell to his knees, blood pouring out the massive hole. Surprise was etched on his face as it hit the ground. A lanky red–boned dog slipped away, head down tail between its legs. There was fear and anger in its eyes.

Morale was dipping rapidly. Two days after the farm, they were already far north of Delphi, where the trail of disks Athelstan had left as crumbs, ended. Papirius' treatment of his troops did not help either. Papirius heard whispers from his men, but he disregarded them. He was Proconsul and any who opposed him would be obliterated. It was near midday when he saw the horseman approach.

Coming closer, he saw the rider was Roman. Titus pointed out what he had sent Quintus and eight others out to do and Papirius congratulated Titus on his forward-thinking, he may just have a lead yet.

The rider, Marcus, came to Papirius and saluted, arm straight at 45 degrees. "Ave, sir!"

"Ave, Marcus. Any news from your group?"

"Yes sir! We have found the barbarian's trail!"

"You what? Where is he!"

He is at least six days ahead of us but there can be no doubt now, where he is headed?"

"Macedonia. We believe we can flank him by turning west around the mountains while this main force chases him north. This way we can keep him in sight as it were until the distance between us is made up.

Papirius threw his head back and laughed. "Good job. Tell Quintus to form a Contuberium, head west and cut the bastard off. He has to come out of those mountains somewhere. Hurry men! We have a rat to catch! We ride through the night," he yelled as he flew into a gallop.

"I will find you, Athelstan." Madness lit his eyes. "I will make you pay for daring to defy Rome."

Chapter Thirty-One

A lone hawk wheeled high over the long sloping mountain valley. The lower reaches were covered with a sea of ripe grasses and their pale heads rippled and swayed like a golden sea. Higher up the grasses and stunted trees thinned until they vanished completely. Above that were the treacherous bare rocky slopes and snow–covered peaks. Cold eyes scanned the valley floor as he hung in the wind; his only care were the small creatures that fed him and his mate. Nothing else mattered including the line of small huddled specks far below. The distant specks moved impossibly slow as they toiled up the steep slope above the tree line. The hawk ignored them. The world of horses and men were of no concern to him. With a sharp snap of his outstretched wings, he caught another updraft and flew away to the south.

A scrawny red-boned dog was using his nose to close the distance between his familiar cabin near Delphi and the travellers. His master had died horribly at Roman hands a week past. He would find a new master, or die in the attempt.

Athelstan looked down and was surprised to see the beast fall into step beside Maehadren.

"What are you doing here?" he asked. A wagging tail was his only answer. He reined Maehadren to a stop and dismounted. The creature was bare bones. The Celt let the creature drink water poured into his hand and he lapped it up greedily. The dog also excitedly gulped down some dried meat. It was starving. He licked Athelstan's face. He smelled like a wet dog.

"Aye fear his owner is dead," Saul commented. Athelstan nodded.

"The Romans are gaining on us and our skinny friend here has been leading them unerringly to us. I cannot blame him. He is alone in the world now." He easily hoisted the dog up onto Maehadren's shoulders and climbed up behind him. The dog fussed for a moment before he sat back and leaned into Athelstan's chest. An impossibly long tongue hung past white teeth in a smiling maw.

"Suppose I call you Roidhn. It means red. Would you like that?" Again, the dog reached up and licked his face twice. "I will take that as a yes." He answered to Roidhn, from that moment to the end of his days.

Twelve days riding through the steep mountains and along the precipitous, narrow ledges proved far more difficult than anyone expected. There were many instances where horses were led single file. The hardest test of all was still ahead. They left the trees that morning and continued upward towards the magnificent rugged peaks. Cold alpine winds whipped long hair into unruly tangles and they had all snuggled deep into their travelling cloaks in an effort to stay warm. Snow and this bitter cold wind were unknown to his companions and it was nearly an unbearable hardship. Roidhn even tucked his tail under his rump and burrowed deep into Athelstan's cloak.

Athelstan was still deeply worried. He knew they had covered most of the distance they needed to in order to keep ahead of the Roman pursuit, yet time had all but run out. Even his dreams were filled with pounding hooves, flying red cloaks and shining brush-topped helmets. This route was their only hope of outrunning them. It would trim the journey from eight days to three with luck. Patches of snow grew deeper and more abundant the higher they climbed. The trail grew fainter and fainter until it disappeared altogether, but Athelstan led them forward, confident that his destination was near. He dreaded what would happen when they arrived at the mountain pass. He did not have to wait long.

A change had come to Constantina as well. She had become even quieter and more withdrawn. She hardly spoke and ate even less. She rode hunched over her horse's neck.

They crept along another rocky precipice hugging the sheer ice-covered cliff face. A misstep anywhere would result in certain death. They rounded a sharp rock wall and the trail widened dramatically. Athelstan called a halt and dismounted. His three companions peered out of their furry cocoons and were staring around in mute shock. For this mountain-bred Celt, the view from here was staggeringly beautiful. Rank upon rank of snow-covered peaks marched north for as far as the eye could see.

His companions were somewhat less than impressed. They stood at the top of the world and stared with horror at the singularly unique feature before them. A deep chasm separated two mountains, the one upon which they stood and the one where they were headed, nine hundred yards away. Joining this mountain to the next was a narrow walkway less than five feet wide. It sat atop a slender fin of stone that looked like a giant knife set on its edge. It dropped away on either side for a thousand feet. A powerful gale blew up one side of the aerial walkway, coiled around the six travellers, before screaming down the other side.

"You are not suggesting we cross here." Constantina's voice was faint in the howling wind.

"Yes, we cross here," Athelstan retorted loudly.

"I am not walking across that," she yelled into the wind at the Celt.

"Of course you are not. The wind would blow you off as soon as you stepped out on to it. That is why you are going to ride across," he explained at the top of his lungs.

Saul looked very concerned at the prospect and his eyes showed it.

They kept flickering back and forth between the slender bridge and the emptiness on either side.

"I am NOT crossing that!" Connie yelled.

"I see," he bellowed, "then give my best regards to Papirius. You should come across him by midday tomorrow." No one looked happy with that prospect.

"We must cross here. It is the only way into the next valley," he explained. "We have got to get off this mountain and someplace warm for the night."

"What stops the horses from being blown off the same way we would?" Saul inquired. His words were ripped from his mouth by the relentless wind.

"Their weight. They also have ten times the balance we do. They can no more fall off this than I can fly. Just lie flat against your horse's neck and hang on tight. They will get you all across if you will just trust them. Remember they do not want to fall off any more than you do.

"I think we need to discuss this before we agree to try it," Constantina shouted.

"Take all the time you like," he opened his arms holding his hands out. "Be aware that the longer we say here, the closer Papirius gets," he moved his right hand. "The Romans are here and we are here," he indicated his left hand. Every minute we spend here…" he moved his hands closer together very slowly showing the distance between them getting smaller and smaller.

She looked at the three men with an expression of uncertainty. Saul looked at Athelstan's calm expression then gave Constantina an imperceptible nod.

"I cannot go across there. I just cannot. I am afraid of heights like this. Athelstan, please do not make me do this," she pleaded.

He knew this would be difficult. "Connie, you can ride with me. Sit in front and lay flat. Keep your eyes closed and you will be fine. I promise." He looked from face to face. Constantina dismounted her horse and his heart sank. For a minute, he believed she had suddenly changed her mind. Instead, she mounted Maehadren and pressed herself against his shoulders and neck. She took two handfuls of his mane, wiggled her bum to settle herself and looked back at Athelstan.

"You coming?" She yelled. He looked at the men and they shrugged their shoulders. After a moment, he vaulted up onto the horse's back. All his feelings for her came rushing back as he pressed her down.

"You are sure this is safe," she hollered. He almost told her the truth.

"Absolutely, just close your eyes and we will be across before you know it," she suddenly turned and kissed him then laid back down.

"You are very brave my love. Just hold on," he kissed her cheek. Before any of them could move, Roidhn crouched low and crossed easily.

He kneed Maehadren and the great white horse stepped out onto the bridge. The wind blasted them with its full fury. Stinging sheets of ice crystals scoured any exposed skin raw.

Heavy hooves rose and fell with exquisite precision. Step by torturous step Maehadren moved across the long span. Stones scattered and skittered off the edge as his iron-shod hooves struck them. Even over the sound of the wind, each hoof fall could be clearly heard.

Saul followed next. Demetrios was last to step out onto the span. Their pace was understandably slow. Constantina had her eyes tightly closed but could not resist a quick look. Her piteous scream of fright tore into Athelstan and as Constantina tried to look up, he pressed her down.

Iola, now riderless, seemed exceptionally nervous and began to buck part way across. She tried to turn and retrace her steps. The panicked beast reared and its hooves slipped and skidded on the frozen stone. A rear hoof slipped over the side and the horse fought to regain her footing. A ghastly shriek of terror ripped from the horse as her other hoof sipped off. There was a horrifying moment where the beast struggled frantically to climb back up. Her hooves bit deeply into the ice, there was a horrifying pause, and a moment later, she was back on top and safe.

Crossing this precarious span took what seemed a lifetime. Constantina was shivering violently. Whether it was from the cold, or from understandable fear he could not tell, but she tensed each time Maehadren placed a hoof down on the frozen rock. From his low vantage point, Athelstan could tell the middle third of this aerial bridge dipped several hundred feet only to rise again near the face of the adjacent mountain. Several inches of snow–covered ice coated the rock in this depression. It had mounded slightly higher in the centre and gently sloping away towards the edges. The second half of their crossing would be made across this treacherous surface.

The slightest misstep here would be fatal. Maehadren held his head and neck low and turned to one side. He kept one of his walnut-sized eyes on the path. Constantina hugged his neck tightly; fists full of his coarse mane and rolling ever so slightly as the horse took one tentative step after the next. Athelstan pressed her down hard against Maehadren's shoulders but risked a brief backward glance at the others progress. He lifted his weight off Constantina slightly and turned to look.

Suddenly Maehadren's front hoof slipped on the ice. The beast abruptly pitched forward and down as he fought to remain standing. Constantina slipped off the horse's shoulders and pitched violently over his head. Time stood still for a moment as she began to fall. A howling scream of terror rang out only to be snatched away by the relentless wind. In sheer desperation, Athelstan lunged for her and at the very last second caught her ankle in a crushing grip. She swung in a long arc past Maehadren's side flailing her arms wildly.

Her weight plus Maehadren's frantic struggle for footing unbalanced Athelstan and he began to slide off sideways. As he fell, he managed to grasp a section of the saddle's leather harness, but he retained a vice-like grip on Constantina's ankle. He hit the ground hard immediately sliding half off the icy lip of the walkway. Maehadren kept walking. Every time he moved his rear hoof Athelstan was hauled along. It never stayed in one place long enough for him to get any footing. Constantina hung upside down at the end of Athelstan's left arm dangling with a thousand feet of air beneath her. The spear wound in his forearm suddenly flared to a white-hot pain. He ignored it all and kept his hold on the Constantina's foot. He would not be able to keep this up for long.

"Stad!" he bellowed at Maehadren to stop, but his orders to stop were blasted back down his throat by the fierce wind. Constantina swung slowly back and forth; he could only imagine her terror. She was thrashing, clawing and grasping for anything solid she could hold on to, but there was nothing but empty air, icy rock and the freezing wind.

Athelstan's fingers were already numb and he knew he was slowly inexorably losing his grip on her leg. His left forearm was screaming agony. No one behind them could do anything but watch helplessly as Connie's life hung in the balance. As Maehadren lurched forward again, it was impossible for Athelstan to regain his footing on the curved icy surface. Unless he did something soon she would fall; it was inevitable. Still, she swung back and forth at the end of his arm like a living pendulum, ticking off the final ghastly seconds of her life.

He pulled on her leg with all his might and hoisted her up alongside his body and she clutched his leg desperately.

"Climb!" he shrieked down at her. "Climb!" She clung to him literally for dear life and was powerless to move. Maehadren jolted forward again and Constantina lost her grip. She swung back out of sight over the edge. She jerked to a stop; Athelstan's arms and chest exploded with agony. He let out a primal scream of agony and impotent rage. He looked down and saw her looking back up at him; eyes wide with terror. She silently shook her head imploring him not to let her fall. He tried to tighten his grip but with the strength failing in his arm and hand, he felt her slip. There was no time left.

"Give me your arm!" he yelled. "Your arm!" She reached up immediately with her long fingers widely splayed. He pulled on her leg with his remaining strength until her fingers clutched at his leg. Then, he let go of her ankle. For a brief instant, she hung freely in the air above a yawning chasm. Then his huge paw closed like a vice on her slender wrist. Her legs swung down adding more momentum to her motion. She grabbed his wrist with her other hand and hung on.

Again, she swung back just as Maehadren took another step. Fatigue told him it was now, or never.

She started her return swing and Athelstan heaved with his remaining strength. Constantina picked up speed. He swung her like a sword, up and over, high above the rocky rim; high over his head and with a final twist by the Celt, flopped her belly down across Maehadren's back. He was reluctant to let her arm go but he had to. His body weight would drag her off again. Constantina scrabbled for grip, but after only a few tense seconds, she regained her seat astride the white horse. The harness was still dragging Athelstan along. He was hanging half on, half over the cliff.

Footing was nonexistent so for a few moments he let himself be dragged, his long hair whipping around wildly. He shook some feeling back into his left hand. Gritting his teeth at the pins and needles sensation. He risked a glance up at Constantina. She was safe and for a moment, he considered simply ending the pain by just letting go. He would slip from sight and they could continue on to the Glade without him. When she looked down, with naked fear for him etched across her face, he rejected these self-destructive thoughts.

He was being dragged along facing outward into the abyss. His own imminent death notwithstanding, the view was spectacular. Blue sky and bright sun provided a stunning backdrop to the surrounding snow-covered peaks. They were glowing like bright islands jutting up from a fluffy white sea of clouds. He wondered if he would enjoy the view as much if he were to fall to his death. 'Probably' he decided since there would be precious little else to do in those final seconds; might as well enjoy the trip down.

He looked down and swallowed hard, then looked skyward and said a final prayer to Epona. Behind his head, he could hear every time the giant warhorse placed his left rear hoof on the ice. It was rhythmic. Thud… Thud… Thud, he counted down the final three steps. Then, just as the horse's hoof was to hit the final time he twisted back reaching with his left arm. The hoof bit into the snow and his fist closed on his fetlock. At the same moment, he let go of the saddle. He slipped down around and under Maehadren just as the great hoof lifted for the next step. The force of being jerked forward along the ice nearly tore his shoulder from its socket.

Sliding on his face across the rough surface, he grasped the beast's tail with one then the other hand. Maehadren continued to walk at a deliberate pace while dragging his master behind him. The wind constantly threatened to sweep Athelstan over the side as he fought to maintain his grip on the slippery ice-encrusted tail. The tiny ice shards shredded the skin of his hands like glass.

With relative security, he rested a moment and allowed himself to be dragged. He looked up and reached for the leather harness strap that goes under the horse's tail. With that hand–hold he was finally able to get to his feet and take a few walking steps behind Maehadren. A moment later he was seated pressing Constantina flat once again.

"Are you hurt?" he yelled into her ear. She shook her head no. He heaved a sigh of relief but could see Constantina was paralyzed with fear.

"Stop jumping off the bloody horse!"

Her head snapped around and fury replaced terror.

"I did not jump…" He kissed her and was chuckling deep in his chest.

"That was fun wasn't it?"

"No! It was not fun, I was terrified!"

"Admit it. That was the most exciting thing that has ever happened to you in your entire life!" He did not have to yell as loud this close to her ear. "You have never felt more purely alive than you do at this very moment. Admit it to yourself." His laughter was infectious. Constantina burst into hysterical tears and laughter all at once.

"It was fun," she admitted reluctantly then swatted him. "You are a wicked, WICKED man! I could have been killed," she sputtered.

"Killed? Rubbish! Do you not know by now that I will never let you go Constantina of Rome? Now, you know you can bet your life on that." All laughter stopped and the two exchanged a silent look that said more than any words could ever convey. As the wind whipped their hair into red and blonde tangles, their kiss transformed all their pent-up fright into pure raw passion and the remaining distance was covered without either of them noticing at all. Yet, something about the kiss was different somehow. She drank him in hungrily.

The journey down the far side of the mountain peak was even more difficult than the approach was. The deep snow was covered with a crust of ice. It had to be broken and tossed aside to clear a path wide enough for the horses to negotiate. The men toiled hard swinging their swords and heaving the frozen slabs aside. It was difficult not to watch the sheets of ice slide down the mountainside and disappear from view into an unseen abyss below. It was more difficult still not to imagine that a single miss-step might propel them down to their death as well.

After a few hours of intense labour, the icy coating became thinner and as they slowly descended it vanished altogether. The knee-deep snow became heavy and sticky–wet. Each step was a struggle in the thin air. Soaking wet, they were all shivering from the cold. Back and forth, they went across the steep mountain face but the farther they descended, the shallower the snow became. Soon great grey patches of bare rock replaced the glittering white mantle of the upper peak until all but a few well–spaced patches of snow remained.

In time, they followed a faint animal trail that, at first, was only visible to Athelstan's keen eyes. As they entered the upper layer of short stunted trees, it became more visible. Struggling through the snow had been exhausting and the party rode slumped over in their saddles. Even the horses stumbled along. Athelstan called a halt and everyone gratefully slid off their mounts and onto the hard ground. They rested awhile and ate the remainder of the dried food. Roidhn laid down, went straight to sleep and began to snore.

"For the next two days we will need to hunt and gather food when we are able," Athelstan announced.

Demetrios looked around dubiously at the rocky terrain.

"Hunt what?" asked Saul. "It is as barren here as it is in the Sinai."

"Sinai? Is that a city?"

"No, it is a desert."

"Here yes," Athelstan agreed. "Not much lives this high up, but lower down there will be more game and a great many edible plants and berries. Do not worry overmuch, the Goddess Epona and her brethren will give us what we need."

"Aye believe in only one God," Saul stated flatly.

"Then, believe in her now. You will soon see she has already provided for all our needs."

"It is a HE."

"Who's a He?"

"My God. She is a He."

"She is? Your God is a He?"

"Yes." There was a pause.

"Oh, good for Her," said Athelstan with a grin.

"Aye am sure He will be delighted you feel that way about Her." They were both laughing.

Constantina snorted with impatience and swatted them both. "How much farther is it to your country?" Constantina asked.

"You mean our country."

"Yes, yes, our country. Do not start that with me!" she scolded.

Athelstan chuckled and sighed. He spread his arms at the distant valley below them. "We have already arrived," he said. "It lies before you. Behold, Gwennderion Glade."

Fatigue had prevented them from looking around before but now they gazed downward. A carpet of green was spread out beneath them dotted with tiny blue lakes. The vista rose and fell over hills and disappeared out of sight in the distance.

"We will travel a bit farther down today and make camp in the upper forests tonight; preferably near a tarn, or mountain stream. By tomorrow evening, we should arrive at our destination."

This announcement gave strength to tired limbs and soothed shattered nerves. They quickly remounted and rode downhill single file. It was not long before a final halt was called and the weary group settled near a fast moving stream that tumbled down from the snows high above.

Constantina immediately started to walk away, Demetrios stood. "I am fine Demetrios. I am just gathering wood. I promise not to go too far."

The Spartan watched her with no small bit of worry. He then looked over at Saul who was chuckling at their antics. Constantina went to 'gather her firewood'.

Athelstan finished unlashing another of the Jew's sheep kills from the packhorse. Easily slinging the one hundred pound beast over his shoulder, he joined Saul. The men knew Constantina had not been eating and worse, she hated the sight of blood, so they would skin and dress the sheep out of her sight. She went one way and they, the other.

"Saul, I am getting a bit worried about Constantina, she does not eat and when she does, she cannot keep it down. I think we may have to stay here tomorrow to let her rest." His long knife slit the sheep open and he began to skin it quickly. "What do you think?" He had come to rely more and more on this man's opinion.

"It is true, she is not eating well and her pallor shows it. However, that is nut what concerns me. Aye can nut place my finger on what is wrong. Unfortunately, we do not have the luxury to wait. We will just have to do what we can to make her comfortable."

"This is difficult country and she needs to eat to keep up her strength," he continued his bloody work. "If only I had something to calm her stomach so she could hold her food down. I wonder what is causing it," he frowned suddenly and sniffed the air.

He looked around. A whiff of something familiar reached his nostrils. His nose turned into the breeze and he began to look behind him. He looked down and his eyes focused on the deep green cover upon which they both knelt.

"Ha! See, Epona provides," he began to pinch leaves off the plants covering this hillside. They gave off a sharp clean smell. Once he had a small handful, he grinned at Saul. "Can you finish this? I may have found something that can help her. I will try not to wound her pride, but you know how indelicate I can be," he winked at his friend.

Saul shrugged. "Yes as Aye have said before, ewe have a gift. Go"

"Then wish me luck," he said with a wave. Roidhn fell into lockstep with Athelstan.

Constantina wiped her eyes and mouth with the back of her hand after the last of the contents of her belly spattered on the bank of the stream. Taking several deep breaths, she stood.

Constantina wiped the dirt off her knees and continued upstream so that she could rinse her mouth out with clean water.

He found her kneeling by the stream drinking. He waded into the water downstream and washed the sheep blood from his hands. Afterward, he rinsed the tiny dark green leaves he had picked. He walked up the stream towards her and gave her a soft smile.

"Today was a hard ride, I'm proud of you. I do not know many men who would be as tough as you, but I am a bit worried about you. How is your wound?" he cocked his head to look into her eyes.

"It is fine."

He reached down, took her hands away from her lap and kissed her palms. "Constantina, do you trust me yet?"

"What is that you wish of me, Athelstan? I have told you before I will not bed you like some common whore," she said without answering his question.

"That was not my question. Do you trust me yet?" he pressed.

"Yes, I do, why?" she asked.

"Constantina, you are not eating well and it is important that you do, doubly important now," he used a veiled reference to her sickness suggesting more than just an upset stomach.

"This land provides everything people need to live and thrive, not just food, but for clothing, homes and medicines. I would like you to chew one of these leaves. Like the poppy leaves that helped your sore jaw and the cut to your ribs, this will help settle your stomach, I promise," he handed her several of the mint leaves with a knowing nod.

Constantina eyed Athelstan warily and then reached for the leaves. She put the leaves in her mouth and began to chew tentatively. It was a sharp, delightfully refreshing taste and she began to chew with more gusto.

"Our healers use this to stop stomach sicknesses caused by bad water or eating the wrong mushroom. Even expectant mothers chew this to stop the early sickness when they are with child," he was pleased. Maybe now she would finally eat.

"Thank you," she said, turning from him. Constantina put her hands behind her back and went back to the pile of wood she had dropped when she threw up. "So what brings you my way? Are you finished with the slaughtering?"

"I will use any excuse to have a few minutes alone with you. Saul can finish with the sheep," he looked up into the trees with an odd expression.

Constantina smiled. "What is it?"

He suddenly cocked his head and looked up into the trees. "Well hello, my cheeky little friends. How long have you been spying on us?" Had he lost his mind? He was talking to no one. He reached into his tunic and took out a handful of hazelnuts.

"I would like to show you something I do not think you have ever seen before," he took her over to a fallen log and they sat down. He dropped a nut into her hand and made her hold her arm outstretched. "Come along my greedy little brothers, it is not often you are fed by a Roman Princess." The stunted trees were filled with tiny birds and suddenly one flew down and landed on Constantina's fingertips.

They were soft beige, with brown crested heads, cream underbelly and reddish-brown feathers on their wings.

Her doe-shaped eyes grew wide as a bird landed. "Oh, my!" When it began to eat from her hand, she issued a small childlike laugh and looked at Athelstan with astonishment.

He grinned back and placed another nut in her hand and as they vanished, more still. Soon both of them were covered in tiny chirping birds. They fluttered in their faces and clung to their hair, sat on their shoulders and arms – all waiting for a chance at one of the nuts.

"They are called the Bold Ones," he watched as she fed each tiny creature and his heart soared hearing her laugh. He knew the mint would work and soon she would be really hungry, but for now, it was magical watching her slowly discover what his simple world.

Constantina's eyes fluttered as rapidly as the little bird's wings. With every bird that approached them, the more joyous her laugh became.

"Bold ones, they are indeed that," she said. "Will they follow me if I move?"

"So long as you have nuts, they will follow you to the ends of the earth," he laughed handing her some more.

"What if I do not have nuts?" she asked. "Will they fly away?"

"Yes, they are fickle."

Constantina nodded. "Let me have some more."

He did and watched her delight as her newfound friends gorged on the nuts. Hiding the nuts, Constantina walked some distance away. Roidhn was ignoring everyone and was spending his time sniffing the underbrush and running through the water.

When she first moved the birds all flew up into the trees in a huge rush but in moments, they swirled back down in a flurry of wings and swarmed around her like a feathery halo.

"No fast movements mind you, you are very big and they are very small." They would all settle on her for an instant before exploding back into the air again. It was an aerial dance that spoke of the old days when man and animal were the same – linked in the wild world.

She looked like an ancient Celtic Goddess come to life before his very eyes. Her auburn red locks swam in the air as birds lifted off still clutching a strand, or two. As a nut was offered, there was an intense flurry of wings and feathers, all aimed at the food. Twenty, or more birds converged and fought for the nut before one lucky bird made off with it. The flock was thinning a bit as those with nuts flew off to eat. One hazelnut would be more than a meal for one of these tiny creatures. Still, Constantina seemed like a wonderstruck child discovering something magical. The sound of her laughter rang like music on the breeze.

He was glad she was feeling better and her laughter alone was priceless. The mint was a great remedy and he was kicking himself for not thinking of it earlier. He began gathering up the wood as she danced and laughed. His whole world was filled with the sounds of her joyous abandon. He hoped it would never end.

Constantina continued to laugh with the birds. She continued to enjoy her time just being a simple girl. Laughing, playing, smiling and running.

One of the tiny birds landed on her left shoulder. Its tiny chirping voice peeped into her ear, 'Dark Fairy' it chirpped just as clearly as that. 'Dark Fairy', it repeated. Its tiny black eye fixed on Constantina's.

It startled her so much she tripped on the hem of her skirt and fell to the ground in a heap.

The tiny bird fluttered in the air above her ignoring the nuts. It landed on her knee as she sat up. It had a kind of wise look and again it peeped. 'Dark Fairy, look for me in your darkest hour and you shall find oblivion.' Then it peeped like all of its kind, quickly collected one of the last remaining nuts and flew off. In a few short heartbeats, Constantina was alone and the birds were gone.

Did the bird just talk to her? Did it just call her Dark Fairy in its shrill little voice?

Seeing her look of puzzlement he asked. "Constantina, did you enjoy that?"

"Yes," she nodded her head. "Yes I did."

"Getting hungry yet?" He was watching her.

Constantina dusted herself off. "Yes, I am. I am starving in fact."

"They have not gone anywhere yet, we are out of nuts. They are fickle."

"Who is fickle," she asked expressionlessly.

"The birds are."

Roidhn sniffed the air and began howling and barking in fright. He vanished at a full run back in the direction of the camp. The horses as well joined in. Something bad was frightening the animals.

Without moving, she stared at Athelstan. Then she blinked and looked around at the trees. It was like she had woken from a dream.

"Romans!" she brushed past Athelstan.

He fell into step with her but as they re-entered the camp, a daunting sight greeted them.

Saul had grabbed his bow and carefully nocked an arrow. His head jerked slightly towards them.

Grey and black wolves poured into the clearing and began surrounding Demetrios, Saul and the animals. Constantina began shaking like a leaf. A silent, zig–zig, dance of agility kept the pack together and always in motion. The sheep carcass sat near the fire and these massive creatures seemed bent on stealing it. Saul had his bow bent and was taking careful aim at one of them.

"Do not shoot!" Athelstan whispered and the wolves danced differently at his arrival.

"Put up your bow, if you shoot that one, they will tear us all to bits. Just remain still. They only want the meat," he began to slowly walk towards the large male.

Its broad head lowered. His face was low to the ground and his ears were plastered to the side of his head. He snarled a clear warning at the Celt. Athelstan snarled right back and with equal intensity.

No one moved. "What are ewe doing?" Saul whispered back Athelstan raised a hand.

"Do not run," he whispered softly. The great creature did not give ground as the man approached and Athelstan did not break stride until he stood beside Saul and the sheep.

"They are not trying to steal our food – they are trying to stop us from stealing theirs. This is THEIR banquet hall, not ours. So we will share our kill with them as proper guests should." His eyes never left those of the pack leader. The dance grew closer and faster. Some of the wolves snapped and snarled at him as he drew closer. Athelstan was transformed. Pack leader gazed at pack leader. Wild, had come to dinner.

Slowly Athelstan drew his sword. For a brief moment, there was a sudden hush in the glade, an inhalation of dread. The wolf leader stopped. The pack stopped. Everything stopped. It was the calm before…

With a sudden glittering stroke, the Celt chopped rear legs off the sheep.

The pack leader jumped back at the sudden movement. The Pack exploded back into motion. The moment had come.

He grabbed and flung the hind over the heads of the wolves and they converged on it. A moment later, they were gone, save the Leader. He had run only a short distance before turning around.

"Go to your pups Phaelan–God. You have provided for us all. You have my thanks." Athelstan turned his head exposing his neck and bowed.

The large timber wolf snarled again then melted away into the forest.

The humans exhaled a collectively held breath.

"Now that our forest brethren have their dinner, let us see to our own," the Celt suggested patting his stomach. Everyone found that after the excitement, they all had deep appetites and Constantina was no exception. She ate heartily. The three men exchanged relieved glances then bent to their own food.

Before Constantina entered the small pine bough hut Athelstan had made, Demetrios asked, "You are unhurt?"

Constantina responded with a nervous smile and a nod. "What did we just see tonight? How did he know the wolves would not attack us?"

"As he is so fond of saying, this is his world and we know so little about it. I doubt very much if this was his first encounter with wolves."

Her eyes narrowed slightly. "This really IS his world, isn't it? He spoke to them as if they would understand him. He is more wolf than we think Spartan."

"I suppose. Still, you still have not answered my question. Are you all right?"

Constantina nodded. "I am unhurt, but he has a real advantage out here. These hills and trees, to him, are like the Vias that crisscross Rome. He knows every rock out here – doesn't he? Don't they both! Saul is in on this too. I have been watching him too."

Demetrios sat near the young girl and took her hand. "What do you mean 'in on this too'?"

She ignored the question. "I think they both knew the danger we were about to be in, long before we were actually in it. I think they can sense things that we cannot."

"Yes. I have seen it too. Do you think they are part of a conspiracy?"

"Perhaps. Saul seemed to smell the pack somehow before they actually made themselves known to us. Did he reach for his bow before the first wolf came into view?"

Demetrios was instantly intrigued. "I did not notice."

"I would bet he did. I do not know how they do it yet."

"Are you suggesting all that was staged? Why would anyone do that?" Demetrios was unconvinced.

"Yes staged somehow, but I had no idea Athelstan would be so... connected to them that way. I think those two actually had a conversation."

"Not possible. Wolves do not talk."

"No? Are you so certain?" she countered. "Let me ask you this one simple question. Why are we here? I know why they are here. What do they want with us? Ask yourself that Greek. What do we have that they want so badly that they drag us here and nearly get us eaten."

"I was ordered to be here. You agreed to come." Demetrios frowned and looked over his shoulder. "Still he knew just what to do didn't he? It was as if the wolves actually knew him and he knew them. He even called one of them by name didn't he?"

Again, Constantina nodded and ducked out of sight into the bower.

"No. I still believe Athelstan is a man of honour Constantina. In his mind, we are in his care. That's all it is. It is that Jew I do not trust," he mumbled.

Chapter Thirty-Two

Unable to sleep, Constantina rose and left the shelter to wander aimlessly away from the camp. Athelstan's words lingered in her mind.

"Connie," she heard behind her. Constantina smiled. It was Saul. She glanced over her shoulder at him but continued walking.

"I just need some time Saul. I pro–"

"Good," he said as he ran to catch up to her. "Then ewe will nut mind me tagging along."

"I want to be alone, Saul. I will be careful."

"If you think Aye am letting ewe go off on your own with those creatures out there…"

"They are called wolves."

"Aye do not care what they are called, it is nut going to happen."

She stopped. "Saul, please."

To this, he sighed.

"Fine, but only ten minutes and if ewe get eaten, Aye swear Aye will do ewe an injury."

To that Constantina chuckled and leaned over to kiss his cheek. "I promise not to get eaten," she said starting to walk again. "Twenty minutes at most."

"Ten minutes."

"Twenty minutes," she said and continued to walk through the huge trees towards the icy stream. As she stood upon the bank, looking at the large bright moon, she was lost in thought.

Constantina turned back to the forest then. Now she saw it, the outline of a large sleek dark creature prowling towards her. She took a step back and as she did, the huge wolf padded into the moonlight. Its head was lowered but it held its tail high and it wagged ever so slowly.

The wolf was massive, sleek and powerful, with a body bigger than her own. It regarded her with penetrating ice–blue eyes. She gasped and backed away. The Wolf moved with her. There was no mistaking; it was stalking her.

Fear shot through her body and she willed herself to stay calm, to think this through. She had no weapon and with every step that took her

275

backwards, the creature narrowed the distance between them. She could run, but with the power of those legs, he would surely catch her. She could scream, but would anyone hear her, let alone reach her in time.

Think! However, when her feet hit the frigid water, all reason left her. She could feel her heart hammering in her chest, could feel her pulse racing. The current strove to unbalance her and sweep her downstream.

She stood, making herself as tall as she possible. Constantina decided to face this wolf and her fate bravely. The wide grey head swivelled and gazed into the trees. "He is here." The words were calm but they awoke the girl's heart. She felt a rush of emotion. The fear left Constantina. The wolf had spoken to her and somehow she had heard him.

"Who?" She followed his gaze.

A low soft growl came from the dark trees above the bank and the Celt stepped into the pale moonlight. The wolf's head swung again in Athelstan's direction and their eyes locked. The Wolf backed up a step, or two away from Constantina and issued a short growl in return. Athelstan gaze did not waver and remained locked with those of the wolf. His senses told him the entire pack was watching quietly from the shadows. Any mistake now could be disastrous for both of them. He addressed the wolf in Gaelic.

"You risk much, noble one, coming between a Celtic man and his woman. She is not your food. She is not your pup."

Calmly he continued to stare at the wolf and walked a circular course away from the wolf but always towards Constantina. The wolf padded in the same circular route away from Constantina but he continued to close on the Celt. They each sniffed the air and barred their teeth. It was a remarkable and silent confrontation.

"You are powerful and wise Phaelan, God of our wolf brother. She is not yours." The wolf lunged with a savage snarl and snapped at the Celt who showed no reaction whatever, save a small frown. Athelstan cocked his head to one side. It was as though a silent conversation was taking place between Celt and wolf.

Athelstan deliberately placed himself between the wolf spirit and Constantina. Here he stopped and so did the wolf. The staring match had not abated. Finally, Athelstan averted his eyes and turned his head downwards and away. The wolf growled again and stretched his forelegs and back in a deliciously sinuous motion. Then the wolf straightened and raised his head. His ears were forward and his wagging tail was held high. He walked right up to the Celt. Athelstan knelt and placed himself eye to eye with the wolf. The beast stopped and sniffed Athelstan's hand, then endured a very brief scratching behind his ears. The wolf bowed again as did the Celt. The wolf then straightened, shook himself and, in a few powerful bounds, was gone surrounded by his yelping, howling, joyous pack.

Alone by the stream, Constantina folded into his arms and Athelstan just held her.

"He was going to kill me," she sniffed.

"But he did not. Nor would he. They do not kill except for food. You are not their food."

"How can you know for sure?"

"We are part of his pack how and they will travel with us for a time. That is the way of things. Everything is possible here. He can feel your pain and has tried to help. In time, I shall speak with Phaelan again. He will not leave you, nor will I. You have formed a bond with him, although at the moment you might not realise it. Kindred spirits find each other in times of need. He can never die Constantina. His spirit, like yours, like mine, is eternal. You should begin to rejoice in that knowledge. You have made an honourable friend – forever."

She sniffed and wiped at her nose with her sleeve. "I will try, but it is so hard."

"That is why you were born strong. Come along my love, you should sleep. You have had quite enough excitement for one day." She blinked at him and stopped him with a gentle touch.

"You just called me your love. I am not your…" He placed a finger against her lips.

"Yes, Constantina; you are. You always will be," she stared at him for a long moment before she let him lead her back to the camp. The wolves could be heard nearby howling. It was both eerie and comforting. Nothing would be permitted to approach their camp tonight. Nothing.

The sun climbed slowly into a clearing sky. The rain clouds scudded eastwards over the mountains. They were awash with brilliant pink, orange, gold and purple. Each colour strove to claim dominance in the sky. A thick fog clung to the lowlands, filling the crevices of the valley like a heavy wool blanket. The small stream gurgled peacefully in the near distance. All around them, the woods buzzed with life, birds singing morning songs as rabbits, squirrels and foxes scurried here and there. The eight men hidden among the rocks paid them no heed.

Theirs was a singular focus. They were not hunters, armed and armoured as they were branded them as soldiers. They bore red and gold of Rome's thirteenth legion. These were the elite of the Legionnaires Equis and the trap they had set for their enemy was perfect and deadly. His few remaining men were set and ready. The journey to get here had been costly with casualties.

These men were not out to hunt animals. They hunted a single, very dangerous man and his tiny band of slaves.

✝

Finally free of the perpetual cold and snow of the high peaks, here in the lower slopes, it was still autumn and the changing leaves left the rolling countryside ablaze with colour. Cool moist air blew clouds of birds south. Geese and ducks flew in wide graceful Vs, while long lines of white swans and herons flew northward beneath them. They passed wild groves of ripe figs, dates, olives and apples. Great stands of walnut and hazelnut trees had their food bags bulging. As they travelled together Constantina, Saul and Demetrios began to learn the names and uses of the countless varieties of leaves and barks, plants and roots, mushrooms and toadstools. Roidhn was nowhere to be seen. He was almost certainly resting and playing with his larger cousins. Throughout the long journey, Athelstan had taught his friends Gaelic. They, in turn, taught Athelstan proper Greek, Latin, and Saul offered language lessons in Hebrew and Aramaic.

It was tentative at first for all of them and, the first several phrases learned had been colourful curses. Athelstan erupted in laughter the first time Constantina uttered one. He was quick to point out that such a demand was probably not something she should repeat and for an hour, she veritably vexed him by repeating it over and over – just like a proper irritating little sister should.

Her very first question caused him to hang his head.

"What is the word for 'Yes'?" she asked sweetly, apple juices dribbling down her chin.

"Neg! There is not one!" He responded dourly and of course, there was not. There were ways to show affirmation of a question, but they were nearly as infinite as the questions themselves.

"Just nod up and down – we will understand."

This caused uncontrollably hysterical giggling from Constantina. For some reason, this struck her as funny. Here was a language with a word for no but none for yes. Still aside from a few oddities, she had an ear for accents and in no time had the complex pronunciation well in hand. Constantina and her men had a similar ear for this strange tongue.

Evenings would see Athelstan sing his songs and listen to those of the others. Saul would sing scriptures from his Torah. They were rich and full of life. He sang joyous songs. They listened to all Athelstan's songs, idle mutterings and repeated them back to him. By now, each could converse passably well in Gaelic, but still, there was no clear word for 'Yes'.

"Teth! Bhur gairdean goirt seadh?" Constantina used Gaelic, seeing him rubbing his left forearm.

He answered her in Greek without thinking, "No not sore exactly, just a… bit… stiff." Athelstan's brow furrowed. "Caite rinn thu ionnsaich uile–siud, caileag? (Where did you learn that, girl?)" His mouth twitched with mischief as he asked – clearly delighted and surprised.

"Thu! Me ionnsaich siud a thu. You, I learned this from you… and all those rapach (filthy) songs of yours. If I were any younger I should be properly horrified by them!" Athelstan was stunned and shocked, then laughed until his ribs ached. Her wide smile lit up the forest with light.

There was a heavy fog that morning and the tiny droplets of water clung to the spider webs like strings of miniature diamonds. The air smelled of moss and humus. They rode through the now heavily forested middle reaches of the mountains. Athelstan felt more relaxed now that they were nearing the relative safety of his mountain valley. One more day of travel would see them safely in the Glade.

He was becoming his old chatty self again and he told his companions stories of his people and their beliefs. They slipped easily through the foggy boles, letting their horses find the easiest path. Soon enough they would be out of the high peaks where the greatest of caution was needed. Athelstan did have an advantage here, however. As a child, his clan had journeyed here when Alexander was still alive. He had a memory of much of this country due to their month-long Samhain celebrations here, nineteen years ago. Then he had been eight years old and hooked up with the visiting children from Macedonia. Many glorious days were spent exploring and playing through much of this untouched wilderness. It was that same year his mother died of a wasting sickness. Seeing these hills again forced his mind to fill with these memories of his childhood.

So it was that his guard was somewhat relaxed as he related to his companions the different landmarks he remembered, where the best swimming holes were and so on. So engrossed was he in his memories of this place he failed to notice the subtle warnings Maehadren was giving him. It wasn't until Roidhn barked and flattened his ears with a growl did Athelstan notice his error. Someone was nearby – and not just one. There were many. The realisation hit him like a physical blow and he brought Maehadren to a halt. People were moving nearby – encircling them. They were hidden in and about the large boulders just beyond their vision in the dense forest. Athelstan raised a hand for quiet, slipped the shiny sword free of his belt and waited for the inevitable onslaught.

Legate Quintus Maximus took slow controlled breaths as the sounds of horses's hooves neared his position among the rocks. Slowly, almost as if they were ghosts from the underworld, shapes began to form before his eyes. With a couple more steps, the horses were clearly identifiable as were the riders upon them. They stopped and as he had hoped, Athelstan was riding the lead horse. Quintus took another shallow breath and allowed it to leak from his nose slowly, silently, his eyes fixed on a spot just before the lead horse. The huge white horse stopped, turned and exposed his right side. That invisible mark had been reached.

Finally, he loosed the arrow, the deadly shaft flinging itself from his grasp and speeding through the air towards its target. He had no doubt by the big warrior's reaction that Athelstan had heard the twang of his bowstring, but it no longer mattered, the trap was sprung. The arrow flew straight and true, striking the Senone's horse behind the right shoulder. Only pure luck caused it to shatter against the Celt's long iron boot knife instead of ripping Maehadren's lungs and heart asunder.

With loud shouts, the Romans sprang from the woods, charging towards the startled horse, the Commander must have been feeling the 'wolf' within him coming to the fore. "Remember," he cried out to Decimus and Julius, "We need him alive. Only he knows where the other children are!"

"Ambush!" Athelstan bellowed and felt the arrow hammer into his leg as he slid from atop Maehadren. Athelstan was instantly in motion. "Take cover." Chaos erupted with horses and riders twisting and screaming in confusion. Landing solidly on the ground, he faced the woods where he could see two Romans approaching; that same boot knife now clutched in his right hand. His eyes narrowed as they closed the net from all sides. With a motion almost too swift for the eye to see, his arm lashed forward, sending the knife hurtling towards one of the advancing Romans. It was an effortless deflection for his great shield and on he came with grim determination.

Then an arrow caught one Roman full in the chest with a sickening thud, sending him crashing to the earth in a soundless heap. With a savage look his face, Athelstan drew his sword and charged the two remaining Romans; a fierce battle howl ripped from the Celt and echoed across the valley as he charged. A plaintive, chilling cry answered it from high in the mountains.

The Roman Centurion noted with a cool detachment that an arrow brought down his second. He knew Decimus was dead, but this was not the time to worry about losses, they still had to bring this enormous creature down. They knew he was the key. Once he was tamed, these other slaves would be easily gentled. With a fierce cry of his own, the Centurion surged towards the Senone, Julius at his side.

The three men met each other near the stream in a deafening crash, their blades flowing against one another in a deadly dance, the cold clang of metal against metal filling the valley. It took only seconds for Athelstan to tear the heavy shields from the Romans hands, evening out the fight. The two men jerked back as they were relieved of the cumbersome but comforting shields. Neither was certain of how long they fought in this way.

Athelstan's blade was faster and more experienced than either Quintus's, or Julius's. His tactics were vastly different and he had a significant height advantage. Only the speed of their combined blades kept the fight fair. "Where in Hades are the other girls, barbarian? Eaten as promised?" the Centurion barked between breaths.

"You will know soon enough once I have deposited you in the next life, Roman. Ask someone there," growled Athelstan.

The Celt risked a brief glance behind him, where he had last seen his friends. They were not in sight. These were relentless professional soldiers. They did not get mad, they did not acknowledge pain, or loss, they displayed no compassion or mercy and they did not intend to lose. It would all be over very soon – one way, or another.

His assessment of the situation was flawed. Demetrios hoisted Saul atop a tall rock as the attack began and in seconds, he was knocking arrows and firing with frightening skill. It took two shots to kill the first Roman and one more to kill a second. Another Roman, seeing Saul take aim again, sprinted around the large rock and began to climb up, in an effort to flank him.

Constantina ducked behind a tree and strung her bow. Constantina took careful aim and felled a man at close range. She watched him die with a wicked grin on her face. She nocked another arrow.

Even as Saul ascended the rock, Demetrios was moving. The Spartan drew his Machaira and advanced on one of the Romans. With a single overhand blow, he clove the Roman shield nearly in half and began a withering frontal assault on his enemy. Blows came rapidly from every direction. The Roman fought back with both skill and cunning, but he was being driven back block, parry and thrust. It was suddenly over. Demetrios' sword glanced off the roman blade and the flat of it glanced off the Roman helmet. It was a brutal blow. The gladius fell from limp fingers and the Legionnaire slumped unconscious towards the ground. The Spartan's final blow ended all pain. He scanned for another target. He looked back towards the rock and his eyes widened in horror.

Saul turned and stood face to face with a Roman soldier. The man had climbed up the rock from the other side. He had his sword raised high and Saul had but a single breath of life left.

"Saul!" Even as Demetrios yelled, the sword descended in a murderous arc.

At that same instant, a ferocious sound was heard and a grey shape hurtled out of the bush and ascended the rock in a single bound. The Lord of the Mountains had come. The soldier did not have time to even look before the huge wolf's jaws clamped down on his throat. The force of the impact hurled the Roman off the rock before the deadly stroke could land. His sword travelled in a glittering arc and it landed with a clang in front of Constantina. A ghastly tearing and rending could be heard amid shrieks and howls of pain and terror. This soldier was a soldier no longer. He was now part of the food chain.

Rodahn and Phaelan, the pack leader came back to watch the rest of the battle. They both sat beside Constantina like loyal dogs. She absently scratched behind Phaelans ears. The fight transfixed everyone. She suddenly realised what she was doing and looked down. The wolf did not move or even blink. He simply stared straight ahead.

As in every fight, things tend to unravel quickly. It was that first mistake that often turns the tide of such contests. So it was here. It happened first to the Roman Centurion.

"Give me your name Roman!" growled Athelstan."

"Give me yours first, barbarian."

"Athelstan Epona, first General of the Senone Multitude," Athelstan said smoothly.

"Legate Quintus Maximus!" he countered.

Ducking a savage blow from the Senones deadly sword, Quintus drove in for a strike at the big man's legs, hoping to bring him down so they could bind him. Athelstan's speed and reflexes were sharp and where before there was a leg, now there was a blade.

Quintus barely had time to react to the quick redirection of Athelstan's sword, bringing his Gladius up just in time to avoid disembowelment, deflecting the blade high above his head. The damage was done, however. The force of the giant warrior's strike knocked him off balance. Struggling to maintain his feet on the snowy ground, Quintus felt his back leg give out beneath him as it slid over the lip of the stream's high bank. It sent him crashing onto his back into the glacial cold water.

With deadly swiftness, Athelstan was atop him, swinging his blade in for a killing stroke, only to have it deflected aside by Julius' sword. To block the strike, however, Julius exposed himself and Quintus watched with a sick feeling of helplessness as Athelstan spun his blade nimbly in his hands and brought it back towards the young soldier in a glittering arc. His blade tip caught Julius just below his chinstrap sending his body to the ground one way and his helmet-clad head into the water separately. No one watched it sink.

Yet, the move gave Quintus the time he needed and he regained his feet, the soaking wet man roared in frustration and charged forward back into the fight, knowing that he was now alone against Athelstan. Some part of him knew he could not win the fight, the other part of him was uncaring. How had his men been so easily bested by the slaves of a barbarian?

The ferocity of his attack caught Athelstan off guard and the big man gave way under the skilful assault. Once back on solid ground the Centurion pressed home his attack. Both men were good fighters; their blades were quick. What the Centurion lacked in experience, he made up for with sheer determination and natural instinct. Nevertheless, even natural instinct is not good enough to bring down such an intensely powerful and deadly warrior when his bloodlust is up.

The fighting swayed back and forth for several minutes, both men's blades licking at the others flesh and drawing blood in small cuts. Athelstan had a bigger advantage over Quintus than skill and experience. It had been a long gruelling chase. He and his men had been fighting exhaustion for weeks. Athelstan, on the other hand, was relatively fresh and rested and the difference was beginning to show. Slowly, inexorably, Athelstan pressed the attack on his enemy and began to drive him back towards the trees. Then, with a deceptively powerful sweeping blow, Athelstan sent the battered Gladius flying from his hand. He landed a heavy kick to the Roman's midsection sending him sprawling across the ground winded.

Athelstan lunged forward and raised his heavy weapon high above his head. With a snarl on his face, Quintus knew that death was upon him. For the first time since the deadly dance had begun, the two men stopped moving. Looking into the unforgiving eyes of Athelstan, he showed no fear, only a slight regret. With a low growl, he spoke to Athelstan. "I am Legate Quintus Julius Maximus."

"Bravely fought Legate – now die with honour!" Athelstan nodded, respect in his eyes as he began to tense to deliver a clean deathblow. Quintus steeled himself for what was to come, his eyes locked upon those of Athelstan, both men's attention so focused on one another that neither of them heard the slight cry of shock from Constantina when Quintus spoke. They had watched from a distance as the battle played out but helmeted Romans all looked alike. Athelstan's blade reflected a watery sun. To Quintus' eyes, it seemed to descend in slow motion when suddenly another desperate cry pierced the quiet that had settled over the valley.

Chapter Thirty-Three

"Quintus… NOOOooooooo!" It was a piteous wail.

Quintus' attention was drawn from the blade that would end his life and he turned his head just in time to see Constantina flying toward him, arms outstretched, hair whipping behind her. It would be his last vision in this life. He smiled and awaited the end. With a jolt, she flung herself upon him, skidding across the wet grasses and soft mud. One arm folded around Quintus' neck and she looked up at Athelstan, "Nooooo, Athelstan! Do not kill him! Pleeeease!" She pleaded with her other hand outstretched towards the possessed Celt.

Shock and surprise lit the Senone's face as Constantina suddenly materialised in the path of a final decapitating blow. The fact that Constantina knocked Quintus aside served to save both their lives. Once in motion, a long sword was quite difficult to halt. A bare instant later, a flailing Constantina tackled Athelstan to the ground as well. His sword whistled inches above their heads and the bloody tip burrowed deep into the muddy ground with a wet sucking sound.

He seized Constantina by the arm and tried to wrench her free of her death grip around his neck so he could properly kill this accursed Roman, but she clung to him fiercely like a cat to a mouse. He succeeded only in sending them both sprawling to the ground again.

"DO NOT KILL HIM!" Constantina howled at Athelstan. He struggled to his feet with Constantina clutching and grabbing at him forcing him away from the beaten Roman. She kissed him fiercely, but he shook his head as a blind, berserk fury still possessed him.

"WhaaaAAAAAAAT?" It was half a question, half a roar of abject frustration. The Senone tried again to dislodge the girl grasping, clutching and kissing him. It was no use.

"WHAT? Do not what? What? Do not KILL HIM? What?? Why in Hades not? He tried to kill us all! He is my bloody enemy for pity sake! ARRRRRRRGH! Will you let me lose!" His eyes suddenly focused on his current assailant as she forced another powerful kiss on his lips. It was Constantina and she was pleading with him. Demetrios held the prone Roman at sword-point while Saul stepped forward and gripped Athelstan's sword hand.

"Stop! Stop. Think what you are doing, Oh please stop yelling and listen.

Stop. Shhhhhhh Stop, stop… please don't kill him. Please don't." Constantina pleaded with him.

He blinked and returned her next kiss with blazing passion. They separated and he had a confused expression on his face. He let Constantina disentangle her arms from him and he took a deep shuddering breath.

Phaelan and Roidhn had silently padded forward and sat calmly beside the prone Roman. The dog only showed his teeth when the Roman tried to move. Constantina dropped across Quintus's chest and held the Roman in a protective embrace. It was only then she discovered she was nose to nose on one hand with a giant wolf and on the other hand a smelly dog.

Never in all his days had something like this happened. Athelstan leaned over the pair, pointed and snarled at Constantina. "Never do that!" He paused his wild eyes searching for something more to add – and finding nothing he repeated: "Never do that!" He was apoplectic!

"Never – do – that again! Ever!" He was angry beyond all reason and none doubted it. He had come within an inch of killing the woman he loved and had pledged to protect. He let out another mighty breath and suddenly sanity returned to his eyes. The scowl remained. Even the blood–covered wolf knew better than to confront an enraged Celt. Roidhn was just happy the yelling had stopped and bounded about like a wiggling idiot.

"Do you know this man?" he demanded. A sobbing Constantina could only nod with her face buried in Quintus, shoulder.

"You KNOW this man?" he asked again incredulous. His head began to nod and he wandered in a tight circle repeating it over and over.

"She knows him! Of course, she knows him. She probably knows everybody in all Rome – in all Italia."

He had been swinging his sword randomly at the sparse undergrowth as he walked and did not come to a stop until he stood over Quintus fallen sword. He bent, picked it up and looked at it stupidly as if the Gladus held some answer to this enigma. His own sword he dragged limply behind him. No one dared move. He settled his shoulders and fixed a hate-filled glare on Quintus.

"I suppose you know all of them." He indicated the other dead Romans. She shook her head, finally looking up and blinking away tears. Constantina broke into his expanding awareness stroking his arm and making noises of some sort. It was only now that the roaring in his ears had begun to fade. Demetrios placed an arm around the Celt's shoulders.

"You won Athelstan. Stand down now. If I have learned anything from you, killing unarmed prisoners is not your way." The Celt clapped a hand on Demetrios' shoulder and nodded.

Peering at Quintus more closely, he began to study his face.

"Get up." He sheathed his own weapon. The Roman got to his feet.

"You are good, better than most, I'll give you that. Did I hear Quintus, it is Quintus right?" The Roman nodded. A deadly calm had replaced rage and a determined looking Celt leaned into Quintus' face.

"I am going to ask you some questions Quintus Maximus, Legate of Rome and you WILL answer them truthfully, or your body will be found here with the rest of your men. Am I clear?" He leaned in almost touching noses with the man; each combatant still fighting to breathe. Quintus just stared him down, his expression of loathing dripped with defiance. This man was unlike any Athelstan had ever met before. He thought the Spartans were a cold and dour lot, but this man's nerve was carved from a solid block of ice. He had faced his own death with unflinching calm and honour. Athelstan could like this man. He quickly dismissed the idea. Quintus remained silent.

"AM I CLEAR?" he roared forcing him against a tree. Quintus nodded once silently; his glare of hatred remained intact.

"How many men have come with you?" he asked.

Quintus stared at Athelstan for a long moment, his eyes still hard. Athelstan could see that a part of him warred against the idea of providing the enemy with any information, but another part knew that the Senone would certainly kill him if he did not. Athelstan was gambling of course. He was betting that while Quintus might die for the republic, but would not willingly die for a tyrant such as Papirius.

"Quintus, this is your final chance. How many men are with you?" the Celt growled in perfect Latin.

"I came with twenty men. Proconsul Papirius rides with a force of five hundred men…" he paused and glanced over at his dead men, a small stab of pain filling his heart for them, "Less the seven now lying dead here and myself, of course," he eyed the wolf nervously. Clearly, he was more afraid of it than he was of the Celt.

His eyes widened at this. He expected less that one hundred.

"So many! Twenty less these seven total thirteen. Where are the rest?"

"Most were lost on the journey here."

"The five hundred, how many days behind us are they?"

Quintus looked away for a long moment. "My men and I left from Delphi with nearly an entire day's head start on Papirius. He follows you. I took a different route – a much longer route. Since I do not know the terrain on the far side of the mountains I cannot say with any certainty. Two days perhaps. Maybe less."

"I see," he paused, just two days was not a long time but perhaps just enough time.

"I assume runners had been already sent to Papirius, so he is now coming directly towards this valley?" Quintus nodded.

"We're very good about that sort of thing," Quintus had a question burning on his tongue.

"Where are all girls?" he demanded. "I only see a sister to one of them. What have you done with the rest?"

"I placed them on a ship back to Rome immediately after we arrived in Delphi. I will not use children to bargain with a madman," he was still angry.

"Why did you take them then?" The Legate was clearly confused.

"I do not answer questions of prisoners. However, in this, you deserve an answer. I did not take them and I have already sworn an oath to personally avenge their abduction. That is all you need to know." Athelstan snarled.

"Swore an oath barbarian? To whom?" Sarcasm crept into Quintus' voice.

"To me," said Constantina. "He swore his oath to me and I believe him," she looked into Quintus' face with a nod.

"How do you come to know my 'sister'?" Athelstan asked suddenly. A brief look of astonishment crossed the Roman soldier's face at this. Constantina still clung to Quintus like a wet garment. His arm was now wrapped protectively around her shoulder. Demetrios had a steadying grip on Athelstan. They would not fight again.

Quintus kept glancing at Constantina. He shook his head, incredulity spread across his features.

"Sister?" he exclaimed, glancing down at Constantina. "She's not your sister." Athelstan now saw that his icy veneer could indeed be cracked.

"ANSWER THE QUESTION!" roared Athelstan. He stepped closer to the Roman.

"How do you know Constantina?"

"This isn't…" Quintus began. Constantina shook her head at Quintus very briefly and tried to interject herself between the two angry men.

Demetrios was caught off guard and grabbed Athelstan's arm in a vain attempt to pull him away.

Saul interceded on behalf of both them. A firm powerful hand closed on Athelstan's shoulder and he was pulled away from Quintus. "Have a care General. Your point has been made. Ewe forget yourself. The time has come for cunning not rage. Go find your knife General."

Constantina's grip on Quintus' waist grew tighter and he looked down at her, his eyes locking with hers as she gave him a slight shake of her head. Nodding almost as slightly, he looked back up at Athelstan. "We grew up together, though I am a little older than her and her sister Con… er, Octavia." He looked at Constantina again.

"Their father…" he stopped as a surge of guilt coursed through him. "Her father and mine were Senators together. Our families have known one another for years. I have known…" There was a pause and he looked at her very carefully. "I have known her all of her life."

He watched both Quintus and Constantina's reaction to his questions and Athelstan's eyes narrowed. Every word Quintus spoke was the truth yet there was more to this story than either of them were letting on. Something else he noticed too. Whenever Quintus mentioned Papirius's name his nose wrinkled as though he smelled something foul.

"And?" He probed.

"And nothing," he countered, "family friends, that is all."

"Yet your family lives on and hers – does not. Why is that Quintus Maximus? Why was it necessary for me to adopt Constantina into my family since she has none? Where is this sister Octavia?"

"No one knows. She has not been seen for years. Ask Papirius if you must. I do not answer for him." Quintus growled.

Athelstan read a great deal into his words and gestures.

"You do not like him, do you? The Proconsul I mean." Athelstan grinned.

"You do not like him one little bit… do you? I might wager to say you might hate him even more than you hate me. Perhaps an opportunity exists here for you if you are clever enough to seize it. It seems certain that Demetrios and Saul will not allow me to kill any more Romans today and I'm certainly not going to let you loose. We have ground to cover, so mount up Quintus Maximus, you are coming with us," he looked at Constantina and then at Quintus.

"You ride with her."

"He will not!" she said firmly and mounted her own horse.

"Gentlemen tie him up and keep your eyes on him. I am glad you are not my enemy – very glad."

Saul and Demetrios collected the Roman weapons and bundled them onto one of the spare horses. The riderless horses were formed into a pack line. Quintus was bound at the wrists and lashed to his own horse.

Constantina stopped her horse beside Quintus. He whispered. "What are you up to? Where is your sister?"

"Shh. I will tell you later. Just keep your mouth shut. It is important."

Quintus gave a tiny nod and fell silent.

The wolf stood nearby. He had silently watched this exchange between the these two. Athelstan nodded to the huge Grey.

"Phaelan, Lord of the Mountains. Resume your appointed path, with my thanks. Hunt well my friend," he spoke in Gaelic and lowered his head. The wolf bowed and stretched again and then like smoke in the breeze he was gone.

What possible good could come from any of this? He issued a low whistle and Maehadren stepped from the trees and walked over to Athelstan. He rubbed his nose and patted his great neck before mounting and the party of eight moved off down a narrow trail into the deepening fog.

He rode in silence trying to come to terms with what had just happened. What had almost happened? Constantina rode up along-side him and leaned in to touch his hand. He was suddenly aware it was shaking and tears ran down his cheeks.

"I'm sorry," she said simply.

"Sorry? Sorry for what?" he sniffed and dragged a sleeve across his nose. His tone was distant.

"I did not know how much you hate this. I'm sorry you were forced to kill for me, Athelstan." The Celt shot her a sharp look filled with astonishment.

"Why – why would you say that? I am a soldier. Killing is what I do."

"No. You cannot make me believe that ever again. You are the kindest and gentlest man I have ever known," her voice was soft. "I see now that you feel killing is wrong at a spiritual level. You bless the game you take for food and thank the Gods for providing it. You let birds eat from your hand. You love me," she looked a bit confused. "Why do you do any of that? You are not a savage or a monster. You have a kind soul. I am very sorry it came to that for you," her insight was staggering.

He was going to deny it but there seemed no point. He simply squeezed her hand back.

"Every life is special and unique, even his. When it is gone, it is gone. The

Spirit survives but the mortal life is gone for all time. Taking a life is the same as giving it. Such things should be left to the Gods. I am but a servant of their will. I do not kill without reason. I can only kill based on the laws of my people as laid down by our Druids," he glanced at her. "It is true I detest killing and do so only when I have no other choice. I defend the helpless, stand witness for the innocent and rid the world of wickedness. That is the pledge every soldier takes before he becomes a warrior in my army. Today I defended you. Each of us hates to kill, but we all do what we must. I am glad you understand."

Chapter Thirty-Four

Breakfast turned out to be a curious affair. They awoke to find Athelstan toiling over a steaming pot perched precariously over a small hot fire. Steam rose from inside and it was accompanied by a rather peculiar smell. He poked and prodded at it with a freshly whittled stick. As his friends began to stir, he clapped his hands with great delight.

"Good morning. I trust you have slept well. I urge you all to try my breakfast stew. It is an old family recipe. It will fortify even the dead for a long day's march." Athelstan was smiling proudly.

He scraped a portion of thick lumpy grey goo onto a board and set it down in front of Demetrios. Connie put her hand over her mouth and nose with a squeak. The Greek looked at it and swallowed whatever had briefly risen into his gorge.

"Been hunting this morning have ewe, General?" Saul asked unable to takes his eyes off the congealing puddle.

"Squirrel and pine mushrooms," he announced proudly. "Try it. There is plenty for everyone." Quintus looked over Demetrio's shoulder and cast a dubious eye upon the stew, then looked at Demetrios with an amused, expectant smile. The sheer anticipation of shovelling some of it into their mouths made starvation seem a most agreeable alternative.

"Dear boy," Demetrios began hopefully, pointedly ignoring the bubbling sewage before him, "should we not be striking camp so as to be on our way quickly? We cannot estimate with any accuracy where the Legion might be at this very moment. And much as I would relish the thoughts of sampling your forest cookery we must agree, can we not, that this… this preparation is – well – disgusting looking."

"Saul?" Saul was eyeing the slop with astonishment.

"Aye am certain it tastes wonderful, friend Ath. Aye fear, however, it is nut Kosher." He scraped the muck onto the ground and walked away.

Athelstan was crestfallen as he once again prodded the semi-solid muck with a dripping stick and examined closely. A wry and apologetic smile crossed his lips.

"Yes," he muttered nearly under his breath. "You are quite right my dear friends – it is disgusting." Without further ado, he tossed the entire contents of the stew into the low bushes. Even Roidhn sniffed it, whined and bolted off with his tail between his legs.

"Even your dog won't eat it," Constantina said.

Athelstan shrugged and strode in the direction of Maehadren while the rest of the company struggled not to laugh out loud. Sadly, they all failed.

They rode through a dark and nearly silent world. Oaks, pines, elms, and firs all vied for dominance, both in scent and height, in this forest of giants. The air here was cooler and the dense fog dampened every surface. It was filled with insects beyond count. Butterflies, kaleidoscopic dragonflies and biting midges joined with hundreds of birds sweeping effortlessly between the towering trunks.

The alders were shedding their leaves and they rode through a veritable golden snowstorm. Occasional, sparkling shafts of light cut through the high canopy and transformed the tiny motes into columns of glittering stars.

The going was still slow. From the peaks high above the lowlands appeared as a tranquil idyllic valley. It showed a soft carpet of differing greens in the upper reaches and an astonishing riot of fall colours below. Yet, the dangerous realities of mountain travel were impossible to ignore and after weeks of travel, the party was desperately weary. There were many obstacles blocking their way. Rockslides, sheer cliffs, precipitous mountain streams and huge fallen trees were, by far, the most common. They went single file, with Athelstan leading the way down along the side of the now raging mountain river.

The ground leveled off and the huge tree trunks were more widely spaced. Some smaller saplings were scattered here and there but the ground was almost devoid of low cover. They stood near the base of a three hundred foot waterfall and the sound if it was deafening. Athelstan felt the hairs on the back of his neck rise and Maehadren shook his head issuing a blast of air from his nostrils. The horse swivelled both of his ears to the right and one great eyeball danced back and forth searching for something.

Saul travelled behind Athelstan and matched the pace he set. He could hear Constantina and Quintus quietly conversing when they could, but could not hear what they were saying. Demetrios had taken up the rear and kept a close eye on the trail behind them. He was quite certain Quintus had lied about how close Papirius actually was. It was something he would have done if their fates were reversed.

The Celt called a halt and dismounted. He looked into the dense trees searching as well.

Constantina called to him. "Is there something wrong?"

His head had turned this way and that and he even seemed to smell and taste the air like a wild beast. Maehadren shook his head again and a full body shiver wracked the creature. He held up a finger for a moment's silence at the question.

"Someone is close by, the horses can sense it," he whispered as he peered into the dark forest. "I wish the trees were thinner."

Constantina looked around as well. She turned to see that not only had Saul dismounted, he had strung his bow. Demetrios pulled his Machaira from its scabbard. Not a good sign.

"I think we should give Quintus a weapon," Demetrios suggested. It was a foolish request of course. Athelstan pondered the idea.

"I will not be surrounded again because I am quite certain we are out-numbered. I am cutting the Roman loose. Give him his sword. Look sharp. I think our shadows have finally arrived," he looked at the horses again. "They will tell us everything we need to know. One of us needs to get Constantina out of here while the others deal with these creatures," he nearly spat the word and glanced at Quintus. He was still tied and carried no weapons.

"If this is another of your traps Quintus, it will go badly for you."

The Roman said nothing. In a quick stroke, Athelstan cut Quintus' bonds and the Legate was offered his sword. He handed it to him hilt first and the Roman took the blade with a grim nod.

"I think they are over there and there." He pointed into the dark fog-shrouded trees. "I think you should go with Connie and keep her safe," Athelstan whispered finally. "Make for the river."

"I agree," Saul had said coming up behind them. " Constantina, go with Quintus he will..."

"No!" she said calmly. "I go nowhere. There is a strong possibility whoever is out there has come for me. We separate; they out-flank us and take me easily. I can only fight so many. No, we stay together and face this together."

A low growl escaped Athelstan but he knew she was right.

The Celt's eyes narrowed as he looked at Quintus again.

"She will fight with you."

"Very well Quintus, you stay with her. Saul will try to isolate one group and take them quietly. This will even things up a bit. Demetrios and I will deal with the others."

"I will fight," the Roman said firmly.

"If I can climb into the trees, I can watch your backs," Connie said. "With the bow, I can make sure no one will come upon you by surprise."

"I think this is a good plan. Stay near the horses if you can, they make good cover," he turned and patted his horse's neck. He walked Connie over to a tall fir tree with its thick cover of fuzzy limbs and offered her a leg up. "You are certain you want to do this?" Athelstan asked. His face was close to hers as he laced his fingers. She nodded and up she went. She scurried up into the thick branches like a squirrel.

Arrows suddenly filled the air and one buzzed past Athelstan's ear. He looked up the tree trunk. "Stay put!" he barked as he turned around. He swept his sword clear of its sheath and raised it. It deflected another arrow up and away. It seemed innocent enough. It was as far from innocent as it could be.

The other two men were already fanning out and closing in on their foe. Maehadren was facing his enemy as he was trained to do and the Celt and the Roman climbed aboard their horses and rode quickly into the trees. Unknown to all, a limp shape slumped out of the branches and landed at its bole in a heap. It all happened so fast. Constantina blinked and tried to stand.

"Athelstan," she whispered softly. She reached for him as he rode away before toppling forward, her eyes fluttering open and closed.

Constantina looked down at the bloody feathered shaft protruding out through a hole in her travelling cloak; its evil tip sticking up out of the front of her shoulder. She whispered his name again and sagged to the ground. He did not see her fall or hear her call his name.

He was already engaging the enemy. This foe was dressed in dark hooded cloaks. Four against twenty was horribly one-sided, but these assassins seemed to have no frame of reference for a highly trained warhorse. Maehadren sliced through a small band of attackers. Two fell and three others scattered. He rode them down and sang as he slew them. Quintus circled around to cut off their retreat. The pair made short work of them.

Saul used his bow to pin the others down while Demetrios engaged them on foot. Sharp swords did their deadly work with precision. It was all over in a few minutes but the damage had been done.

He had not seen a thing; no one had. She lay crumpled under the fir tree.

"CONNIE!!" Athelstan shrieked and let out a deafening howl of pure savage panic when they finally found her.

He looked down and saw a spreading pool of fresh blood and his own blood suddenly ran cold.

Constantina was slumped face down; her arm outstretched in her final appeal for help. He rolled her over and lifted her into his arms.

"No!" he squeaked under his breath. His eyes were already beginning to burn. "Connie?" He fingered the arrowhead and watched the steady drip of blood from its ugly feathers. The shaft had entered under her right breast and protruded out her right shoulder inches from her ear.

Drip. Drip. He blinked. He looked closely and she drew a rough breath. She still lived!

"Connie? Can you hear me? Do not die!" It was issued like a command.

The men stood looking down in mute shock.

This could not be happening. This was all a dream. Yes, that was it. He would wake up to find her sleeping back in the warm soft bed that had been provided for her while in Athens. Yes, that was it. This was all a very bad dream, but what was taking him so long to wake up.

The sounds of her coughing made him focus on her face. The sight of the blood beginning to spill from her chest ripped him back to reality.

"Shh. Stop that now." Constantina scolded him. Her voice was weak and growing weaker.

"No. Be quiet, save your strength."

"I am going to die here."

"Die? From that little scratch. Never." Athelstan lied.

Constantina's eyes fluttered closed and the hand he held went limp. He stared at her. The rise and fall of her chest had stopped. He lightly shook her. She did not stir.

"Constantina," Athelstan said shaking her again. There was no response. "Constantina, Constantina!! No!! No!!! Oh Please NO!!"

He touched the arrow jutting out from her chest and knew it was all but hopeless. In all his days, he had never seen anyone survive something like this. He had failed to protect her and she had paid a terrible price for that failure.

He lowered his head to her breast and choked back a sob.

Thump-thump! Thump-thump!

He lifted his head and looked around, astonished. "She's alive," he whispered. "Her heart is still beating," he said. Athelstan ripped open her cloak and shirt – her modesty be damned and looked closely at the wooden shaft protruding from her chest. It was a square rather than a flat, or round arrowhead. Another bright red drop formed on the feathered shaft.

Chapter Thirty-Five

"Can you hear me? Connie! Answer me!" She was swimming in and out of consciousness.

Saul ran his hand through Constantina's blonde curls and his dark eyes met weak green ones. "What am Aye going to do with ewe?" he asked. "Do ewe even know what the words 'stay out of trouble' means?"

Saul stood with Quintus. Saul's face blanched and he sighed. He stood behind Athelstan and whispered in the man's ear. "Has the blood begun to flood her lungs?"

Athelstan shook his head. "Not yet."

He showed no sign of concern but the feathered shaft had gone in at a strange angle. He could feel the still shaft under her skin. It had entered her body beneath her right breast and seemed to have travelled over her ribs to exit through the top of her shoulder.

She winced as he put pressure on her collarbone. It was solid. A relieved breath exited the big man. In a soft whisper, he said, "You are a very lucky young lady," he quickly looked under the bandage on her side. It was still very raw looking.

"What was that for?" Constantina said.

"Just checking. Save your strength."

"For what?" Constantina asked.

"To live." Athelstan responded, "or have you forgotten my promise to you."

"What will we do? Can she be moved? Do we set up camp here amongst the dead?" Quintus asked. He handed his sword to Saul, Athelstan noticed.

"I think we have to move her. This weather will not hold and I do not want her left out in a cold rain. We will need to get her into the caves. They are not that much farther below us. I hoped to have reached them today, but we are running out of daylight.

"Constantina, we're going to take you somewhere you can rest while I go get help. I need to trim this arrow first. It's going to hurt sweetheart – a lot," he drew the boot knife. "Let me know when you are ready."

"I am."

Saul and Demetrios bent close to Constantina and held her firmly.

Quintus saw what Athelstan was about to do. "What? No! Do not hurt her."

"Leaving it like this will be harder on her than removing both ends."

He quickly sliced off the flights and the head.

Constantina stiffened, her face went pale and she passed out.

The sound of howling in the distance made him look away. There in the brush, were the wolves from before. Rodahn sat quietly with them. "Have they taken to following us?" Saul asked.

"They have taken to protecting us, Saul. There is a difference. They have no difficulty telling friend from foe."

"We will have to secure her tightly to your back. Can you stand being tied up once more Legate?"

"I can stand it."

Athelstan unpacked his medicine bundle and took a packet of leaves; the same leaf–packet he had her chew when they first met. He slipped it past her lips. "Constantina just lie here for a few minutes and chew this. The pain will ease."

He was looking at the feathers of the arrow and although he recognised the bird they came from, he knew these birds did not live in southern Italia, only in some areas of Northern Hellas. The square tip was hammered bronze. Romans used iron and created flat, leaf-shaped arrowheads. These arrows were Macedonian.

This was not right. He frowned at the men and glanced around.

Saul saw the way the Celt looked at the arrowhead. "Your mind is spinning. Let me in."

"Walk with me," he took his friend by the arm and headed towards Quintus. Demetrios stayed with Connie.

"So far I have believed that these men are Romans and have been trying to kill me because of the threat I pose to them. Look at this bronze arrowhead, shaped like a sling bullet, plus Swan feathers for flights."

Saul looked closely at this evidence.

He stooped over one of the dead attackers and looked at his arms. The backs of his hands were tattooed in a black rose pattern. "Where did this man come from?"

"Axum," Saul whispered.

"You are certain?"

"I am certain."

Saul looked at the tattoo again.

"Athelstan, has anyone else who attacked ewe had these markings on their hands?"

"Yes, I think the ones at the Inn did, why?"

"This is the marking of the Axum. They have not been followed us, they have been following her. Now they have found her. This is the price ewe have begun to pay for talking to that beggar in Athens. We have a brief advantage here. They now think she is dead. This buys us time. The survivors will need to report back."

"But those men at the inn carried Roman coins and these carry Macedonian

296

coins," he hefted the strange looking coins and passed them to Saul. His mind was now at work rearranging the odd pieces to this puzzle. "So this is not your man Quintus?" Athelstan asked. The Legate shook his head.

"We do not need to mark ourselves to know we are Roman. We give ourselves names."

"Considering how hard it was for me to catch up to you, it would be safe to say Connie and I are the only two Romans left on this side of the mountain," he stated flatly.

Athelstan looked up sharply at the reminder that his love was, in fact, Roman.

"So Axum is a country then and not a person," he commented in a grim whisper.

"Axum is not just a nation. It is a city, a fortress, but more importantly, it is a vast organisation. It seeks to gather control over every nation." Saul explained.

"How?"

"Aye seek. When Aye find, Aye will know."

"Who is in charge?"

"They have a leader, but no one knows much about him. Their leader keeps to the shadows and wears a hooded cloak to protect his identity. He is called The Hooded Man. When you join his ranks, to prove your loyalty and to show your allegiance, you are forced to endure a gruesome set of tests. Those who survive are tattooed in just this way and live only to do his bidding."

"Now I understand."

"Did ewe look closely at the men who attacked ewe at the inn then?

"I did not, I was too angry. I found Roman coins in their purses and believed what I was being shown. I think it would fair to wager they bore these marks too."

Saul nodded, turned and walked back towards the horses. It left Athelstan looking at Quintus.

"Quintus, arm yourself, sir," he said. "I am putting my trust in you that you will not turn on us. Do not disappoint me." There was some menace in his voice but Quintus nodded his agreement. They hoisted Constantina behind him and lashed the two together tightly.

Riding downhill was tough on Constantina. Each hoof–fall was jarring and he knew she was suffering greatly. "Patience, it will be over soon," he whispered. He was doing his best to keep her from moving.

She grunted but did not speak. Her head rested limply against his shoulder. The pain was often so unbearable she would pass out only to awake and pass out again. It was a vicious cycle but one that was unavoidable.

Then as the sun finally set, a vast dark opening could be seen in the mountainside. Surrounded by heavy rocks, it beckoned to him like an old friend. He brought his horse to a stop. "We're here, Connie, time to rest now," he lifted her down from the horse's back and she was limp in his arms.

"I am ready," she whispered. "Death – it comes for me now."

"Death has much better things to do than to bother with the likes of you. You will have no such visitors tonight." The men rushed back and forth carrying gear into the cave. Saul and Demetrios went in search of firewood.

She grimaced from the pain of being laid down on the hard ground, even though they had made a pallet of clothing for her.

Quintus was setting a hot fire close to the wall where Athelstan had laid Constantina. His white fur was wrapped around her and tucked it under her chin. His hand cupped her chin and a serious look came over him.

"This Axum has much to answer for and it will answer to us both."

Constantina whispered. "Leave him alone. He is too powerful. Even for you." she said softly.

Her eyes closed and a peaceful expression settled over her.

"She is asleep. We need to watch her carefully." I will leave at daybreak to go for help."

Saul stood beside the Celt. "She has lost much blood, Aye am not sure if…"

"This wound is serious, but it has pierced nothing inside. She was up a tree and the arrow came straight up at her." He stopped and reflected on what he just said. "I was the cause of this."

"No, you were nut."

"That arrow should have slain me. I knocked it aside without a thought while I was still under that tree." He looked at the sleeping girl. The pain in his eyes was obvious.

He sat alongside Constantina for a time and watched her sleep. He had made a mess of everything. How could he have been so blind and arrogant to think he could fight an entire nation alone? He had realised too late that they defend their interests ferociously. They would have hundreds – even thousands of operatives loyal to them. He was blind to it all. His failed mission had blinded him. His arrogance had blinded him. His love for her had blinded him. His blindness had probably cost Constantina her life.

Saul came up and put his hand on the man's shoulder. "We trust ewe, Celt. Aye know you will help Constantina. Ewe are committed to crushing those who want to hurt her. Aye am proud of your efforts friend Ath."

He had no words for him save a grim nod. "I will leave at dawn. Saul, I would like you to come with me when I leave, you too Quintus. We have much to discuss before we arrive in the Glade. Your reception will not be an easy one I am afraid, but I'm sure you understand why." Quintus nodded grimly.

Athelstan looked at Saul. "We have an advantage over this Axum of yours, you know. They have no idea what a cataclysmic mistake they have made by attacking the woman I love. Axum seem to kill for sport. They seem to think this is just a game they can win. None of this is real to their soldiers. This is all about to change. It will become very real for them once I find them."

Demetrios smirked. "I am sure they will, but I would like to stay here."

"I hate dividing our forces like this. Very well, then you stay and Saul you come with me. Get what sleep you can now," he leaned back against the wall beside Constantina and looked down at her. Her face was peaceful and he sighed. He would save her – no matter the cost.

Morning did little to brighten their moods. A light rain fell softly. It would be a grey day. Sitting beside her in the cave, Demetrios bathed her forehead with cold water. A fever took her quickly and she was restless. He had wrapped both spots where the arrow protruded from her breast and shoulder, with clean dressings.

Saul stirred a warm broth of dried meats and herbs.

Athelstan opened a small glass phial and dripped a few drops of eye-watering oil on the cloth. He added more to the broth.

Immediately the musty cave smelled like a forest after a spring rain.

Saul's eyes widened as he caught a whiff. "Whew!" he exclaimed standing up suddenly in an effort to get clear of the fumes.

"What is that?" he asked.

"Oregano." Athelstan sniffed. "This is oil made from the leaves of a local weed. If there is an infection in her, this oil will help her fight it. I have put a few drops in her broth as well." Concern lit his face as he leaned in.

Connie moaned and Athelstan cooed and shushed at her like she was a fretful child. By the gods, this girl was lovely. His heart ached at the likelihood of losing her because he could not protect her from his enemies. She was right. She would have been far better off alone.

She was struggling to sit up. He helped her and urged some of the pungent broth down her throat. Her nose wrinkled at the taste but she took more immediately.

"Harichandan?" Connie whimpered, her voice jagged and broken. Her breathing was shallow but regular.

"No Connie," he blinked and sat forward. "It's Athelstan?" She had no idea where she was, or what was happening.

"Harichandan?" she whispered the name again. "You are near. I can smell you."

Her soft unfocused eyes fluttered open. "Harichandan," floated from her lips again.

"I am faithful," she whispered. Pain clouded her features. She took some more broth.

"I know you are Connie. Try not to talk."

"It is yours now Harichandan. The Market. I am ever your servant. Rome has fallen to you," she called out.

"Thank you for that." He looked up in confusion. The others could make no sense of it either. "It will save me waging a great war."

"Our child will know you."

"Child?" Athelstan asked.

"No. No. Please do not leave us. We need you. Please stay." She slumped back into unconsciousness.

Athelstan stroked her hand and mopped her brow as he listened to her strange dream. Was she was reliving a moment in her past, or was this a prophecy of the future?

"Harichandan? That name. Does it mean anything to you?" Demetrios asked. Quintus shook his head. Saul was frowning.

"It sounds familiar but Aye can nut place it."

"I have heard that name before. It is the proper name of The Hooded Man. I learned it in Athens when I chatted with those knife fighters."

"Ah, yas Ath, ewe are right. But how does Constantina know this name?"

"Papirius?"

"If that is true, then the world is in very great danger," Saul nodded.

Demetrios wiped her brow with a dry cloth and touched her forehead. "She seems cooler. It is a powerful medicine."

"If Aye had nut seen that with my own eyes, Aye would never have believed it," Saul whispered.

"It is simple magic from our Gods," Athelstan said simply. "It is time for us to go. Demetrios, you will not be disturbed here. People will come by midday tomorrow. Get her to drink as much of this broth as you can." He nodded but never took his eyes of Constantina.

Harrowing would scarcely describe their precipitous flight down the mountainside towards the lowlands. A heavy rain had fallen during the interminable night and the ground was slick and treacherous. Saul of Jeru–Salam and Quintus Maximus of Rome trusted each to their own Gods as vast cliffs plunging thousands of feet were narrowly averted in their haste to find help for Constantina.

They kept the river to their left and by late morning, the land had begun to change. The river grew wider and the terrain became more level, but there were still the numerous rock falls to skirt and marshy mosquito-infested bogs to wade through. Finally, the trees began to thin out and wide–open grassy plains replaced the narrow clefts and dangerous drop-offs. They had finally reached the valley floor.

With Saul on his left and Quintus on his right, they raced north through a golden sea of wild grains. Harvest had already begun. The river wound lazily around several low hills but the riders rode up and over them. Gwennderion Glade lay only a few miles ahead. A wall of trees loomed before them and Athelstan finally reined Maehadren to a walk. Foam streaked the beast's neck and shoulders and he could feel him heaving huge gulps of air.

"Stay close to me, especially you," he turned to Quintus. "There will not be many who will be glad to see a Roman Legate. Ignore the comments if you wish to see the dawn. We will have to go see my King immediately I fear, but that will be a very short meeting. I will send help for Constantina before we meet with him." His expression was grave and lines of worry etched his face.

"Right now Constantina is my only concern," Saul commented. His face just as grave. They entered the dark moist eaves of the forest and the temperature dropped noticeably. A wide road gently snaked around the ancient boles and mosses hung from the limbs like the wispy beards of old men. The brightly coloured leaves rained down forming wide halos around each tree; red here, orange and yellow there, creating a riotous tapestry that disappeared in every direction. Every sound was muted in this surreal place. The track was paved with grey-blue shale but the ancient trees muted even the clip-clop of the horse's hoofs. It wound along for several miles before a bright opening could be seen in the distance.

Once finally free of the trees, a staggering sight greeted them. The river tumbled out of the forest as if in a rush to be free of that silent world. It wound down into a vast lake. Colourful tents and huge pavilions covered its eastern shore, all arrayed in roughly circular patterns. They surrounded inner rings of more permanent dwellings of free-standing stone foundations, daub and wattle walls, capped with conical thatched roofs. From their centre, coils of smoke climbed upward briefly before joining the wind in its wild flight east. Every building was perfectly circular and each one varied in size based on its use. A clan pole or standing stone stood precisely in the centre of these rings of buildings. Each was decorated with family colours, war trophies as well as all manner of protective amulets, runes of power and glyphs of warding. Hundreds of such communities dotted the plain east of the lake. They formed an unbroken carpet of humanity until they completely disappeared out of sight in the distance. Livestock roamed freely. Children ran and laughed joyously. Men and women were about their business in a random and chaotic dance. Domesticity reigned. Life flourished in all its complexity.

A pair of towering rune–covered standing stones stood on either side of the slate road. Next to the monoliths were long poles containing the standards of many different clans. As they passed between them, Athelstan selected one specific standard. It was predominantly green and blue like his clothing but had long streamers of many colour combinations. Feathers and foxtails festooned the odd standard. Holding it high, he carried it down into the valley.

It did not take long for the trio to be spotted and a troop of horsemen raced up the long slope towards them. There were twenty garishly dressed wild-haired ferocious-looking men surrounding them and for a moment, it did not look good at all. Most of the men simply looked from Quintus to Saul and back in sheer astonishment. One of them, clearly in charge, rode up to the trio and looked at Athelstan with a deep scowl.

"It is about time you got back," he growled.

"Why, did you miss me that much?" He threw a wet kiss in the man's direction and a slow grin appeared on Athelstan's face. The hulking creature that addressed them mirrored it.

"Menniob, my old friend. Not dead yet? I am disappointed." They clasped hands.

"Dead? Hardly! My ancestors could not stand me when they were alive; I doubt their opinion of me has changed much, now that they are not. Where have you been General? The King was getting ready to turn Hellas on its ear to find you… the crazy bastard." He spat punctuating his disgust.

"Worse than in Milan?"

"I am sorry Athelstan."

Menniob was not one to hold his tongue and his comment was filled with both venom and grief. Athelstan listened carefully. "Never mind that now. We have wounded in the high caves of Phaelans Fang. You know the ones." Menniob turned and looked back at the snow-covered peak in the distance. They turned and continued quickly down toward Gwennderion Glade. Athelstan continued.

"Find the Druidess Caileigh and get her and a troop of men up there. Now! Tell her it is a wounded woman and a Spartan is tending her."

"Find my men – you know who I mean. Tell them I have returned and have them meet me inside the Great Hall when I arrive. Have them ready," he shot Menniob a knowing look. A pair of riders broke away from the procession and galloped away down the hill to obey Athelstan's orders.

"Inform the King of my return. Alert all the Clan leaders to be in the Hall in one hour. I bring news," he glanced at Quintus. Another group broke off and thundered away.

"I want it clearly understood that Quintus Maximus is not a prisoner but an envoy from the Republic of Rome and he will be treated as one. I will personally deal with anyone who offers him any insult. Am I clear?"

Menniob glanced at the Roman who kept his gaze stoically forward. "It is clear, General. I suspected there is a story here and no mistake. I look forward to hearing it… I will pass the word." Menniob looked over at Saul and visibly resisted the urge to touch his deep caramel–coloured skin.

"And you sir. I have never met a man like you before. Where are you from?"

"Aye am Saul from Jeru–Salam. Aye seek."

"Do you now. I wish you health and bid you welcome to the Glade. A rescue party is being assembled. We will find your friends." Saul looked at Athelstan.

"There is none better, Saul. If Menniob says he will do a thing, I know he would rather die than fail. That is why he is one of my best commanders. That is why I trust him like a brother like I trust you. You must have faith that the Gods… er that your God, Jehovah, will protect her until then." Saul's sharp look spoke volumes but he nodded. It was all that could be done.

Menniob nodded to the three riders before spurring his own horse and pursuing his men down the slope.

"I'm not going to enjoy this part of the ride, am I?" Quintus asked casually.

"I would think not. Once we arrive, you will be held, not as a prisoner but as a guest. The difference though might seem a fine one at first. Naturally, your movements will be restricted at first, but you will not be locked up. I promise you that."

"Are you planning to marry Constantina?" Quintus bluntly asked. He studied the Celt closely.

"If she will have me, yes I am," he replied and looked forward again.

"She is not what you think."

"Few women ever are," said Athelstan.

Athelstan looked ahead and there was a long pause. "You have proven to me that you can be trusted; that your word is as important to you as mine is to me. In a different world Quintus, I might be willing to call you friend. I needed to tell you that." The Roman looked at him with surprise.

They travelled northward along the eastern shore of Lake Ohrid following the same grey paving stones. The cool wind off the water bore a fresh sweetness that seemed to clear the tired mind. They wove through one clan encampment after another. Athelstan called many by name and they all seemed jubilant of his return. The trip took time since Gwennderion Glade was really an entire valley and Lake Ohrid was no small body of water. It was a glittering jewel of deep blue forty miles long and just less than fifteen miles across.

They travelled through fruit groves and beneath towering nut trees of every description. Wild grains mixed with oats and barley was being cut; the sheaves stacked for drying and flailing. Great fields of root vegetables filled much of the intervening areas and each clan was busy harvesting these 'Forever Gardens' in preparation for the Samhain festival and winter. Even the water was alive with boats and the men hauled up small nets and tossed untold numbers of fish into their long reed boats. The women gutted and dried them on long wooden racks. Each clan had a different predominant aroma. The festering woad piles used to make the blue colouring for tattoos were particularly pungent.

He passed a low hill and looked at it in horror. Nine men were staked spread–eagle on the ground and soldiers prevented their families from getting close. He rode up to one soldier and the man straightened as he recognised the General.

"What is going on here? Why are these men being executed?" Athelstan demanded.

"Treason against their King," he answered smartly.

He looked up at the poor souls. "Release them and have them tended immediately."

The soldier looked at his General and hesitated. "The King will not like this sir."

"I am not in the habit of repeating myself and have no interest whatsoever in your opinion. Cut them loose, or join them yourself. I will deal with the King." The soldier looked indecisive. Athelstan's scowl deepened.

"At once sir," he turned and ran up the hill. Many of the soldiers guarding this hill turned to look at the General before they began to obey.

That was not the only horror on the road. As they passed through a stand of sacred oaks, the dead dangled from low and high branches amidst a murder of crows, a conspiracy of ravens and a gulp of magpies. The crows and magpies fought for scraps. The Ravens fought for the souls. Beneath all lay many dead and dying birds. They fought for life. All would lose here today. Athelstan waved an arm and let out a piteous howl. The birds exploded in a flurry of feathers and squawks of outrage into the air.

The men had been garroted, hung and bled with cruel slashes to their throats. It was the ignoble end saved for the criminals in the Celtic world. Athelstan reigned in Maehadren and gazed up at them for some time. They swung in the breeze like macabre decorations. A low snarl slipped past his lips.

"What is it?" Saul asked in a soft voice.

"The wicked are hung and bled so. We do this so they cannot join with their ancestors in the afterlife. Only criminals are treated in such a low manner, not kin."

"These men are – are your family?" Saul was shocked. Athelstan ignored the question and looked away in disgust.

"Never kin. Never," he whispered.

News of the General's return spread like wildfire through the semi-permanent encampment. A flurry of activity ensued. The news sprang from clan to clan in an ever-widening circle. Even a mile, or more from the walled Royal enclosure, they were being swarmed by hundreds of people. Many cheered but many more had grave faces. It was clear that his people had been suffering greatly. Athelstan knew the cause but said nothing. Considerable verbal abuse was aimed at Quintus offering single combat but like a true soldier, the Roman stared stoically forward and ignored them all. Despite the tone, no one dared to touch the General's Roman companion. No one! They rode along under a growing cacophony of angry voices but one look at the general's face told them, intervention would prove a deadly adventure.

After an interminable length of time, they finally arrived at the nearly symmetrical horn of land jutting out into the lake. In fact, night was falling. A twenty–foot high wooden palisade wall enclosed it. A crowd of some two thousand strong now strained and jostled to get a glimpse of this odd pair riding with their Army General. Great events were unfolding and no one wanted to miss a single second.

They approached the Royal compound. It was walled along three sides and open to Lake Ohrid on the fourth. There were four huge enclosed structures. Each was comprised of a square of four long halls forming a square each with an inner courtyard. Separating them were two wide roads forming a cross running north/south and east/west. There were three gates, one in the north and two others east and west.

They rode through open eastern gates and along the wide straight road leading directly to the Royal Hall. It was still a long journey past the throngs. Royal Guards and warriors stood lining the road but the compound was nearly filled with people. He scanned the crowd and noticed several men he recognised. He flashed them a simple sign and they nodded before slipping free of the crowd. He was pleased. It would be comforting to have some family nearby for this meeting with King Trahearn.

A rough cheer went up as the Athelstan slid from his steed and he slapped several men on the shoulder before entering the Royal Hall. Saul and Quintus accompanied him, one at each shoulder.

For the people, it was a grand day. Their General had returned with help against the Romans. He had even captured one. It was still unclear what sort of help he brought. They stared at both Quintus and Saul with naked curiosity. He talked quietly for a few moments to a man at the entrance to the Hall. The castellan's eyes widened and then widened even more. He looked at the pair of men with Athelstan before turning and motioning for the doors to be opened. He took several steps inside and banged an ornate staff on the floor three times.

"Your Majesty! General Athelstan has returned. Accompanying him, may it please your Majesty to receive, Minister Saul, a delegate from the city of Jeru–Salam and Legate Quintus Julius Maximus, Commander of the Legion Equis and ambassador from the Republic of Rome!" An unpleasant ripple swept the packed room. It was filled with representatives from every clan occupying the glade – predominantly nobility, clan chiefs and their sons as well as a handful of personal guards for each. They were a wild-looking shaggy, painted, collection of men. The Royal Guard was also at hand and surrounded the raised dais containing the seated king.

"Stay right beside me and say nothing. Your very lives depend on it," he whispered to his two nervous companions.

A foaming, mad King peered at him with naked suspicion painted across his haggard face. His brother had aged terribly and he was drawn and thin. Greyish white skin hung from his cheeks and the room bore the stale smell of decay. He was rotting from the inside out.

"Athelstan?"

"Sire," Athelstan spoke in a booming voice and began his walk forward. Saul and Quintus joined him a half step to the rear.

"Has that traitorous dog dared to return HERE?" The King stood and fixed an icy glare on approaching Celt.

"I have your Grace!" His voice shook the rafters. Murmurs of anger swept the room.

"What foul plots have you hatched with that Spartan Witch?" squeaked the king in a high reedy voice.

"None whatever, your Grace!"

"Where are the soldiers you were sent to bring back?"

"T'was a fool's errand. None will come your Grace!"

"What are you doing with this Roman dog? Is he a pet?"

"He is not your Grace. He is an ambassador. He is to be treated with respect, your Grace. I shall slay any who offer him the slightest hint of disrespect. I swear this by the Gods." The Kings eyes widened at this.

"You have disobeyed me at every turn."

"I have not your Grace. I have been ever faithful."

"Where are the hostages?"

"I freed them at once, your Grace. I shall not be forced to commit acts of cowardice and disrespect against children, not even by you."

"Freed them? FREED THEM? I WANT MY HOSTAGES!" He was getting worked up again. Foam and spittle coated his long beard and spattered wetly on the floor while he spoke. A paroxysm of coughing ended the stream of questions for the moment.

Athelstan did not react to his words but continued to approach the throne with slow measured steps. Quintus and Saul still followed a half step to the rear as the crowd closed in behind them. Saul's eyes darted to and fro at the assembly while Quintus remained stoic and stared at the Senone King. Athelstan came to a halt and he bowed down on one knee before his Sovereign. His companions followed his lead and also knelt. As suddenly as the tirade had started, it was over.

"Why were you gone so long dear brother?" Trahearn asked sadly. "Menniob is a traitor, you know and so is Cedric. Everyone in here has betrayed us. They are all against us. Damn their black traitorous hearts to the underworld! I have had most of them executed." He snarled spat and began to cough again.

Athelstan did not move as the thick, greasy spittle struck him. He remained on his knee with his head and eyes cast downward.

Trahearn stood unsteadily and stepped up to the kneeling warrior. "Get up, get up," he slurred impatiently. "Who is this you have brought before me?"

"Envoys and ambassadors all, your Grace," he murmured in his soft whisper. "Allies of the highest order." Only Saul heard and gave him a brief sidelong glance. He watched Athelstan close his hand around the hilt of his great sword. Athelstan glanced at Saul and the Jew shook his head almost imperceptibly. He knew.

"What was that? What did you say? Why did you bring that Roman pig in here? I should have you both flogged and hung." The King nearly gagged on the word 'Roman'. He stamped his feet like a little boy throwing a tantrum. "GET TO YOUR FEET! I demand to know wha…"

A soft baritone voice interrupted the King with three simple words. "Goodbye – old friend."

Athelstan suddenly stood and in a single fluid motion drew his great sword. Athelstan swung his weapon in a brutal, murderous arc.

King Trahearn's head suddenly sprang from his shoulders spraying a geyser of blood. The head hit the floor with a hollow sound before bouncing to a stop by the throne. The body collapsed spattering Athelstan, Saul and Quintus in a forceful fountain of blood. Both Saul and Quintus were struck dumb in shock at the sudden brutality and their faces showed it. Quintus braced himself to be killed on the spot.

The crowd gasped in absolute shock and horror and just as suddenly was stunned into absolute silence. Athelstan bent and placed both of his hands in the gushing spout of blood coming out of the decapitated body of the King. He stood and faced the assembly he clapped both his hands against his own face leaving two bloody handprints. He uttered a long eerie inhuman howl that was painful to the ears. He bellowed at the roof… "The King is dead! Summon the Druids!"

Chapter Thirty-Six

The first to move was Trahearn's personal guard but two–dozen blueand green clad men – Athelstan's men – swiftly stepped forward to counter them. There were brief scuffles but most people took several steps away from the General in abject horror. This was the last thing anyone would have expected from King Trahearn's half–brother and most trusted companion.

With Royal blood dripping from his face and hair, he began to chant an ancient prayer.

> Orchil, our Earth Goddess is under the
> Brown earth in a vast cavern where she weaves at two looms.
> With one hand, she weaves life upward through the green grass; with the other hand she weaves death downward through the mould;
> And the sound of that weaving is called Eternity,
> And the name of life in this green world is called Time.
> Through it all, Orchil weaves the weft of Eternal Beauty,
> That never passes from this land.
> Her soul is change.
> Earth Mother, welcome our brother Trahearn Livy to your tapestry and give him peace.

He calmly retrieved the Kings head and carried it casually by the hair. Blood bubbled out of the neck soiling the stone floor. The dead face bore a somewhat surprised expression.

"I will speak to you again soon, old friend," he whispered as pandemonium erupted throughout the Great Hall. Some cheered outright while others wept. An equal number were furious and stormed from the Hall while others rushed in. He had stirred a monstrous hornet nest.

Athelstan stepped over the body without a second glance and said simply, "Bury him with honour." A crown hung carelessly from the arm of the throne and Athelstan left it hang there. He placed the King's dismembered head, gently on the throne next to the crown. The room was suddenly a hive of activity. People began running in and out and in moments the entire Royal compound was in a state of chaos.

"Cedric!" Athelstan called. "Find Cedric and bring him in here. What news from the Macedonian King?" He asked a stunned open–mouthed aide.

"They sent a delegation, General… er, Your Majesty. I am told we have reached an agreement with… them." His eyes flickered to the headless body. Athelstan held up a hand.

The man fell silent. "I am not your King – just answer the question. Where are the Druids?" The King's aide looked bewildered.

"The Druids? At once, Majesty…ah, General." The poor man was beginning to look pale.

"Well go find them. NOW! Tell them to meet me here. We have a small matter to deal with." The attendant vanished, visibly relieved to be doing anything rather than standing under Athelstan's intense gaze.

He raised his arms and in a loud voice, he addressed the crowd. "Hear me! The reign of King Trahearn is ended. I have done what we all knew had to be done. His actions have dishonoured us all. If they are willing, the Gods will cleanse us of his evil deeds! Trahearn had lost his ability to rule and so as a true child of Senone, I have released him from the burden of his madness. His wickedness is over. He is finally free to enter the next life. Let his ancestors welcome him around their fires so he may stand beside them with honour until his spirit's return." Blood dripped from Athelstan's fingers.

"Until his return." The crowd repeated.

A grizzled warrior in greying beard and moustache shouldered his way into the packed room; a huge smile spread across his face. Deep laugh lines ran from beneath his eyes around his cheeks and down his face. Expressive furrows framed the corners of his mouth.

"Athelstan?" He bellowed.

"You have finally returned. Thank Epona." The older man glanced about, stepped over a headless body and asked innocently.

"What's going on? Where is the King?" Athelstan indicated Trahearn's body with a jerk of his head, he indicated the body.

The old veteran turned and looked down with a frown. "Ah… I see. You thought this through I suppose. You had a good reason I trust?" Athelstan nodded but put up a hand for silence not bothering to elaborate.

"So what do you need of me sire?" There was this to be said about old Cedric he adapted quickly.

"Enough!" Athelstan suddenly bellowed and the din in the room ebbed somewhat. He turned back to Cedric. "I want no more of this 'sire' talk."

"I am afraid you will just have to get used to it – Sire. You were his half–brother after all. He had no other immediate kin." An old and all too familiar voice behind him silenced every other voice in the Hall. Athelstan's face became grave and he turned this bloody visage towards the speaker.

Vestorix, Arch Druid of the Senone Celts… the most powerful person in the Celtic world stood facing him – holding the Moldavite Crown in both hands. With him were members of the Druidic council dressed all in white.

There was a flurry of activity. More of Trahearn's blood was collected and mixed with goat milk and mead. Vestorix placed his hand on Athelstan's shoulder.

Athelstan shook his head in confusion and frowned ever so slightly. "No!" he whispered at the white–beard. "Do not do this."

"Kneel before your ancestors Athelstan Epona of son of Senone." He winced at these words but sank to his knees at the Druid's command. This was the one man who could not be disobeyed. His was the final word. His was the only word.

"Athelstan Epona, by the wisdom placed within me by Gaia the Earth Goddess and by the decree of our ancestors, I pronounce you to be the rightful King of Senone," he placed the gold and green gem encrusted crown onto the shaggy mane and touched his forehead three times with his own balding pate. Vestorix accepted a shallow bowl with the blood and milk mixture. He handed it to the kneeling warrior.

"Drink! Let the power of your fallen brother flow in your veins and take your rightful place among the great rulers of our people." Athelstan drank and handed the bowl back to the Arch–Druid.

"Arise and greet your people, your Majesty. Long live the King!" Vestorix shouted.

"Long live the King!" The crowd shouted back and a great cheer erupted.

He was physically and spiritually drained – stunned in fact and felt icy cold inside. He was trying to comprehend what had just happened. He had anticipated being hacked to bits for what he had done, but not this. That he might be made King, had never once occurred to him. Saul nudged him and he blinked at the Jew. His eyes focused and widened.

"Mobilize the Army, General Cedric! You now command the multitude. I want this valley secure enough to withstand a mounted assault by nightfall. The compound walls need shoring up to form work teams. This place could not defend against a herd of cows let alone an army. Round up the King's councillors and hold them. I will have a word, or two with them shortly." The old warrior looked at him strangely.

"Army? What army?" Cedric asked looking around.

"The Roman Army – the Macedonian Army – the Axum Army, take your bloody pick. They all seem rather annoyed with me at the moment." Athelstan placed an arm around Cedric's shoulder and handed him the crown. "Here, take this. Keep it safe for now."

"How big a Roman army?" Cedric asked as Quintus came to stand beside him. Cedric looked Quintus up and down, crested helmet, golden armour, red cloak, gladius and all. "You're a bloody Roman," he stated.

"Legate Quintus Maximus of the Equis Legion of Roma, meet my first cousin Cedric Epona, first General of the Senone Multitude." Both men nodded formally at each other. "Let's not get too chummy, you two are at war after all." Both men leaned away from each other slightly.

"So what is HE doing here?"

"Funny you should ask. He travelled here with Proconsul Papirius Aurelius Cursor and a small handful of his finest cavalry formerly under the command of Quintus Maximus here. A few hundred, or so I should think should still be alive by the time they arrive. We travel with Papirius's wife Constantina and Ptolemarch Demetrios of Sparta. This is Ambassador Saul of Jeru–Salam."

"Papirius is positively apoplectic with our recently departed King. I am equally certain he just as angry with me. No matter, you have your orders." Athelstan grimaced slightly as he held up Trahearn's head. Keep this safe as well. He should rest in the Grotto."

"Proconsul Papirius? Not THE proconsul Papirius of Rome?" Cedric joined in with Athelstan's mirth but slowly his smile faded and a horrified expression crawled across his face.

"The very same."

"Wait! You are serious?"

"Yes, I am. Have you ever known me not to be? It is difficult not to anger people when you steal their children and use them as a bargaining tool." mumbled Athelstan through a hastily grabbed mouthful of bread and cheese.

"Aw! Bloody Hell! So, what is this Axum Army? I have never heard of them," asked Cedric.

"That - is less certain. Damn dangerous is all you need to know. So keep your wits about you." Athelstan nodded towards Saul and motioned to a long table of food and wine.

"You should eat something. You have not eaten all day. Saul will be leaving with Menniob and his men, Caileigh's people as well."

"To go where? Wait a moment. What do you mean First General of the Multitude?" Cedric asked.

"Oh, do try to keep up old friend. I can't very well be the General anymore now can I?"

Cedric's brow furrowed as he plunged deep in thought. He muttered, "No, I suppose not but…"

"One of our companions is injured; shot by an assassin and we had to leave her in the mountains. She is being hunted by something called the Axum. I do not know why yet. She is Roman. Menniob is forming a rescue party and Saul; you will be going with them. We need to retrieve her and get her back here safely.

Saul looked at Athelstan in surprise. "Ewe are nut coming?"

"No Saul, I cannot. I have to stay; it is far too dangerous for me to leave right now. You saw what just happened. What I have just done could easily spark a civil war. I must prevent that from happening if I can. It is critical that Constantina has a secure place to recover. You understand." His expression was calm but his tone was intense. He appeared, at this moment, every bit a barbarian King. Saul nodded.

"What about him?" Cedric referred to Quintus. Athelstan looked long and hard at the Roman and the Centurion returned his gaze steadily.

"Find him quarters inside the walls of the compound. See to his needs and keep him safe. No weapons! He is a guest, not a prisoner, you understand. I have come to understand not all Romans are... unreasonable. He and I have come to an understanding." They held each other's gaze and Quintus gave a knowing nod to the new King before being disarmed and led away.

Chapter Thirty-Seven

The Druids and ruling council of clan chiefs both had summarily rejected his plan of facing Papirius in single combat. His reasons for engaging the man alone were sound. He knew it and they knew it. It was the honourable thing to do, but argue as he might, they were adamant. He would not be permitted to fight Papirius. It was just too dangerous.

He listened to them all staring at the Moldavite Crown swinging absently from a forefinger. Another graybeard began to extol the dangers that could be faced by the King while in combat with Papirius. Ground Squirrels! If a warrior should misstep into one of their numerous burrows, it could, in his opinion prove disastrous. Athelstan's patience with these moaning and aged hand wringers came to an abrupt end.

"Enough!" He slammed his hands on the table and the sound echoed off the rafters of the Great Hall. "I have been fighting battles like this from birth! From that moment forward I have been preparing for today. How can you not see that? I have defeated tyrants and madmen, bands of outlaws, rival clans and invading nations. I have gentled them all and never once has anyone ever suggested to me that I might take a misstep into a bloody rodent hole! NO! I ride upon the shoulders of the White Horse Goddess. She has swept me from one divine victory to the next and the only thing my enemies can do is weep. I was not defeated by them and I will not be defeated by this old man and his ragged band of thugs," his voice thundered through the hall. A grizzled hard–looking man stood and pointed a finger at Athelstan.

"What makes you think I am going to let my sons and my brother's sons fight and die for you in the first place? We have no requirement to help you fix your mistakes," Ocatis, an irascible old clan chief, bristled. He stood before the new King, feet apart and hands on hips. In two strides, Athelstan crossed the distance and grabbed the surprised man by the beard.

"Because if you do not, Ocatis I will personally hack you to bits here and now and find someone among your kin with enough backbone who will," he released the man's beard. "Choose!" The two men glared at each other for a moment before the clan chief huffed and sat back down. Athelstan swept the room with his eyes looking for any others who would question his authority.

None dared.

"It is decided. Go make your preparations according to my instructions. I will join you in the field shortly. I have something of importance to attend to." Clan chiefs left the hall grumbling. Druids and other nobles remained.

He cast his gaze over the remaining men. "I was told there is a treaty with Macedonia to sign? Let me see it." A page produced a scroll and handed it to his King. Vestorix bent and whispered into his ear. He nodded his understanding.

"Tell General Cedric and the Macedonian delegation to attend us," he settled back into a plain wooden chair and began to read. The ornate throne was situated prominently but Athelstan would not sit in it. His brother's blood still stained it.

A young noble stood and cleared his throat nervously.

"Your Majesty, this agreement assures us that we can live here in peace. We believe this is the best way to avoid a fight with our new neighbours. As you can see…" He was interrupted.

"Sit down," Athelstan commanded dangerously and the man did. Athelstan stood and locked eyes with the nobles.

"I want something clearly understood right now. I called this meeting. You are here at my bidding, not the other way around. No one is to talk during my meetings unless you are spoken to directly. You have all played at being advisors to Trahearn but none of you was man enough to tell him the truth."

"Now wait just a moment." A man stood. "We have done everything necessary to aid the former King and he was well pleased with…"

"And you have done a terrible job of it, too. If it were in my power I would dismiss you all for your dishonourable advice to him, now shut up and sit down." The noble's mouth opened in response to the King's rebuke but he slowly regained his seat.

Athelstan tossed the scroll onto the throne. "Imagine my surprise when a frightened band of little girls were delivered to me in Athens. I can forgive him. He was insane and could not see things clearly, but you could see things all too clearly. Was it your council that prompted this operation? Have you any idea what those Goths did to those children while in their tender care? Some of them were as young as seven years of age! Seven! Do you think they will ever recover from that? Your council caused their misery. I sent them back home where they belong. Is it your intention to ignore Rome's legions and wage war against their children instead?" He dared anyone to contradict him. Many heads were cast down in embarrassment.

"You claim to advise the former King and still I find good and loyal men staked to the ground and hanging from tree limbs. I am within a heartbeat of ordering that you replace those men on the Hill of Torment. At the very least it would give you time to think; something you all seem incapable of doing now." The doors opened and five garishly dressed Macedonians entered. The new Senone General in full battle dress followed them in. He motioned that they should approach Athelstan. Cedric came and stood beside Athelstan.

They recoiled at the bloody handprints on his face

"I am King Athelstan. I just beheaded my brother. I trust, by now, that news has already reached your ears. It pleases me to see that King Cassander wishes to forge an alliance with us. I have the agreement here," he picked up the scroll.

"It pleases us as well your Majesty. I am Parmenion, chief negotiator for our government," he produced a quill and ink flask.

"All that remains is for you to sign it and we can be on our way," he held out the quill so Athelstan could sign. The king looked at the quill and then at Parmenion without expression. The Macedonian shrank back from him and nervously rejoined his associates.

Athelstan asked, "Is it your council that I should not read it first?"

"Yes," the fop began.

"Yes? I should not read it?"

"No. Oh, of course. Read it, don't read it as you like..." There was a hint of dismissive annoyance in his voice.

"I would prefer if you addressed me as 'Your Grace', or King Athelstan. Whichever falls from your tongue more easily. Snicker again and I can assure you of two things. You can join my former King and one of these..." his eyes slowly scanned the other Macedonians. "One of these people will take your place. I trust I am being quite clear."

"Quite clear, your Grace."

Athelstan opened the scroll and started to read. He began to walk into the grand hall; his eyes never left the document. It took some time to read and he read every single word. His casual walk took him to the grand hearth. Every eye in the room was fixed on the new Senone King.

After a long time, he finished reading the document and rolled it up.

"This is a very interesting document. I have never seen one quite like it before. There are a few points I would like to touch on – so that I understand them fully."

"Such as?" The speaker was a small pinch-faced man dressed like he was going to some grand ball. There was thinly veiled exasperation in his voice. Clearly, he found the new king to be a little slow.

"It says here that your kingdom's treasury is to receive the Senone King's weight in gold annually in rent for this tiny bit of land we stand on. I am now the King so you must be pleased to have my weight in gold rather than that of our former King. I believe I weigh about fifteen stone. I think two hundred and ten pounds of gold could be easily found here. Do I read this correctly?"

"Yes, your Grace."

"I see. There is also lots of talk about the previous agreements between Alexander of Macedon and the Senone nation. He was a fine commander and a shrewd negotiator – a man not easily replaced. You would agree?" Heads nodded. Athelstan nodded as well. "I have read these agreements and they are a bit vague in places, but my advisors have explained them to me and I understand the basics details of what they contain." Parmenion rolled his eyes. Athelstan paused a moment before continuing.

"In its entirety, this agreement deals with military matters almost exclusively, with a few minor exceptions. It indicates a rather sizable downsizing of our armed forces from their current levels, to roughly five thousand soldiers and places the defence of these lands squarely in the hands of the Macedonian army. This is to become an outpost for some twenty thousand of your forces on the borders of Illyria and we would build suitable accommodations to house them as well as provide food and all necessary items to make their stay here comfortable. Did I understand that correctly?"

"Essentially correct your Grace," their leader stated flatly. The others nodded their agreement.

"I see also it mentions non–aggression pacts and installs mutual defence agreements between us. It states clearly that we are not to expand eastward, nor south, or north beyond this valley. It also states that we would be required to come to your aid if called upon to do so, by King Cassander. Would that also be a fair assessment in your opinion?"

"It would your Grace." The Macedonian delegates began to glance at each other with some confusion. "This agreement is quite standard in all of our dealings with barbar... er, rather neighbouring states. There is nothing out of the ordinary within it."

"Oh! Is it now? Standard? That is a pity. What of free and fair commerce between us? We lie on the trade routes both north into the Goth territories and south into Greece as well as east to Persia and beyond. How will we conduct trade with our neighbours? What of freedom, of religion? Our Druids will ask if they have the freedom to travel and minister to the clans. I also noticed that nowhere is there any mention of Macedonia having a mutual non–aggression pact with us. Is it your intention to wage war on Senone?"

"NO, your Grace."

"I do not believe you, sir." They were at once crestfallen. He had quickly pointed out all of the conditions missing at the command of Cassander."

"Nor does it mention anywhere that Macedonia would come to our aid should the Illyrians or for that matter, the Dacians, the Thracians, the Praetorians, or even the Islamic, tribes who, incidentally surround us on all sides, should decide to wage a war of conquest on us. So let me say something about this agreement..."

With a casual motion, he tossed the scroll into the flames and returned to the front of the room. The Macedonians were in abject shock at his action.

"It is utterly unacceptable from the first word to the last. Go home. If it is Cassander's opinion that this is a fair agreement, he needs to bang his head with a rock. You tried to take advantage of my brother's mental infirmity and very nearly succeeded. When Cassander is ready to come to an equitable agreement with me, then I will be only too pleased to welcome him. HIM and him alone. None of you will pass into these lands again." These men blanched at his words.

"We cannot tell him that. He will kill us."

"Either he will, or I will! Take your pick. Know this, if I kill you, it will be very unpleasant indeed. Tell him this so he understands it clearly. Gwennderion Glade is now part of the Senone nation and we will defend it. Inform him that all current treaties between us are now in abeyance. I care not at all if this is to his liking! He should have sent honest men to negotiate with us! When he is ready to treat us in a civilised fashion I am willing to listen, but now he must present himself personally. He will personally apologise to me for – that," his head indicated the fireplace. "And he will do so on his knees. If Cassander fulfils these requests, I might even let him live as my personal slave."

"I will not speak to any more of his ill-mannered minions," he tossed one single drachma on the floor. It made a hollow ringing noise as it slowly spun to a stop. The Macedonian envoys stared in shock at the dull, worthless iron coin.

"PICK IT UP!" Athelstan bellowed. Two of the envoys lost their water. One was brave enough to pick it up.

"Take that in payment and give it to your precious king. Tell him that the 'king of dogs' will not get my weight in gold for us to live here. We do not rent land; we are Celts. We dare take what we need and we occupy this land because it suits us to do so. We will defend this land against any who seek to take it from us. Those who do not like that can go to Tartarus. Remind him as well, that if one Senone soldier can prevent him from taking a simple walled village like Athens, imagine what might happen to his world should I release the multitude upon it. If he chooses war, I will give him a war he cannot begin to imagine. We will gut his army, kill his people, sack, loot his cities, and decorate my Clan totem with his head. Nothing of Macedonia will be left standing save what placed there by very the hands of the Gods. You tell him that! This meeting is over. Escort these men to the borders of the glade. If they offer you any trouble at all, if they so much as utter a single word – kill them all and send the Dog King their heads in a sack." He watched as the stunned Macedonians were escorted from the hall. Outside a small entourage of blue and green clad guards fell into step behind them.

Athelstan's gaze swept over the nobles who remained. Many looked at the King with horror on their faces, the others with ill-concealed anger. "I know you all. I will remember what was almost done today. You are dismissed." One by one, they turned and left, many conferring in whispers as they left. Once the hall was empty, he sat wearily. "Cedric, have your men take down the bodies hanging in the southern oak groves and bury them with honour. Then, when the moon is full in the sky, take those traitors who just left and hang them. All of them. If anyone offers you resistance, hang them too."

"Hanging them might prove very dangerous, cousin. All of those men are from powerful clans." Athelstan shot Cedric a look.

"More dangerous than letting them plot my murder? More dangerous than letting them plot civil war? I am sure that is their plan. Hang them. I need to set an example of what I will and will not tolerate. My intention is to make it clearly understood that a warrior now commands this nation. Oh, and Cedric, we are and always will be family, cousin. My name is Athelstan. Use it." Cedric smiled.

Chapter Thirty-Eight

'It must be a dream.' Her mind struggled to make sense of her surroundings as she slowly awakened. Surely she had died. Shot through the chest with an arrow is always fatal. Her eyes fluttered open and Constantina stared up at a brilliantly colourful, slightly slanted ceiling. It took some time for her eyes to focus before she realised she was inside a massive tent. Her right arm was bound tightly to her chest and there was a throbbing pain under her right breast and the top of her right shoulder. All her ribs on the right side burned unmercifully.

Voices could be heard everywhere, both inside and out. Since the pavilion was partitioned into dozens of small rooms like hers, no one was in sight. All she could think of was that she needed to find Saul and the others. With a Herculean effort, she rolled onto her side before sliding her feet out of bed and onto the floor. She stumbled past the cloth walls, out through the large tent's entrance and was greeted by a sight that brought her to a complete stop.

Her mouth dropped open and she had to steady herself against one of the tent's massive support beams to keep from falling. Spread before her, was a sight of astonishing beauty. She stood overlooking a wide valley. The lower slopes were covered in a riotous tapestry of red, orange and gold coloured trees. It seemed that every leaf of every tree had been painted a different hue. Halos of their fallen leaves ringed the base of each one giving the forest an unreal, almost unearthly quality.

Further up the steep slopes, the green trees returned and they were just as bright and vibrant as their colourful cousins below. The mountain peaks high above were dusted white and added the perfect accent to this visual confection. The mountains cupped a vast lake in a gentle embrace. The blue lake stretched away to the southern horizon. Hundreds of sails dotted its deep blue surface as men plied the waters for fish.

Although the shoreline was a hundred paces away, Constantina felt her toes snuggle into the warm sand surrounding the healer's pavilion. The vista might have been startling but that feeling of warm sand under feet gave her a powerful sense of contentment. She suddenly became aware of the throngs of people, children and animals milling about. Many slowed as they passed to look at her or to call out a greeting of welcome, or prayers for a swift recovery. Everyone smiled at her and many bowed, or curtsied awkwardly.

She looked around and saw the healer's tent was a part of a large complex of tents and stone, thatch-roofed buildings. It was protected on the land by a tall wooden palisade wall with dozens of watchtowers. It was a semi-circle enclosing over six hundred acres and almost a mile of sandy shoreline. Several gates led to the surrounding forests and fields of the Glade beyond.

The gates were open wide allowing people to come and go as they pleased. A sight beyond the gates caused a sudden intake of breath. What looked like some kind of crop from this distance was, in actuality, a sea of men. They were Senone soldiers and they covered the ground for miles. It looked like a seething crawling anthill that had been stirred with a stick. Constantina's good hand went to her mouth to stifle the gasp of surprise. Being told about the Multitude was one thing but to suddenly see it was something else entirely.

A throng of people stepped out of the largest of the simple stone structures. They followed a tall man. It was too far away to hear what was being said but she knew by his gestures and smooth long-legged gait that it was Athelstan. He was pointing here and there issuing orders. The people surrounding him bowed one by one and scurried off to do his bidding. A slight frown crossed her brow as she watched. He said he was General of the Army, but the people around him were acting like he was their… King!

A cold sensation clutched at her chest as she suddenly realised that they had been so easily deceived. She pushed the thought down. A warm hand on her shoulder caused her to physically jump.

"What are you doing out of bed?" asked an older woman. She was of an indeterminate age with white hair and pale eyes.

"Come along back inside. You are in no fit condition to be walking around yet."

"Who are you?" she asked shrinking away from the touch.

"I am Caileigh, child. I am the healer here. Please do not be frightened. You are going to be just fine." the older woman took Constantina's bandaged arm and walked her back inside.

Constantina glanced back over her shoulder for one last look.

"Where am I?"

"You are safe. This is called Gwenderion Glade. It is our home. It is now your home too as I understand. Your understanding of our language is remarkable my dear. Have you lived among Celts before?" She helped Constantina back to her bed and helped arrange pillows. She ignored the question save for a brief shake of her head.

"How much do you remember?" Caileigh's shrewd eyes took a quick measure of Constantina's condition."

"I remember travelling in the mountains. I remember a Greek, a Jew and a Barba… um – I remember Athelstan. Where is Quintus?" Just thinking about him brought her to a stop.

Caileigh's eyes narrowed briefly. "I do not know that name. That you remember anything is very good. Is something troubling you? Are you worried about your injury?"

"I am fine."

"Who is Quintus?"

"He is my – friend."

"Oh, you mean that Rom... I suppose we all have our prejudices. Forgive me."

Constantina flashed a weak smile and waved off the slight.

"How did this happen?" Constantina asked with a pleasant look.

"I removed the shaft of an arrow. You are very lucky to have survived."

"An arrow? May I see it?"

"Yes, I suppose so." Caileigh went to retrieve the shaft.

Her body still ached and the pain filled her to the point where she wanted to scream. Nevertheless, she had to maintain her composure.

Moments later the healer returned with the shaft. Constantina took it and looked up.

"Where is the rest of it?" Constantina sniffed it and wrinkled her nose.

"I do not know."

"What is that smell?"

"Oil made from a herb. It is for fighting an infection."

"Is it really?" she mumbled as if recalling an old memory. She held up the arrow shaft. "May I keep it for a little while?"

"Of course. Try not to tire yourself. It is sleep you need right now."

"Thank you for your kindness."

The white-haired woman's face took on the look all mothers get when a beloved child is trying to hide something. She sat on the edge of the bed. "You are welcome. It will take all of your strength to heal after this and it simply will not do to have you fretting about something. But if you say nothing is amiss then I shall take you on your word," she checked the bandage under her right breast and the top of her shoulder.

"I was afraid of this, your wound has opened. Let me re-bandage it so we can let you get the rest you need. Are you hungry?" Constantina nodded.

Her fingers moved with practised efficiency as she removed the now bloody bandages. She did a strange thing. Gently she touched Constantina's wound under her breast with her finger and began to hum, or chant. The tune had a haunting quality to it. When she removed her finger the bleeding simply stopped. She bandaged Constantina's chest again, lashing her right arm over the thick pad. Caileigh checked the fresh bandage on her ribs as well. This was healing nicely.

A bowl of steaming soup was brought to her but even with the healer's help, she could only manage a few bites. "Get some rest, you can have some more when you wake up."

Constantina frowned. She did not know this woman or these people. "Thank you Caileigh–child. Where did you learn how to do this?"

The woman looked at her seriously. "Just Caileigh if you please. I am a Witch. I am a wise woman, a healer of my people and it is my business to know these things." There was no pretence in the ancient's tone. She spoke her mind and it was almost certainly the truth. The Druidess waited on the edge of Constantina's bed.

"Why did he bring me here?" she asked in a barely audible whisper.

"To save your life of course." The elder explained patiently. Constantina sighed and sank into her pillows.

"Laigh samhach lass. (Lie still girl.)" A woman's voice filled her ears. It was calming but strange somehow. Constantina drew a breath and moaned at the dull pain in her chest. Her last thought was of surprise. They had been talking in Latin.

"Caileigh, she's awakening." Constantina's eyes fluttered open to a surprising sight. A weathered and heavily lined face hovered above hers – a familiar face. The woman was dressed all in white. Her hair and eyebrows were just as white. She remembered this face from a dream she had. Was it a dream? She had three young women with her also dressed in white. These girls were only slightly older than she was. Assistants she reasoned.

Constantina was more confused than frightened when she opened her eyes. She firmly believed she would die from the arrow.

The moment of confusion passed.

"I know what you are," Constantina whispered.

She spoke in heavily accented Gaelic. "I am delighted to hear you say that. Am I who I think I am?" She had an enigmatic expression but with a kind smile and the same calm eyes as Athelstan.

"Who would know better than you?" Constantina answered in a hoarse whisper.

The old woman laughed. "That is true Constantina."

"So I have been told, please call me Connie," she said in Gaelic. Caileigh's eyebrows lifted in surprise.

"Thank you, Connie, I will. Your mastery of our language is quite remarkable. There is someone here to see you." She motioned to someone behind the curtain.

A familiar face appeared. It was Quintus. Gone were the trappings of a Roman Legate. He was now dressed like any other Celtic man.

"Quintus! What are you..." Constantina winced in pain as she tried to sit forward. The pain in her chest caused her to fall back to the bed. "Must you always be so stubborn?" he asked.

"Learn from that my dear. I do not want you to try to move just yet. We had quite a time getting that arrow out of you." The older woman placed a warm hand on Constantina's brow and nodded at Saul. "Her fever is gone. I believe the worst is over," her smile lit the room like a summer sun.

"I will go for now and let you speak with your friend for a few minutes, but I will be back soon. Summon Athelstan. Inform him that she is awake," she patted Constantina's right hand that was bound tightly to her chest. Caileigh turned to Quintus.

"NO excitement!" It was not a request and he knew it. She nodded once in finality.

They waited until the Healers had departed.

"You have to find out something for me," Constantina whispered, "What am I doing here?"

"I do not take orders from you. Why are you pretending to be..."

"Shhhh! Answer me!" she gasped, her voice raw and scratchy sounding.

Quintus leaned over to give her a ladle of water. She sucked it down greedily.

"I know exactly why you are here."

"Well?"

"It is because of your sister."

"What about her?"

"It seems she agreed to be his..." he leaned close and whispered in her ear.

Horror flashed across her features. "What?" she mouthed silently. "Oh, isn't that just like the doe-eyed slut? Quintus, you have to get me out of here. I am simply not going to stay and become breeding stock for these animals. Where are we, exactly?"

"South of Illyria and west of Macedonia. We are in the village of the Senones. Athelstan was not only able to bring these healers to you to assist with the surgery needed to save your life, but also to bring you to the land of his people. In addition, before you ask, Athelstan is attending to some important business. He will visit you when he can."

"No! Listen to me. This is not what I agreed to. I have been tricked into coming here. I have been lied to from the beginning. You have got to get me out of here and away from here now." There was some obvious confusion in her voice and her head lolled from one side to the other as she spoke.

"Who has lied to us? Athelstan?" Quintus asked.

Constantina shook her head weakly. "No Harichandan."

"What makes you say that?"

"He told me he was a general. Is he their King? Why would he send me all the way here? I could have easily taken care of it on the trail. I would not have been shot and I would not be lying here bound up like a prisoner. What game is he playing?" She tried to sit up again but the pain was too great and she slumped back with a groan. "He knows, doesn't he? Help me get up!" she commanded.

Quintus's face took on a sad look. "No – Constantina. You are precisely where you need to be and no one has lied to you. Until the moment we arrived here, Athelstan was, in fact, the General of the Senone army. When we arrived we were admitted to the Royal Hall and King Trahearn Livy was there to greet us."Quintus gave a slight shudder and fell silent.

"Where is this mysterious King Trahearn then? Why is Athelstan pretending to be their ruler?" She was confused.

"He is not pretending. I have witnessed many things in this life as you know all too well, but nothing can rival what I saw happen here that afternoon." Quintus shuddered visibly.

"He executed his King without a word – without any warning. I believe he whispered something, but my Gaelic is still not that good. He beheaded the King in front of the entire assembly. The Druids proclaimed him King on the spot." Saul heaved a sigh.

"He executed his own King?" Constantina was shocked and aghast. Her mouth was open and once she realised it, she shut it with a snap. "Why?"

"I have no idea. He gave no hint to me what he was going to do. He just stood and took his Kings head with a single clean stroke. He kept the head for some future use. It was... well, it was absolutely the most barbaric thing I have ever seen. Every word he has said to you has been the truth. I firmly believe his tongue would jump right out of his mouth if he were to utter a lie."

As if by magic, the hide doorway parted and Athelstan stepped into the partitioned room. There was a worried look on his face.

"Hello there," he said kneeling and taking her free hand. A soft smile lit his face. "Causing trouble already I hear." She shrank from him visibly. She seemed terrified.

"You have heard."

"Yes, your Majesty."

Constantina nodded. "Let's end this Majesty talk. Athelstan will do."

"What have you come to tell me?" she asked weakly.

"You are getting rather fat. I am not certain this cot can take all that weight," she swatted him in mock protest and moaned at the effort it took.

"I do not mind telling you I was worried about you. Leaving you in that cave was the hardest thing I have ever done in this life. I will not willingly leave you again."

"Harder than taking your King's head?" her tone was icy.

Athelstan blinked in surprise. "You heard that part too?" He looked over his shoulder. "Quintus, of course." Constantina had an odd expression on her face.

"What is troubling you?"

"Besides the fact that you decapitated a head of state and usurped his title? I can't imagine," she sniffed. "You are absolutely NOT going to carry his head around, or bring it here to show me!"

"What? Carry it around? What do you think I am?"

"I do not know what you are, now do I? I need to think. Please just go."

He nodded and wiped his nose with his sleeve.

"I must attend to a rather pressing matter anyway but I will come back and see you this afternoon."

Her face fell at his expression.

"What is it you need to attend to?"

"Not what, who. Papirius has arrived and I must go to meet him now," her face went pale.

"Do not go. Send your army. You are their King. Command them!"

"This is too important for me not to face him."

"I am coming with you. I want to see his face."

"Out of my way!" Caileigh demanded an instant before she reappeared through the cloth opening. "Get out," her head jerked towards the doorway.

"Only after I do this," he leaned over and kissed Connie on the forehead. Connie swung at him but missed. His cloak swirled as he turned and left.

Caileigh looked at Constantina. "He is very handsome is he not?"

"Yes, I believe I am!" came the response from beyond the doorway.

Chapter Thirty-Nine

The cool autumn breezes blew through the wide plain directly to the south of Gwennderion Glade. Four men stood in a deep field of grass, Athelstan among them. Blonde braids covered in talismans of protection blew across his face. At his side were three men, Saul, Demetrios and Quintus Maximus. Summer grasses had gone to seed and the chest–high reddish fronds undulated like a tranquil sea in the freshening breeze. The scent of morning dew and impending rain gave the air a delicate sweetness.

King Athelstan stood tall and proud and bore a grim expression. In his hand, he held the Royal Standard of Senone and upon his head sat the moldivite crown. The standard, festooned with brightly coloured streamers, feathers, furs and decorated skulls, gave him great comfort. The crown bore green gems that glittered in the muted light. He had waited a long time to meet with the architect of the attack on his homeland, the murder and rape of his people. That time was now at hand.

He glanced at Quintus. An uneasy peace had developed between these two men. Athelstan could not say he liked or even trusted him. There was respect. That accounted for a lot. The reverse also seemed to be true. Quintus was to be torn. He had a duty to the Republic of Rome to kill its enemies wherever they are encountered. Athelstan clearly qualified as an enemy of Rome, but Quintus had made a promise to Constantina not to kill him. The time was rapidly approaching to see which oath held more weight.

In the distance, a pair of red-caped outrider scouts appeared from the dense trees a mile distant. They rode well out into the field before they noticed the four motionless men. They came to a stop before both turned and retraced their path back into the forest. The long chase was finally over.

Less than half of the five hundred men who began this chase came into view in the distance. Their journey across the mountain spine had been very costly indeed. The race had taken its toll and they were a ragged, tired looking lot. Still, they formed up handsomely and with the Proconsul at their head, approached the four lone men. Titus rode beside the Proconsul. He could see the nervous confusion on the soldiers' faces. After all they had endured, this open field was where their quarry had decided to stand and fight? It suited them very well.

An eighty-yard long column of horses and men reigned to a stop sixty feet from Athelstan and his three attendants. An old man resplendent in his red and gold armour, helm and cape dismounted and marched towards the Barbarian. Papirius' arms opened and he indicated the valley of wild grass. He feigned confusion.

"What? What is this?" he asked with a smirk. He indicated the empty field around them.

"Papirius – you do not mind me calling you, Papirius? So good of you to come; I see you received my note." Athelstan smiled.

He looked the fur and armour covered Celt up and down and studied his tall standard with some interest. "So, you are this Athelstan I have heard so much about. Somehow, I thought you would be more…" he issued a snort of derision. His personal disgust of Celts was evident in his tone. "Where are they? What have you done with them? Must I have my men search for their bodies, or have you eaten the last of them?"

Athelstan frowned as if thinking. "Them? Oh, you must mean those lovely young ladies who dropped in for a visit. I have to say they were much too young to be travelling abroad alone. I sent them home," Athelstan answered smoothly. "After all, it's not like I am a… barbarian."

"What? Papirius exploded. "Sent them home?" the Proconsul sputtered.

"Yes, yes home, back to their families where they belong of course. I do wish you would at least try to keep up. Even now they are tucked safely in their mothers's arms... warm, safe, secure..." he feigned exasperation.

Papirius seemed genuinely confused. "You kidnapped the girls only to send them home? I do not understand. Why?"

"I..." Athelstan began softly, "did not kidnap anyone. The Senone King ordered that action to occur."

"Then he will die next!" Papirius thundered.

"You're too late. He is already dead."

"Who is king now?"

The big man nodded. "I am…" he winked at Demetrios.

"You made the children send these to their mothers? It was a cruel and heartless act," he exclaimed, brandishing and proffering the girls's letters. Athelstan accepted the sheaves of paper and looked them over carefully. They fell from his fingers and blew away in the wind.

"I did and it was, but what would you know about cruelty and heartlessness? No matter, it worked and it has brought you here to me," still his voice was calm.

"What did you hope to gain with these, besides your death here in this field? These slaves of yours cannot help you now. You must have known I would come Barbarian - now here I am!"

"I did and in fact, I counted on it. Now here you are. Yes, here, so far from hearth and home and safety. I could not be more pleased. Oh and these fine gentlemen who stand with me they are not slaves. They are my friends," the Celt said smiling.

Papirius looked more closely at the three. "You have fallen somewhat in stature Quintus Maximus. No matter, when I deal with this tiny rabble, I am sure I can find something for you to do in Rome."

"Like decorate a cross on the Via Appia, Proconsul?" Papirius snorted with humour.

"Just so – yes."

"Proconsul, I have so looked forward to this meeting. Shall we exchange pleasantries all afternoon, or can we talk a while?"

"You are mad! Since I came here expressly to kill you, I will do so and be gone from this accursed place." Papirius reached for his sword.

"Oh, we will have plenty of time for that later. No need to rush back to Rome on my account. As I understand it, Rome is managing just fine without you. Perhaps you should have stayed home after all instead of coming all this way 'expressly to kill me'." The Celt glanced at Quintus.

"In truth, I have it on good authority that you are to be replaced as Proconsul by unanimous proclamation... ahhh what was that fellow's name again, Quintus? Oh, that's right. It is none other than Quintus Maximus here! It would seem, Papirius, that you now owe this man your allegiance," he nodded happily and shrugged.

"Quintus?" The Roman roared. "Replace me? Impossible!" Athelstan allowed his paranoid mind to work on that for a moment. His mouth worked without sound. Hate cascaded towards Quintus who stood silent – motionless.

"Why you disloyal, traitorous dog. I will have you skinned. Skinned!"

"Capital idea, Papirius, you do that. I do believe if there were more Romans like you, there would be fewer Romans – like you." A smirk crossed Athelstan's lips but his pun was lost on his enemy. "Or would the reverse now be true. Perhaps Quintus here should have you skinned? No matter."

"It is probably for the best - you really were not a very good 'evil despot' were you? You know as evil despots go, you were sadly lacking. I think your heart was not really in it. Imagine, just a few well-chosen words from me into the ears of children and you came running like a loyal dog to heel. It shows me that you are not competent enough to herd pigs let alone govern Rome. Now you are in a place where you can do the most good for the Republic and the world."

Naked fury at the unaccustomed rebuke reddened Papirius's face. "Really? Tell me then what is so special about this place? It is an empty field."

"Do you not recognise your own grave? You stand upon it now."

"Ha! My grave." A cackling laughter filled the air. "You overestimate your chances today Senone. There are over 200 loyal knights at my command and you have only four men. I have wasted enough time with this nonsense. Prepare to die," he drew his gladius and took a step towards the King.

Saul stepped forward with a naked scimitar in his hands. With a loud clash of steel on iron. Papirius was quickly disarmed. It happened in the blink of an eye.

Titus, bristling with anger, drew his gladius and kneed his horse forward. Saul acted in the same heartbeat. A wicked looking knife suddenly appeared in his left hand then just as quickly vanished with a flick of his wrist. It rematerialized buried hilt deep in Titus' throat. Surprise and pain fought for dominance on his face as the Gladius slipped from his numb fingers. The light faded from Titus's eyes and he slowly slumped forward. With a final bloody gurgle, he fell from his mount onto the ground and moved no more. His horse simply walked past Athelstan and calmly began to graze. A murmur rippled through the ranks of the Roman Equis.

Athelstan tisked and wagged a finger in negation at the astonished older man. His tone was grim.

"No, Papirius, it is you who have overestimated your chances here. I am not the simple stupid animal you take me for. Once again, you forget where you are. You do not command here, I do. Wild is my name and in the wild is where you stand. I am King of the Elder race. My influence extends to the trees, to the winds and to all the creatures that call this land their home."

"I have heard these stories before and those are just tales told to children to keep them from wandering off. I will not be frightened by old myths." Papirius scoffed.

"I am one man, that is true. I am a man who commands the very ground upon which you now stand. You think yourself safe because you bring some ragged band of smelly horse–thugs along? You are not. You believe your words are to be obeyed simply because you utter them? It is an illusion. You are not safe here Papirius of Rome any more than that lackey of yours was – far from it. Your words make no sound here. I wield magic so powerful you can scarcely comprehend it. You dare stand before ME, filled to overflowing with swagger and piss? You do not understand your peril. I can call up an army from the very grass around you." His intense stare was having its effect and Papirius looked about nervously for a moment before letting a slow smile cross his lips. Athelstan nodded sadly.

"Nonsense. No one can make an army simply appear out of nothing, or I would have done so myself. The truth is that your people died upon the swords of the Illyrians. Your women now service their soldiers." His men laughed nervously at his joke but they too looked around with uncertainty. Papirius turned to accept his due like a common actor.

"Very well then. Behold the power of a Celtic King and despair," he turned a full circle with his arms outstretched and chanted in Gaelic. Some of the mounted warriors chuckled at the bizarre antics of this wild man. He completed his turn and raised his standard high overhead.

"Sons of Freedom, Arise!" He bellowed and plunged the staff deep into the ground. A moment later four thousand Celtic warriors appeared in an unbroken sea around them. It was as if they sprang forth out of the very earth. All their faces, hair and clothing had been whitened with ashes and it gave them an unearthly aspect.

A deafening howl of rage erupted at the same instant and the Celts began to bang weapons on shields. To a man, they rushed forward to form a tight impenetrable ring around the Romans and their King. The effect was absolutely devastating. Quintus looked around and the colour drained from his face.

The ordered ranks of Roman cavalry disintegrated instantly as the men fought to get their mounts and their brutally shattered wits under control. Papirius's eyes opened as wide as they could and his knees very nearly failed him. What seemed like certain victory had been mercilessly snatched away.

Athelstan's face darkened menacingly. He walked around the stunned Papirius. "Can you see your grave now Papirius? Your road back to home goes through them and us and me. You will never see Rome again and I can feel Rome rejoicing already." The Proconsul gaped but remained speechless.

In a loud voice, Athelstan began.

"Papirius Aurelius Cursor, you are personally responsible for the attack on my lands and people. You have unlawfully sanctioned the deaths of Senone women, children and old men too weak, or feeble to defend themselves. The Gods have delivered you into my hands for judgment. I, Athelstan Epona, rightful King of Senone, hereby condemn you to death for your treachery." A giant cheer erupted from the Celts.

"Justice will be served today and because your own ego was too large to comprehend the depths of your stupidity, I will now rid the world of you. However, there is the small matter of your men. I am assured by Quintus Maximus, that they are good soldiers. It is my judgment that they should be allowed to return home unharmed. I do this for three reasons. First, I hold them blameless and in truth, they have likely suffered enough already just bringing you here. Second, they will tell Rome what has happened here today. Third… it is the civilised thing to do. Tell your Senate this; Senone will defend her people, she will defend her lands and she will exact a full and merciless accounting from her enemies. Mount up Proconsul Quintus Maximus. Mount up. You're leaving here forever." he commanded and pointed south. The mounted Romans looked around unsure what to do.

"Leaving? Why are you doing this?" he asked in a whisper.

Athelstan leaned forward and answered in kind, "Because I must let you go. Be the leader I know you are. Go. Now, or join him in death."

"Quintus looked at the host of ashen soldiers surrounding him. "You really do wield magic!"

"Yes, I really do. Ponder this. Only my enemies need fear me. My friends do not. Be a friend for both our sakes."

Before the Legate mounted Titus' horse and took his place at the head of the column he said, "Have a care Celt. Constantina - she is not what she appears to be." Their eyes met.

"Few women are," Athelstan called back.

Quintus nodded and saluted Athelstan. "You are a man of honour. I will remember you." He turned and spat on Papirius who was trying to remount his own horse. Quintus kicked him in the face, turned and led the Legion Equis from the field. Before he travelled more than a few yards he turned and called back.

"Should we meet in battle again, I will kill you."

"I fear it is your fate to try."

A corridor of jeering Celts opened to the south. The Romans needed no further urging and the red-cloaked soldiers calmly filed away to the howling protests of Papirius. He was red-faced and shrieking. When they were out of sight, the Proconsul turned back to Athelstan. Naked fear was in his eyes.

"I am so glad we have had this little chat." Athelstan turned and began to walk away. "We really must do this again sometime," he called over his shoulder.

"Wait! You cannot leave me alone here!" Papirius pleaded crying in terror.

The King stopped and turned. "My dear Proconsul, I would not dream of leaving you alone here.

He turned his back on Papirius for the final time. He raised his battle standard above his head.

"Take him!"

A tide of bloodthirsty men poured over the helpless Roman. On his walk, back to the glade Athelstan and his friends collected bunches of wildflowers for Constantina.

"Saul remarked, "Ewe have an interesting way of creating enemies."

"It is a gift."

Chapter Forty

"Dead? The One is dead? Are you certain?" the Hooded Man asked.

"She took an arrow in the chest. The arrow was meant for the Celt. Aye saw her fall before Aye was forced by that monster and his Roman lackey to withdraw. Aye am an assassin after all nut a warrior. Aye have never seen anyone survive such a wound. Those creatures ewe sent with me were worthless, cowardly dogs. Aye spit on their graves. Once the fight began, they scattered and died quickly," Acaph commented casually. He was the only man who was not frightened to be in the presence of the Exalted One.

"So you did not see The One die. Ve vonder – perhaps confirmation of this can be found," he hissed. "Go into their lands – quietly – and find out for us. Somehow Ve have our doubts."

"Master, nothing could be more certain. She could nut possibly have survived." Acaph oozed confidence.

"So far nothing concerning this Senone animal has been certain. Everything has gone badly. The assassins failed because of that man. The kidnappers failed because of that man. The trackers have failed because of that man. He must be a vizard of some sort. Ve are never thvarted, yet this man has thvarted us at every turn. Ve will not take anything for granted. Ve vant proof, The One is dead. You vill bring us this proof," the Hooded Man commanded.

Acaph inclined his head. "As ewe wish Master. Aye will bring ewe either proof she lies dead, or Aye will bring her back to ewe alive."

"No. If The One does live, tell her everything The Other has told us. Tell her to take the beast for a husband. Bring vord back to us. Ven he is comfortable in his skin, then bring her back to us. Ve will be in that house in Pella. Bring proof to us there."

"As ewe wish, Master, however this time, Aye will do it my way if it pleases ewe. Directing fools is not something Aye find enjoyable. Too many complications for my liking." Snake sneered.

"Very vell. Keep in mind the price of failure. This time ve vant results, not excuses."

Acaph chuckled. It was a cold humourless sound. "No need to worry Master. Ewe know me. Aye never fail."

✝

Caileigh's serene face showed some concern as her charge refused to have more than a few sips of the steaming broth. "Listen to me my child; you have suffered a terrible injury. You must try to eat. It is important you start to regain your strength."

Constantina was the worst kind of patient anyone could have. She had known that for a long time. Saul frequently told her that. Holding the cup in her hand, she sipped and then groaned, her stomach turning in knots. "I will try again later," she said resting back against the pillows. "I am just not up to it now."

The older woman gently felt Constantina's cheek with the back of her hand like mothers have done to daughters since the beginning of time. "Na stamagan ti – teth!" She said over her shoulder and an aide jumped to make a hot mint tea for her stomach.

"Have you been feeling like this for long?" she asked Constantina suddenly.

"Not very long, I imagine. Why do you ask? Athelstan gave me some leaves to chew that helped when my stomach got queasy like this."

"He remembers his lessons. I am so happy." She was handed a clear tea that brightened the room with its pungent smell. "Did the leaves smell like this?" she asked bringing the cup close to Connie's nose.

"Yes," Constantina said drawing back a bit. "This is much stronger smelling than the leaves were. Are you going to make me drink this?" Constantina said frowning down into the cup.

"Yes. Let me help you sit up." She reached behind Constantina's back and lifted her up. A gentle, virtually unfelt hand strayed to her lower belly. She felt Constantina's stomach muscles clench as she sat up. Caileigh felt something else too. "Here, have a small sip," she instructed holding the cup up to her lips.

"Must I?" Constantina asked. "It is just so strong. Can't I simply just rest again? I am very tired."

"It will help. Please, just a small sip."

Constantina took a sip of the pungent drink. It helped make her stomach feel better.

"Where did you get this cut?" She probed Connie's ribs.

"That? I don't remember."

Caileigh frowned and felt Connie's head.

"What are you doing?"

"Did you hit your head in that fall? One simply does not forget a wound like this."

Connie simply shrugged.

"Connie, I have something to tell you." The older woman's wise grey eyes fastened on Constantina.

"Can it wait? I am just so tired. I do not seem to have the energy to do anything other than sleep."

"Not at all. I know how difficult this has been. This could make you happy, but it can wait if you would rather," she motioned that Constantina should have one more sip.

Constantina lifted to drink from the cup and began to feel slightly better. "Happy?" Constantina asked surprised. "What is it?"

"You are carrying a new life," she placed her hand back on Constantina's belly. "Here. You carry his child." she watched her reaction closely.

"New life?" Constantina asked. Her hand then went to her belly and she repeated again. "New life?" she said in shock. "Oh no, this cannot be."

A soft chuckle rippled through the Druidess like a gentle rain. "The Gods and I disagree. I may not know their minds but I can spot the glow of a 'mother to be' at a distance and in absolute darkness. You must have really hit your head. There is no mistake Constantina. You are pregnant." A knowing smile lit the old woman's face.

Both of Constantina's hands went to her belly. "I am going to have a baby?" she whispered in stunned disbelief.

Strong hands restrained her from standing. "You should not try to move. There can be no doubt. It is his child and I can tell it is strong within you."

"But I have not... I mean we have never..." she paused and thought this through. "Please, I have to go."

The Druidess helped her stand. "I know this must come as a surprise, but any new life must be seen as a joyous gift from the Gods. You have been selected above all others to nurture this life. That is how special you are to them. Everything will be fine. You will see."

"A child? I cannot have a child," was all she could say. Clearly, she appeared not to know understand how this could have happened.

"Again, the Gods and I would disagree. When are we going to tell him?" Caileigh advised.

Constantina said. "We cannot tell him anything."

"He will need to be told at some point. Not because he is the father, not because he is King. He has shown a profound dislike for secrets. I can tell him for you if you would prefer."

She swayed with sudden dizziness. "NO! I beg of you, say nothing to him."

"Say nothing to whom?" A cheery question came from the doorway. "Should you be out of bed?" Athelstan stood inside the healer's pavilion clutching a bundle of wildflowers and stray bits of grass. He was in an exuberant mood. Demetrios was with him.

Struggling to remain standing, Constantina looked at Caileigh in fear. It was very clear that she say nothing.

"What is wrong? Please say nothing to me about what? What are you hiding?" He walked forward to help Caileigh return Constantina to the bed. Worry had instantly replaced jubilation. Caileigh quietly took Demetrios aside.

"I am fine and what makes you think we are talking about you?" she asked not fighting either of them. "You know how stubborn I am. Are those for me?" she asked changing the subject. Athelstan nodded.

"My Uncle?" she quiried

"Your Husband you mean? It is done." It was delivered in a flat tone. She gave a curt nod.

"HUSBAND?" she shook her head in surprise. "Quintus?"

"I let him go. He once again leads his men."

A thin smile crossed his lips as he handed the perfumed blooms to Constantina.

"If I am not mistaken I asked a question that someone is going to answer right now," he glanced from Constantina to Caileigh. "What is going on here?" He had a look that precluded defiance on anyone's part. "Well?"

Constantina frowned. "Do not take that tone with me," she said defiantly.

"Or with me!" Caileigh barked. She spun on her heel and marched away. Demetrios intercepted her.

In the background, Caileigh and Demetrios began a quiet conversation. He glanced at Constantina and gestured to his own ribs.

Caileigh blurted out, "Seven weeks ago? No. Not possible, three at most."

"I was there." Demetrios corrected, "It was seven." Caileigh stared at him in confusion.

A long silence followed before Athelstan whispered. "I had no right to speak to you like that. I can see that something is wrong and if you let me, perhaps I can help fix it." He sat on her bedside and took her hands gently in his. She pulled them away.

She shook her head. "Ha! You cannot fix this. Damn you, Athelstan, damn you. Why do you have to be so…?" she said lowering her head.

"Well if it is not me, then what is it? Did someone offer you an insult? Is it your wound?" He paused a moment. "Is it this place? I know it must seem crude and brutish but we are a simple people trying to live a simple life in peace," he hung his head. "You must hate it here."

Her mood softened. "It is nothing of the sort. Your people are kind and friendly. They have taken very good care of me."

He was baffled and his face showed it. "I do not understand," feeling genuinely helpless to discover what was troubling her. He shrugged and was silent.

"I am fine. This is a woman thing. It is not your concern," she said touching his face.

He realised it had been a long time since she had done that. She was looking at him again as if for the first time.

"Come on then, lie back and rest." He let her settle into the pillows. He used his fingers to brush her hair. She reached up and pulled the collar of his shirt aside.

"Tell me about those tattoos. They have a meaning I suppose?"

"Yes. They tell the story of my life." He opened his shirt. These show that I am firstborn to a noble family and that I have a younger sister."

"Sister? I don't recall you talking about a sister. What is her name?"

"Rowena – Ro. I have not seen her for a long time." Connie nodded.

"This one is given to a boy when he comes of age and enters the army. Some recall events both past and future. I will soon be given a mark proclaiming me King. It will go here." He pointed to his breastbone. He looked at her for several heartbeats.

"I am glad I met you, very glad," he said suddenly and handed her the cup of soup.

Constantina reached out to touch his chest and arm. "I think I am too," she had a faraway look in her eyes. "We are very different," she said returning to the present, the look was gone and a smile returned as well. "What are you going to do today?"

"I am doing exactly what I want to do today. I am talking to the most beautiful woman on earth. The question really is, what has everyone else planned for me to do today. Frankly, I have no idea and care even less," he knew she needed her rest but it was just good to be here. "I should let you sleep. We will have plenty of time to talk once you are stronger."

She nodded. "I will miss you, I think."

"You say that now, but I will probably become quite a pest." He brushed her button nose with a forefinger. "I am going to meet with Saul and Demetrios. There are some things I need to discuss with them and yes, we will probably be talking about you."

She smiled. "Really? What about?"

At that moment, a soldier entered and whispered something in Athelstan's ear. He glanced at the man and nodded.

"A great number of things actually. I would like to ask Saul and Demetrios to retrain those forces that will accompany us to Milan. I expect King Cassander will either bring another team of negotiators or an army. I want to be ready for either. Moreover, you will be getting out of here soon and proper quarters need to be found. Saul will help arrange things to your liking," he smiled. "I am also going to find out if you are ticklish and where." A wicked twinkle flickered in his eyes.

She seemed puzzled. "Ticklish? What makes you think I am ticklish?" she asked.

"Just a premonition. We shall see. Just rest now. Is there anything you need?"

"No."

He kissed her forehead and then her lips. "Sleep well. I will see you when you awake."

Constantina watched him walk away and her hands went to her belly unconsciously.

"Going back to Italia are you?" she whispered then closed her eyes and fell fast asleep.

Chapter Forty-One

Demetrios had waited patiently for a time when he could be alone to speak with Saul. He placed a hand on his shoulder and motioned the Jew to follow him. They came to a stop in a line of pickets where horses grazed on second cut hay. They stamped and nickered noisily.

"What is it, my stoic friend?" Saul asked with an easy tone.

"I overheard you back in Athens."

"Did ewe now."

"Yes. Is it true?"

 "Is what true?"

"What you said to Leonida about Athelstan."

"Aye always strive to tell the truth friend Demetrios." The Greek shook his head.

"We are not friends Saul. I have told you that before. We have never been - friends. I think it is important that you understand that."

"Aye see. Very well then, what did ewe hear?"

"Queen Leonida asked you, 'Why did you not want her to tell Athelstan what you really are?' What did she mean by that? What are you that she would ask such a question?" Saul's eyes narrowed slightly.

There was a pause.

"Now is nut a good time for ewe to know this Demetrios."

"Yes, you said that before too. You said, 'For now, Aye will be the pilgrim - who seeks.' You also said, 'Aye will be a friend who he can count on. In time, he will discover the truth.' I do not believe you are his friend at all. So, I ask you now, what do you seek? What is this truth you keep so carefully guarded?"

"It is a truth given to me by my God. Aye can nut say more," Demetrios was about to speak but Saul held up a finger. "Have a care Demetrios. Ewe are about travel down a very dangerous road."

"So are you Saul. Know this, if you ask Athelstan, he will respect your secrecy."

Saul seemed taken aback by this. "My secrecy?"

"He will take your secret to his grave if you ask him. It is not necessary for you to dig that grave for him."

"Ewe know this for certain?" Saul's expression was one of deadly intensity.

"I do. Saul and I will tell you this also and be forewarned. If you do plan to dig graves, 'Friend Saul', dig two of them. The second will surely be for one of us." Demetrios left Saul to ponder his words. The Spartan hoped they would be heeded.

†

Athelstan stepped out and the late afternoon sun was bright. A cool wind blew down from the mountains and his nose told him that the first snows would soon be here. His earlier meeting with Cedric and Demetrios went well. The two men seemed to like each other from the moment they met. Demetrios was much harder to read than the Celt. They began immediate preparations to select and train an elite force of fighters. If any battle with Macedonia were to occur, these soldiers would be left out of it.

A nobleman of one of the clans hurriedly closed on Athelstan. He seemed agitated.

"Lord Gwelf, is it?" Gwelf nodded. "We think there is a spy in the compound. A guard has reported seeing someone climbing the western wall, but he disappeared."

"Find him and have him brought to me. Gather whatever manpower you need. Do it now. Do it quietly." Gwelf nodded and fled at a full run. Athelstancast about for a senior commander. Menniob was tending his horse.

"Menniob," he called. "We have an intruder. He came over the west wall. Gather the guard and help Lord Gwelf and his men find him." Menniob nodded and drew an ox horn from his saddlebags. He blew two long blasts and one short one. The effect was like stirring an ant nest.

"What does he look like?"

"I would suspect, like someone you have never seen before. Now GO!" He grabbed a soldier running past.

"Find ten good men. Arm them and set them to guard the infirmary." The man gave a curt nod and charged off. Even from a mile, Athelstan could see the newly built gates being closed and barred. Whoever this intruder was, he might be able to get in, but not out. Athelstan turned full circle very slowly. Sentry stations were being strengthened. Trackers were already getting final instructions and heading off in all four compass points. Everything was being thoroughly searched. Athelstan stood and waited in the shade of an elm tree.

"They'll never find me you know," said a voice. Athelstan flinched. He knew the voice immediately. He shook his head.

"What makes you think we're looking for you? "

"I would be mightily hurt if they were not."

Athelstan turned around with an expression that was part scowl and part smile. Behind him, a most curious creature lounged easily against the elm trunk. He blended in so well it was difficult to tell where the tree ended and where the man began.

"Lord Greynoc! You old Mongrel," Athelstan exclaimed with ill-concealed delight. The two men embraced warmly.

"The very same my Lord Athelstan! I am astonished you remember that far back. Are you going to call off the search now?"

"No indeed. I am going to order my army to beat the bushes with sticks until the intruder is found."

"Then we should repair indoors. I would hate to have to kill your entire army one man at a time armed only with the first man's stick." They walked toward the Royal compound.

"I suppose I should call you King Athelstan now? Athelrix?" said Greynoc.

"Athelstan will do quite nicely. I took your advice."

"You followed your conscience, you mean. I offered you no advice."

"You helped me see clearly."

"It is the duty of the aged to do so. I will now offer both my condolences to your nation and my congratulations to you."

"I graciously accept both, sir."

As they walked, those who saw them came to a complete stop. Many of them just stared. Others shook their heads and rubbed their eyes to clear the strange vision. Their King was walking and talking with a bush. The bush was also walking and talking to their King. It was proving difficult for many, to determine which was worse.

As they approached the doorway Athelstan called out, "Make preparations, a room for our guest and a feast in his honour. This is Lord Greynoc leader of the nation of Rhaetia. Lord of the mountains and the forests. King of the Invisible people. Let all who see him, make him welcome. He is a friend. It is by his kindness alone that I live."

Nothing could have jolted Senone more profoundly that discovering a creature of legend was suddenly walking among them. The title King of the Invisible People shot through the compound. Many did not believe it at first. The Great Hall filled with the curious like it had sprung a leak. Soon the doors had to be shut.

"You are going to be a bit of a curiosity here."

"Wait until they discover some of my people have been in your compound for the last five days. You might want to tear your walls down and try again. Setting walls flat upon sand…" Athelstan frowned and made a gesture that suggested they dug their way under the walls. Greynoc nodded.

"Oh, my dear friend, you might want to keep those two bits of news to yourself." Athelstan called out. "There is no intruder. Call off the search. Pass the word."

Day turned to night and an additional five strangely attired Rhaetians were welcomed warmly into the hall. They sat with Athelstan and Caileigh in places of honour at the head table. They ate, drank and sang until quite late.

"Of course it goes without debate that I am delighted to see you again

Greynoc. Still, I have to ask, how are the twins and why have you come here?"

"They are in good health and it is because of them that I am here. Several weeks ago, they told me I had to come. They said you were in danger."

"I am always in danger. Did they say in danger from what?"

"They didn't say. You know how they are. I was sent here to protect you," Greynoc grinned. It was like looking at a wrinkled tree.

"You are aware I am surrounded by a huge army."

"Yes. What if you are in danger from it?"

"I can't argue with that logic."

"My people are on their way. It will still be weeks before they arrive. Ludmilla and Ratia say do not do anything rash until they get here."

"That might prove difficult. I am going to get married."

"Ah, that is wonderful." He clapped Athelstan on the shoulder. "Does she know yet?"

Athelstan's face fell slightly. "Well, no not exactly." Greynocs' eyebrows rose slightly.

"Still, you found a nice Senone girl. I am happy for you." The tree wrinkled a little more.

"She's a Roman girl actually." The tree suddenly unwrinkled.

"A Roman girl? Do you think that's wise?" Greynoc's asked.

Athelstan just shrugged.

Constantina huddled under the heavy bedding against the crisp bite in the air. Night was falling earlier now. The crispness of autumn was in the air. Braziers of glowing coals kept the real cold at bay. She drifted in and out of sleep. Her dreams were closer to nightmares. The pain in her chest and side was abating but, when she tried to move, there were moments of stabbing pain that astounded her.

The pavilion of the healers was silent. Indeed, it seemed almost empty. As she hovered just above sleep voices came to her from another area. One of them had a familiar tone to it. She could not hear the words but they were being spoken in an elegant and precise manner. She had heard someone speak like this before but she was still too tired to make a connection. Connie strained to hear.

"No, it is much too late for visitors. You can see her in the morning." This was spoken by one of Caileigh's young assistants and it was tinged with irritation.

"Of course. How insensitive of me dear lady. Aye beg your forgiveness. Until tomorrow then." The healer's reply was in the form of a short gasp. Footsteps slowly approached. Someone was quietly searching behind all the screens. She huddled deeper into her bedding and held her breath. The curtain to her alcove was slowly drawn back and someone in a dark cape and hood leaned in. The intruder sniffed the air, slipped inside and closed the curtain behind him.

"Ewe are - awake?" His voice was a precise and cultured whisper.

"Acaph?" Constantina hissed. "You have come at last."

"As commanded by the Master, Aye have come to find The One. Aye have come to be certain, The One still lives and to speak with The One." He was beautiful with a perpetual grin. His steady gaze was mesmerising. His resemblance to Saul was staggering. Only a close friend would be able to tell them apart.

"Well, it is about time. Give me my cloak. I am ready to travel. How did you get in here?"

"Presumably the same way Aye will get out."

"Are you not worried about the guards?"

"Does the wolf worry about the sheep?" asked Acaph. Constantina struggled to sit up. The cloaked figure gently pushed her back into her pillows. His left hand glittered with rings of sapphire and gold.

"Ewe are commanded - to remain here," he said with a mischievous twinkle in his eye.

Constantina gasped, "Stay? I cannot stay."

"Ewe are commanded - to play your part a while longer. Ewe are commanded - to wed the Barbarian King and keep his attention focused on - ewe rather than on what - we are doing." There were significant pauses in his speech pattern that set him apart from anyone else she had ever known.

"I will not wed that – that creature!"

"Are ewe certain? Ewe know the price of disobedience." He smiled sweetly and waggled a slender blade before her eyes.

She glared at the blade with horror before nodding in silence. The cloaked figure smiled and wiped the bloodstained knife on a fine white linen handkerchief. The cloth was casually tossed into the glowing brazier and he watched it burn for a few moments.

He bent low over the bed. "When the time is right, Aye will come for ewe and ewe will be reunited with our Master - once again.

She turned her head away.

"Here is what ewe need to know from - The Other." He whispered in her ear.

As he spoke, a single tear rolled down her cheek. Her twin was dead.

It was still deep night. Greynoc and his men stood by the open gates along with Athelstan, Demetrios and Saul.

"No dear boy, I will not presume on your hospitality any further by staying inside stone rooms. In truth," he said conspiratorially, "they make me feel like I lay in an empty tomb. My men and I will make our bowers in nature as we have always done. In the morning, we will be gone and rejoin those travelling here. I will be back soon enough with Ratia and Ludmilla. I wonder what your Gentle Mothers will make of them," Greynoc mused.

"I am sure they will be made most welcome. A special place will be prepared for them. All will be in readiness for their arrival."

"Then I will take my leave of you, friend Athelstan. We should arrive by Samhain unless we are delayed. It has been a pleasure to make your acquaintances, gentle folk."

"As it has been with us," Demetrios nodded and Saul bowed.

"At least take an escort. Bandits can be dangerous." Saul advised.

"Bandits will have to find us first," he said with a wink. Saul inclined his head

"As you say Greynoc. It is good to see you again." The Rhaetians turned and walked out the gates. The guards closed them and slipped heavy bars into place.

Athelstan and his men retired for the night. It had been a magical day. The first he had spent since coming down from the mountains. The first since he became King. Thoughts of that day still came to him in a rush and a blur. His mind had been so fixated on saving Constantina; he had scarcely given a thought to what might happen after he killed his King. Now that she was safe, he relived that moment over and over especially in the quiet hours of darkness. He had scarcely slept in days.

Then there was the real possibility of rebellion. Trahearn had loyal followers. Many members of several noble families now fed the crows and rats as they swung from ropes on the hanging trees. Something would have to be done before a full civil war erupted. So far, he had been a dreadful King. At the very moment when total exhaustion wrapped its silent cloak over him, there came a frantic pounding on his door.

"M'Lord!" It was Menniob. "M'Lord, come quickly. It's the infirmary. Caileigh begs you to come. There has been a death!"

Athelstan sat bolt upright and pulled on his leggings. His mind could only think of one person injured badly enough to have succumbed. His mouth went dry as ashes. He flung open the door and Menniob was hard pressed to keep up with him. They ran a third of a league in a cold drizzle. He had no shirt and was barefoot. At the infirmary, there was a chaotic tangle of activity. People were coming and going at a full run.

He slowed to a walk as he reached the entrance to the infirmary and the heavy flaps were thrown open. He immediately stepped into Constantina's alcove. She was sitting up with her knees drawn up under her chin – crying.

"Thank Epona, you are alive. Are you hurt? What happened?" She shook her head.

Caileigh arrived and she was wiping tears from her eyes. "Here." Athelstan turned.

"What has happened?"

"It is Euphemia. She has been killed."

"Your young assistant?" Caileigh nodded. "What do we know? Who did this?"

"We do not know yet. The only person in here was your friend. I came in and found her like this. Why would anyone kill a young girl like this? What danger could she possibly be?'

"Show me."

Euphemia was lying on the ground. A tiny pool of blood had collected under her left ear. Someone has plunged a narrow blade deeply into her ear and sliced her brain. She would have been dead before she started to fall. That was not the horror. She stared upwards in death with empty eye sockets.

Athelstan hugged Caileigh in a tight embrace. "We will find out who did this," he whispered.

Caileigh sobbed and nodded. Athelstan indicated silently that the body be taken away.

Athelstan returned to Connie's bed. She was under heavy guard and she was still shaking uncontrollably.

"Alright, please try to calm down. What can you tell us? Did you see anyone?" She nodded and wiped her nose.

"Get this thing off me. Get it OFF! Get it OFF!" she demanded hysterically. She began clawing at the bandage holding her arm in place.

"Alright. I will take it off. Just hold still." Someone handed him a knife and he started to cut the fabric away. "What do you remember?" She watched as the binding fell away. Once her arm was free, she lunged at Athelstan and wrapped her arms around his neck. For some time all she could do was cry. He held her tight and murmured softly to calm her. Once her tears tapered off, she looked up into his eyes. The tears finally stopped and she sniffed to clear her nose. A clean cloth was handed her.

"He said he was going to take my eyes. I have never been so scared. He showed me... He showed me... Oh by the Gods, he showed me the girl's eyes. He told me I had pretty eyes. He wants my eyes. He is coming back for my eyes. I have to get out of here." She struggled to stand. Athelstan held her close.

"No one is going to take your eyes. He will not hurt you, Connie. He will not. Look at me." She looked up. "He will not hurt you. I will not let that happen."

Her eyes widened. "It is him!"

"What?"

"The way he talks. He speaks just like Saul. Aye – Ewe – Nut... The same accent. They must all be in this together. He must be a spy. He must be. He sent that man to kill me. Why?" She was getting frantic.

"What did he say to you? Try and remember."

"He said he was coming for you. He said that your enemies were nearby and you would never see it coming. He told me you are no King, just a poser who had no business sitting upon a throne. He wanted you to know he would take everyone you trust and love away from you before the end. He said he would take me last. How did he know? I need to go home now. Do not make me stay here. Please do not make me stay here."

"Did he tell you his name?"

"Yes. He made me repeat it over and over. All I could see was the tip of his bloody knife getting closer and closer to my eyes." She shuddered. "Acaph. He said his name was Acaph and that he was coming for you. He said he was coming for all of us. I am so scared."

"You have done very well Connie." He motioned to one of the guards. "She is being moved into my rooms immediately. Set a twenty-man guard team, fully armed, four shifts, night and day. Find Saul and tell him we need to talk." He passed a weary hand over his eyes. "I must be getting too old for this."

"You're not leaving me!"

"No. I will see you safely tucked into bed in my... our rooms. I am not leaving your side until then. You will be safe there."

Caileigh came in with a cup of steaming liquid. Connie drank it down. She visibly relaxed after a few minutes. Bundled up tight against the cold Athelstan carried her into the stone-walled compound.

"Athelstan? Can you forgive me?" she whispered.

"Forgive you? For what?"

"I love you but in the last few weeks, I have treated you very badly. I have been very scared and the longer we travelled, the more frightened I became. I have been taking it out on you. Can you forgive me?"

"With all you have been through, can you forgive me?" he whispered back. She nodded silent and exhausted.

He was shivering from the cold when he re-entered the Great Hall. Servants were cleaning up the remains of the party. He headed directly to the Royal apartment. By the time he pulled up the furs and kissed her forehead, she was fast asleep.

Chapter Forty-Two

A bleary-eyed Saul slipped into the Great Hall. Aside from Athelstan seated on his throne and a squad of Royal Guards at the door, the Hall was empty.

"Aye was asleep. What is so important that it could nut wait until morning?" Athelstan's face went hard.

"One of Caileigh's assistants Euphemia has died."

"Yes?"

"What do you know of this?" Now it was time for Saul's face to harden.

"So far, only that one of the healers has died. How did she die?"

"You don't know?"

Saul looked around. The guards had closed and stood guard at the door. Athelstan leaned forward and was glaring at Saul.

"What is this? Why do ewe question me like this? Have a care how ewe answer."

Athelstan stood and closed the distance between himself and Saul. "No, YOU have a care! If it was not you, then a countryman of yours has paid us a visit. He speaks with the same accent as you do. He killed Euphemia, he took her eyes and was asking questions of..." At that moment, the doors opened. A soldier ran in and came to a stop.

"Sire, we have found something. You should come."

The soldier led them back to the healer's pavilion. People had begun the task of packing the summer structure for the winter. By the time they arrived, all work had stopped and a crowd was growing outside.

There was a bloodstain on the ground where Euphemia had died. A small group of people, including Caileigh, were standing around Constantina's pallet.

Saul bent down and picked up a curious item that lay near the blood. It was a single briar rose. Black as night it was and wholly unseasonal in this realm. He dropped it like it had burned his hand. He ground it under his sandal.

"What do you know of this, Saul?"

"A black rose. It is a message for me alone." Saul looked up and looked over his shoulder. "It is here," Saul breathed.

Athelstan looked up, angrily. "What?"

"Axum. It has come."

The King stood. "What has come?"

"That which Aye seek. It has come."

"Acaph?" Athelstan asked. Saul nodded and placed both hands on the King's shoulders. He nodded gravely.

"Ewe know his name?"

"I know a great many things, Saul. I know that this Acaph is from Jeru-Salam. I know he is your countryman. What does he want with us? Is he Axum?"

"He is a great number of things, foremost among them, he is my brother."

"He is the brother you spoke to in Athens?"

"No. He is one Aye do nut speak of. It is nut good that the Gatherer has come among us. Ewe are in grave danger friend Ath-el-Stan. We all are. Take your King to safety and guard him well. Aye will be back, or Aye will nut. My God alone must now decide. Aye must find the Gatherer and lay him low, or perish in the attempt." He kissed the King on both cheeks, turned and fled the Hall.

"Stop!" Athelstan commanded. "Follow him. Do not let him out of your sight. Bring him back here along with anyone he meets!"

Saul did not have to search. He knew where Acaph would be waiting. The area would favour this trained killer. He knew when he had found the appointed place. The Senone guards were easy to evade.

"Shalom — Brother," came an all too familiar whisper from the near total darkness.

"Aye fear that peace between us will nut be possible, this day," Saul said. There was a tinge of sadness in his voice. A younger copy of Saul of Jeru-Salam stepped into the small clearing. There was a refined and cultured grace to his movements. He carried a long flat box.

"Aye as well have waited for this moment to arrive as we both knew it would." The younger man stepped forward and placed the ancient box on the ground in front of Saul.

It was ornately carved of wormwood and inset with mother of pearl. There was a split, double hinged lid that the newcomer opened. He stood and stepped back.

"Aye recognise that box Acaph."

"So ewe should, it is yours."

Inside were two identical knives. The silver and onyx handles bore a family crest. The blades were engraved with two halves of a Hebrew prayer – Yizkor – half on one and half on the other.

כי אני רוצה מבלי ,המורה שלי שהלך לעולמו העליון שלו ,זכור הנשמה של האבא שלי לחייב את עצמי עם נדר לתרום צדקו

ועם ,תהא נשמתו כרוך בקשר חיים עם נשמות אברהם יצחק ויעקב ,ובזכות זה .למענו אמן ,ונאמר ;צדיקים אחרים שנמצאים גן עדן

The prayer read:

May God remember the soul of this man who has gone to his supernal world, because I will - without obligating myself with a vow - donate charity for his sake. In this merit, may his soul be bound up in the bond of life with the souls of Abraham, Isaac and Jacob, Sarah, Rebecca, Rachel and Leah and with the other righteous men and women who are in Gan Eden; and let us say, Amen.

Saul did not have to read it. He had seen this inscription since he was a child. He knew the words by heart.

"It is fitting that ewe bring these blades," Saul said with reverence.

"It is equally fitting that we use them now to put an end to our dispute. Too long has it sat upon my soul," countered Acaph.

"Our father who sits with God would approve, Aye think," said Saul reverently.

Acaph nodded. "Are ewe now ready to embrace him in the presence of our God?"

"Aye am. Are ewe also ready to embrace him in the presence of our God?"

"Aye am. As eldest, it is for ewe to select first." Acaph stated.

Saul bent and looked at both blades. He sniffed them and looked up, "Poison?"

Acaph inclined his head, "The Puff Adder. It is our way," Acaph said.

"It is our way."

Saul chose one blade and then Acaph took the other.

"So it comes to this. Would that we could have foreseen this as children," Acaph mused.

"The end comes for us each in our appointed time brother. Remember me with reverence to your offspring as I shall also do," Saul countered. The niceties had been completed. Only one thing remained.

It is said that a knife fight is like the trunk of the tree. It is that from which all other branches of warfare stem. Axe, sword, spear and lance, all need close combat at their foundation. When all these aspects of war are perfected and brought together in the dance of a knife fight, the tree flowers beautifully. To perfect the knife fight is to perfect the personal art of war.

They twirled, dipped, rolled, sprang in and out using an unspoken language all their own. This language involves both their bodies and an external source: their enemies mind. While fighting, they had to control every minuscule part of their bodies while also learning how to time their own movements and divine the intentions of their foe. It forced the fighters to consider their environment in a different way. One mistake and the dance would end abruptly.

Their feet whispered in the long grass. The steel blades whistled though the air. The poisoned tips came within a hair's breadth of contacting flesh and blood, but each time, their flesh was left pristine – untainted. Their breathing became more laboured yet the ferocity of the battle increased in tempo. Each thrust was blocked. Each riposte was parried. The tiny clearing was filled with a staccato of ringing steel against steel. The blades of the knives were all but invisible.

There was no pause. No quarter was offered or expected. Not a word was spoken. Not a single movement — wasted. In the end, one man would walk away tasting of the free air of life. The other would remain where he fell until the ending of the world.

Saul saw that opening he sought and pressed his advantage with a hard lunge. Acaph saw a similar moment and sprang forward also to take advantage. There was a sharp ring as the two blades met and held.

Saul cocked his head to the left slightly. Acaph did the same from his side. These men were so evenly matched that the knives met point to point. Two powerful thrusts were stopped. One stopped the other on the head of a pin. Their eyes met and in that briefest moment, the fighters smiled, each giving a slight bow to the other. Each acknowledged the others skill. They stepped away and began to circle again.

"Why did ewe leave, Acaph?" Saul asked. "We might have avoided this day."

"Aye can serve one master with grace, but Aye will nut serve a lesser man."

"Aye am nut a lesser man. Aye was your better."

"In station only brother, nut in skill as Aye am going to show ewe now."

It was a bold move on Acaph's part. With a snap of his wrist, he hurled his knife at Saul. Saul moved his head aside and the knife whistled past his right ear. Now Acaph was unarmed. Saul took a single step forward to finish the fight.

The tip of Saul's tongue and lips started to grow numb. Acaph stood motionless. Saul looked down and watched a single drop of blood fall past his nose to the ground. It struck a golden alder leaf with a tiny splash. His fingers went to his earlobe and came away bathed in crimson.

He took a second step. It was unsteady and with the third step, he faltered and fell. The pale autumn grasses swam upwards towards his face and he felt the sensation of them tickling his nose.

Acaph took Saul's knife from his hand and set it on the ground. He studied Saul's face for a moment before saying a final two words in parting.

"Shalom — Brother." Saul's eyes closed. He took a final shuddering breath before becoming very still.

Acaph licked one of the knives. He replaced the knives in the box and latched it closed. He lay down beside his brother, took his position on the ground, and slipped unconscious. Two cloaked and hooded men materialized from the gloom of the forest. They cut Acaph's ear, gathered up the knives and the unconscious Saul, and calmly walked away.

Chapter Forty-Three

The early morning's tumult was indescribable. All of Senone had been shocked into chaotic activity. Military commanders rushed in and out of the royal compound. Everyone was shouting orders. A lifeless shape was carried in. Constantina could not see who it was. Caileigh was fighting tears as she shouted for quiet and order. She got neither. Tersely, she ordered the apprentices to bring herbs, boil water, and prepare poultices. Constantina heard the word poison several times. She was certain of the source but not the victim. Everyone from cooks to nobles all jostled for space within the narrow hallways.

If it was the King who fought for life, Constantina believed it was only a matter of time before suspicion fell upon her. The time had come to leave this place. Her death at the hands of these savages would hardly further the cause she had committed to so long ago. Her Master would have to find another way to punish these unbelievers.

She quickly dressed. Several packets of the pain-relieving leaves were set on a small table in Athelstan's room. She grabbed them all, stuffed them in a sack she found in a pile of discarded clothing and slipped out of the room. With everyone focused on the wounded man, she was all but invisible. It could be hours before she would be missed.

Her next stop was the kitchen and there were only three people inside working. No one noticed her grabbing hot bread and a heel of cheese. These, she also crammed into the sack. With careful steps, she headed for the entrance. Not a single person noticed her leave. Not a single person tried to stop her. She simply walked away and her tiny form melted into the trees.

Athelstan looked down at the still body of Saul. He was ghostly – a faint translucent spectre. In death, he projected both a simplicity and a complexity that beggared all words. Death did not become him. Long deliberate strides drove him away from the campfires and into the slate-grey morning. He was in an absolute state of shock and did not want to be around people. His legs took him out of the royal compound and randomly away. He scarcely noticed where he was going, or even that he was climbing. Even in the early dawn, the autumn riot of colour was evident. Thick carpets of leaves lay upon the ground like halos around the tree trunks. He kicked at them idly as he stormed up the twisting trail.

The air cooled suddenly as he passed the tree line. The higher he climbed, the louder the roaring in his ears became. Small stunted bushes and mountain grasses would have jumped clear of the fiery king if they could. He swept past them all – unseeing – uncaring.

Then the climb was over and he reached the hill's domed rocky top. This hilltop covered a vast area and a smooth path ringed its circumference. The King slowed and took a breath. He simply would not accept that Saul was dead.

Athelstan finally stopped and looked around. He was actually surprised to find he had climbed the Hill of the Four Winds. This ancient path had been walked by countless generations of Senones. Four stone seats had been carved into the living rock of this hill long ago. Each seat faced a different direction and he discovered he stood before the Raven seat facing west. The Swan seat faced east and it was where the path up the hill ended. The southern facing seat was decorated with images of Wolves and the northern seat bore the antlers of the Stag.

He stared at the ancient chair for many long minutes as his frustration grew to an explosive level. He suddenly turned and released a deafening howl.

"Why?" he asked. The crisp empty air did not respond at first. "Why did he die?" A faint voice answered him.

"Not dead." whispered the wind. "Only dormant, like the trees." The sound of a female filled the air around him.

He spun on his heel to see who spoke but the hill was empty. He stared at the empty stone seat. It was covered in twigs and dead leaves. He felt entirely forsaken.

Weariness had descended upon him and had settled heavily in his chest. He sat in the Raven Throne and buried his face in his hands. He rubbed his eyes with the heels of his hands and shivered slightly at the rising wind. With a low groan, he leaned back and rested his head against the cold stone of Raven's breast. When he opened his eyes, a shimmering being stood before him. It was a woman and he could see the grey scenery clearly through her. Something familiar tugged at him as he looked at her. "Do I know you spirit? Why do you torment me? What do you know of me that would bring you here at this hour to mock me?"

She smiled. "I know you very well Athelstan Epona. Perhaps I know better than you do."

He blinked at the insubstantial ghost. "You are Celeste? You are the spirit of my mother?"

She smiled. "I have borne the name Celeste and many others too," she said and moved closer. "It is good to see you again, my son.

"Why do you come to me now? Have I not been worthy of your presence until now?"

"You have never been unworthy of anything," she said stepping closer so he could make out her features. "I come to you now because you have need of me, today."

He nodded and then did recognise her. "Perhaps I do need your council today. It is good to see you again," he smiled at the spirit. "What am I to do

Celeste–spirit? I have lost someone dear to me today."

She smiled at her son. "Why then, do you not seek her?" The word seek stung him.

"I cannot. He has joined his ancestors this day."

"You did not answer my question. I know the nature of your loss, but it is not the loss you think. An item of great value is lost in a dark place, while you sit in the light and mourn the living."

He sat perfectly still. "I do not understand you. You speak in riddles."

"Prophecy is like that. I only speak the truth. An item of great value carries your heir. Find it and bring it into the light."

"How I can mourn the living?" The spirit stood motionless.

"Heir? I am to be a father?" The spirit nodded again.

"Do not let the 'treasure' fade to dust. Beware, the 'curse' is very near at hand." The spirit began to fade. Athelstan sat forward as these words sank into his brain. He was about to ask a question when the vision faded. He caught a brief glimpse of a gentle smile before it was gone.

The words of the twins came forward. 'The item of great value.' 'One is a treasure one is a curse.' At last, it all made sense to him. Constantina was indeed the treasure and this monster Acaph was the curse. Nothing could be clearer now.

He sat for what seemed like a short time pondering the words of Celeste. A day had passed in the space of an hour before he came back to himself.

A scent reached his nose. He turned and sniffed the air. He had no time to waste on random smells and turned to head back the way he had come. He smelled it again and it triggered a memory.

He stopped and the scent reached his nose again. Was he going mad? He could not keep her out of his mind and now her delicate scent was filling his nose. Would there be no end to this? He turned to retrace his steps back and another apparition greeted him. Constantina stood several yards away looking at him. He blinked and realised this was no apparition. " Constantina? What are you doing up here?" He was not sure if he should be happy, or furious. She was dressed in a simple shift, sandals, and light cloak. She shivered in the biting wind. He suddenly understood. This was no ordinary girl. She was exceptionally tough to have made it all the way here in her condition. "Constantina!" He sprinted towards her.

Chapter Forty-Four

With a shudder, she slumped to the ground. Blood loss had finally taken its toll.

He wrapped her in the white fur cloak and laid her down out of the wind in the shelter of the Ravens' wings. She was shivering uncontrollably. Her lips and fingertips were turning blue.

"What are you doing?" she asked

"If you think for one heartbeat that I am going to let you freeze to death up here you are very much mistaken. You bleed." He settled down beside her and she clung to his warmth.

An odd snuffling sound could be heard. One could hear the creature long before it came into view. Once he caught sight of the pair, Roidhn broke into a joyous waggling run and tackled Athelstan. He wiggled and sniffed the Celt, licking him wildly. Then he turned his attention to Connie. His attitude changed instantly. He sniffed the wound oozing blood and gently touched it several times with his tongue. He climbed into the white fur with her, took a position behind her back and snuggled close. He still smelled like wet fur.

Constantina's breathing slowed as exhaustion finally overtook her. Athelstan continued to rub her hands and arms, warming them.

He waited until she was asleep before settling. He listened to her soft breathing and listened to their hearts beating. Three hearts - one sound. They beat in simple unison. He found that fact calming somehow. As he lay his head down next to hers, he kissed her cheek. "I love you, Constantina. Sleep well, sleep deep, you have earned it," he breathed.

Dawn was bright but cold. He lay cocooned with Constantina. Her tiny form was entwined around him and her breathing was soft and regular. He stretched carefully and peeked out of the fur. He smiled at what he saw but pulled the fur back over his head.

He felt Constantina stir. She stretched like a cat and winced in pain. A contented smile lit her face as she looked at him before she curled up in a tight ball against him with a satisfied sigh. Roidhn had not moved all night but as Connie stirred, his wagging tail was clearly audible.

"Mmmmm. Good morning my love," she purred. The tail wagged even harder.

"Roidhn, I am pretty sure she is talking to me." Roidhn wiggled out of the furs, stretched, yawned and with nose to the ground, waddled off in search of adventure.

"Did you sleep well?" He brushed a stray curl from her face.

"Mm-Hmm," she whispered. "I did sleep well for the first time in months." She touched his face. "You are a puzzle."

"Yes, I am," he had a mischievous smile as he pulled back the furs just far enough to let her see out. She gasped at what she saw and sat straight up with astonishment. He pulled the warm fur over her shoulders while she looked all around. They looked out over a landscape that was a brilliant luminous white. It had not snowed, but during the night, an ice fog had moved into the valley. At this height, it had covered every leaf, twig and blade of grass in a feathery white frost. The valley below lay unseen beneath a soft mist. Dawn had bathed the whole scene in a pale golden glow.

"What has happened here?" There was some panic in her voice.

"Shhhh. Everything is fine. This is fairy magic Constantina; this is your magic."

"My magic?" She looked around with big eyes and an overwhelming sense of wonder. "What do you mean?"

"Last night you embraced this land for the very first time and it has embraced you back. You are to be its Queen, Constantina. That is not a dream. When we wed, you will wear a crown. Did you dream last night?"

Her demeanour turned serious. "I did dream. I was dancing and spinning in big circles. I wore a glowing white gown and white slippers. I was dancing on air. A crowd danced with me but I could not see their faces. You were there too. You, but not you… am I dreaming still?" Her head twisted around again.

"No, you are awake and what you see now is very real. While you slept, the Frost Fairies came to dance with you; they welcomed you to this land and into their world. You saw me in your arms but you were dancing with the Fairy King. What you see is the result. All traces of this night will vanish with the morning sun, but for now, enjoy the beauty. This is His gift to you alone."

She looked around. "Nothing in my life could have prepared me for this. This really is a land of magic." The trees with their colourful leaves sparkled where the sun caressed them. Rapture overcame her and she began to laugh and cry.

He helped her stand. A wild halo of hair streamed all around her head. She stepped gingerly across a frosty carpet of leaves. It felt as though she was utterly connected to every living thing. She could feel life vibrating all around her. Every detail was in sharp focus.

There was not a hint of wind and her breath puffed out in visible clouds that hung in the air for a moment before fading away. A spider's web, frosted white, captured her attention. It was a miraculous work of art and she spent some time studying it. She giggled when the frost vanished beneath her delicate touch.

"It is so soft and cold," she said in wonderment. With arms wrapped around her in a self–hug, she turned in a final circle before running back.

"Oh, Athelstan!" Constantina was breathless. Even this little bit of exertion was taking its toll. "This is the most amazing morning of my life. No one has ever; no one could ever have given me a gift like this," her face glowed with happiness. "But you did," she gave him a tender kiss. "Thank you."

He just smiled and held her. As the day grew brighter, the frost melted away.

"You know there are going to be some people who are very annoyed with us at the moment. We should go."

"I was very afraid of you."

"I know you were. Was it because of the way I became King?"

"Yes."

"I did not want to become King. I simply needed to remove the old one."

"Until they remove you the same way?"

"Perhaps. However, I think not. Let me ask you, what are you doing up here?"

"I was running away."

"Why?"

"I suddenly realised I might have to stay here," she admitted.

"Well, you did say, 'Not a sister.' What else then?"

Constantina frowned. "Not a sister? Am I missing something?"

There was a pause. "No, Not at all."

"Where would you have gone?" he asked.

"Home. Back to Rome."

"I suppose now that Papirius is gone, you can go home. Is that what you want?"

She shook her head slowly. "If the truth be known, I am beginning to like it here. I feel I can be myself here. I feel I can trust the people here and not be an unwilling slave to the Republic."

"Now that you are no longer a wife to the Proconsul, you would be free to become my…"

"WIFE?" It was half exclamation and half question.

"My wife, yes. If you choose not to become a Queen, then my other offer still stands."

"You mean you want me to become your wife."

"Only if you want me as a husband."

"What other offer?"

"Sister? Become my sister – adoption, remember?"

Clarity bloomed on her features. "Sister! That's what you were referring to a moment ago. I misunderstood you. You must think me quite the fool."

Athelstan smiled. "No. Never a fool. You have been through a great deal and now to learn you are pregnant. I fully understand. I will admit, though, I was beginning to wonder who you were."

"I have been a bit distracted. Can you forgive me?" He just nodded and picked her up in his arms. "It is time we go."

Constantina looked around. The sun had risen and the Fairy Magic had faded away.

He carried her down the hill across fog-shrouded land to the Royal compound wrapped snugly in furs. They stoically braved the stares of both the curious and the outraged. There was the usual flurry of activity that heralded their arrival. He waited as a calm serene Druidess tucked the contented, smiling girl into her bed and smoothed the sheets. She had no reaction when his bloody shirt was found keeping her chest wound closed. It was discarded and the injury re-bandaged.

"Is there anything I can get you, my dear?" Caileigh asked.

"No, thank you. I am fine now," she said with a quick look at Athelstan.

"Good." The woman straightened and placed her hands on her hips. "I have something I would like to say." Athelstan's heart clenched. He recognised her tone and the stance. Athelstan raised a hand absently to silence her.

"Caileigh, I have to prepare for a funeral of a dear friend."

"Now just a moment…" Caileigh began.

Athelstan turned away from her and spoke to the men behind him. "I do not know what his funeral rites are so he will have to be content with ours."

"Excuse me but…" She tried again. He partially turned and held up a finger to silence the Druidess a second time. Her face darkened dangerously.

"Shush for a moment. I do know his God is named Jehovah and we should beseech him on the deceased's behalf."

"EXCUSE ME, YOUNG MAN!" Caileigh shouted.

"Just a moment, can't you see I need to plan a funeral?"

"Why, did somebody die?" It was a very familiar voice. Athelstan turned and found Saul looking positively lifelike.

"You are not dead!" exclaimed Athelstan. He gathered a surprised Saul up in a bear hug.

"Aye might be soon if Ewe do nut release me," he gasped.

He released his friend. "Why aren't you dead?"

Caileigh fixed him with a hawk-like gaze. "He is not dead because I saved his life, that's why."

"She did. Thank ewe dear lady."

"You are quite welcome sir." Athelstan and Saul turned to leave.

"NOBODY move!" The two men froze in place. "I will deal with you in good time," she said poking Athelstan in the chest. "Saul will you do this old lady a kindness and please get back into bed?"

"Oh, Aye feel quite well now and Aye…" he began.

"SIGH. I am so sorry dear. I phrased that as though it was a question. Get back to bed. NOW, before I carry you there!" Her tone was emphatic. Saul did as he was told.

"Is she always like this?"

"ALWAYS!" Caileigh retorted.

That same gaze was now turned on Constantina.

"My dear, over the last few days I have risked both life and limb to get you into that bed alive. I will not mention the precipitous journey I was forced to endure to climb those mountains to find you. Nor shall I burden you with the even more harrowing one to bring you back here alive. It took all night to remove a two–foot long shaft of wood that had violated your body. If not for our intervention, you would have certainly died my dear. Yet, only hours after you wake up you are bellowing orders that you are leaving. Then to make good on your threat, you run off into the forest alone wearing the thinnest of nightshirts." Caileigh was trembling with outrage.

Constantina sat up. "I? You! No one EVER speaks to me thus."

"There is a first time for everything my dear, and NOW is that time for I just did – speak to you thus!"

"Then I am leaving!" Constantina started to rise.

"Don't you dare try to get up young lady! You will be in that bed for the next three days even if I have to lash you into it! Believe it!" Constantina slumped back down into the pillows and pulled the blankets up to her chin. "Three days."

"No, I will not stay here another second," Constantina whined petulantly. Athelstan shook his head in warning but to no avail.

Caileigh's eyebrows rose. "Would you like to try for four days, my dear?" Caileigh was impossible to intimidate and her force of will was simply undeniable.

Constantina shook her head mutely and settled deeper into her pillows.

Caileighs head slowly swivelled until she glared up at the King.

"And YOU!" She spat. She stalked over to him like a cat closing on a field mouse. She stood toe to toe with Athelstan. She craned her neck painfully to look up at him and he bore an expression absolute dread. She barely reached his ribcage, but nonetheless, she filled the room.

"WHAT were you thinking making love to such a badly injured girl all night long out there in the freezing cold? Are - you - out - of - your -mind?" Athelstan opened his mouth to respond but Caileigh had already turned her back to him.

"SILENCE!" she roared. "Not one more word! You could have killed this poor girl out there… alone and defenceless against such a heartless, rutting, brute of a man." Caileigh sat on the edge of the bed and took Constantina protectively in her arms.

"King, or not, you should be ashamed of yourself. I am sorely tempted to take you across my knee and thoroughly tan your backside with a willow switch!" Caileigh was livid.

"But Caileigh, he actually…" Constantina began but the Druidess turned and patted her hand and shushed her sweetly.

"There, there my dear, I know. You will be safe from him now. I will make sure he does not come anywhere near you ever again. If he does…" She shot Athelstan a chillingly wicked look. "I will happily transform him into something even more cold-blooded than he already is," he saw Constantina's smirk and give a helpless shrug of her eyes.

Athelstan pointed towards the door. "I am just going to… ummm." Caileigh waved her hand dismissively.

"Yes, yes get out, get out. Go polish your crown, or something equally unimportant," she smiled kindly at Constantina and gently took her hand.

"Now how about you join me in a nice warm cup of tea my dear? You have had quite an adventure haven't you?" Connie nodded. Athelstan beat a hasty retreat.

Chapter Forty-Five

Banished!

Athelstan had been banished from his own suites, banished from the great hall, and banished from the entire Royal compound. The guards had orders NOT to admit the King for any reason unless he was actually dying. Even then, entry would be subject to Caileigh's personal discretion. Saul was released from Caileigh's tender ministrations the following day. Even he was denied re-entry to the hospital. Saul told Athelstan about the fight and filled him in with most of the details.

"Who is this Acaph?"

"He is my brother. A twin. We are indistinguishable one from the other."

"Was he one of the men I saw you speaking to in Athens?"

"No."

"What happened to him? Where is his body?"

"Aye cannut say. Aye would say if Aye knew. Aye do nut know, so Aye cannut say. Had Aye been allowed to track him after the fight, things would be different and we would know something of value."

With the Samhain festival, now, only days away, the entire glade was a beehive of activity. As king, Athelstan was shouldered with the burden of directing the official preparations.

Huge bonfires were being laid along the twenty miles of lakefront. Each, complete with three rings of logs arranged around piles of fuel for seating. Spaces between the log rings allowed access from one ring to another. The inner circle would hold the dancers, entertainers and musicians. They would cavort at an energetic pace, throughout the night. Thousands would take part. The second row would find families gathering for the food and festivities. The outer ring was for young lovers. There they could enjoy the music and singing; they could watch the dancing and acrobatics without being greatly disturbed by it all.

Stickmen made of poles lashed together and dressed in extravagant and gaudy clothes sprang up everywhere. Cloth heads with funny and grotesque faces completed each of the crude statues. They were designed to scare away evil spirits from the homes of the living. In Athelstan's world, Samhain was the single day of the year when the veil between the land of the living and the land of the dead becomes the thinnest. During this one night, the spirits of the departed could cross over and roam freely among the people of the world. They come to frighten children, play pranks on the adults and visit with their living relatives. People wore gaudy, grotesque, or animal masks to confuse the spirits. They would leave a plate of sweets outside their doors so the spirits would eat and go away satisfied. So while their customs were many, their goal was singular – fellowship with the living – both in this world and in the next.

It was a special time in the Celtic year. Harvest was over. Soon winter's heavy snows would cover the valley and the lake would freeze solid. A thousand acres of grains were reaped and the fields prepared for winter. Turnips, carrots, nuts and dried fruits filled the massive storage burrows to overflowing. Wild game was so abundant, smoking huts were pushed to the limit. Tanners were buried in hides of every kind. Cow, deer and mountain sheep were the most common large hides. However, the hides ranged from hedgehogs to wild boars; badgers to mountain cats, muskrat, mink, skunk, otter, squirrel and everything in between. They were piled in great heaps at every tanning station.

Leagues of fish racks covered the eastern shoreline as Lake Ohrid gave up its bounty. Boats with huge nets plied the lake while armies of knife-wielding workers cleaned, washed and salted the tender white flesh. Dyers, weavers, blacksmiths, bowers, fletchers and artisans of every ilk toiled at a frantic pace. Gangs of children scoured the edges of the forests for the heavily laden beehives. Once found, skilled bee handlers relocated the hives for the winter. They carefully collected the honey and wax. Candles and sweet cakes were treasured end products of this dangerous task.

Not to be forgotten were the breweries and meaderies. They worked feverishly to supply the huge quantity of spirits likely to be consumed over the winter. Each individual meadery boasted that the finest meads came only from them alone. It was due to their superior honey–producing bees. Since each believed their claims to be the only valid ones, feuds would break out regularly.

Livestock roamed freely in the Senone world. Cattle, sheep and goats moved in slow herds from one green patch to the next. Dogs chased cats. Sows chased dogs – and rams chased ewes and anything else they wanted. The wild, laughing children made grand games out of riding these cantankerous, humourless goats, which inevitably led to injuries. These tough little boys stoically walked off most of the cuts, scrapes and bruises, but the occasional broken bone arrived on Caileigh's doorstep. She would kindly listen to the whole tale nodding sadly at the highlights; skillfully set and immobilise the injury; then sternly admonish the youngster from games likely to cause death. She would kiss their foreheads then send them home to recuperate with Epona's blessing.

Caileigh was a marvel. She tended the sick and injured alike. It seemed she had a potion or ointment for virtually every ailment. In the course of a day, she would see people with rheumatism, infections, cuts, burns and broken teeth from fist fights. Caileigh was doctor, dentist, surgeon, councillor and alchemist all rolled up into a fierce, wiry little package. She treated every soul alike. From the very young to the aged, from the insignificant to the important, she offered an interested ear and advice that was both firm yet kind. Everyone listened to her advice and called her 'Gentle Mother'. It did not take Constantina long to realise that even though Athelstan was King of these people, Caileigh's word was law. Constantina liked the idea of a strong woman keeping all these wild men under control.

So it was that one evening during dinner, Constantina asked between bites, "Caileigh, if you directed Athelstan to so something, would he have to obey you?"

Caileigh sat back in her chair and her wise eyes looked at the young queen-to-be. She pushed back her board and heaved a contented sigh.

"That is a surprisingly intuitive question, my dear. I will not insult your intelligence with any, 'why do you ask ' nonsense. I know precisely why you ask," she smiled at Constantina.

"I do not believe I will answer the question, however. The answer is far more complex than the question's simplicity might suggest. I might tell you that the answer is both yes and no. But being obtuse, or flippant would also insult your intelligence," she was being honest. It was clear she was trying to explain something fundamental to her culture, in a way that someone unfamiliar with it, might understand.

"No, ultimately he is not compelled to obey me, but in actuality, yes he will obey me. He knows what is good for him and by extension what is good for the nation. That might be too simple a truth, but the reasons behind that truth would take a lifetime to explain."

Constantina nodded slowly. "I think I begin to understand. What can you tell me about him as a man? How long have you known him?" She asked past a mouthful of spiced goat.

"I have known Athelstan all his life. I was midwife to his mother and I helped him into this world," she said. Her eyes showed that she recalled fond memories. "What can I tell you about him? He serves life – all life, everywhere. I cannot think of a better description for him. The fact he would not abandon you is so typical of him. I have never known him to do something without careful consideration, nor have I ever seen him shy away from adversity. He is not afraid of things he does not understand, he is drawn to them with a cat's curiosity." Caileigh took a sip of tea as she paused in her reminiscence.

Constantina listened intently. "He does seem to lack the healthy sense of fear that most of us have."

"That may be an illusion. Athelstan understands fear well enough but he does not allow it to walk with him. To him, fear is the ultimate lie and oh how he hates lies. I have heard him say that the truth may not always be pretty but an ugly truth is always better than a pretty lie. I can tell you with certainty Constantina; he will never lie to you – not ever. He would sooner cut out his own tongue." Caileigh stared intently at the Roman. "You are in love with him are you not?"

Constantina simply nodded shyly and looked at the older woman with large green eyes. Caileigh smiled softly and raised an eyebrow.

"Then what are you doing sitting here talking with an old crone? Go to him. There is no need for you to stay here any longer." Constantina's face brightened but she quickly replaced it with indifferent calm.

"I do not sit with an old crone. I sit with Senone personified and there is no place I would rather be right now. I can never repay your kindness Caileigh," she kissed the Druidess and a tear formed in the witch's eye.

"You just did child, you just did."

Chapter Forty-Six

It was Samhain. In the darkness of the night sparks from the huge bonfire rose in tight columns high into the air. Dozens of white-clad dancers spun in wild abandon about it. Athelstan was huddled in conversation with Caileigh. He was not sitting, but bent over her shoulder and spoke into her ear. Constantina sat on one of the logs surrounding the fire and for the moment, she was alone. Saul stood several feet away talking bowmanship with a fascinated young Celt.

Vestorix, the Arch Druid resplendent in his white robes, began the Samhain ceremonies. With his arms outstretched to the heavens he chanted...

"Grant us, O holy ones thy protection;

And in protection, strength;

And in strength, understanding;

And in understanding, knowledge;

And in knowledge, the knowledge of justice;

And in the knowledge of justice, the love of it;

And in that love, the love of all existences;

And in the love of all existences, the love of all faiths,

And in the love of all faiths, O holy ones, let us embrace all that is good in this world.

Awen! Awen! Awen!" The last, a deep drone of Ah–Oh–En, resonated into the very bones of those who heard it. Vestorix paused briefly then asked,

"Who will hold my hand?

Who will send the energy on to weave a circle of light in this place?

I call on the light,

I call to the Gods and to the Goddesses.

I call to the four corners of the Earth,

Strengthen this circle and let its power grow,

Let the love of family past and present enrich us in this place!

As it was in the past, so let it be now and forever more."

"Now and forever more," chanted the crowd.

"Let the powers attend as I am about to open a Grove of Druids in this place. The first duty of Druids assembled in the Sacred Grove is to proclaim peace in the four corners of the earth for without peace our work here cannot proceed." He began assembling items, a smoking cauldron of peat, a horn of mead, a sprig of wintergreen and placed them on an altar in front of the fire.

As the fire blazed up with multicoloured tongues of flame, a cool hand touched Constantina's shoulder. A pale skinned, middle-aged woman came and sat beside her.

"Welcome to the Glade my dear, I hope you are enjoying yourself."

Constantina smiled at the woman beside her. "I am," she said softly. The woman had lovely white hair and eyes the colour of the sea.

"I am very glad you are here to see all this. Oh but I am being rude. I am Celeste Epona. Athelstan is my son," she smiled and offered Constantina her hand.

"His mother? Tell me how is it possible that you are here? I was told you were…"

"Dead? Yes, it is true, I passed from this world long ago, yet I am here now because it is Samhuinn." –she used the old word. "I have seen how my son looks at you. Why do you try to deceive him?"

"Deceive him? What makes you think I am deceiving him."

"He loves another. Why are you here in her place?"

The pale lady surprised her. Constantina went cold to the bone.

"Who are you?" Celeste asked.

"I am Constantina."

"No, you are not. You cannot deceive the dead, my dear." Celeste's face darkened. "Who are you?" Her voice had changed. It was like an icy wind.

"Constantina," she repeated.

"LIAR!" Celeste spat.

"LIAR!" The apparition flowed in on the wind. The ghost leaned in closer and closer repeating over and over. "LIAR! LIAR! LIAR!"

Her voice raised in volume and pitch with every word. The ghost drew nearer with every word.

"Get away from me!" The terrified Roman shrieked.

The ghost pounced and the girl fell to the ground with a horrified scream. Celeste faded into nothingness. Everyone within hearing turned to see what was happening.

Constantina scrabbled away from something unseen and continued to scream. Several women rushed to her aid and helped her stand. For a moment, she looked around in fear expecting the spirit to reappear. People were asking her if she was hurt. Constantina drew a deep breath in an effort calm he pounding heart.

"I am fine," she said. "I am fine, truly," she said at last. "It was just a silly dream." With a final look over her shoulder, she settled back down on a log closest to the fire. Her left hand ached and she realised she was clutching something tightly. She looked down and opened her hand. Sitting in her palm was a fat hazelnut. She very nearly threw it away. Curiosity prevented her. A new life, much different from her old one had suddenly presented itself. Perhaps this was an escape? Perhaps this was a real chance at peace.

Vestorix continued the solemn ritual by circling an ornately carved altar by the fire three times holding an ancient sword in the palms of his hands. He stopped, facing eastward and partially drew the blade. With a deeply resonant voice, he spoke.

"Let there be peace in the East!" He slammed the blade back into its sheath and then bowed very low touching his forehead to the weapon. He then walked a quarter circle to face the south, redrew the sword partially and repeated his words.

"Let there be peace in the South." Again, he slid the blade back into its sheath and bowed. This was repeated two more times for the West and the North before he finally placed the sword on the altar. He stood statue–still for a long time deep in meditation before speaking again.

"Let these powers attend as I open a Druidic Circle. The circle is consecrated and the Gods and Goddesses of our people are now in attendance."

"Blessings be!" intoned the assembled crowd.

"As it was in the deep past so it is now. This day of Samhain (Sowain), in the Druidic tradition, marks the end of this Golden Year and the beginning of a new year, restarting the cycle of time. In this season, the harvest is brought from the fields. The Sun, our father, descends into darkness and the Earth, our mother, dons her brown garments of mourning. The veil between the worlds grows thin and our ancestors draw close. Their voices whisper to us in the autumn winds. As we stand among the fallen leaves and the grey and golden light, let us remember the past and its lessons and gather a harvest of wisdom to bear us through winter to the new spring to come."

"Let it be so," said the crowd in reverence.

"On this day I invoke Ceridwen (Karowen) the goddess of wisdom, keeper of the cauldron of transformation, mistress of the cycles of change. Ceridwen, Ceridwen, Ceridwen. Join with us in the circle of this Grove. Grant us your blessings and receive from us our blessings in return. Watch over us and over the living world; protect, cherish and guide all existences in the turning of the year's wheel now before us."

"Grant us your blessings," intoned the crowd.

Vestorix took a horn of mead from the altar and held it high.

"I take up the Hirlas horn in the presence of the goddess. I bear offering and augury of plenty. From the green realms of the Earth Mother, the spirits of nature gather gifts for our sustenance each in our own place in the wheel of the turning year. On this day of Samhain, behold the horn of plenty, emblem of the abundant gifts of nature and the sprig of evergreen, in recollection of the year that is past and hope for the year that is to come. In these symbolic gifts, may there be blessings upon the Earth forever."

"Blessings be upon the Earth," the crowd whispered.

Vestorix lowered the horn, drank from it and returned it to the altar.

He then took up a sprig of wintergreen.

"From the Earth, her never failing promise, from the Holy Kindreds, their gifts of will and grace, we receive with thanks the evergreen of enduring life. From all that is given, we give in turn." He placed the sprig back on the altar.

"From those who have established the turnings of the silent stars, who place the seal of their blessing on the living Earth and lift up its children to inscrutable heights, have given to all without tribute and without price; may we be worthy of that which is given."

"May we be worthy," came the refrain.

"We have received the blessing of Ceridwen."

"Blessings be."

"Let the powers attend as I proclaim a Grove of Druids now exists in this place. Peace prevails in the four quarters and throughout the Grove. Let any power remaining from this working be returned to this place for its blessing." He drew the sword and held it aloft.

"I now invoke the Sword of Swords!
From the rising sun, three rays of light;
From the living Earth, three stones of witness;
From the eye and mind and hand of wisdom,
Three rowan staves of all knowledge;
From the fires of the sun, the forge;
From the bones of the Earth, the iron;
From the hand of the wise, the shaping;
From these, Ex–Halabre;
By the Sword of Swords, I pledge my faithful service
To the living Earth our home and Mother.
Awen! Awen! Awen!" He put the sword down, turned and strode away without a backwards glance.

A rush of young women approached the flames and placed their nuts in specific places between the coals. Constantina stepped up to the fire and as she did, everyone about stopped to stare. Saul looked at her and smiled. Only Saul, who actually took the time to talk to the Celts about their customs, knew what she was doing. He stood and watched the scene quietly, holding his breath in anticipation. Some of the girl's hazelnuts exploded and one by one they took to their heels to chase down the man of their dreams. Other nuts smoked, burned and blackened to glowing embers.

Even Athelstan looked up from his talk with the Druidess to watch what Constantina was doing. The nut blackened quickly in the glowing coals and began to smoke. Time passed slowly and a small crowd was now watching the Roman stare at the fire. Her heart sank as it began to burn but as she was about to turn away, there was a tremendous explosion. Everyone around the fire jumped at the sound and watched as a tower of sparks rose skyward. There was a moment of stunned silence and even Athelstan was looking up at the bright swirling motes. He looked back at Constantina with a surprised look on his face.

Saul smiled when it happened. He knew what it meant. Constantina's eyes fell upon Athelstan and the Druidess. Caileigh had a large bright smile and was wiggling her fingers at Athelstan mimicking a running motion. He straightened and kissed Caileigh on the forehead, then waved at Constantina.

There was little time for confusion as the crowd cheered and urged her to catch her man and take him for her own. Athelstan was already moving away from the fire towards the trees. It would seem that the chase was on.

Constantina did not understand and looked at a woman who was standing nearby. She was grinning at Constantina. She heard the crowd chanting. "Run – run – run."

Athelstan knew she could not run far since she was still getting her strength back, so he turned toward a special place he knew. It was nearby down a well-travelled path and even in the dim light; she would have no trouble following it. Roidhn loped along beside Athelstan. After a short march, he arrived at the top of an ancient stone staircase leading down into a deep grotto. There, waiting for him, stood a familiar old friend. The grey-eyed wolf calmly watched him descend. He stopped several feet away from the creature and lowered his head. The wolf did the same.

"I am honoured that Phaelan has given us time so we can speak together. Welcome to Gwennderion Glade. It pleases me greatly to finally welcome the God of wolves among us." There was great reverence in his voice.

The wolf nodded. "You did not run." It was a statement. The voice in his head was clear.

"I did not."

"Does she chase you?"

"I believe she does, yes."

Athelstan blinked as the wolf stood up and changed into the spirit of a pale-eyed God-King. He was tall, strong and dressed in the same furs that cover his children. Athelstan lowered his head to the shimmering spirit.

"Why did you share your food with my children in the mountains?"

"It was not my food. It was your children that shared their food with us. They gave us the gift of life. I thank them and you for that."

Kamenawati walked away from Athelstan to look up at the night sky. "Your ways are strange Man-King. Still, you treat your people as I do mine. I have watched you." This woman, what makes you think you are worthy of her love?"

"I am not. Yet, what I think matters not. She gives herself freely; I cannot love her more and I shall never love her less. It is now for her to choose. If she chooses me, I shall show her what love can be."

"Are you certain she is the one you want?" Phaelan asked facing the man.

"Yes. I will have her."

"Often wanting what you do not have and having what you do not want are not always different."

"Is that not a contradiction."

"It is, but it also often true."

"You are the second spirit who has suggested this. Should I not take this woman as my mate?"

"You should do as you deem prudent. I do not advise humans. That cousin by your feet is a kind and gentle one" Phaelan-God bent and scratched Roidhn between the eyes. Roidhn was in a canine version of rapture. "Any man who is kind to both wolf and dog is blessed by the gods."

"When we meet in the next life, I shall stand proudly beside you among the honoured dead. Celt to Wolf!"

"Until then great King, fare you well."

The man was once again a wolf and it bounded away up the stairs and into the night.

She came through a low opening in the boughs of an ancient pair of cedar trees. As she passed under them, two intricately carved monoliths roughly five feet in height announced the start of a curving stairway leading down into a deep wide grotto. Water fell from the far rim in a gentle stream to the damp floor below and ran away in a small channel under the grotto's walls. From the top of the stair, she could see him – waiting

Constantina flowed down the steps like a soft mist over the hills and she stopped about ten feet from him. "Did I win?"

He walked the ten feet and took her shoulders. "Yes, you have won. I shall never run from you again, only towards you," he looked up at the Harvest Moon rising over the rim of the grotto. The light shone onto the pair. " Constantina, do you hear that music?"

"Music?"

He gently cupped his hand over her other ear and a soft wind–like music began to sound in her head. Constantina smiled. It seemed like it was the first time in months. His touch always felt so good to her. "Yes," she resting her head on his chest. "I can hear it. What is it?"

"That is Moonlight. It is the sound of our spirits dancing," he began a slow tender dance with her.

Constantina moved with him as he danced with her. Her hands were on his chest as they danced. After a time, she began to sing softly to the music she heard in her head. Pulling back, she looked up into his face. "Our spirits singing? I do not understand."

"You will my love, you will. This music is for us alone. No one else can hear it. No one else can feel it," he paused in his dance and took her hands in his. He looked at her very closely and fell to a knee.

"Constantina, Lady of Rome, you know that I love you. You know that I will always love you no matter what happens. You are the only star in my night sky. Will you marry me?" His wild mane was silhouetted in the soft glow and behind him above the rim of the grotto shone the full moon and one bright star.

Constantina watched him. "Athelstan?" She blinked and blinked again. Her hands began to shake softly as he held his and tears filled her eyes. "Marry you! I have thought long on this I want to but..."

"I have spoken to Phaelan. He came to me this night," he paused suddenly at a loss for words. "We have his blessing."

She wiped at her moist cheeks as he proposed to her. "The Wolf? Oh, Athelstan, I must not. You do not really know what I am," she said pulling her hands away from his, she shook her head, lifted her skirt intending to run back up the steps of the grotto.

A gentle hand stopped his fawn from running. He turned her and kissed her lips softly. She moaned at the touch. She could not help it and did not try.

"Do not be afraid of this, Constantina."

Once she had regained herself enough to speak, she said, "I am a Roman. I will only hurt you and those you love in the end." her voice was shaking now.

Roidhn licked her hand and was wagging his tail.

He smiled down at her and shook his head. "No dear heart, you will not. We can do this and if the omens are true, we must do this for the sake of both our nations. You say that your people's security and happiness are important to you. They are to me as well. We can end this war.

Her tears streamed harder from her eyes. "You have been so kind to me. I cannot stay here and you cannot come with me. I must go home. You must stay here." she said turning away from him.

His arms encircled her waist from behind and his hands closed over hers on her belly. "I am the Senone King and yes, I must regain my people's homeland for I have pledged to do so. But there are ways to do this without war."

She turned around and looked him full in the face.

Athelstan took her hands from his cheeks and kissed each palm. "Do you not see? A great ruler deals with the problems at hand but he must not dwell on them. A great ruler provides what is best for his subjects and his nation in five years, ten years and fifty years. A great ruler provides for the nations security and happiness now and for a thousand years after he is gone. I mean to do that for Senone just as you shall for Rome." As he spoke, his large hands gently rubbed her belly. That calm soothing baritone was like a soft warm blanket. "Let me be that ruler. Marry me."

"In the short time I have known you and your people; I have learned many things that will change how I live – forever. You are not the beasts I was told you were. Together you and I will be richer for the time we have spent together. But that time is over now. I must leave you. I cannot stay here." It was difficult to ignore those riveting eyes.

"Constantina, change is the only thing that remains constant in this world. You say I am a King and so I cannot be with you. Yet you forget it was not by choice that I am King. I accepted the Crown because the people demanded it of me. I have accepted it during a time of crisis and so long as I am King I shall be a mighty one indeed." His voice rose and that wild beast she referred to strained to be unleashed. A long sigh escaped him.

"But if my being King means I must lose you, then they can choose another to be their King. I rule by my free will. You are that important to me. You must know that this is true. Constantina, our child needs to know a father is there to love and protect him. I shall be that father, even if that means leaving behind all that I have known. I will be that father and that husband. Marry me."

Athelstan brushed a stray hair from her cheek and kissed her forehead. "Listen to what your heart is now screaming at you, Constantina. There is nothing more that you can say, but yes. Marry me."

"Athelstan, it is not the simple. There are things you do not know about me."

"Of course. Love is always like that. Marry me – now."

"But Athelstan…"

He placed a finger on her lips. "There will be no more maybes. There will be no more doubts, no more fears and no more heartache. Just this one time will you stop and listen to your spirit?" There was a pause. "Was I wrong

Constantina? Do you not want to be happy?"

"Of course I do, you know I do."

"Then say yes, love. Put your hand in mine and give me the strength to do what I have pledged to do for both our countries. Marry me. Damn it girl for once in your life stop being so confoundedly stubborn."

Her hand reached for his. "Yes, my love. Yes."

"You said yes?" he laughed. Constantina could not help but laugh too; his joy was contagious. He lifted her high in the air and twirled her in a great circle. She was folded into a gentle embrace; her feet still high off the ground. He kissed her long and deep.

"You said yes," he released her and turned his face to the sky. "SHE SAID YES!" He bellowed at the heavens. His joy was explosive. Then he calmed and kissed her again. "You did say yes?" He breathed.

"Did you think I would not?"

"There was a tiny moment." He indicated a small gap with his thumb and forefinger.

"You have become my world," her happy smile lit the dark grotto like a midday sun.

"I shall never forsake you, Constantina. Not in this life, or the next."

Looking at her he started to laugh again, a happy joyous sound that echoed off walls of the grotto. His hand went to her belly. "We shall have many beautiful children and I pray they all have your kind eyes."

"As long as the girls don't grow scruffy beards, I will be content." Her laughter was the most beautiful music.

Chapter Forty-Seven

Turnip lanterns lit the path she walked and they cast an orange light on her long dress. It was cream coloured linen, embroidered in gold at the neck, hem, cuffs and bodice with runes for long life, happiness and fertility. A veil of gossamer draped her face held in place by a diadem of silver and precious stones. Those auburn curls were arranged loosely and woven into the long tresses with yellow and purple wildflowers. A procession of twelve maidens led Constantina to the sacred grove as children dashed, laughed, and played games in and out of the trees.

Constantina followed the women down the lane and was in amazement at what she was seeing. The lanterns, the flowers, the children, and women were magical. The wedding to Papirius was steeped in tradition; this ceremony was much less complicated and so very refreshing. She smiled and stepped into the sacred circle.

Vestorix and Caileigh awaited the procession and the maidens took up places around the circle. Everything was in place and proper. Saul stood beaming. Druids did look a bit odd in the ceremonial Celtic costumes but she knew they would endure anything to be here. She looked around and everything looked perfect, everything except for one thing. Athelstan! He was missing and nowhere to be seen. Constantina looked at Caileigh for some guidance and looked puzzled.

She smiled as she looked Constantina over. "You are beautiful my dear; the very vision of a royal bride," she said softly. "Now, go ahead and call for him. He is a man after all and has to be reminded of even the simplest of things."

Constantina blinked. "Call to him?" she asked. "But how?" she asked turning towards the lane she called out, "Athelstan. You're late as usual. Attend me this instant."

"I am here," came the response and he came up the path to her smiling widely. Gone were the trappings of his office and he wore a simple blue-green tartan leggings and vest over a white long–sleeved shirt. His hair was free of braids and amulets. Constantina was the bright flower today and he would have it no other way. He strode to her side and kissed her tenderly on the forehead.

"You look so beautiful Constantina…" His voice caught in his throat.

"I love you," she breathed softly.

"I do too!" he kissed her deeply again. Soft laughter coursed around the assembly. In a clear voice, Caileigh raised her hands to the heavens and began.

"Blessings be and merry meet one and all. We are here today to join Constantina daughter of Rome and Athelstan, son of the Senone together as one. They have asked you here to share in their joy and to declare their love for one another before you as a community."

Vestorix spoke. "What is your desire, Athelstan? Why have you come?"

"I have come to wed Constantina and to take her as my wife for now and forever."

Caileigh turned to face Constantina. "What is your desire, Constantina? Why have you come?

It was only after Caileigh turned to face her that Constantina said. "To be his until there is no longer breath within my body."

Taking a crystal wand, Vestorix dipped it into one of four bowls and sprinkled a few drops of water on and around Constantina and Athelstan.

"Repeat after me," he said. Athelstan did.

"I Athelstan of Senone do come here of my own free will, to seek the partnership of Constantina of Rome. I come with all love, honour and sincerity, wishing only to become one with her, the only one I shall ever love. Always I will strive for Constantina's happiness and welfare. I do so swear before this congregation of men and the Gods."

Caileigh took the wand and repeated the action. She looked at Constantina smiling. "I think you have words of your own to say. Speak them now my child."

"You are my world dear heart, my love, my life, my joy. You fill me with an unexplainable feeling of… I do not know what," she said with a soft bell-like giggle. "I was lost before you and like the sun on a cloudy day you have come into my life and shown me what is good and holy again. I want only to spend my days loving you and my nights making love to you for as long as we both shall live. "

Caileigh dipped the crystal wand into a second bowl. She sprinkled two gold rings with the water and took them up, handing Constantina's ring to the Athelstan and then his ring to her.

Vestorix took up a smoking bowl and ceremonially bathed the pair in the smoke. As he did so, he chanted.

"As the grass of the fields and the trees of the woods bend together under the pressures of the storm, so must you both bend when the wind blows strong. Know that as quickly as the storm comes, just as quickly may it leave. Yet you both will stand strong in each others presence."

"As you give love, so too will you receive love. As you give strength, so too will you receive strength. Together you are one; apart you are nothing.

"We each understand that no two people can be exactly alike. No more than any two people can fit together, perfect in every way. There will be times when it will seem hard to give strength and to give love. But, see then your reflection in a woodland pool, when the image you see looks sad and angered, then know it is the time for you to smile and to love. It is not fire that puts out fire."

Caileigh took up the chant.

"In return, the image in the pool will smile and love. So, change your anger to love and your tears to joy. It is not weakness to admit a wrong; moreover, it is strength and a sign of eternal growth."

"Love, help and respect each other forever. The constant circle of love you share is symbolised in these rings. Let them be a token of your friendship and the partnership you have come to celebrate on this day. When the waters are rough, let these rings remind you of the ebb and flow of life. Let them remind you of the happiness you feel at this moment and let that memory soothe your spirit."

"You may now exchange the rings as a token of your lifelong bond." Athelstan took Constantina's hand and slipped the plain gold ring on her finger.

"This is a token of my love for you. With this, I marry you and take you to my heart. I shall never forsake you for another. That is my pledge to you, Constantina," he kissed her hand.

"This is a token of my undying love for you. Just as the circle is unbroken so too will my heart be connected to yours. Just as the circle goes on without end, so too will my love and devotion to you. I shall never forsake you for another," she said slipping the ring on his finger.

Caileigh spoke. "If there are any things that the bride and groom would wish to say to one another, this is the perfect time for such a thing."

Athelstan took Constantina's hands. "When I first laid eyes on you, you were a grubby little guttersnipe. How little I knew then that I would be standing here today, with my heart in the clouds and you in my life. I can say to you now, that it was a very good day."

Constantina opened her mouth to speak but could not. All she could do was cry. She reached forward and kissed him several times, which ended with laughter.

He gathered her into his arms and kissed her with passion and tenderness. He had tears in his eyes and made no attempt to hide them. Caileigh said laughing. "You may now kiss the bride," he broke for the briefest of seconds to say, "I already am kissing her... and I'm not quite done yet either." Laughter and loud cheering greeted this but he made good his statement and drank in her soft lips and delicate scent. He finally pulled back and looked into her eyes for a long time before looking up again.

The Druids joined hands and announced. "It is with great happiness that I pronounce you married and present you to the community as husband and wife. May you always remember the love that brought you here on this day and may the God and Goddess of Nature bless this union. So Must It Be."

A great cheer rose from the small assembly in attendance but it was taken up by a nation. Soon the Glade rang with music and laughter. A great party was about to begin in their honour and the people rejoiced. Athelstan led Constantina into the circle. They extinguished the smoking bowl with earth and each drank of the water. Then, it was over. He held her close and for some reason, he could not take his eyes off her. She was so beautiful and so happy; he wished this moment would last for her forever.

Vestorix spoke one last time.

"The web of life is an endless circle. It cannot die; it can only change form.

What was begun as two, is now completed as one. Welcome home these energies borne.

The circle is open but unbroken. So Must It Be!"

Chapter Forty-Eight

By the hundreds they came, clan chiefs, warlords, simple labourers offering up congratulations for their new King's marriage. There was music and dancing, juggling and feats of magic to delight the masses. Food and drink were laid out in vast abundance and no one wanted for anything. Now with the sun setting and storm clouds moving in, it was time to take the celebrations inside. They would celebrate for many days.

It was a magical day to end a golden year. The Senone people felt a new hope dawn. They had a strong and powerful King and now he had a beautiful and clever Queen. It helped mute the last mad days of King Trahearn and the Roman occupation of their homes. Today it seemed the very Gods smiled down at the people. Anything was possible now and the nation rejoiced.

As the first few fat drops of rain began to fall, Athelstan, together with Saul and Demetrios, made their way back towards Athelstan's forest home. In truth, it was little more than a long sod–covered stone house. It tunnelled deep into a hillside at the foot of the eastern mountains. It was set well back from the lakeshore and surrounded by pine and cedar trees. A winding path led to the doorway and it had been lit by hundreds of small turnips hollowed out so a lit taper could burn inside.

People lined the route and handed bunches of mistletoe to Athelstan for his new bride. Soon his arms were full of red berries and he could carry no more so the overflow went to his two groomsmen. He was very comfortable with his people and accepted slaps on the back from soldiers and commoners alike. He nodded at the sage advice of the venerable as they offered up their secrets to a long and happy marriage. He bent to receive the kisses of maids and crones as they wished his union would be a fruitful one. His approach could have hardly been any less of a secret and their long walk took on the air of a carnival.

He stopped some feet away from the doorway. Inside Constantina awaited her husband and once he stepped through that door, he would never be alone again. It was something he had scarcely imagined only a few months ago. How quickly the Gods can change one's path. A smile of pure contentment crossed his face as he turned and gestured to the throng arrayed behind him, stepped up to the door and knocked three times, with his foot.

As was tradition, women chosen to attend Constantina during this time of waiting always remained until her new husband arrived. While it is unclear why exactly they do remain, it seems that part of their job is to direct the often heavily inebriated husband towards the bed. It is hoped the wife can manage the situation from there. Today this would not be necessary. The King remained sober.

The door opened and a soft yellow light beamed out across the wide path. The ladies gathered up the masses of flowers and took them inside. Once relieved of their armloads of flowers, Athelstan turned to his two friends. He grasped each in turn and pressed his forehead to theirs.

Saul, he kissed on both cheeks. "It is impossible for me to make you understand what you men have come to mean to me. Not only because you are honourable men, but because I have come to trust your judgment in things. I have come to look upon you as more than friends. You shall always be welcome at my fires. Yet what I am most grateful for is your blessing you have given to this marriage. I can never forget such a gift. My thanks is all I have."

Demetrios nodded and Saul smiled. Demetrios nodded. "I am glad your paths crossed in Yithion. As you said, that was a very good day."

"I am too, but I do believe it is time for us to part." He smiled at the trio.

The women in the room stared at Constantina in awe. The feeling of so many eyes on her was a bit unnerving. She wanted to lower her head, play with her hair, something. Instead, she tapped into her training and stood there proud – regal. Her hands hung at her side. Her long blonde curls flowing about her head, the crown of flowers still atop the loose wild mane.

The gown she wore was long and was made of gossamer that reflected the flicker of the candlelight. The soft green looked lovely against her pale tone and hair. It had a low neckline, tying up between her cleavage, with the long strands of ribbon. Someone had said it was so the King could unwrap her like a present. That erupted into a whole chorus of laughs and giggles. It just made her feel like she should run and hide.

It was strange standing in this room. Everyone here knew what she was about to do and everyone here had no qualms about commenting on it... however bawdy. In Rome, this was a private affair; here in Athelstan's world, it was a celebration.

"He will be arriving soon," one of the women said. Then all eyes fell upon Constantina again.

At that, the woman calmed. "Now child, is there anything we can get for you before we leave?"

To her surprise, Constantina said something she was not expecting. "A drink and a strong one." Giggling broke out. They pointed to a large barrel of Mead.

The sound of the door closing caused all within the dwelling to hush. Ten women took their places before Constantina. With a nod to her, they approached Athelstan. Each woman placed a different item believed to engender a long and healthy marriage in Athelstan's hand. The last woman placed a ring of flowers around his neck to match the one Constantina had on her head. She smiled at him and he winked at his bride standing there in all her finery. She shifted from one foot to the other

"Today was a lovely day for a party was it not."

The room was bathed in soft candlelight and Constantina was stunning. He could scarcely catch his breath at the sight of her. He nodded. "Yes it was," he said a bit sheepishly. "Too bad about the rain, though," he could not take his eyes off her.

"From what I am told it always rains, here," she said and felt even more nervous.

He held out his hand to her. "You are the most beautiful woman I have ever seen Constantina."

Now that he was standing before her and complimenting her, Constantina tucked her hair behind her ear because she needed to do something with her hands. He reached for her and she reached for him. She placed her soft smaller hand in his. "This party will never end for us."

"I do not want it to."

He gathered her up in his arms and held her tight for a long time. "I know our ways must seem very strange to you, but it's all over now. Outside, the world no longer exists; it is only you and I."

She did not hesitate. Constantina wrapped her arms around his waist and sighed at the strong chest underneath her cheek. Constantina blushed at his words.

"Was it that obvious I was terrified?" she sighed.

"All new brides are terrified. I would not have it any other way," he laughed. "This way you will remember every second of our wedding. I know I will never forget this day." She laughed.

"It is not that your ways are strange it is just that my ways are so very different. I enjoyed myself. Your people are wonderful and I am proud to now be a part of your world," she said.

He tilted her head up and kissed her softly. "I have something for you on your wedding night. He took out a long wooden box and handed it to her. Inside was a simple necklace of lapis lazuli and sapphire. "This has been worn by the matriarchs of my family for generations. It belonged to my mother and her mother before her. Now it belongs to you," he fastened it about her neck and held her at arm's length. "It suits you," he said with a gentle smile.

Constantina looked up into his face. She remembered the ghost and looked at the necklace with some trepidation. "Oh Athelstan, this was your mother's? I could not possibly!"

"It is just another of our strange ways, then, but it is yours now that you are my wife. You will pass it to our daughter when her time comes and she to hers. It is so we are always remembered throughout the ages. Does that make sense to you?" She smelled so good and having her this close had a profoundly calming effect on him. He looked into her eyes again and brushed some hair from her face. His heart hammered in his chest just looking at her. He traced the curve of the necklace along her neckline. He had to kiss her again.

"Thank you I shall treasure it always," she said placing his hand on her belly.

When his lips touched hers, she reached up to meet him halfway.

"Love me like this forever, Athelstan."

"How can I not?" he asked with a mischievous grin. He let his cloak fall to the floor and gently lifted her into his arms. Constantina's arm wrapped around his neck as he carried her, her body trembled in rapt anticipation. He carried her into the back and lay her on the deep eider–down mattress. He stood before her and untied his tunic.

"Once I fight my way past some of those flowers and ribbons, I will prove it that you." He kissed her deeply and began to untie her gown.

"I am told I am to be unwrapped like a present," she said with a wiggle of her eyebrows.

"Is that right? Well far be it for me to disappoint all the wise women of the village. I should never hear the end of it," he laughed and began to do just that. He punctuated each pull and tug with tickling. Each gossamer layer had its special challenges for the King but he persevered and soon his precious present was suitably unwrapped. He bent to kiss her neck and shoulders with a tender touch.

Constantina's eyes fluttered closed. Desire awoke and spread through her like wildfire. She panted out. "My King."

"My Queen, the time has come for me to find out just where you are ticklish. I warned you I would," he tickled her and she squealed in delight as she tried to fend him off. He laughed and inhaled deeply as her heat rose to his nostrils. Hunger flared in him. She was so irresistible when her eyes grew hooded and she bit her lower lip. Soon she would release that wild creature she kept so tightly reined in. A frown crossed his brow for a moment as he continued to nibble and kiss his way down her perfect body. He lifted his head a moment and consciously sniffed the air. His frown deepened. "Can you smell that?" he asked softly.

"Umm," Constantina moaned. The heady scent of wood smoke filled the air.

"I can," she said, gathering up the blanket to cover her body. "Athelstan, it smells like smoke."

He sat up torn between making love to his new bride and seeing what the cause of the smell was. "Did we knock over a candle?" He had to check. It would hardly do for the newlyweds to burn alive due to simple carelessness.

"Wait here." He left her huddled in her blanket and quickly scanned the three rooms. There was no sign of anything amiss, but no mistake; the smell of smoke was growing stronger.

He tried the door. It did not move. It was locked from the outside. This was typical of Celtic Honeymoons brides and grooms are often locked in, sometimes for a month. This was to ensure that a child would result. It was hardly necessary here. He tried the door again.

"Is it locked?" Constantina stood behind him. She held a portion of her dress to her chest. The silk hid very little

"Not for long," The Celt crouched and launched himself at the door. He hit it full force and it erupted outwards in a cloud of splinters

Naked, he stepped out into the icy rain. The rain was being blown by an ever-increasing wind. He sniffed the air and smelled smoke. To the south, an angry red glow lit the low clouds. Athelstan knew that, next to a landslide, a forest fire in the mountains was extremely dangerous. Fire follows the smoke.

The new Queen could smell the choking smoke coming. It burned her eyes and throat. It looked like the coming of the sun. In the early dark of night, it was not. Placing her hand on his shoulder, she stood a little off to his left. "Did you hear any thunder, or lightning to accompany the rain?" she asked.

"No, I did not." Athelstan seemed distracted.

It was just then that Saul, Meniob, and Cedric arrived. The older man was puffing hard.

"What caused the fire?" Athelstan asked, turning and leading them back inside the small hut.

"No one is sure yet. It isn't coming from any of the clans. It is much higher up in the trees. This could be a prelude to an attack," Cedric offered. Athelstan turned to Menniob. The man believed it was a possibility.

"Wait here," he said to the three men as he pulled Constantina back into their small bedroom. When he turned to her, she saw the mask of concern cover his face. "You need to get dressed. We have got to get out of here. Now!"

Even from over a half mile away, a massive explosion shook the ground. "Hurry!" She jumped at the sound. "What was that?" she asked. He could tell she was scared, yet all that showed was outward calm; a fact that amazed him.

"Trees explode when they burn!" He said as if that answered the question.

As quickly as they could the pair dressed, he in his white tunic and dun trousers, she in her long white gown, minus the flowers. He took Constantina by the hands and wrapped a cloak around her. "Ready?"

"Almost," she said, slipping on her slippers and lying on the bed. She raised her knees to her chest. "Gather the bottom and cut off the excess," he looked at her puzzled for only a brief second, but nodded and did so. When she stood the gown hung to her ankles allowing her to run without holding her skirts.

"I am ready now," Again he took her hand and returned outside. The five of them left the cabin. "I need a report," he said to the men.

"No one knows yet what started it; they're busy getting people out of the way," Menniob said. They fell into step alongside Athelstan and stepped out into the cold rain.

"I want to know how this started. Fires do not start by themselves, especially not on a rainy night. There has been no lightning." His long strides took them downhill towards the lake. People appeared and he issued orders calmly. "You men with axes, start cutting a fire break there, there and there," he pointed up the slope. "Cut another one there. Drag as much dead brush away as you can," he addressed another clan chief's son. "Make sure everyone uphill and downwind from the fire gets down to the lakeside. You know how quickly this can change direction. GO!" He went.

"Constantina, there are going to be people hurt fighting this and I need you to organise the rescue teams and the healers." The smoke was getting thicker around them and in the distance, a terrible roar could be heard.

"I would like you men to help her take care of all this. Order your subjects, my Queen. They will obey," He was slowed to a stop and turned his head towards the raging forest fire. "but you stay near the water." His head snapped around. "Promise me."

She stood in awe at how her new husband took charge of things. He was a king. He could do nothing else. She nodded at his orders. She kissed him quickly. "I promise." She launched into action.

"I will need cots, clean water, and dry cloths," she commanded. "I will need special salves for burns and bandages. It is imperative that no dry brush surrounds us. And even more important, is that there is a large ditch between the fire and where we seek shelter. You bring the woulded there." she said to a few of the men.

"Saul you go with the men to build the ditch, Menniob you help some of the women heat buckets of water and have it on hand if we need it. Cedric, see to it Athelstan stays out of danger."

Athelstan smiled as she continued downhill towards the lake with her team. He took one last look at her before disappearing southward into the heavy trees and the flames.

Hours passed without count. Clutching cloaks tightly against the driving rain Constantina and Caileigh ran towards the next building pressed into use as an infirmary. They ducked inside and saw two men each with terrible breaks of their legs. As well, one of them had been burned across his back. Even though they were injured and in pain, none passed up the opportunity to wish Constantina a happy wedding night. These were a remarkable people.

"I'm getting too old for all this running about," Caileigh stated flatly.

Constantina smiled at the old woman. "You have done well tonight. Just like, I am sure, you have always done well for your people. I am honoured to have you here beside me. You lend me the strength I do not often have."

"You are stronger than you think Constantina, never forget that. You are as strong as the people who follow you. Look around and tell me you are not strong and loved," she wiped hair from her eyes.

"What you believe to be a lack of strength is only a lack of confidence and that will come with time." Someone yelling in the distance interrupted her. She heaved a deep sigh and groaned as she stood. "Shall we see what more we can do, Majesty?"

Constantina smiled at the old woman. Turning they saw a man running towards the pair. He looked distraught and frazzled.

A man stopped in the rain a few dozen yards away and wailed at the sky piteously before sinking down onto his knees head down face in hands sobbing. "OH someone please help," he shrieked.

Constantina came to comfort the man. She froze in recognition.

He looked up face wet, eyes red. "It's my daughter and she's all Aye have left!" he sobbed and clutched at the ladies skirts. "She's trapped, up there and I cannot get her loose," he showed a seized claw-like right hand that was obviously useless. "Oh please come. If we all pull, Aye know we can move the branch covering her. You must come now, you must! Please, she's only five."

The look he gave Constantina was chilling. She felt her heart break, knowing what was to come.

"I can manage this, Caileigh. You stay here where you are needed."

"I am not so old as I look child. Lead on sir."

They helped the man stand. "Show us the way to your daughter."

He gasped in relief and immediately led the two women away from the lake and into the dark trees. His only comments were to hurry. "It's not far now. Just over here," he said finally gesturing into the dark silent trees.

Then he finally stopped and turned. His supposedly maimed right hand now held a wickedly curved knife and Constantina could see the evil grin cross his face. "That is far enough old crone," he growled at Caileigh, "Aye have no further need of you, it's her He wants. He wants her back now." A cold snicker was heard as he stepped towards the Druidess.

"Wants who back? What is going on here? Where's your daughter?"

"The Axum wants what is his returned to him. He wants his Octavia back."

"Octavia?" She looked at the Queen. "You?"

She nodded sadly. "I am not Constantina. I am her sister, Octavia. I have been lying and spying on all of you. The Hooded man is my master. And this is Acaph. The man with the knife sneered and chuckled madly.

Saul stepped from the shadows.

"Saul, thank the Gods you are here. They are trying to kill me," Caileigh exclaimed.

"Gentle Mother, Aye am nut Saul. Aye am his brother Acaph, and those who seek to kill ewe and your King - will succeed - evidently." A wicked looking knife dropped from his sleeve into his hand. "We have nut met although Aye have watched ewe sleep."

A look of horror filled her eyes. Caileigh attempted to run one last time.

Acaph leapt forward and slashed Caileigh across the arm with his knife. She immediately clutched at the wound and fell to the ground.

"Stop it!" Octavia screamed. "Let her go! She does not need to die."

Acaph whirled on Octavia with a feral snarl of insane hate and hammered the butt of his knife against the side of her head. Octavia sank to her knees, the blood dripping into her mouth from her head wound. She turned to him. "Why?" she asked not sure why he was doing this.

Maniacal laughter ripped the still air. "Oh, ewe will find out why soon enough my dear. He will tell ewe why. Oh yes, He will tell ewe and ewe will not like it either."

Octavia winced in pain at Snake's grip in her hair. She saw Caileigh cradling her arm and felt tears in her eyes. Had to try to stay... conscious. Her eyes fluttered once, then twice. She had one last conscious thought.

"Athelstan!" She expressed it in a whisper. The wind swallowed it.

It had taken nine hours of cold wet backbreaking labour of a thousand, or more men to fight the mountain blaze. During their assault, he had ordered men to fall back three times as the fire jumped their fire lines at treetop level. In the end, the rain did more to put it out than any efforts of man.

Athelstan was exhausted, dirty, scraped, scratched, burned and furious. Someone had deliberately set this fire in a place where it was guaranteed to cause the most damage and loss of life. Looking down at the source of the blaze, he kicked at a still glowing log. A large fire pit of rocks surrounded a dead tree. Sixty men stood with him, each was as dirty and battered as their King.

"I want the person who set this found and brought to me." It was a low growl and the expression on his face brooked no failure.

"Sire, over here." Athelstan was already moving towards the man. He was pointing down at the ground. Under an unburned cedar tree were hoof marks. Sheltered as they were under the heavy boughs, the rain had not washed them away. Athelstan examined them with a skilled eye.

"This horse has been shod with iron shoes and it has left a very distinctive mark with its left hind hoof. The one who did this must own this horse. Find the horse that left these marks and bring me the son of a bitch sitting atop it. I will roast his black heart!" With a jerk, he turned and headed towards the lake. "Spread out and see what else you can find and report back to me in two hours." No one followed him as he disappeared downhill.

Dawn was turning the black sky a cold grey. Like the other men, he was covered in woodchips, soot, mud, and dry pine needles. His hair, moustache and clothing were singed and he carried a double-headed axe easily over his shoulder. At the water's edge, he dropped the axe and waded waist deep into the frigid lake. He ducked under the water before erupting with a howl in a shower of freezing droplets. He used handfuls of sand to scrub some of the filth off his body.

A voice from shore called. "Athelstan, there you are!" The stocky troll of a man was clearly agitated as he waved at the King.

"Cedric," he acknowledged his new General wearily. He could not remember a time he felt more tired. "Have you found the idiot responsible for all this?" He asked before disappearing beneath the surface again.

"We have been trying to find you, we have looked everywhere," he was clearly worried about something.

"Find me? Find the one who started this fire. I was up there with the men working the fire lines. Why what's happened? He pointed with a frown.

"It's Caileigh... she's been murdered – butchered in fact." He looked at the ground. "It looks like pieces of her were – eaten."

Athelstan froze in disbelief water dripping from his long braids. He waded towards shore. "Caileigh? Murdered? What in Hades, are you talking about? Eaten? Eaten by who?" He thundered. "You are in charge of security here. You command an army! How did this happen?" He looked past Cedric and a small crowd had gathered. They all stared at him with sad worried expressions.

"That is not all." The General said gravely.

His withering look locked Athelstan in place. "...Not all? There is more? Speak up man!" the King demanded.

"We have searched everywhere. I have parties searching the shoreline and the hills but with this rain, they have nothing to track. We have checked all the buildings but no one has seen her for hours. She has simply vanished Sire."

His face fell and a cold hand clutched at his chest. "Vanished?"

"Queen Constantina Sire. We found this by the Druidess's body." In his hand was the blue stone necklace he had given his wife only a few short hours ago.

His mouth turned to ashes and his voice caught in his throat.

"Constantina?" He breathed incredulously. "Someone had set the forest ablaze just to capture his new bride. Caileigh was caught up in that, and paid..." His voice broke.

Athelstan bellowed in impotent rage as he realised what had happened. The sound of it echoed off the mountainsides. A wave of lake water preceded him as he closed on Cedric. He took the General him by his beard. Athelstan's voice was low and dangerous.

"Assemble the Multitude! I want her found! Do you hear me? Find her! I do not care how; I want her found. I do not care if you have to lift every rock, or tear down every building in the civilised world to do it! I want her found! If there is any resistance – sweep it aside. Let nothing stand in your way. Nothing."

He released Cedric's beard and wrapped an arm around his shoulders. "I want all the port cities and harbours watched. You know what I mean. Release the Multitude! Send teams to every known landing spot in Hellas and Illyria, no matter how small. She must not leave this land. I want her found and the men responsible for this crime brought to me. Find me this Axum... this hooded creature. No one does this to us. NO ONE! They shall taste our wrath. We shall turn their world to dust. I swear it by the Gods. As of this moment, the Senone nation is at war. We shall visit upon Axum, a form of Elder World savagery that has not been seen for a thousand years."

"Sire!" Cedric said with deadly calm. He strode off issuing orders as he went. He left the King standing by the shoreline - alone with his fury.

An expression of pure hatred slowly crossed Athelstan's face. His eyes went dead, merciless. He looked up at the heavens.

In a savage whisper, he said, "You wanted a war with us? Very well, war you shall have. You cannot begin to comprehend what is to come." His look turned feral.

"Hooded Man!" Athelstan spat. "We run from you no longer."

END OF BOOK 1

The Moldavite Crown

Second in the
Celtic King Saga

M. F. Harding

Preview

A soul–chilling shriek of horror ripped through the dark halls of the estate. Athelstan sat bolt upright in bed, wide-eyed. Kaliope had snuggled in beside him and also sat up blinking. A second scream followed the first, and before the sound died, the Celt was out of the bed, and through the door into the dark hallway. Kaliope followed her new master at a full run.

Servants, and other household staff hurried towards the sound, everyone was converging on the suites of their mistress. Saul joined him in the hallway at virtually the same moment. Without a word, the two half–naked men raced to Lady Amyntor's, rooms. They were clogged with people. However, they did make way for the determined Jew. As he bore down on them, and Athelstan fell into step behind him.

They found the Lady Amyntor standing surrounded by members of her personal staff. She was looking at something lying on the floor. The hovering women were trying to calm her, but to no avail. She shook uncontrollably, and was crying in terror.

It was a rose. It was the colour of blackest coal. Saul stooped, picked it up with a cloth, and examined it closely. A sniff warranted a nose wrinkling in disgust. A scowl darkened his already serious face. He put it down on a table just, as carefully. "Lady Amyntor, where did ewe get this?"

"Wha… The Rose? It was left. Over there on my bed," she continued to sob. He went to the bed, and began a careful examination.

"Did you touch it?"

"Yes, I flung it away from me."

Aside from the colour, it seemed to be an ordinary rose. Athelstan did not understand her reaction. He picked it up, and gave it a sniff. It had a peculiar sour smell. One he could not identify at all. That bothered him.

Stefanos arrived, sweating, and puffing. He had obviously run from some distance away, and he rushed to her side. "Lady! What happened?" He gasped.

"Where are my boys?" She demanded. Everyone turned, as the children finally burst into the room. Once they were safely in her arms she began to calm down. She showered them with tears, and kisses.

"Thank the Gods you are alright!" She seemed badly frightened. The Celt looked at the rose again, and was perplexed. Saul returned with the pillow. Some dark smudges marred its white surface.

"What happened?" Stefanos repeated. Every eye in the room fell on Athelstan, and the Black Rose he was holding. The Guardian stared, as the Celt held it up, for him to take. Saul ripped it from his hand, and tossed into a burning brazier.

"It is the Black Rose. They only grow on the bodies of the dead. That is why they are black; they feed on blood. Never touch one, and never hand one to someone. In Jeru-Salam, it is a curse. It is the sign of death."

"Oh Stefanos... It's him isn't it? He has come, for us again." Lady Helen whispered. The Guardian nodded grimly.

Athelstan seemed to be the only one in the room who had no idea what anyone was talking about, so he, asked, "Who in all Hades left that on her pillow?"

Saul turned, and answered, as a strange man in a grayish–white cloak entered the room just as Saul said,

"The Axum!"

A sinister-looking cloaked, and hooded figure stepped out of the deep shadows. With a clear strong voice the stranger said,

"The Hooded Man!"

About the Author

M.F. Harding is both a author and a historian. His love of the Celts, their Druidic faith, combined with his interest in archaeology, has placed him in a unique position to write this history-based adventure. He selected the 3rd century BCE because the classical world was in a state of flux. The Greek Empire is fractured. Alexander the Great is 14 years dead, and the rise of Rome seems imminent. The entire world has taken a deep breath waiting to see what is to come. What indeed?

Research for this book has taken him over two decades and he has been aided every step of the way by friends, family, and academics worldwide. He has peered into the long forgotten nooks and crannies of history and has personally challenged many of the beliefs concerning ancient Druidry and the elder race of Celts.

He currently lives on the west coast of Canada with his wife Barbara and is working on book two, The Moldavite Crown.